Overleaf: Land-Use Management Areas in the Pinelands National Reserve. (Map adapted by Tina Campbell from Plate 28, Pinelands Comprehensive Management Plan, 1980.)

The Pinelands Comprehensive Management Plan divides the 1.1 million acres of the Pinelands National Reserve into eight land-use management areas. The primary purpose of these designations is to protect valuable undisturbed, or minimally disturbed, natural and cultural resources by directing development toward areas near existing settlements. The management area designations are also intended to encourage agriculture and recreational uses of appropriate lands.

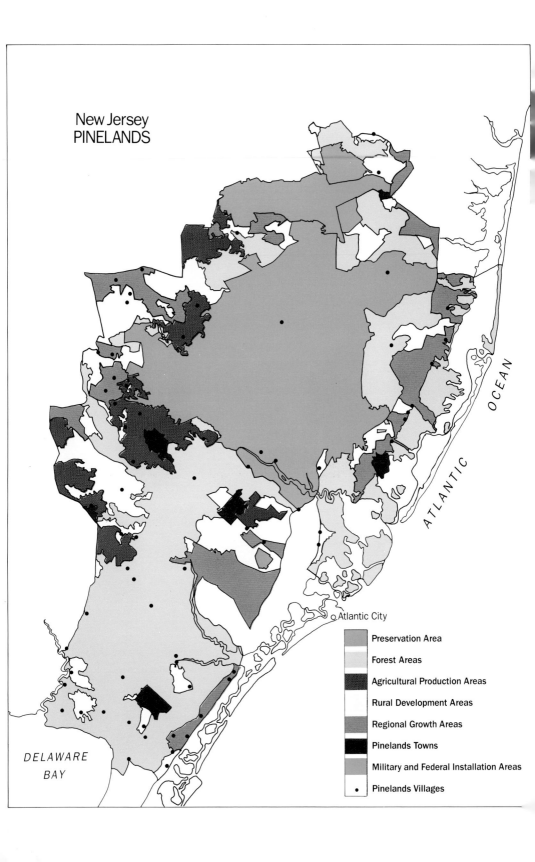

New Jersey
PINELANDS

ATLANTIC OCEAN

ATLANTIC

DELAWARE
BAY

Atlantic City

Preservation Area
Forest Areas
Agricultural Production Areas
Rural Development Areas
Regional Growth Areas
Pinelands Towns
Military and Federal Installation Areas
• Pinelands Villages

Protecting
the New Jersey
Pinelands

A New Direction in
Land-Use Management

Edited by
Beryl Robichaud Collins
and
Emily W. B. Russell

Rutgers University Press
New Brunswick and London

Library of Congress Cataloging-in-Publication Data
Protecting the New Jersey Pinelands.
Includes index.
1. Land use—Government policy—New Jersey—Pine
Barrens.   2. Pinelands National Reserve (N.J.)
I. Collins, Beryl Robichaud.   II. Russell, Emily
Wyndham Barnett, 1945–.
HD266.N52P566   1988   333.75′09749′6   87-36958
ISBN 0-8135-1267-0   0-8135-1275-1 (pbk.)

British Cataloging-in-Publication information available

Publication of the paperback edition was made possible by a grant from The Fund for
New Jersey.

Contents

Support Actions. Assessing the Economic and Fiscal
Support Programs. Conclusion

Illustrations and Tables

Tables

Preface

One of the nation's largest, and most radical, land-use management experiments for resource protection is being undertaken in New Jersey, in the very midst of the heavily urbanized East Coast. Covering more than one-fifth of this small state, the New Jersey Pinelands was declared by Congress in 1978 a National Reserve, and innovative means were designed to protect its unique resources from the encroachments of modern life. Bypassed by land developers for hundreds of years, the area that is today the Pinelands National Reserve is an extraordinary, near-wilderness region within a few hours drive of more than thirty million metropolitan-area residents.

Long before colonists settled the East Coast of the United States, geologic and biologic processes created in southern New Jersey an intricate mosaic of very arid, sandy uplands and an assortment of marshes and swamps intertwined with slow-moving streams. These natural habitats continue to nurture a treasured variety of plant and animal species that owe their presence to successful adaptation over thousands of years during which humans were too few to influence natural selection processes. Even after several hundred years of settlement by Europeans and despite fairly severe uses of the resources, the Pine Barrens ecosystem maintains its resiliency.

Twentieth-century technology and the demands of a much larger and faster-growing population, however, have placed new stresses on the Pine Barrens ecosystem, endangering its stability and threatening to cause irreversible impacts on its natural resources. In the 1960s a handful of individuals recognized the national significance of the region and convinced thousands of others that a huge jetport and an accompanying urban complex should not be allowed to obliterate the heart of the Pine Barrens. Fewer than twenty years later, Congress signalled a new direction for land-use planning in the United States by designating the New Jersey Pinelands as a National Reserve, to be managed under an innovative program that provided an alternative to inclusion within the national park system.[1] Within a year New Jersey's Governor Brendan Byrne appointed a regional commission to prepare a master plan for Pinelands protection, and secured the land from harmful development in the interim. In January 1981 the creative and comprehensive management plan for the Pinelands National Reserve, approved by New Jersey's governor and the U.S. secretary of the interior, became effective. The plan sets forth land-use regulations for about one million acres of land stretching over seven counties and fifty-six municipalities; more than half the land in the reserve is privately owned.

Rooted in the greenline parks concept, the Pinelands legislation provides federal funding for a limited program of land acquisition and calls for a local, state, and federal governmental partnership interwoven with active public participation to manage use of private property in the reserve. In the context of a living landscape, one where many people live and some earn a living, the Pinelands Comprehensive Management Plan (CMP) sets forth a strategy, standards, and regulatory mechanisms to govern land-use; by legislative mandate its design is strongly conservation oriented. Agriculture and recreation are encouraged under this plan; new residential, commercial, and industrial development are permitted only if they can be accommodated at no destructive risk to critical land and water resources. The CMP is also the first attempt in this country to implement the concept of transferable development rights on a significant scale.

The bold measures taken to protect the Pinelands did not occur fortuitously or overnight. Although plans for a jetport and a new city were defeated, in the 1960s and 1970s the vast, largely empty Pine Barrens tract was an inviting target for other development schemes. Pristine surface waters became polluted, and it appeared inevitable that the same would happen to the huge aquifer of pure freshwater that underlies the region. It took two decades of hard effort to gain passage of federal legislation establishing the reserve, and another half year to win effective implementing legislation from the state of New Jersey. During this time many plans for land-use in the Pine Barrens were proposed and debated. An early state-initiated attempt to exercise regional advisory influence over local land-use decision-making failed to provide adequate resource protection. Controversies over proper use of the Pine Barrens were bitter, with conservationists pitted against land speculators; developers; builders; large landowners; farmers; and many local, county, and state officials. It took extraordinary vigor on the part of a handful of conservationists to win broad public support to convince federal and state legislators.

Since January 14, 1981, all land-use decision-making for the one million acres of New Jersey Pinelands has been guided by the Pinelands Comprehensive Management Plan. Not everyone has been happy with the results. Large landowners, land speculators, and builders have had their expectations thwarted. Farmers worry that their land will become worthless. Disappointed owners of small lots are not able to develop their land as they had anticipated or, in some cases, even build as they had planned to do for their own use. Many local officials are dismayed to see their authority over land-use decisions eroded. Even environmentalists show dissatisfaction, as some who fought for the plan are now uncertain that the program as currently implemented is restrictive enough to save the Pinelands.

Because the Pinelands National Reserve represents the first federal attempt to protect a sizable area outside the national park system, there is widespread interest in the nature of this land-management effort and its outcome. If the greenline park concept is proved viable here, there are many other places in the United States where it may offer the most appropriate means for protecting a landscape with significant resources. The Pinelands experience also is of international importance. In 1983 the United Nations, through UNESCO's Man and the Biosphere Program, identified the Pinelands Reserve as one of the world's outstanding natural areas. It was designated a unit of UNESCO's International Network of Biosphere Reserves which presently contains 261 units in 70 countries. The Pinelands Reserve is recognized as a key model in the network, illustrating the biosphere concept of combining conservation with accommodation of a wide range of human resource needs. Thus, assessment of the success of the Pinelands protection effort serves the interests of those particularly concerned with the protection of the ecological integrity and cultural resources of the Pine Barrens landscape as well as of a broader constituency seeking a land-management strategy and organizational and procedural implements applicable to other situations throughout the world.

To serve both these interests, three objectives were established for this book:

> To trace the genesis and the substance of the legislative foundation for the protection of the Pinelands

> To describe and assess the land-use management strategy and supporting programatic and procedural mechanisms being implemented in the Pinelands National Reserve

> To identify the environmental, social, economic, political, and legal consequences of the Pinelands Comprehensive Management Plan as implemented, and to draw from these experiences lessons transferable to other land-use planning activities.

As a backdrop for understanding the land-use regulatory program and its impact, the book starts with a description of the Pinelands landscape, highlighting its unique natural resources and the imprints of human use of these resources, past and present. Interrelationships between resource use and the ecosystem's capacity to maintain its essential characteristics are discussed. The next two chapters review, in chronological order, the events that led to enactment of federal and state legislation—the National Parks and Recreation Act of 1978 and the New Jersey Pinelands Protection Act of 1979—and the content of these legislative mandates.

Chapters 4 and 5 trace the activities of the Pinelands Commission from its inception through the preparation of the Comprehensive Management Plan. The regulatory mechanisms used by the commission in the building moratorium period are reviewed and their effectiveness analyzed. The process of plan writing is described, with particular attention given to ecological, social, economic, political, and legal issues. Involvement of the public in the plan preparation process is discussed. Chapter 6 summarizes the contents of the Pinelands Comprehensive Management Plan, synthesizing its land-use management strategy and substantive and procedural provisions. Note is made of actions taken to amend the CMP.

Chapters 7 through 10 present a topical rather than a chronological treatment of the four principal phases of CMP implementation. The first of these deals with the establishment of an effective intergovernmental partnership to manage the reserve and includes a description of the certification process through which municipalities and counties bring their master plans and ordinances into conformance with the Comprehensive Management Plan. Chapter 8 analyzes the procedures for the regulation of development under the CMP and reviews six years of experience under the regulatory programs. The strategies used in the land acquisition program and in the management of public lands in the Pinelands are the subject of Chapter 9; the economic and fiscal programs and the degree to which these cushion the adverse effects of the land-use regulatory program are explored in Chapter 10.

The final three chapters are evaluative. Chapter 11 assesses both the legal foundations of the Comprehensive Management Plan, and the legal and legislative challenges that have been made and their outcomes. In the next chapter, the environmental, social, economic, and political consequences of the current Pinelands land-management program are reviewed and assessed within the context of its legislative objectives. Forces that presently influence the effectiveness of the Pinelands protection efforts (and those that may do so in the future) are considered. Finally, lessons are drawn from the New Jersey experiences.

This book is written for a wide audience, including legislators, administrators, and professionals at all government levels who are, or will be, involved in regional land-use planning activities, as well as their numerous counterparts in the private sector—developers, land speculators, planners, lawyers, economists, and environmental scientists. Members of special-interest groups can also profit from knowledge of the Pinelands experiences—local, state, and national conservation and environmental organizations; sportsmen's groups; building industry associations; farm bureaus; and taxpayers associations. This book can also serve an instructional purpose for students who seek careers in public administration or resource management. And, finally, the authors hope that all who share their love for the New Jersey Pine Barrens will find the book of interest.

August 1987

Beryl Robichaud Collins
Emily W. B. Russell

Acknowledgments

Many people gave assistance to the authors of this book during its seven years of manuscript preparation. We thank collectively all of the residents of the Pine Barrens; public officials; and representatives of environmental, building, farm and other organizations who took time to share with the authors their experiences with and reactions to the Pinelands planning and program implementation efforts. We thank also members of the Pinelands Commission who were always willing to explain the rationale of their decision-making. The commission's executive director, Terrence Moore, and his two assistant directors, William Harrison and John Stokes, provided easy access to commission documents and, most cooperatively, made themselves and other staff members available for numerous interviews.

Many reviewers also helped the authors by their independent evaluations of manuscript drafts. For their careful scrutiny of the entire manuscript we thank Norma F. Good, Ralph E. Good, Mark B. Lapping, and William A. Niering.

Linda Howe shaped individual author drafts into much more readable text, and also edited the bibliographic material. Most of the book's maps and graphs were designed and produced by Tina Campbell, and David Borrelli supplied many of the photographs.

For financial support of individual research projects which contributed to the book, we first thank Rutgers, the State University of New Jersey. The university supported Russell's study of the Pinelands Commission activities in 1980. The author especially thanks John M. Cooney, executive assistant, Office of Rutgers Community Affairs and Leland G. Merrill, Jr., Center for Coastal and Environmental Studies, for their encouragement and advice on that project. Additional university funding for research analyses of development review activities was provided to Beryl Collins. She thanks Norbert P. Psuty, director of the Center for Coastal and Environmental Studies, and Ralph E. Good, the center's director of Pinelands research, for financing this work and for providing typing and other administrative services to the authors. The National Park Service, through J. Glen Eugster of the Mid-Atlantic office, provided funding to Beryl Collins for research studies of development activities in the Pinelands Reserve coastal area and of the commission's enforcement activities.

Finally, it is the Fund for New Jersey that made possible the integration of the individual research projects into a comprehensive text that describes and evaluates the significance of the Pinelands protection efforts.

The grant provided by the fund and the interest of its director, Robert P. Corman, provided the encouragement needed to complete an evaluation of the innovative land-use management experiment being conducted in the Pinelands National Reserve. We hope that the completed product fulfills the expectations of the fund and of the many individuals who contributed to the work.

List of Contributors

BERYL ROBICHAUD COLLINS, Center for Coastal and Environmental Studies, Rutgers University, New Brunswick, N.J. 08903

JAMES K. CONANT, The Graduate School of Public Administration, New York University, New York, N.Y. 10003

NORMA F. GOOD, Center for Coastal and Environmental Studies, Rutgers University, New Brunswick, N.J. 08903

RALPH E. GOOD, Division of Pinelands Research, CCES, Rutgers University, New Brunswick, N.J. 08903

PETER J. PIZOR, Department of Environmental Resources, Rutgers University, New Brunswick, N.J. 08903

EMILY W. B. RUSSELL, Department of Geological Sciences, Rutgers University, Newark, N.J. 07102

CHARLES L. SIEMON, Siemon, Larsen, & Purdy, Chicago, Ill. 60606

ROBERT A. ZAMPELLA, Pinelands Commission Staff, New Lisbon, N.J. 08064

Protecting
The New Jersey
Pinelands

Introduction

1. The Landscape of the New Jersey Pine Barrens

Beryl Robichaud Collins

Norma F. Good

Ralph E. Good

The New Jersey Pine Barrens presents a truly unique landscape. Past geologic and biologic evolutionary processes have created a combination of natural land features with particular associations of living organisms, plant and animal, found nowhere else in the world. Overlaid on the landscape are distinctive imprints of past and current human use of the resources.

In contrast to the majestic redwoods of West Coast forests, the dominant tree in this region of New Jersey, the pitch pine, typically grows crooked and scraggly, sometimes in dwarf form. Early European colonists described the region as "barren land" because of the infertility of its soils compared with those in neighboring areas. Thus came the region's common name—the Pine Barrens.[1] In its low relief there are none of the deep canyons or high mountains that characterize many of our national parks. Today's hurried travelers on route from Pennsylvania or New York to Atlantic City or other shore resorts often see the Barrens as a vast, monotonously flat, sandy wilderness forming a striking contrast with the urbanized surroundings. But those who have taken a canoe trip on one of the rivers, hiked along the Batona Trail, or visited Chatsworth, a small village in the heart of the Pines, at cranberry harvest time carry away a different image. Almost always this is one of amazement that an area as beautiful and remote as the Pine Barrens still exists in the megalopolis that stretches from New Hampshire southward through New Jersey to Virginia.

Location, Boundaries, and Size

Located in the fifth smallest and most densely populated state of the nation, the New Jersey Pine Barrens lies within easy access of thirty million metropolitan residents. New Jersey itself nestles between the cities of New York and Philadelphia, its population concentrated in two large clusters, one in the northeast adjoining the New York metropolitan area and the other adjacent to Philadelphia in the southwest. Connecting these two population centers is a heavily developed transportation corridor of railroad tracks and multiple-laned north-south highways, that is said to carry the largest traffic volume in the world. This corridor splits New

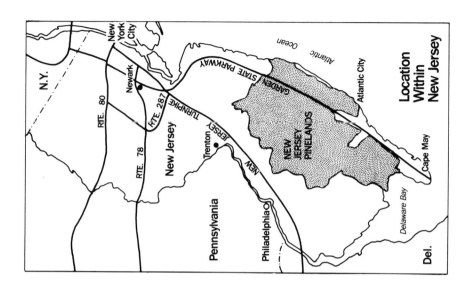

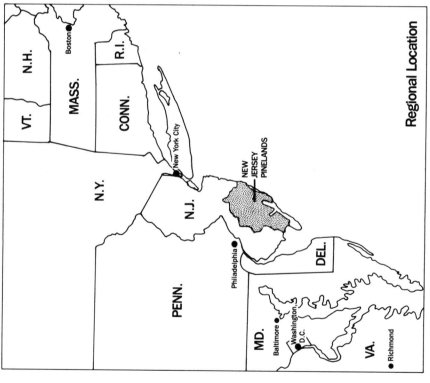

Figure 1–1. Location of the New Jersey Pinelands. Maps by Tina Campbell.

Jersey almost in half. To the southeast of it are the Pine Barrens and the seashore (Figure 1–1).

When measured by scientists as an ecosystem, the New Jersey Pine Barrens totals about 2,250 square miles (1.4 million acres), almost 30 percent of the state. The federal government designated as the Pinelands National Reserve a smaller land area of 1,719 square miles (1.1 million acres). An even smaller region, 1,460 square miles (934,000 acres) was delineated as the Pinelands Area by the New Jersey legislature and placed under the management responsibility of the Pinelands Commission. The boundaries of these several designations are shown on Figure 1–2. The term "New Jersey Pinelands," or simply "the Pinelands," refers to that part of the Pine Barrens landscape protected by federal and state legislation. However measured, the Pine Barrens or Pinelands is larger than the state of Rhode Island, and exceeds many national parks, including Yosemite, the Grand Canyon, and the Great Smoky Mountains.

To the east of the Pine Barrens is the heavily used ocean shore of New Jersey; this is served by the Garden State Parkway, which forms much of the eastern boundary of the state-designated Pinelands Area. The larger federal Pinelands National Reserve stretches eastward across the parkway into the coastal area and southward to Delaware Bay.

That the Pine Barrens survived as it did into the twentieth century is attributed to its location—outside the main East Coast north-south transportation corridor and not within easy commuting distance of either New York or Philadelphia. Another reason is that adequate supplies of more fertile land were available for agriculture in nearby areas. Recently, however, new patterns of development have brought intrusions into the Barrens. These will be discussed in Chapter 2. In the following pages, characteristics of the Pine Barrens landscape are described—its natural ecology and the human imprints (political, social, and economic) upon it.

Ecology of the Pine Barrens[2]

To ecologists, the New Jersey Pine Barrens probably is best known as home to the vocal, purple-striped, green Pine Barrens treefrog; the miniature curly grass fern; and numerous other curious and rare plants and animals. (The scientific names of plants and animals mentioned in this book are listed in Table A.1). It also is a place of cedar bogs, swamps with masses of yellow-spiked bog asphodel, sandy uplands with clumps of the white-flowered pyxie moss, and fields of the fragile blue Pine Barrens gentian. Hydrologists, and legislators, acclaim it for overlying one of the few unpolluted aquifers on the East Coast.

Figure 1–2. A Comparison: The New Jersey Pine Barrens, the Pinelands National Reserve, and the Pinelands Area. The boundaries delineated for the Pine Barrens follow those drawn by Jack McCormick and reproduced in Richard T. T. Forman, ed., *Pine Barrens: Ecosystem and Landscape* (New York: Academic Press, 1979), p. xi. Map by Tina Campbell.

Pine Barrens

But the Pine Barrens is more than just an aggregate of unusual plant and animal species and a reservoir of pure water. It is a very large and unusual ecosystem within which are nested a multitude of varied, but inextricably linked, subsystems of natural and human origin. The biotic components of this ecosystem—plants and animals—evolved over long periods of time as they interacted with each other and with the abiotic elements of the system—soils and water—and reacted to the stress of disturbances, both natural and human-induced.

Today's landscape has its origin in geologic history dating back perhaps five million years. Since then, the land-forming processes of deposition, erosion, and sea level changes have molded the region's topography, determined the geologic material from which its soils are derived, and formed its ground and surface water systems.

Geologic Formations, Topography, and Soils.   The Pine Barrens is sited on the Atlantic Coastal Plain, a physiographic province in the eastern United States that extends northward to Cape Cod, southward to the tip of Florida, and then westward across Alabama, Mississippi, Louisiana, and Texas to Mexico. In New Jersey, distinction is made between the

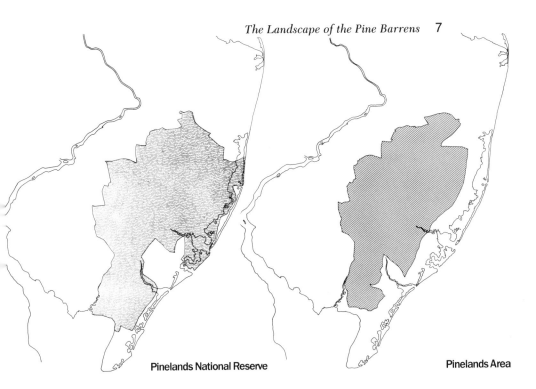

Pinelands National Reserve   Pinelands Area

Inner and Outer Coastal Plains. Although both have their origins in depo-
sitions of clays, silts, sands, and gravels, they were formed at different
times. The younger Outer Coastal Plain, on which the Pine Barrens is
located, is much sandier than the Inner Coastal Plain and thus less fertile.

Geologists give names to distinctive and mappable units of geologic deposits, and the particular formation at the surface throughout most of the
Pinelands is known as the Cohansey Sand. The Cohansey, as it is usually
called, overlies an earlier deposit, the Kirkwood Formation, which is exposed only along the region's northern and western borders. Overlaid on
the Cohansey are localized patches of later deposits, the most important
of which are the Beacon Hill, Bridgeton, Pensauken, and Cape May
formations.

Past geologic events have created in the Pine Barrens a landscape of
low relief marked by occasional gentle undulations, with neither steep
ridges nor deep valleys. Much of the region is less than one hundred feet
above sea level. Still, visual contrasts in topography have led to landmarks
identified locally as hills and even mountains. Apple Pie Hill, capped with
Beacon Hill gravel, has the highest elevation in the Pines, just over 200
feet. The Forked River Mountains are slightly lower.

Soils are formed primarily from the disintegration of surface-deposit and parent-rock materials. Because the nature of soils greatly influences plant growth, the character of the Cohansey—the principal formation underlying the Pine Barrens—is important. The Cohansey is an unconsolidated deposit, meaning that its constituent particles are not cemented together into rock form. The relative fertility of soils derived from such parent material depends upon the relative proportions of clays, silts, sands, and gravels in the mixture. The greater the percentage of coarser particles (sands and gravels) in the soil, the less its capacity to hold water and the nutrients most needed by plants—nitrogen, phosphorus, potassium, calcium, and magnesium, for example. Soils that developed from the Cohansey and from patches of later deposits typically have a high proportion of coarse sand particles and a low proportion of clay, making them droughty (having poor capacity for retention of moisture) and low in nutrients. This characteristic of high soil porosity has two dimensions. First, it is a limiting factor on plant growth, and, second, it means that the soils are chemically inert, incapable of filtering out waste contaminants whether they originate as agricultural fertilizers, pesticides, wastewaters from septic systems, or leachates from landfills. Soils with more clay have a greater capacity to filter out bacteria and trap or chemically alter solutes and particles as wastewater percolates through the soil to the ground water table.

Soils scientists identify thirteen major series (classes) of soils in the Barrens.[3] One of the most common series, considered characteristic of the region, is the Lakewood series, a droughty, low nutrient, and very acid soil with pH values in upper soil regions registering only 4.6. The Lakewood soil resembles infertile soils of colder regions and like them is considered a podzol, that is, a soil in which all the finer particles and organic material have leached out of the upper soil horizon, bleaching it gray as compared with the darker lower soil layers. The Barrens also, however, has areas of more fertile soils with higher clay content (the Sassafras Series, for example), and these have been used successfully for the culture of fruits and vegetables.

Ground and Surface Water Resources.   Underlying the Pine Barrens is a huge natural aquifer of potable freshwater. Equivalent to a lake of about 2,000 square miles in surface area and thirty-seven feet deep, this aquifer is believed to have a storage capacity as much as seventeen trillion gallons. The Cohansey and the Kirkwood formations each has large water-bearing layers alternating with confining clay layers that form aquifers; the two systems are interconnected. Within the Pine Barrens the Cohansey serves as the principal source of water supply. In coastal areas, where the shallower Cohansey is more vulnerable to saltwater intrusion, the Kirkwood is the more highly utilized aquifer.

The Cohansey aquifer creates a shallow water table, usually no more than twenty feet below the land surface. Where the water table intercepts the land surface, as it does in many places, a stream or a wetland is formed. The source of groundwater replenishment is precipitation, which is rapidly absorbed by the sandy surface and percolates quickly to the shallow water table. About half of the average forty-five inches of annual precipitation goes into the groundwater system; the remainder is returned to the atmosphere through surface evaporation or plant transpiration. Excess groundwater discharges from the aquifer directly into local streams or moves more slowly through deeper horizons to discharge into major river basins.

In the Pine Barrens, natural surface waters occur mostly as rivers and streams (Figure 1–3); almost all the lakes and ponds have been created artificially by damming of streams. Streams are fed mainly (90 percent) from groundwater supplies, and for the most part flow eastward on a gentle slope to drain into barrier bays, which are important feeding, spawning, and shelter grounds for aquatic life. Three large river basins drain much of the land eastward to the Atlantic ocean—the Toms River Basin in the north; the Great Egg Harbor River Basin to the south; and, between the two, the Mullica River Basin, the only one to lie wholly within the Pine Barrens. Another large basin, the Maurice River, drains southeast to Delaware Bay, and the Rancocas Creek, whose headwaters rise in the Pine Barrens, flows westward to the Delaware River.

Because of the low topographic gradient, streams are typically slow moving and shallow; often they are narrow enough to allow streambank vegetation to form a continuous canopy over the water. For the most part, the waters are pure but are an unusual brown, or tea, color. This distinctive coloration comes from a chemical complex formed by the oxidation of dissolved iron mixed with decomposed organic materials. Stream waters that have not been disturbed are acid, typically with a pH value of less than 5, and low in levels of nutrients and dissolved solids. Disturbed streams are less acid, with pH values that exceed 5, and register higher levels of nutrients. A key measure of a stream's nutrient load are levels of nitrate-nitrogen, a pollutant that has been associated with health hazards to infants and that is also a good indicator of the presence of other contaminants more difficult to trace. In undisturbed streams, nitrate-nitrogen concentrations may average only 0.05 parts per million (ppm), which is extremely low.[4]

Nature has created in the Pine Barrens a remarkable, but very fragile,

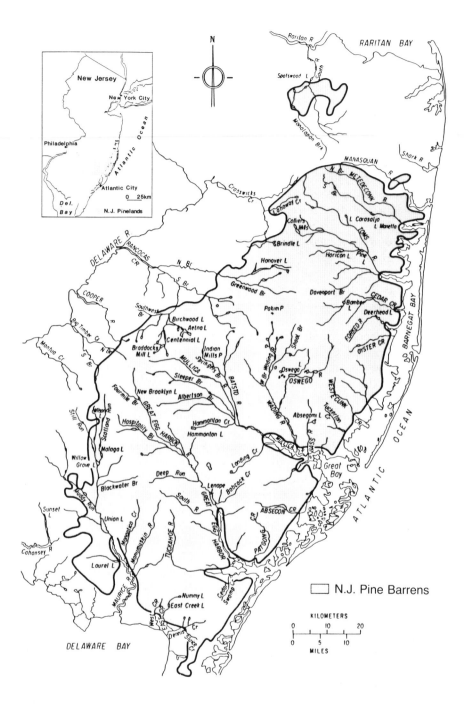

Figure 1–3. Rivers and Streams of the Pine Barrens. Map modified by Michael Siegel from Forman, 1979.

system of hydrology. The very attributes that give the system its functional capability—high soil porosity and interconnectedness of ground and surface waters—also make it vulnerable to damage. Contaminants in wastewaters and leachates can easily enter the system, pollute ground and surface waters, and destroy the particular habitat conditions that permit the characteristic plant and animal species to maintain themselves.

Genesis of Biological Distribution Patterns.   Geologic processes have created a diversity of habitats for plants and animals. The sandy, dry uplands are at one extreme; at the other are the wetlands. In some cases uplands and wetlands are joined through transitional zones of varying moisture. In other cases the two meet along abrupt boundaries. Sometimes small irregularities in the soil surface or variations in water table levels produce an upland habitat as an enclave within a wetland, or enclaves of wetlands in depressions within uplands.

The vegetation and its associated animal communities present today have evolved over thousands of years and reflect the success of particular species in invading, and maintaining themselves in, the various habitats that characterize the Pine Barrens. Upland plants must have tolerance for sandy soils with few nutrients and little water-retention capability; wetland vegetation must thrive in acid waters with low levels of nutrients. Together with evolutionary selection for these habitat preferences, various past climatic events as well as wildfire have molded the present patterns of plant and animal distribution in the Pine Barrens.

Influences of Past Climatic Changes. An epoch of glaciation known as the Pleistocene started about 1.8 million years in the past and ended only about 14,000 years ago. During this period at least three of the four major ice advances reached New Jersey. The last, known as the Wisconsin, stopped just ten to forty miles north of the Pine Barrens. Although the glacial ice did not encroach on the area, it is believed that in the late Pleistocene, when the Wisconsin ice was present, the climate of the Pine Barrens was considerably cooler, and probably wetter, than it is today. Many paleobotanists believe that at this time the region was covered by a forest similar to the present-day spruce-fir boreal forest in northern New England and Canada. A few believe that the climate was so cold that an Arctic type of tundra vegetation existed here. In either case, the assumption is that the Pine Barrens plant and animal populations as we know them today developed only after the Wisconsin ice began to melt about 14,000 or so years ago.

When the glacial ice started this final retreat from New Jersey, the sea level was still low and the ocean far to the east of its present coastline, making the coastal migratory path for both southern and northern species much larger than it now is. During a warm post–glacial period, plants and animals of southern coastal regions expanded their ranges northward, with some colonizing the Pine Barrens. To a lesser degree, range expansion from the southern Appalachians also proceeded northward, then east to the Pine Barrens. The climate then cooled again, and though there was general subsequent southward retreat of flora, many of the southern species continue to survive in the Barrens.

These events are strongly reflected in the present-day flora, and to a lesser degree in animal populations. Although many of the plant species present in the Pine Barrens are found also in surrounding areas, an unusual number (109) are southern species that reach the northern limit of their range in the Barrens; turkey beard, pyxie moss, bog asphodel, and the Pine Barrens gentian are examples. Another fourteen species are northern plants that reach their southern limit in the Pine Barrens. One of these, the broom crowberry, which once had a wider distribution, now occurs only as remnant populations. In addition to the Pine Barrens, the broom crowberry is found only in New York's Shawangunk Mountains, in small areas of coastal Massachusetts and Maine, and on more northern coastal sites in Canada. The distribution of curly grass fern is even more limited; while found also in Long Island bogs, it typically occurs much farther north in coastal areas of Canada. Still other plant species are found only in the Pinelands and a few southern locales.

Certain groups of fauna also reflect the influences of past climatic events. A number of species of moths and butterflies reach their northern or southern limits in the Pine Barrens, and an unusual number of the region's fish, amphibians, and reptiles have decidedly southern affinities. The Pine Barrens treefrog is reported outside the region only in North Carolina and Florida; the carpenter frog, the northern pine snake, and the eastern mud salamander are only a few of other species of fauna that reach their northern range limit in the Pine Barrens.

Evolutionary Adaptation to Wildfire. Because of the particular nature of the soils—sandy and droughty—wildfires have always been a common phenomenon in the Pine Barrens. Fires, caused by lightning and spread by high winds, probably have swept across the flat uplands since before prehistoric humans roamed the state. Only streams and wetlands served as natural fire breaks. Some believe that the Indians burned the Pine Barrens forests to improve hunting conditions; certainly ever since European colonization humans have accidentally or intentionally set fires here. Today thousands of small wildfires still occur each year—for example, in spite of fire control measures, on one weekend in 1963 more than 150,000 acres of woodland were burned.

Some plant species are structurally more insulated from heat than others and therefore are less susceptible to fire damage. Also, some trees and shrubs are able to produce stem and/or root sprouts quickly after fire damage, while others have little or no resprouting capability. Seeds of some plants are destroyed by fire; the seeds of others germinate more quickly when heated by fire, or when left on the relatively bare soils exposed by fire. The present flora of the Pine Barrens reflects the evolutionary success of particular species in invading the region and maintaining themselves competitively in the presence of frequent fire. All dominant species of upland trees and shrubs are fire adapted, though to varying degrees.

Generally, fire on uplands in the Pine Barrens favors the pitch pine and its less abundant evergreen associate, the shortleaf pine. Both have relatively thick bark and can send up new shoots from the base if the top of the tree is killed. Young pine seedlings, which cannot establish themselves where there is a thick accumulation of leaves and other litter on the forest floor, develop successfully when fire consumes the litter. Among the many species of oaks that are native to the Pine Barrens, there is wide variation in resistance to fire damage. All have considerable ability to resprout after fire, but the smaller, so-called shrub oaks (the blackjack, scrub, and dwarf chestnut oaks) are able to survive more frequent fire than the taller, tree-form oaks (black, white, chestnut, and scarlet). Wetland species of trees, though less exposed to fire, are more readily killed when fire does occur. Frequency, intensity, and seasonality of fire have played a strong role in determining patterns of vegetation in the Pine Barrens.

Fire also has affected distribution patterns of animal populations. In the short term, local populations may be extirpated by fire. More important, in the longer term, animal populations are affected by fire-caused changes in the composition and structure of vegetation. A change in forest composition from oak to pine, for example, or the reverse, affects those animals that utilize only one of these groups. On the other hand, when acorn production in scrub oaks is stimulated by fire, some species of mammals and insects will benefit more than others. Also destruction of forest canopy and understory layers alters available nesting and feeding habitats of birds.

Plant Species and Communities.   Although a single tree, the pitch pine, appears to dominate the vegetation of the Pine Barrens, the landscape shows striking patterns of contrasting plant growth. Botanists have identified more than 1,000 plant species that grow in the area, and ecologists describe a rich variety of upland and wetland plant communities (or vegetation types).[5] Although the pitch pine tolerates a wide range of moisture, most species have more rigid requirements for water and differ in their abilities to tolerate extremes, whether of excessive water or of drought. For this reason, soil moisture plays the primary role in habitat differentiation in the Pine Barrens.

Upland Vegetation. In the uplands, where the water table is generally more than two feet below the soil surface, patterns of forest vegetation involve varying combinations of different pine and oak species. Though in numbers the pitch pine is the most common tree in the Barrens, a second pine, the shortleaf, occurs abundantly in some locations. A third pine species, the Virginia pine, is found on the western and southern fringes of the Pine Barrens. Black oak is the most abundant of the larger-growing oak trees, but chestnut oak, scarlet oak, southern red oak, and white oak also are common. Blackjack oak, post oak, and the scrub oaks represent smaller-growing oak species.

Ecologists identify two broad classes of upland forest, with many gradations or subdivisions within each class—pine-dominated (or pine-oak) forests and oak-dominated (or oak-pine) forests. The differentiation between these two major classes is made on the relative proportions of pine and oak trees. In typical pine-dominated forests more than half of the trees are pines, while the rest are representatives of the tree-form and shrub oaks. In the central part of the Barrens, blackjack oak is the most common associate of pitch pine. Heath shrubs—black huckleberry and lowbush blueberry in particular—may form an almost continuous understory. With the exception of bracken fern, wintergreen, and cowwheat, herbs are sparse on the forest floor. Most pines grow only about thirty-five feet tall, and individuals are spaced sufficiently far apart to allow considerable light to penetrate into the woods.

Oak-dominated forests are quite different. The trees average forty to fifty feet in height and their tops come together to form an almost closed canopy. Although pitch pine and shortleaf pine are present, the larger tree oaks are more abundant. North of the Mullica River the black oak is the most common species, and to the south, the southern red oak. Chestnut oak, scarlet oak, and white oak vary in abundance from site to site. The post oak, which may be a canopy tree in this type of forest, outnumbers the blackjack oak. The shrubs and sparse herbs that occur are the same species present in pine-dominated forests.

Oak-dominated forests are more prevalent south of the Mullica River and in western areas, and pine-dominated forests are common in the central area of the Barrens. Ecologists believe that frequent fire, clear-cutting, and poorer soils explain this pattern of distribution. In a woods with litter and shade on the forest floor, oak seed germination and seedling development are more successful than pine seed germination and seedling development. Therefore, unless fire (or clearcutting) opens up a forest and burns away the litter, older pines will not reproduce themselves and the forest eventually will be dominated by oak species. Where fires occur at intervals of about forty years or less, the more fire-resistant pines will be favored.

A striking variation of the pine-dominated forest occurs near Warren Grove, Ocean County, in several areas (totaling about 12,400 acres) collectively known as the Pine Plains. This is the home of the world-renowned dwarf, or pygmy, pine forest. Here multiple-stemmed pitch pine trees grow densely, but often no more than four to six feet tall, making it possible to look out over the top of the forest canopy. Along with the stunted pitch pines are blackjack oaks and scrub oaks, all growing no higher than the pines, as well as mountain laurel, sheep laurel, black huckleberry, and sweet fern. The lower-growing shrubs and herbs may include broom crowberry, false heather, sand myrtle, and pyxie moss.

The distinctive character of this dwarf forest is probably the result of very frequent fires over hundreds or even thousands of years. Under such conditions the tree oaks, which are not found in the dwarf forest, would not have been able to maintain themselves, because they bear viable seed only on stems twenty years or more in age. The pitch pines present in this forest are genetically differentiated from other populations of the species.[6] They are less upright, of shorter growth form, and produce cones at an earlier age. Unlike other pitch pines, whose cones open to disperse seed normally at maturity, the pitch pines growing in the dwarf forest have closed (or serotinous) cones that open to disperse seed only at high temperatures, such as those occurring during a fire.

Wetland Vegetation. Wetlands make up 15 to 20 percent of the Pine Barrens and occur mostly in the headwater areas of drainage systems and as wide bands along rivers and streams. There is a concentration of swamp wetlands around and south of the Mullica River and its tributaries, and in the coastal marshes on the eastern edges of the Pinelands National Reserve. At these sites the soils are poorly drained and the water table is high enough (about two feet or less from the surface) for a sufficient period of the year to be beyond the tolerance range of most upland plants. The variety of vegetation types and plant species, however, is greater here than in the uplands. Though pitch pine tolerates a wide range of moisture and is present, even abundant, on some lowland sites, other species not found on the uplands have been able to compete successfully and achieve dominance in certain wetland communities.

The most distinctive, though least common, type of swamp vegetation is the white-cedar forest found in narrow bands along the streams. Often these forests are called cedar "bogs" because of their accumulations of peat. The narrow, conical southern white-cedar trees grow tall and straight and so close together that they form a dense canopy, making the bog interior dark and difficult to penetrate. Between the hummocks on which the cedars stand, the water is covered with spongy mats of sphagnum moss and usually littered with fallen logs. Many rare and beautiful plants grow in more open areas of the bog—the highly prized curly grass fern, the insectivorous sundews and pitcher plants, and a variety of other herbs. There is a great variability in other tree species in a cedar swamp. Pitch pine, red maple, blackgum, or sweetbay, in particular, may occur in sparse or abundant numbers. Shrubs such as the leatherleaf, sheep laurel, dangleberry, swamp azalea, and sweet pepperbush may form a dense understory or be present only in sparse numbers.

Though cedar swamps were once very abundant, there are now only about 21,000 acres left in the Pine Barrens. Cedar is extremely susceptible to fire injury, does not resprout after stems have been killed, and can reseed itself only under certain specific conditions. The combined effects of fire and logging have favored the development of hardwood swamp forest on sites formerly occupied by cedars. In the Pine Barrens these hardwood swamps are dominated by a variety of the red maple tree known as the trident maple, for its three-lobed leaf. Two other deciduous trees, the blackgum and the sweetbay, are also abundant, and some sassafras, gray birch, and pitch pine are also usually present. In the fall the brilliant crimson foliage of the maple and blackgum and the yellow leaves of the sassafras make a sharp but pleasing contrast to the evergreen pine forests. The hardwood swamps have abundant shrubs (generally the same species as those that grow in sparse numbers in cedar bogs), but neither the variety nor the abundance of the herbaceous plants of the cedar swamps.

Ecologists identify several types of pitch pine forest that grow as transitional vegetation between the hardwood or cedar swamps and the upland pine- or oak-dominated forests. In the pitch pine lowland forests, pines account for as much as 90 percent of the forest canopy trees, and typically grow crooked and not more than twenty-five feet high, although if not damaged by fire they may be taller. Leatherleaf often forms much of the shrub growth, and there is a rich ground cover of ferns and herbs, including turkeybeard, golden club, wintergreen, and several species of orchids.

Treeless plant communities are also found in the wetlands. Inland freshwater marshes, locally known as savannas, once covered thousands of acres, but now are reduced to limited areas. The marsh plants include lowland broomsedge, bullsedge, and other grasses and grasslike plants. Shrub thickets, called spungs (or spongs), grow along stream channels or on pond margins, or form bands around depressions. Leatherleaf or high-bush blueberry, or mixtures of the two, along with sheep laurel and staggerbush, are the typical plants in these spungs; sphagnum moss and chain fern form a nearly complete groundcover.

Animal Species and Their Patterns of Distribution.   Many of the same habitat conditions that determine the patterns of plant distribution in the Pine Barrens explain the presence, or absence, of certain animal species. In particular, some species of fish, amphibians, reptiles, and insects can compete more successfully in the low-nutrient, slow-moving, acid-water habitats of the Pine Barrens than in surrounding environments, and some species of burrowing snakes and of mammals do well on the sandy soils.

Their species variety and population numbers make insects and other invertebrates the most common fauna in the Pine Barrens. The high acidity and low nutrients of soils and waters, however, are limiting factors for some species. Earthworms, for example, are not usually found in the Pine Barrens, and tree snails are not present because of the lack of calcium for shell-building. The available habitats have favored certain insect groups, including moths and gall wasps, which feed on pine and oak, and tiger beetles and velvet ants, which inhabit sandy areas. As a group, insects and other invertebrates are an essential link in ecosystem food chains; the system could not function without their presence. Of particular interest to nonscientists are the brightly colored moths and butterflies, of which about a hundred species reach their northern or southern limits in the Pine Barrens (CMP, 89). Four other groups of animals deserve further attention: mammals, fish, amphibians and reptiles, and birds.

Mammals. Thirty-five of the forty species of mammals in New Jersey are resident in the Pine Barrens. An additional four species of bats migrate through the area.[7] All the mammals are widely distributed, and none is limited to the Pine Barrens. One of the species now present, the beaver, vanished from the area by about 1820 because of overhunting, but was recently reintroduced. There are now more than one hundred active beaver colonies in the Barrens. Three other species once found in the Pine Barrens—the wolf, bobcat, and black bear—are no longer present.

The white-tailed deer, the most conspicuous species, is the only Pine Barrens mammal classed as large—having a body length of more than 3.3 feet. Twelve more with an adult body size (excluding tail) of from 10 to 30 inches are considered of intermediate size. These include the opossum, eastern cottontail rabbit, woodchuck, beaver, muskrat, red fox, gray fox, raccoon, mink, striped skunk, river otter, and eastern coyote, a newcomer to the periphery of the region. The remaining species are all small, with one, the masked shrew, measuring only 2 inches in length. These small mammals include five insect eaters (the masked, least, and short-tailed shrews and the eastern and star-nosed moles), one carnivore (the long-tailed weasel), three species of breeding bats (the little brown and big brown bats, and the eastern pipistrelle), and thirteen rodent species (the eastern chipmunk; the gray, red, and southern flying squirrels; the rice rat; the white-footed, house, and meadow jumping mice; the red-backed, meadow, and pine voles; the Norway rat; and the southern bog lemming).

Beavers, otters, weasels, minks, muskrats, and many of the smaller mammals favor the lakes, streams, and wetlands as habitats. Deer prefer shrub thickets that alternate with open areas such as abandoned fields; in winter, however, they seek shelter in the dense white-cedar swamps, where their excessive browsing has interfered with the growth of cedar seedlings in forests that have been cut over or burned. The gray fox and the red squirrel, both abundant, prefer the upland forests, as do the chipmunk, flying squirrel, raccoon, and red fox—the latter two particularly common in woodlands near farms.

Fish. Fish, particularly, are sensitive to acidity of water, and of the seventy species of freshwater fish reported in New Jersey only sixteen are characteristic of undisturbed Pine Barrens streams.[8] These species, which flourish in acid, low-nutrient, and slow-moving stream waters, are not commonly found in other areas of New Jersey; rather, the Pine Barrens fish fauna is more closely associated with that of southeastern North America.

Many Pine Barrens fish are strongly patterned and are sought after for aquariums. This is particularly true of the blackbanded sunfish, the species said to be most characteristic of the Pine Barrens. Marked with striking black and straw-colored bands, this fish is found in most streams and lakes. Two other sunfish typical of the region, the banded and the mud sunfish, prefer cedar-water habitats. The eastern mudminnow, yellow bullhead, pirate perch, ironcolor shiner, and swamp darter are common fish along stream margins. The pickerel is distinctive as the only large native gamefish.

At the periphery of the Pine Barrens, where waters are less acid, additional fish species are found—the golden shiner, white sucker, banded killifish, mummichog, redbreast sunfish, pumpkinseed, white perch, and yellow perch. Several species of marine (anadromous) fish, including the blueback herring, alewife, American shad, and striped bass, spawn in the lower portions of the larger Pine Barrens rivers, but do not enter the more acid upland streamwaters.

Amphibians and Reptiles. Considering its northern location, the Pine Barrens has an unusually rich and diverse community of amphibians and reptiles (herpetofauna). Of the fifty-nine species reported in the Pine Barrens, there are eleven salamanders, fifteen toads and frogs, twelve turtles, three lizards, and eighteen snakes.[9] Only four of these are introduced species, now successfully reproducing themselves—a frog, two turtles, and a snake. Although most of the species are widely distributed over eastern and northeastern North America, many reach the limit of their ranges in the Pine Barrens, and an unusual number have decidedly southern affinities. Some zoogeographers believe that these probably arrived during warmer postglacial times and have been eliminated from areas surrounding the Pine Barrens because of habitat destruction.

Seven species found in the Pine Barrens occur nowhere else in New Jersey—the Pine Barrens treefrog, the carpenter frog, the ground skink, and four snakes (the northern pine, northern scarlet, northern red-bellied, and corn snakes). Two more species (the eastern king snake and the rough green snake) are confined mostly to the Barrens, although they have been found in a few fringe areas. Of the nine species, the Pine Barrens treefrog and the northern pine snake occur only in isolated populations outside New Jersey; the other seven species occur in other states along the Atlantic Coastal Plain.

Both upland and wetland sites are important for maintenance of the herpetofauna populations. To survive, salamanders, frogs, turtles, and certain snakes need access to ponds, streams, or wetlands. Upland forests provide breeding sites, food resources, and shelter for numbers of lizards, snakes, and some salamanders that breed in woodland wet depressions. Disturbed sites such as gravel pits and abandoned fields or building structures serve as breeding grounds for fourteen species of herpetofauna.

Birds. Ecologist Jack McCormick identified 144 species of birds that regularly breed or reside in the Pine Barrens; this count was later confirmed by Dr. Charles Leck, although he noted that many more species could be added to the count as transients.[10] McCormick suggested that considering the adequacy of food resources, the species total does not indicate an unusually rich diversity of birds in the Pine Barrens. The uniformity of tree heights in upland forests and of the heath shrub layer appear to limit the type of nest sites, nest materials, and perches available and this in turn restricts bird species distribution.

The rufous-sided towhee is the most abundant breeding bird in the upland regions, with the gray catbird more common in the wetlands. The wild turkey, once abundant, became extinct in the Barrens because of unrestricted hunting; recent attempts to reestablish it appear successful. A permanently lost species is the once abundant but now extinct heath hen, the eastern race of the prairie chicken.

Common in all upland habitats are two birds of prey (the turkey vulture and the American kestrel), two game birds (the ruffed grouse and the bobwhite), and several birds of southern affinity (the Carolina chickadee and, in lesser numbers, the Carolina wren and the northern mockingbird). The species most likely to nest in pine-dominated forests are the towhee, the pine and prairie warblers, the brown thrasher, and the whip-poor-will. Among birds that appear to prefer the oak-dominated forest as breeding sites are the screech owl, downy woodpecker, blue jay, Carolina chickadee, tufted titmouse, red-eyed vireo, ovenbird, and black-and-white warbler. Breeding species in the cedar swamps include the gray catbird; eastern wood-pewee; yellow-throated vireo; common yellowthroat, American redstart, and several other warblers; and song sparrow. Red-winged blackbirds are abundant in the marshes and shallow lakes; streams attract green herons, various ducks, and spotted sandpipers. Numerous other species are found in the Pine Barrens in nonbreeding seasons. In winter the dark-eyed junco, mourning dove, rock dove, and downy woodpecker are typically present, along with many species of waterfowl, these latter varying with the amount of open water and freezing weather. During the spring and fall migratory seasons additional species pass through the Pine Barrens; there are impressive flights of hawks (especially the sharp-shinned hawk) and large numbers of warblers, thrushes, and sparrows.

Fire appears to have some influence on bird populations. Eastern bluebirds, whose overall population has declined, show increases on sites that have been burned. This is true also of the common nighthawk and the chipping sparrow. Conversely, populations of towhees and brown thrashers appear to decline as a result of fire.

Human Imprints on the Landscape

The typical picture of the New Jersey Pine Barrens is one of wooded uplands and wetlands interrupted only infrequently by blueberry fields, cranberry bogs, and small settlements, and crisscrossed by miles of narrow, winding sand roads. This scene best characterizes the central Pine Barrens (the area north of the Mullica River); to a lesser extent, it also describes the land in the south, which also is heavily forested and sparsely inhabited. The human population of the Pine Barrens is concentrated on the northern, eastern, and western perimeters. Large agricultural operations are located on the more fertile lands along the western and southwestern edges, with an important farming outlier in the Hammonton area.

Though a relative wilderness in the midst of a large metropolitan area, the Pine Barrens is home to many people. Some work within its boundaries, but many more travel outside each day for their employment. Others, who lived and worked in other areas of the state or the county, have come to the Pine Barrens to retire. Visitors by the thousands also come from outside the area, a few to harvest blueberries, but most to canoe, hunt, or enjoy other outdoor recreational pursuits. The landscape of the Pine Barrens bears strong human imprints—political, social, and economic—of both present and past interactions with the natural resources.

Political Institutions and Influences. That political boundaries do not necessarily coincide with those delineating ecosystems or distinctive natural resources is well illustrated in the Pine Barrens. New Jersey is divided into twenty-one counties, and further subdivided into 567 municipalities (or townships). The state-designated Pinelands Area and the larger federal Pinelands National Reserve include portions of seven counties, with most of the land falling into Burlington, Ocean, and Atlantic counties. The 1,460 square miles of the Pinelands Area encompasses eleven municipalities entirely and varying portions of forty-one more (see Table A.2). The reserve stretches into 4 additional townships. Thus the Pine Barrens is a patchwork of local political units. For most of its history, New Jersey has had a strong tradition of home rule. Until recently most governmental revenues were derived from local property taxes and most governmental services were administered at the local level. Though the enactment of a state income tax in the late 1970s lightened the property tax burden, more than 40 percent of all state, county, and local expenditures still are supported by local assessments on property. Thus, home rule tradition remains a dominant influence in public decision-making processes. Certainly, in the Pine Barrens support for the principle of home rule has been a powerful force in molding a framework for the protection of the region.

Control of land-use activities in New Jersey rests primarily with each municipality, which is required to adopt a master plan as a prerequisite to establishing municipal zoning ordinances. Although New Jersey's county governments play a minor role in the procedures that govern land-use activities, county political organizations can wield enormous influence over general land-use policy through their domination of nominations for county boards of chosen freeholders as well as for the state legislature.[11]

Combined with New Jersey's strong tradition of localism is a long-standing north-vs.-south cleavage that had its origin in the division of the land by the British into two colonies—East (or North) Jersey and West (or South) Jersey. North Jersey, oriented to New York, is described as being "more industrialized, highly populated and liberal, while the south (oriented to Philadelphia) is more rural and conservative."[12] Politically, all land south of a line drawn from south of Trenton east to Point Pleasant has been considered the South Jersey domain. In 1980, in nonbinding referenda, a majority of voters in these five southern counties endorsed the notion of secession from the state. The action was in response to a well-organized publicity ploy to politicize the feeling that "South Jersey has gotten the short end of the stick" regarding representation in state appointments and share of the budget.[13] Expressions of sectionalism have always clouded discussions of Pine Barrens issues; as recently as 1985 a South Jersey public official claimed that residents of North Jersey were trying to stake off the Pine Barrens for their own recreational use and reserve its valuable groundwaters as a clean water source for North Jersey.[14]

Patterns of Settlement.   Just how many people live in the Pine Barrens has yet to be determined. According to the 1980 census, about 495,000 individuals lived in the fifty-two municipalities that are included, wholly or in part, within the state-designated Pinelands Area. However, the boundaries of these municipalities do not correspond exactly with the boundaries of the Pinelands Area; indeed, for the most part, human population is concentrated outside the area's perimeters. Perhaps not many more than 300,000 individuals, if that many, actually live in the Pinelands Area. Washington Township, a municipality of 107 square miles in the core of the Barrens, had a 1980 population of 808, a density of only eight persons per square mile. The adjoining municipality of Woodland Township, only slightly smaller in area, had a density of twenty-four people per square mile. Eleven additional municipalities entirely within the Pinelands Area had population densities of less than one hundred per square mile. These are striking numbers when one considers that the overall population density in New Jersey in 1985 reached 1,000 people per square mile. In the Pinelands Area, municipalities with the highest population densities are either in the west or northwest—Berlin Boro and Township, Medford Lakes Boro, and Wrightstown—or in the northeast—South Tom's River, Lakehurst, and Beachwood. Despite experiencing rapid growth in recent years, the municipalities on the fringe of Atlantic City, according to 1980 Census counts, still have relatively low densities.

More than fifty discrete settlements (as opposed to legally incorporated municipalities) within the Pinelands Area have been identified as traditional Pinelands villages or towns (Figure 1–4). Various writers have suggested that Chatsworth in Woodland Township best represents this traditional Pine Barrens settlement. Calling it the capital of the Pines, John McPhee described it in this fashion almost twenty years ago:

> From the air, two miles away, Chatsworth is not visible under the high cover of oaks and pines. The town consists of three hundred and six people, seventy-four houses, ten trailers, a firehouse, a church, a liquor store, a post office, a school, two sawmills, and one general store.[15]

Though its population has grown slightly, recent years have brought little change in Chatsworth. It might be noted also that McPhee's inventory failed to include the remains of the abandoned White Horse Inn (or Shamong Hotel), which in the nineteenth century catered to stagecoach travelers, and later belonged to the Italian prince who founded the huge lakeside Chatsworth Club. In the early 1900s the Chatsworth complex attracted the elite of society from New York and Europe. It later was abandoned and the club destroyed by fire.

Natives of the Pine Barrens have given distinctive names to many places of local interest. Some identify natural land or water features—Apple Pie Hill, Double Trouble, Stop-the-Jade Run, Gum Spung, and Hog Wallow. Others mark the location of former structures or hamlets—Quaker Bridge, Martha Furnace, Sim Place, and Ong's Hat. The last was derived, according to one version, from the name of a young man who "while considerably in liquor" threw his high silk hat into a tree where it remained for many months.[16]

The settlement of South Jersey and its cultural and ethnic groups have been studied by geographers, historians, sociologists, human ecologists, and folklorists.[17] Particular attention has been paid to a single cultural

Trenton

Camden

Jackson

Wrightstown
Juliustown McGuire
Birmingham Pemberton
Evansville
New Lisbon
Browns Mills
Vincentown
Buddtown
Presidential Lakes
Marlton
Lake Pine Medford
Medford Lakes
Taunton Lakes
Chatsworth

Tansboro
Albion Jackson
Atco Dunbarton
Cedar Chesilhurst
Brook Waterford Works
Blue Braddock
Anchor Elm
Williamstown Winslow
Hammonton
Cecil Nesco
Folsom Green Bank
Elwood New Gretna
Newtonville
Landisville Egg Harbor City
Buena
Mizpah
Milmay Leeds Point
Dorothy Oceanville
Estell Manor
Cumberland English Creek
Port Elizabeth Sculliville
Tuckahoe Corbin City
Dorchester Belleplain
Leesburg Petersburg
Heislerville Delmont Woodbine
Eldora
Dennisville
South S. Seaville
Dennis Clermont
Swaintown

Lakehurst
Whiting South Toms River
Pinewald
Barnegat Pines
Forked River
Waretown
Warren Grove Barnegat
Manahawkin
Cedar Run
West Creek
Parkertown
Tuckerton

Atlantic City

City Populations

○	Up to 1,000
●	1,000-5,000
☉	5,000-10,000
◉	10,000-25,000
◎	25,000-50,000

0   5   10   15
miles

Figure 1–4. Settlements in the Pinelands National Reserve. Map by Tina Campbell.

group, the Pineys. Although recent studies suggest that earlier images portraying the Pineys as hillbillies, remote and isolated from surrounding social and political institutions, are in error, a clear definition of "Piney" remains elusive. Indeed, in her search to define "Pineyness," Nora Rubinstein reports that she came full circle:

> "Pineyness" was based on geographical location, at various stages in life, with birth-place being of greatest significance. [It also included] ancestry, age, occupation, economic status, family ties, and an amorphous quality many comprehend, but few can define. . . . From geography and language, ancestry and occupation [it has come to mean] . . . a feeling for family, but most important, for the land, for the experience of "being" in the Pines. [The elusive Piney] is just over the horizon, or as Janice Sherwood said, "a little deeper in the woods than you are."[18]

Jonathan Berger and John Sinton, who have given us vivid descriptions of Piney lifestyles, emphasize that Piney cultural values are no different from those of rural people in other mid-Atlantic sections and include a love of place; a central role of family in social transactions; Christian morality; seasonal activities such as farming, hunting, fishing, and trapping; and high participation levels in local politics and in volunteer organizations such as the farm bureau and ambulance and fire companies.[19] Pineys depend heavily on use of the region's natural resources for their subsistence; they hunt, fish, clam, crab, and trap for food and cut wood for heat. A few still earn a reasonable living by "gathering"—collecting whole plants or parts of plants for sale to nurseries and florists. Traditional Pineys no longer make up the majority of the population of the Pine Barrens. Far more numerous are the residents of the western, northern, and eastern areas. These people do not depend on local resources for their livelihoods, and for this reason are sometimes identified as outsiders, not true Pineys.

Natural Resource Use.   Of the more than one million acres in the Pinelands National Reserve, only 9 percent is considered developed land; another 5 percent is used for agriculture and the remainder (86 percent) is forest or wetland (CMP, 127). All but 10 percent of the developed land is in residential use; there are no significant industrial activities or commercial centers in the Pinelands Reserve. Residential development is primarily single-family housing, and commercial development is confined mostly to small retail shops and service businesses located along highways. There are only sixteen operations employing one hundred or more workers, the largest employer being the federal government, which operates the Fort Dix, McGuire, and Lakehurst bases in the northern part of the reserve and a federal aviation technical center in the south. Much of the 48,000 acres within these federal installations is still forested.

Major north-south transportation arteries are generally on lands to the west and east outside the state-designated Pinelands Area, although one of these, the Garden State Parkway, to the east, does pass through the Pinelands National Reserve. A wide band of heavily-used east-west road and rail facilities connecting the Philadelphia-Camden metropolitan area to Atlantic City bisects the Pine Barrens. The Pinelands is probably best known for the hundreds of miles of two-rutted sand roads that crisscross the region.

Scenic rivers and walking trails attract thousands of canoeists, hikers, trailbikers, and nature lovers to the Pine Barrens. Two federal wildlife refuges in the reserve—Brigantine and Barnegat-Holgate (now known as the Edwin Forsythe National Wildlife Refuge)—and an additional 275,000 acres of state-owned forests, parks, and wildlife management areas provide varied opportunities for fishing, trapping, swimming, camping, and hunting—especially deer hunting. In the interior woods are several hundred small camps used by hunting clubs; in season "the woods reverberate with horns and shouts of the deer drives."[20]

The Pine Barrens is more than just a place for living, however, or for recreational use. Major economic activities—agriculture, timbering, and mining—also take place within the region, and all are dependent on use of the natural resources.

Cranberries, Blueberries, Fruits, and Vegetables. Berry culture is an integral element of the Pine Barrens landscape. Both cranberries and blueberries are native plants that flourish on highly acid, low-nutrient, sandy soils with high water tables. Though wild berries were used as food by the Indians, commercial berry culture did not start in the Pine Barrens until 1835, when the first cranberry bog was planted. Now more than 12 percent of the nation's crop comes from here.

Cranberry bogs are shallow basins, dredged and then diked on all sides so that they can be flooded to prevent early frost damage and winter kill and to aid in the harvesting process. Mechanical equipment is used to shake loose ripened berries, which then float to the surface where they are collected for sorting and packing. Only about three thousand acres of bogs are required to produce New Jersey's share of the national cranberry crop; however tradition has it that for every acre of bog, growers need ten additional acres of upland to ensure that the critical resource—a reservoir of unpolluted water—is available in adequate supply when needed.

Figure 1—5. A Typical Scene in the New Jersey Pinelands. A sand road stretches through an upland forest dominated by pitch pine trees. Photo courtesy of the Pinelands Commission.

Figure 1–6. Wetland Habitats in the Pinelands: The impounded Forge Pond at Batsto in Wharton State Forest, site of the Batsto forge built in 1781. Photo by David Borrelli, courtesy of Wharton State Forest.

Figure 1–7. Dwarf Pine Forest on the Pine Plains. Multiple-stemmed pitch pine and blackjack oak trees grow no more than four to six feet tall, making it possible to look over the top of the forest canopy. Photo by Ted Gordon; copyright Pinelands Commission.

Figure 1–8. Wetland Habitats in the Pinelands: View of cedar bog along the Wading River. Photo by William W. Leap; copyright Pinelands Commission.

Figure 1–9. Batsto Village: The restored Batsto mansion. The earliest portion of the home was erected before 1800 to serve as the residence of the ironmaster. Photo by David Borrelli.

Figure 1–10. Batsto Village: Aerial view of the restored village of Batsto in Wharton State Forest. Batsto was an active ironworks community from the 1760s to the 1860s and also served as a munitions center during the Revolutionary War. Photo courtesy of the New Jersey Department of Environmental Protection, Wharton State Forest.

Figure 1–11. Batsto Village: Restored homes of workers at the Batsto forge. The architecture is characteristic of early South Jersey building. Photo by David Borrelli.

Figure 1–12. Wildfire in the Pinelands. For thousands of years wildlife has been a natural occurrence in the Pinelands. Frequent burning is essential for maintenance of pine-dominated forests. Photo of wildfire in Atlantic County, May 1971, taken by Carl E. Owen, New Jersey Forest Fire Service; copyright Pinelands Commission.

Figure 1–13. Cranberry Culture in the Pinelands: Mechanical harvesters are driven through the flooded bogs to knock ripened cranberries off the vines. Photo by David Borrelli.

Figure 1–14. Cranberry Culture in the Pinelands: The floating berries are directed into a small area at the side of the bog and then loaded mechanically into a truck parked on the bog dike. Photo copyright T. Stephan Thompson.

Figure 1–15. Recreation in the Pinelands: Canoeing on the Oswego River. Photo by Robert Hastings; copyright Pinelands Commission.

Figure 1–16. Recreation in the Pinelands: Hiking on the Batona Trail. Photo courtesy of the Pinelands Commission.

Active cranberry bogs, along with their supporting reservoirs and drainage systems of dams, gates, dikes and ditches, add much to the landscape diversity. The few remaining local cranberry sorting and packing houses testify to the role that berry culture has played in the past. Settlements formed around these operations with housing for workers, tool sheds, storage barns, garages, and often a company store.[21] In Whitesbog, for example, the remains of one large cranberry village can still be seen.

Whitesbog was also the headquarters for the series of breeding experiments that spawned commercial cultivation of blueberries in New Jersey. Starting in 1911, Elizabeth White worked with F. V. Colville to select the best of the local wild-growing plants as initial breeding stock. Now New Jersey is the second largest producer of blueberries in the nation, and much of its crop is produced in the Pine Barrens. Today the area of blueberry cultivation overlaps that of cranberry culture, and extends farther to the south. The largest blueberry operations are located in the Hammonton–Egg Harbor area.

Where there is a higher clay content in the soil and a lower water table, a tree fruit industry has developed. The orchards, apple and peach, are located in the southern part of the Pine Barrens; one center is on land lying between Berlin on the west and Hammonton and Egg Harbor City on the east and another is in the Vineland area. A variety of vegetable crops is grown on the same soils. Both types of cultivation, however, require substantial liming to reduce soil acidity and large quantities of fertilizer to increase soil nutrients, particularly nitrogen. Runoff from limed and fertilized fields has affected the water quality of local streams, which show higher level of nutrients and higher pH values (lower acidity) than typical undisturbed Pine Barrens streams.[22] Berry culture, it should be noted, though more compatible with the Pine Barrens environment, also requires use of fertilizers and pesticides.

Timbering. Though there are about 750,000 wooded acres in the Pine Barrens, state foresters bemoan their low yield of forest products. In 1977 New Jersey's state forester reported that the entire region yielded about 0.09 cords per acre (or about 1 cord for each 10 acres); he described this as "an appallingly low figure."[23] Poor soils, frequent fires, and repeated wood-cutting since Europeans settled the area are responsible for the condition of the forests today. For example, most current oak trees originated as sprouts after fire or cutting; as a result, many have developed two or more trunks from one root crown. Such multiple-stemmed trees have less resistance to insect and fungus attack and are more susceptible to having their tops snapped off by strong winds. Pines are crooked and few have been allowed to grow to the heights of trees that early settlers reported seeing. Furthermore, extensive cutting has dramatically reduced the acreage of white-cedar swamps.

The uses of timber from the Pine Barrens were many. Lumber, tar, and pitch were taken to supply the early ship-building industry; oak, cedar, and some pine saw-logs were used for home-building in cities and towns outside the region. More pine provided fuelwood and charcoal needed to heat homes in early Philadelphia, New York, Newark, and Wilmington, as well as to supply the industries that flourished in the Pines during the century from 1760 to 1860. Although by the 1860s coal had generally replaced wood as a fuel, fuelwood continued to be, and still is, taken from the Pine Barrens. Today pine is also used for pulpwood and some lumber. Cedar, however, because it is rot-resistant, continues to be the most valuable wood of the region; it is used for posts and poles and, in sawn form, for shingles, boat-building, and a variety of other uses. No area of the Pine Barrens has escaped being cut; state foresters estimate that since European settlement, the forests of the Pine Barrens have been cut over at least five times.

The impacts of repeated cutting combined with those of frequent fire are reflected in the structural appearance and species composition of the present forests. Clearcutting in upland woods (as distinct from selective thinning), together with fire, favors pine, because pine seedlings develop best in open areas. In the lowlands, regeneration of cedar forests is favored after a clearcutting, if seed trees are available nearby.

Mining for Sands and Gravels. Geologic formations—the Cohansey and the overlying deposits that are responsible for development of the particular soils and vegetation that characterize the Pine Barrens—have provided a rich source of gravels and sands. For hundreds of years these deposits have been mined to supply local needs for road development and industry, particularly the glass industry. According to a survey made by the National Parks Service in 1984, there are seventy-five active mining sites, involving more than 15,000 acres of land, within the boundaries of the Pinelands National Reserve. These activities are located mainly in Ocean, Burlington, Atlantic, and eastern Cumberland counties.

Though an important feature of the economy of South Jersey, mining operations are in the eyes of many a blight on the landscape. Land is levelled and stripped of its natural vegetation and soils, and often surface and ground waters are disturbed. In the past, gravel pits have been abandoned without any attempt at restoration and, in a few cases, the pits have been converted to use as landfills without appropriate action to prevent the contamination of ground water by the leachates.

A Century of Industrialization. Thousands of years ago prehistoric people, and later the Indians, left marks on the landscape of the Pine Barrens by intentionally, or accidentally, setting fires. They also may have altered the natural relative abundance of particular animal or plant species by hunting and gathering for food. Although traces of these activities remain, their impact on the resources was almost nil compared with that of European settlers and their descendants.

The smelting of iron ore began in the Pine Barrens in the 1760s. Furnaces were built to process bog iron, which develops when rainwater soaks through the forest litter and becomes acid enough to leach iron out of the clays. This dissolved iron then travels through the groundwater to streams, where it is oxidized, precipitated, and finally deposited on stream banks. Bacterial action cements the iron precipitate and sand grains together into a crust called bog iron.

During the late eighteenth and early nineteenth centuries, as many as twenty-nine furnaces and forges were established along the major drainage systems in the Pines. Batsto became a munitions center for Washington's armies during the Revolutionary War, and the area "was dotted with sizable communities built around ironworks, paper mills, sawmills, glass factories, brickmaking establishments, cotton mills, and grist mills."[24] In the mid-1800s, competition from furnaces in Pennsylvania, which were close to supplies of superior ore, coal for fuel, and rail services for transport of finished products, ruined the Pine Barrens iron industry.

The paper industry, which had grown up during the same time, continued to flourish for a few more decades. The community that developed around the prosperous Harrisville plant, for example, was famed for the rows of gas-illuminated ornamental lamps that lined its main street. Eventually, the Harrisville paper operation failed, as did other industries in the Pines. By the end of the nineteenth century, factories, forges, and villages had been abandoned, and today only ruins of the once-thriving industrial activities remain. These are the ghost, or vanished, towns of the Pines.

The century of industrialization had significant impact on the landscape. The iron forges and furnaces consumed huge amounts of charcoal, which was made from cordwood and smaller trees. To supply local industries as well as the export demand for fuelwood and charcoal, the forests of the Pine Barrens had to be cut repeatedly. Fires ignited accidentally from the furnace, forge, or charcoaling activities also took their toll. Impoundments of streams made one or two hundred years ago to supply power to local industries still exist and influence drainage patterns. And, finally, the sand roads and now-abandoned railroad lines that connected the early industrial operations with their supporting services (including tavern stops) determined the paths along which settlement took place during the following century.

Land Speculation: The Aftermath of Industrialization.   When the demand for iron and charcoal dropped off, a century of industrialization in the Pines came to an end. Although glass has remained an important industry in the economy of South Jersey, it moved from the center of the Pine Barrens to more-settled fringe areas. This abandonment of early industrial sites left the area open for unsound land-speculation schemes.

Unscrupulous real estate promoters, through high-pressure salesmanship, sold hundreds of thousands of unusable small homesites or farm lots to city dwellers who had little knowledge of the worthless property they were being offered. Lots were staked out on paper only and, as transportation to the Pine Barrens was not easily available, even for residents of New York and Philadelphia, naïve investors bought without visiting the development site.

The most notorious of the land speculation schemes was Magic City—Paisley—which was to be developed on a 1,400-acre tract in the heart of Barrens, between Chatsworth and Tabernacle. In 1888 the first advertisement for Paisley appeared in New York newspapers. It announced the availability of house sites and of small plots of the "finest" farming land.[25] Homesites were priced at $50 to $100 each and a five-acre farm lot could be had for just $175. Buyers were assured that property values would increase with the promised development of community buildings, a hotel, colleges, sanitoriums, factories, and even a music academy. By 1895 more than 10,000 house lots and 216 farm plots had been sold. Only twelve dwellings and one small factory, however, were ever built in the Magic City—and a small cottage was dubbed the Paisley Inn. Few buyers ever ventured into the Pine Barrens to see their investments. Most of those who did came by railroad and hack, had difficulty locating their lots, and returned home sorely disappointed. The Magic City was eventually abandoned, as were most of the other high-flying speculative schemes. Roads that had been cut have been overgrown with brush and only an occasional street sign marks the dreams of the past.

Although a few communities, such as Medford Lakes, Browns Mills, and agricultural settlements around Hammonton and Vineland, owe their existence to speculation, the principal result of these schemes has been confusion of title claims. There were more than 400 unsound land-promotion schemes in the Pine Barrens, from which more than one million individuals suffered losses.[26] In ten Burlington County townships alone 180,000 lots existed as paper subdivisions only. Typically each was no larger than twenty-five by one hundred feet. These worthless land divisions eventually became a problem for municipal officials and led to fraudulent land claims, some of which are still being tried in court. Much of the property became tax delinquent, and, in New Jersey, townships are required to pay county and state assessments on all property even if delinquent. To avoid such payments, some municipalities tried simply to lose the records of the lots for which no taxes were being paid, thus removing them from the tax rolls completely. When the state finally took action to force municipalities to account for every parcel, tax-delinquent property owners could not always be located. As a result, many titles to Pine Barrens property still are clouded.

Resource Use and Ecosystem Stress

The Pine Barrens ecosystem is dynamic. Changes in interrelationships among and between plant and animal populations—including humans—and elements of the physical environment—soils and water in particular—may change individual ecosystem components, biotic or abiotic. Human use of the natural resources adds a powerful dimension to this potential for change.

No sure knowledge is available of the natural landscape as it existed prior to European settlement, but scientists do believe that with minor exceptions today's vegetation types have existed for thousands of years. It is likely, however, that prior to the intensive exploitation of the woodlands by humans there was a greater diversity in both the size and age of trees in the pine- and oak-dominated forests. Certainly there were many more larger and older specimen trees. There remains evidence of individual white-cedar trees that had attained the age of 1,000 years and of whole forests that had survived for 200 years. On the species level is more evidence of change. Presettlement vegetation did not include 270 plant species and an unknown number of animal species that are now present and reproducing themselves in the region. On the other hand, a large number of native plants and animals have been extirpated, and many others with declining populations are now reported to be endangered or threatened species. Human actions have created a variety of new habitats for plant and animal species in the Pine Barrens. Abandoned cranberry bogs, mining pits, agricultural fields, iron forges, and railroad right-of-ways have been quickly colonized by invading plants and animals, thus helping—along with small settlements, agriculture and timbering operations, and frequent fires (whether intentional or accidental)—to make the Pine Barrens a more diverse landscape.

There are limits, however, to the amount of human disturbance that the ecosystem can withstand without changing its essential characteristics. Increased nutrient loading of the interconnected ground and surface water systems, both from new development and from agricultural land runoff, and decrease in the water acidity from the liming of lawns and fields, allow noncharacteristic species of plants and animals to outcompete traditional members of aquatic and wetland communities. Survival of characteristic fish and herpetofauna, such as the Pine Barrens treefrog, for example, depends on the existence of acidic waters. When nutrient levels, particularly of nitrate-nitrogen, rise above the normal range, invaders from plant communities outside the Pine Barrens replace native species and the composition of wetland communities is altered. A further stress on the ecosystem comes from pumping of groundwater beyond safe yields. Such pumping can change ground water levels and so directly affect both stream flow and the differentiation of wetland from upland habitats. This, in turn, will alter patterns of plant and animal distribution.

Frequent fire, as has been noted, is a natural stress in the ecosystem to which the characteristic plants and animals have adapted themselves. Changes in this fire regime, mostly by human-initiated fire prevention, causes a disturbance in the system. Over the past four decades, improved fire-control measures have sharply reduced the total number of acres burned annually in the Pine Barrens and increased dramatically the intervals between burnings.[27] Because pitch pines depend upon regular burnings to maintain their abundance, however, such a fire prevention program will change the components of the ecosystem. Pitch pines will decrease in abundance and oaks will increase. Ecologists speculate that, in an extreme case, this may result in a landscape more appropriately described as the "oaklands." It could also cause the disappearance of the famous dwarf pine forest.

Tighter fire-control measures, increased pollution of streams, and greater demands on groundwater supplies are directly associated with increased development in the Pine Barrens. Of particular scientific concern is the fragmentation of the natural ecosystem into smaller-sized, often isolated, units to accommodate development. This may, in turn, reduce the number of native species and the genetic diversity of the entire system, thus diminishing its capability to adapt to changing environmental conditions and ultimately to survive.

At the time of European colonization the New Jersey Pine Barrens stretched uninterrupted for about eighty miles from north to south, and thirty miles east to west. Since then the fringes of the region have been nibbled away by development, and intrusions into the interior have dissected the natural communities of vegetation and animals into smaller patches. The immediate local impacts of such fragmentation may be readily apparent in the extinction of a rare species or the disappearance of a particular vegetation type, but the total, long-term impact of these changes on the Pine Barrens ecosystem as a whole may not be quite so easy to see for some time. The complexity of ecosystem processes and the spatial and temporal heterogeneity of patterns of biological distribution often obscure single small changes. But in the aggregate, small changes can have dramatic effects on the continued viability of natural communities, and particularly on those communities that reflect the essential character of the Pine Barrens.

Starting in the 1950s, concern about threats to the ecosystem from development led to heated discussions of appropriate resource use and ultimately to legislative action to protect the Pine Barrens landscape.

2. The Backdrop for Pinelands Legislation

Beryl Robichaud Collins

U nusually strong environmental legislation to protect the New Jersey Pinelands was enacted in the late 1970s. To understand the reasons why this happened, one must look at events that occurred in preceding decades. Therein lies the genesis of both federal and state legislative actions.

Until the late 1940s the population of the United States, as of other developed countries, was concentrated in metropolitan areas. Following World War II, there was explosive growth—in population, in number of households, and in the economy. At the same time, innovations in ground and air transportation and in communication technology were developing and were providing a stimulus for populations to disperse and for industries to decentralize by moving away from increasingly crowded and expensive metropolitan areas.

The Pine Barrens, with a population in 1950 of only sixty-five people per square mile, was not to be immune to the impacts of this growth and dispersal trend, which has continued into the 1980s.[1] Before World War II the Pine Barrens was considered a hinterland—remote from the population clustered near the New York metropolitan area and close to the city of Philadelphia. But beginning in the 1950s eyes began to turn toward the Pine Barrens as a potential area for development. At the same time, interest in conservation of the Pine Barrens was also evolving. Inevitably, land-development and resource-conservation goals clashed.

The 1950s: Seeds of Conflict Are Planted

From 1950 to 1960 the population of New Jersey increased by about 25 percent, with the greatest growth occurring outside the older urban areas. None of this early population diffusion had an immediate impact on the Pine Barrens, however. Even the opening in 1955 of the first segment of the Garden State Parkway did not appear to threaten the Barrens with development. The parkway brought the northern part of the Pine Barrens within a two-hour drive of New Jersey's New York metropolitan area residents. Initially, most were interested only in faster access to shore recreational facilities; eventually, however, the parkway and the decentralization of industry would make living year 'round at the shore a practical reality for many.

The shortening of the work week after World War II had given people more leisure time. The need for additional facilities for outdoor activities became recognized, and in 1955 the state responded by consummating the long-delayed acquisition of 100,000 acres encompassing much of the Mullica River basin in the Pine Barrens. This tract became the Wharton State Forest. It offered a wide variety of recreational opportunities, and would introduce many people to the Pine Barrens. In so doing, it would also foster interest in conservation of the region.

Growth of Conservation Interest.   Since the days of European exploration, the New Jersey Pine Barrens has been of great interest to naturalists. Early descriptions focused on the distinctive plant life and the contrasts in vegetation and soil fertility between the Barrens and the surrounding land. In 1911 Witmer Stone, a Philadelphia zoologist and naturalist, made an extensive floristic study, which he used to delineate the boundaries of the Pine Barrens as they then existed. These were refined by John Harshberger, a plant geographer, also of Philadelphia, who in 1916 published a map and comprehensive description of the types of plant communities found in the Barrens.

In the mid-1940s Dr. Silas Little started a long and productive research career at the United States Department of Agriculture's Northeast Forest Station in Lebanon State Forest in the Pine Barrens, where he demonstrated the need for setting controlled fires to maintain the dominance of pine trees. At about the same time, at Rutgers University, Dr. Murray Buell, a distinguished ecologist, established one of the country's early academic programs in ecology. Many of his graduate students were to undertake research projects in the Pine Barrens. One of them, Jack McCormick, inventoried the vegetation in two watersheds. His work still provides the most complete ecological information available about plant communities in the Pine Barrens, and his delineation of the boundary of the Pine Barrens as it existed in 1957 remains an authoritative guide for the region.[2]

Complementary to these scientific research studies, and equally important, have been the findings of field naturalists for whom the study of the Pine Barrens has been a full-time avocation. These experts regularly comb the Pines and identify critical habitats of the many species of flora and fauna. In 1957 a group of such individuals was called together by Joe Truncer, who then worked for state parks and forests operations. Truncer wanted a committee that could advise the state on botanical issues associated with the development of the Wharton tract.[3] Out of this committee came the first public-interest group dedicated to the protection of the

New Jersey Pine Barrens—the Pine Barrens Conservationists. Among its members were Dot and Brooks Evert, Eileen and Lou Hand, and Elizabeth Woodford, all of whom worked tirelessly over a long period of time to protect the Pine Barrens. At first, the Pine Barrens Conservationists concentrated on preparation of flora and fauna inventories and establishment of nature trails and educational programs. Members of other conservation organizations joined in these efforts, including Mort and Betty Cooper, leaders of the Ocean Nature and Conservation Society, and Frank Mc-Laughlin, director of the New Jersey Audubon Society and spokesman on statewide wildlife conservation issues. The primary focus of the Pine Barrens Conservationists and their associates quickly changed, however, when in the late 1950s Burlington County officials proposed that a major airport be sited in the Pine Barrens on land in Lebanon State Forest.

County Proposal for a Jetport in the Pine Barrens.   South Jersey, other than the Camden-Philadelphia area, did not immediately participate in the postwar economic boom. The explosive state population growth of the 1950s—an increase of more than one million people—was accommodated for the most part in new suburban areas close to existing urban centers. Although, as noted above, there was an upward surge in demand for vacation and year-'round housing in coastal communities, there was little other development activity in the southern counties.

County and local officials, however, were eager for South Jersey to share in the economic resurgence. In the mid 1950s, even before the Port Authority of New York and New Jersey initiated preliminary studies on the needs for additional airport facilities, Burlington County Planning Director George Rogers proposed that "the Pine Barrens would make an ideal site for jet travel in the northeastern United States."[4] His suggestion was heartily endorsed by the Burlington County Board of Freeholders, which in 1958 announced preliminary plans for an international jet terminal that would occupy 16,000 of the 22,000 acres within Lebanon State Forest in the heart of the Pine Barrens. The county then applied for a federal grant to finance engineering surveys for the project. The Civil Aeronautics Administration, however, refused to endorse the county's proposal, saying that from an air-traffic control standpoint, it was "neither economically sound nor practical."[5] This did not deter Burlington officials, who continued to press for consideration of their plans.

In December 1959 the Port Authority announced that it had selected the Great Swamp (in Morris County in northern New Jersey) as the site for a new jet airport. The immediate, explosive opposition to this choice by area residents set the stage for what would be a decade of controversy about the possible use of the Pine Barrens as an alternative site for the airport complex.

The 1960s: A Decade of Jetport Controversy

The 1959 Port Authority report that identified a need for another major airport in the New York–New Jersey metropolitan area pinpointed the Great Swamp site as the only one out of fifteen possibilities that met all its defined criteria. The Port Authority claimed that none of the South Jersey sites it had considered, including two in the Pine Barrens, satisfactorily met air-space and ground travel-time requirements. This finding immediately raised controversy in two quarters and for completely different reasons.

First, residents in Morris County joined together in an extraordinary effort to oppose the siting of a jetport in the Great Swamp. In so doing, they took on the powerful Port Authority, which heretofore, under the authoritarian management of Austin Tobin, had been widely acclaimed for its effective role in developing bridges, tunnels, and marine and air terminals in the metropolitan area. The fascinating story of this fight to save the Great Swamp from airport development has been told by Cam Cavanaugh.[6]

Second, Burlington County officials wanted the airport badly and enlisted neighboring Ocean County as a partner in their effort to site the jetport in the Pine Barrens. On February 23, 1960, the Burlington County freeholders created by resolution a Pinelands Regional Planning Board, as an instrumentality of both Burlington and Ocean counties, and charged it to prepare a "comprehensive long-range plan for the development of the Pinelands Region . . . and to formulate an action program for carrying out the content of the plan."[7] Although the planning region was restricted to within the boundaries of Burlington and Ocean counties, it encompassed an area of 950 square miles. Ocean County officials quickly endorsed the action. State legislators and the entire congressional delegation, feeling the pressure from Morris County residents, also vigorously supported the county's proposal and asked that the Port Authority reconsider the Pine Barrens site for the new airport. The newly appointed Pinelands Regional Planning Board also pressed hard for this reconsideration. Ultimately, its actions served as a catalyst to stimulate a widening public interest in the Pine Barrens, an interest that in turn led to the development of a strong opposition to the jetport plans.

Pinelands Regional Planning Board.   The eleven-member Pinelands Regional Planning Board (including five appointees from each of the two counties and one representative appointed by the state Commissioner of Conservation and Economic Development) was supported by federal, state, and county funding. In 1962 the board engaged Herbert H. Smith of Trenton as its consultant. Smith began by testifying before a state senate committee investigating the Port Authority. Smith's testimony countered that of Austin Tobin, who was arguing that the Pinelands region was not a feasible area for a new metropolitan jetport. Smith then focused on the preparation of a plan for the Pinelands region. He pointed out that the Pine Barrens had not yet been caught up in the "nightmare of the development cycle" and that several alternatives existed for the region—on the one hand, it was "capable of absorbing tremendous growth stimulated by an input such as a jetport"; on the other, it might "be conserved as a wildlife preserve and recreational resource"; or it might be developed according to "a combination of these alternatives."[8] Smith advocated development and sparked a bitter conflict over land-use in the Pinelands.

In June 1965 the Pinelands Regional Planning Board adopted the land-use plan, which had been developed by Smith and handsomely packaged in a 41-page report. The plan called for a jetport that would be the largest airport in the world. Occupying 32,500 acres, it would cover more than four times the combined area of the then existing three major New York–New Jersey airports. Commercial and industrial enterprises would ring the jetport area. "New City" would be built on another 10,800 acres of forested land. Designed to provide for 250,000 people, New City would become the third largest city in the state. Additional traffic would be accommodated by construction of new highways, and existing roadways would be expanded. Figure 2–1 illustrates this elaborate plan.

Though the plan also called for expansion of state park holdings, it showed a total lack of consideration for the value of existing natural and cultural resources and for the impact of development on surface and ground water quality. The jetport would obliterate the famous dwarf pine forests and an entire state forest; New City would destroy both critical plant and animal wetland habitats and the natural and cultural features of the Forked River Mountains. Although its plan was eventually rejected, the Pinelands Regional Planning Board left a significant mark by giving the first official recognition to the principle that "development problems do not confine themselves to municipal boundaries" and that "the Region must plan . . . not as individual communities alone, but together."[9]

The State's Role in the Jetport Controversy.   Governor Meyner incurred the wrath of Morris County residents when in 1961 he vetoed a bill to prohibit the establishment of a jetport in Morris or six other northern

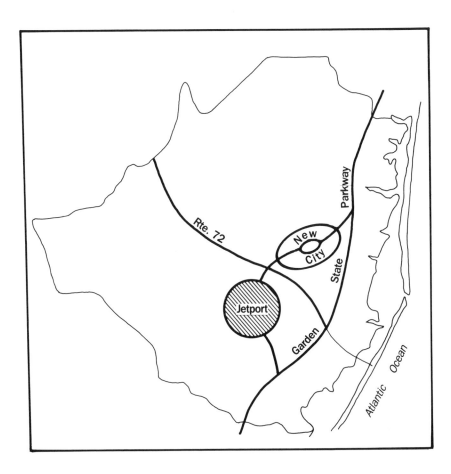

Figure 2–1. Plans for a Jetport and New City in the Pinelands. The Pinelands Regional Planning Board proposed that the Pinelands be the site for a huge international airport and a new city. Drawings show the location of the proposed development and the skyline of the city as visualized by the Planning Board. Map and drawing by Tina Campbell.

counties, while Governor Richard Hughes, who succeeded Meyner in 1962, found it politically advantageous to oppose location of a new jetport in either Morris or Hunterdon County. Throughout his eight years in office, however, Hughes did push for consideration of a South Jersey site, believing it would be economically advantageous to the state. He tried several times, but without success, to change the negative attitudes of both the Federal Aviation Agency (FAA) and the Port Authority toward the Lebanon State Forest site, which had been proposed by Burlington and Ocean county officials.

In 1967 Hughes appointed a blue-ribbon committee (officially named the Governor's Economic Evaluation Committee for an Intercontinental Airport for New Jersey) to identify the need for airport facilities in the state and to make recommendations for action. On the committee were twelve executives from leading New Jersey businesses. A thirteenth member was George Rogers, the former Burlington County planner who had originally proposed the Pine Barrens as a desirable jetport site. Funded by industry, the committee engaged consultants, who in 1968 produced a lengthy document known as the Blomquist report, which concluded that immediate construction of a major intercontinental jetport in New Jersey was essential for the health of the state's economy. Of the seven sites they studied (the Great Swamp area and six in South Jersey), the McGuire/Lakehurst site in the northern section of the Pine Barrens best met committee criteria.[10] Governor Hughes, however, was unable to convince Alan Boyd, then U.S. Secretary of Transportation, to endorse and to act on the Blomquist recommendations, nor could Hughes get the state legislature to act on the Blomquist recommendation to create a semi-autonomous jetport authority with the power of eminent domain, and so the proposal died. Hughes' successor, Republican William Cahill, was elected at least partly on the basis of his position that "New Jersey does not want and does not need a new global jetport, and we will not implement it."[11]

Public Opposition to the Jetport Plan.   Although not one member of the public voiced any objections at the February 1960 meeting during which the Burlington freeholders created the Pinelands Regional Planning Board, the body that would propose siting a jetport and a new city in the Pine Barrens, steps had already been taken to organize opposition to the jetport project. The Citizens' Committee to Save State Lands was formed to prevent development on public or private land of important recreational or conservation value. Brooks Evert, a business executive and member of the Pine Barrens Conservationists, chaired the new group, which included representatives of the New Jersey Audubon Society, the Federation of Women's Clubs, New Jersey Garden Club, the Conservation Council, and the Sportsmens League.

This committee represented the first organized effort to widen public awareness of the Pine Barrens resource values, which it did through effective publicity releases and a letter-writing campaign directed to public officials on county, state, and federal levels as well as to other community and national citizen groups. Although the committee focused on opposing the jetport in Lebanon State Forest, it also successfully prevented the use of 1,200 acres in the state-owned Wharton tract as a National Guard Tank Training Area.

Additional public-interest groups soon sprang up to oppose efforts of county officials to promote development of the Pine Barrens. One such spinoff was initiated by Richard Thorsell, then director of the New Jersey Stony Brook–Millstone Watershed Association. Thorsell pursued with the U.S. Department of the Interior and with New Jersey's Senator Harrison Williams various means of protecting the Pine Barrens by national certification of the area. Interior suggested that the status of national monument be sought. In March 1965 a Pine Barrens National Monument Committee was formed, chaired by Brooks Evert, and it immediately enlisted national conservation organizations in the efforts to secure national recognition for the area. An attractive multicolored brochure describing the outstanding natural features of the Pine Barrens was widely circulated. Members of the New Jersey Department of Parks and Forests and of the New Jersey Audubon Society joined in the push for monument status. Effective petitioning of congressmen moved the Department of the Interior to assign the National Park Service to perform new ecological studies of the Pine Barrens.[12]

In 1967 a coalition of interested individuals and conservation groups, such as the Pine Barrens Conservationists and the New Jersey Audubon Society, was organized under the name Federation of Conservationists United Societies, or more commonly, FOCUS. Under the leadership of Mort Cooper and Robert Litch, the coalition's initial effort was a two-pronged effort—to interest Congress in protecting the region and to oppose the establishment of a Pine Barrens jetport. Litch also served as editor of *The Pitch Pine*, an informative newsletter covering all past and scheduled events affecting the Barrens; readers were alerted on how and when to influence designated decision-makers.

The Federal Planning Initiative. In 1967, in response to the pressures for designating the Pine Barrens as a National Monument, the National

Park Service (NPS) was asked to perform additional scientific studies. NPS commissioned Dr. Jack McCormick, then with the Philadelphia Academy of Natural Sciences, to look specifically at the 365,000 acres in the central Pine Barrens that was threatened by the jetport development and to delineate the boundaries of an ecosystem that would "include representatives of all significant features of Pineland natural phenomena . . . and had the potential for research and educational uses."[13] As a result of the study, McCormick suggested that the Wading River and its associated watersheds—an area of about 160,000 acres—had scientific values of national significance, and he recommended that another tract of 8,000 acres of wetland in Wharton State Forest also be considered as a Natural Landmark.

The Secretary of the Interior's Advisory Board on National Parks, Historic Sites, Buildings, and Monuments agreed with McCormick's recommendations and requested that the National Park Service suggest methods by which the Pine Barrens values might be protected. This action dismayed county and local officials and their supporters, who were advocating the Pinelands Regional Planning Board plan for development in the Wading River watershed. Newspapers quickly supported the officials and reported local resentment stemming from fears about possible loss of tax revenues if more land were to be placed in public ownership. The Ocean Nature and Conservation Society reported that at one mass meeting of "mayors, property owners, marina operators, cranberry and blueberry growers, sportsmen, and conservationists . . . tempers flared, faces were red, fists clenched, and a very tense and charged atmosphere pervaded the room. Shouts of 'keep the Feds out' and 'this is a home rule state' and 'we want to run our own show' were heard."[14]

Burlington and Ocean county freeholders scheduled public meetings at which representatives of the National Park Service explained the scope and direction of their studies. The upshot was that in October 1968 both counties appointed a Citizens' Advisory Committee "to place at the disposal of the National Park Service the ideas and knowledge of a broad segment of the citizen population of both counties."[15] It included a number of county and municipal officials, representatives of agricultural, conservationist, and sportsmen's interests, the state director of the Department of Economic Development, and the administrative assistant to Congressman William Cahill, who was to become the next governor. But with more than forty members, the committee was unwieldy, and so the task of reviewing the National Park Service work was delegated to an executive committee, which was to play a powerful role in determining the next step that would be taken to protect the Pine Barrens.

National Park Service Report: Alternatives for Protection. Early in its work, the National Park Service decided not to recommend that the Pine Barrens be designated either a national park or a national monument, as had been originally proposed. Neither designation would be economically feasible, for neither would permit continuation of the indigenous agriculture, timbering, and mining activities, which the Park Service thought did not adversely affect the aquifer. Instead, it proposed that the state take the lead in working out a comprehensive plan and suggested four possible outlines for such a plan. All focused on protecting the Wading River area that McCormick had studied, but each offered different options regarding the size of the protection area and the management roles for federal and state governments. Two alternatives called for designation of a national scientific reserve, either of 175,000 or of 245,000 acres; another option was a state forest or a national recreation area of 267,000 acres; and the fourth option called for a state Pinelands region of 373,000 acres.[16]

Recommendations: Citizens' Advisory Committee. Through its executive committee the Citizens' Advisory Committee immediately began to develop a response to these Park Service recommendations. Not surprisingly, this response reflected the membership on the executive committee, which was heavily weighted with county officials (eight members). Three other members represented agricultural interests, two represented the Pine Barrens municipalities, another two the conservation groups, and one was a spokesman for sportsmen. The remaining committee member was Congressman Cahill's representative.

Of the alternatives presented by the National Park Service, the committee favored the establishment of a Pinelands Region of 373,000 acres under state control as well as state acquisition of another 25,000 acres (the dwarf forest areas) at an estimated cost of $10 million. Preference for state rather than federal control over the region was emphasized because it would permit more home rule and reimbursement to municipalities for tax losses on public lands. The committee delineated very specific recommendations for the mechanism through which the state would exercise planning and management control over the region. They suggested creation by the legislature of a Pinelands Environmental Council with power to plan, review, and influence the course of development within the area. The council was to be modeled on the Hudson River Valley Commission, with the significant exception that the Pinelands Council was to consist of designated representatives of local interests rather than of gubernatorial appointments. The executive committee recommendations were approved by the full Pinelands Citizens Advisory Committee and became the basis for state legislative action in 1971.

The 1960s End on a Note of Optimism. By the end of 1969 the threat of a jetport facility in the Pine Barrens had evaporated. The airlines, the FAA, and the Port Authority had all rejected consideration of sites in South Jersey. Expansion of the existing three major metropolitan airports was in progress. As it ultimately turned out, new technology soon permitted international jet flights to originate and terminate in cities west, north, and south of New York; the New York–New Jersey area was no longer the only passageway to Europe.

The jetport controversy had focused national attention on the protection of the Pine Barrens. At the same time, John McPhee's widely publicized book, *The Pine Barrens*, provided eloquent testimony in support of protection for the Pines and sounded a dire note of warning about the development threats. The decade also saw the emergence of strong local and statewide environmental interest groups, whose efforts would be needed in the next decade to ward off new threats to the Barrens.

On the local level, both the Pinelands Regional Planning Board and the Citizens' Advisory Committee agreed that a regional planning approach was required to protect the valuable resources of the Pines. As both agencies were dominated by county and municipal officials, this was a hopeful sign, but as events in the next decade were to prove, effective regional planning was not an easy goal to reach in the Pine Barrens.

The 1970s: Decade of Land-Use Planning Conflicts

In 1970 an euphoric note was sounded by President Mort Cooper of FOCUS, the conservation organization that, with other support, had successfully warded off powerful efforts of county and local officials, the business community, the press, and a former governor to site a large jetport in the Pine Barrens.[17] The new governor, Republican William Cahill, was committed to a platform of "no international airport in New Jersey" and was even sympathetic to the establishment of a Pinelands regional planning body as recommended by the Citizens' Advisory Committee. Cooper suggested that, for the moment, attention could be turned to other environmental issues.

By the mid-1970s, however, the harmonious note on which the decade had started had turned discordant. The hope that the newly created Pinelands Environmental Council would satisfactorily reconcile multiple land-use interests was shattered. From the outset, the gulf between the interests of developers, large landowners, farmers, and local and county officials seeking new ratables on one side and those of conservationists and recreationists on the other was just too wide to be bridged by a new, but still locally dominated, regional planning body with no regulatory authority.

Pinelands Environmental Council. The 1972 state legislation that established the Pinelands Environmental Council (PEC) was drafted by the Burlington–Ocean County-appointed Citizens' Advisory Committee.[18] Burlington County legislators sponsored and guided the bills through the legislative process. As prescribed by the enabling legislation, twelve of the fifteen PEC members were appointees of county freeholders (including one freeholder, three mayors, one sportsman, and one conservationist each from Burlington and Ocean counties). Two additional members represented the cranberry and blueberry growers' associations, and one individual was appointed by the state commissioner of the Department of Environmental Protection (DEP). Not only was the PEC local in its representation, but also more than half of the initial appointees had served on the parent body—the Citizens' Advisory Committee.

The council had jurisdiction over about 320,000 acres of the Pine Barrens in southern and eastern Burlington and Ocean counties, mostly the area that had been threatened by the development plans of the Pinelands Regional Planning Board. The legislative charge to the PEC favored resource conservation, especially water resources, which were to be protected from misuse and pollution. In addition, the council was to conserve the scientific, educational, scenic, and recreational values of the Pine Barrens and to preserve and promote its agricultural complex. Compatible land uses were to be encouraged in order to improve the overall environmental and economic position of the area.

To carry out this mandate the council was given two powers. First, it had authority to develop "a coordinated, comprehensive plan" and second, it had authority to review development in the region, determining within a 90-day period whether or not a project was in substantial conformity with the council's plan. If during this review the PEC found that a project would have "an unreasonably adverse effect" on scenic, historic, scientific, recreational, or natural resources, the council was to report its findings to the public agency having development approval power. Although the Council's role was only advisory, it could delay a development project until its review was complete. The legislature provided an initial appropriation of $100,000 for the PEC, with the understanding that there would be annual additional state and county funding; it failed, however, to pass a companion bill that would have provided $10 million for the acquisition of 25,000 acres of critical areas identified by the Citizens' Advisory Committee.

In its first meeting the PEC elected as its chairman Garfield DeMarco, a cranberry grower, owner of more than 9,000 acres in the Pinelands, and for many years chairman of the Burlington County Republican party. De-Marco had chaired the Citizens' Advisory Committee and had been in-strumental in getting the PEC enabling legislation passed.

Offices were set up near Browns Mills in the Pine Barrens. In its first years the PEC funded studies on environmentally significant areas, spon-sored public information and educational programs featuring lectures and tours, and established priorities for acquisition of public land. In 1975 the council released to the public a draft of its regional plan that had been prepared with the aid of consultants. Thereafter, and for the duration of its existence, the PEC was to be embroiled in controversy.

PEC Plan for the Pinelands. The commissioner of the New Jersey De-partment of Environmental Protection, David Bardin, in a scathing letter addressed to Council Chairman DeMarco, called the PEC plan "a land-speculator's dream," while Jack McCormick, the ecologist who had par-ticipated in the recommendations that had led to the formation of the PEC, said that the plan was "wholly unsuitable." [19]

The plan divided the land under PEC jurisdiction into two principal categories, the first of which was designated Areas of Critical Regional Concern. This category included tidal marshes, freshwater wetlands (de-fined in a rather vague fashion), the dwarf forests (the Plains), and part of the Forked River Mountain area. All other vacant land fell into the second category and was considered "potentially developable." [20] The plan further suggested a housing potential in the whole PEC area of about 167,000 new housing units with a consequent population growth of about a half million people—this in a region that at the time had a population of 7,500. If sewers were available, there was no maximum density set for units per acre; without sewers, housing density would be limited to two units per acre.

The plan emphasized the need to respect "traditional rights and owner-ship and use of land," but it failed to recognize the impact that the per-mitted development would have on water quality and on the ecosystem. In this respect the PEC plan was no better than the Jetport–New City plan proposed by the Pinelands Regional Planning Board in the preceding decade.

Aftermath of the PEC Plan. Despite the PEC claim of open-mindedness about recommendations for improving its plan, its original pro-development bias alienated irrevocably many conservationists, including both mem-bers of the U.S. Department of the Interior, who had been tracking the regional planning effort since the 1960s, and officials in the newly elected state administration of Democrat Brendan T. Byrne. PEC chairman De-Marco quarreled bitterly with Byrne's DEP Commissioner David Bardin over the PEC plan, and after 1975 no state funds were appropriated for the council's operations. It is said that DeMarco ruled the council with an iron fist, though not without heated opposition from the state's representative on the council and from Floyd West, mayor of Bass River Township and an outspoken advocate of greater protection of the Pines.

From 1975 until the day it closed its doors in 1979, the PEC was on a downhill slide. Its executive director, Joseph Portash, was forced to resign in 1976 after being indicted—in his capacity as mayor of Manchester Township—for taking a payment from a large developer without performance of services. In 1977 Garfield DeMarco, pressed by conflict-of-interest charges stemming from his various land holdings in the Pines, resigned as chairman of the PEC. Thereafter, DeMarco actively opposed any federal or further state legislation to protect the Pine Barrens.

In 1978 Mort Cooper, the conservationist from FOCUS, succeeded DeMarco, and Richard Goodenough, who had extensive experience in state environmental operations, succeeded Portash. But it was too late to change the tarnished image of the PEC. Development pressures were bearing heavily on the Pine Barrens and many were beginning to recognize that, if the Pine Barrens was to be successfully protected, more effective regulatory action would be needed.

Population Dispersion and Development Pressures. During the 1960s the population of New Jersey increased by about 16 percent, or some 1.2 million people. During this same ten-year period the population of the Pine Barrens grew by nearly 60,000—a 36 percent growth rate. In the 1970s New Jersey's population growth slowed to less than 3 percent overall. Nevertheless, migration to suburban and rural areas accelerated and all of the counties having land in the Pine Barrens grew at a faster rate than the state average. Ocean County in the 1960s gained distinction as being the nation's fastest growing county. In the 1970s it continued to be the state's fastest growing county, alone accounting for 70 percent of New Jersey's population growth. During this decade the population of the Pine Barrens region increased by 96,000, a growth rate of 43 percent.

Initially, the state's population growth extended out from the New York–northeastern New Jersey and the Philadelphia metropolitan areas along established highway networks. For the Pine Barrens this meant development on the northern and western perimeters, a pattern that has had the cumulative effect of shrinking the region's boundaries. At the same time there was little pressure for the siting of new economic activities in the Pines, though one threat, which failed to materialize, did cause an uproar. In 1976 the Department of the Interior leased rights for off-shore oil and gas exploration in the Baltimore Canyon. If substantial petroleum resources were to be discovered, there would be heavy demand for construction of supporting infrastructure and housing, both along the coast and reaching into the Pine Barrens. There would be further threat if pipelines were constructed on a direct route across the Pines from drilling areas to refineries along the Delaware River. Exploration efforts were unsuccessful, however, and the offshore development threat evaporated.

Since mid-century, development of individual single-family homes had nibbled away at vacant land in the Pine Barrens. The 1970s, however, brought a new pattern of residential development, presenting a much more visible threat—the development of whole new towns and retirement communities. In 1972 a developer's request to build New Town, a city of 80,000 or more, near the banks of the Wading River in rural Bass River Township, was denied by local officials because of objections by Floyd West and other environmentalists. But the choice of South Jersey as a desirable location for retirement communities was not thereby ended. Indeed, New Jersey has become the fifth most popular retirement state in the Union (after Florida, California, Arizona, and Texas); this preference stems in great part from the availability of large tracts of relatively inexpensive rural land within an hour or two of New York and Philadelphia. Ocean County, with more than half of the state's retirement communities, has the largest concentration of such development outside Florida and the Southwest. As explained by an Ocean County official:

> The relationship between municipalities and retirement communities is a happy one. We give them one of the lowest tax rates in the state and in return they put no strain on our court, police and education systems while their spending supports an awful lot of jobs. It's your ideal population.[21]

Initially, retirement community development centered in northeastern Ocean County, but in the mid-1970s the focus had shifted southward, primarily to Manchester and Berkeley. Each of these towns has considerable acreage in the Pine Barrens. Later, because retirement communities need no strong linkage with centers of employment, cheaper land in the heart of the Pines was to become attractive to developers. By the mid 1970s one large retirement community, Leisuretown in Southhampton, had invaded the Pine Barrens, and plans for several additional large developments had been drawn. Another project of 4,500 units was planned in the forested area of Manchester Township and a second of equal size was planned for rural Woodland, where a developer had acquired more than a thousand acres. Some even feared that if the Army were to abandon Fort Dix, a "New Town" would be built in its stead.

In 1976 New Jersey's voters approved a referendum legalizing Atlantic City casino gambling and triggered another demand for development in the Pine Barrens. Atlantic City, located on a barrier island, is less than ten miles east of the Pines. State officials had hoped that the influx of jobs and investment dollars would revitalize Atlantic City, which had lost its popularity as a tourist resort. By 1978, when the first casino opened, a frenzy of real estate speculation had already reached into the Pines. It was estimated that by 1990, twenty-two casinos employing more than 30,000 people would be in operation. Housing for this immediate group and for the thousands more employed in casino-related businesses would require residential development on the mainland extending southward into Cape May County, northward into Ocean County, and westward into relatively unsettled Atlantic County municipalities. Today, although a demand for new housing has developed from the casino-gambling activities, it has not developed at quite the speed that had been predicted. Nevertheless, the combined development pressure from all sources underlined the inadequacies of the PEC's development review authority.

Development Regulation under the PEC.   In New Jersey, municipalities have the principal authority over land use within their boundaries; counties are vested with only minor power in this area. Understandably, however, municipalities may lack a regional perspective, and in the endless quest for more ratables planning board officials frequently fail to consider environmental problems that development may cause, even within township boundaries. In the 1970s most townships in the Pine Barrens lacked adequate expertise to assess properly the impact of development on the region's resources. Many municipal master plans and ordinances as written allowed huge potential for development growth. In such a context, the role of the PEC in guiding development was critical.

Despite the loss of state funding, the PEC used private contributions and county money to continue to review commercial, industrial, and multiunit (five or more units) residential development projects proposed for within the 320,000 Pine Barrens acres over which it had jurisdiction. This review could include a public hearing. The council's recommendation, which was not binding, was then transmitted in writing to the developer and to the public agencies having power to approve the project.

Although the PEC lacked authority to reject proposed development, it occasionally was able to persuade a developer to modify a project design to improve protection of resources. In a few instances, projects were even withdrawn or rejected on PEC advice, but most often PEC findings were ignored. For example, the minutes of a September 14, 1977, PEC meeting reported "Lacey Township totally ignored the Council's recommendation" to reject a mining operation. But for the most part environmentalists (and a few council members, Floyd West in particular) complained that the council approved too much development. Testimony by Morton Cooper, then PEC chairman, on February 22, 1979, reflects the divergence of attitudes toward PEC development review actions. Cooper proudly noted that the PEC had been able to convince the developer of the proposed Burrs Mill Ranch Estates in Woodland to agree to dedicate 25 percent of his 1,025-acre tract as a conservation easement. Environmentalists, on the other hand, bitterly opposed any development at all on the whole tract, which was a critically sensitive wetland and which drained into a long-established cranberry bog. The Burlington County Health Department also expressed reservations about the project because few of the proposed lots could support septic systems. Although the Woodland Township Planning Board approved the project, the Pinelands Commission later rejected both it and the 4,500-unit ROC community proposed in Manchester (known as the Warwicke project in the PEC files), which were under PEC review at the time that the council was discontinued.

The development review actions taken by the PEC, together with the shortcomings of its 1975 management plan for the region, eventually led to accusations that the council was "an impotent group composed of land barons and vested interests."[22] Such accusations, as well as the fact that PEC had jurisdiction over less than one-third of the Pine Barrens and no real power within its area of authority to stop development, provided convincing evidence to many federal, state, and local officials as well as to environmentalists that new and much different regulatory mechanisms would be needed to protect the Pine Barrens. Within a short period of time a host of suggestions for stronger protection measures were advanced.

The Federal Challenge: Concepts for Preservation.   Dissatisfied with the actions of the PEC, leading environmental groups met with the Department of Environmental Protection in 1975 to identify priorities for Pine Barrens protective actions. The New Jersey Audubon Society suggested that it was time to get back to a joint federal-state effort. David Bardin (the commissioner of the DEP who had strongly criticized the PEC management plan) agreed, and in October 1975 he met with Nathaniel P. Reed, the Department of the Interior's Assistant Secretary for Fish and

Wildlife and Parks. Reed apparently was impressed with Bardin for he immediately issued a memorandum to his three agency directors—in the Bureau of Outdoor Recreation (BOR), the Fish and Wildlife Service, and the National Park Service:

> The Pine Barrens constitute the largest undeveloped stretch of land on the eastern seaboard. But it is area susceptible to development, and so far no sound plan to keep it intact has emerged. New Jersey's Commissioner of Environmental Protection, David Bardin, is interested and energetic; thus, there seems to be ample opportunity for a joint Federal-State program to preserve the area. With the BOR taking the lead, I would like the three bureaus to form a small task force to pool information and approach and prepare a broad option paper for me.[23]

The federal task force report, entitled "The Pine Barrens: Concepts for Preservation," was issued in April 1976 and received widespread attention. The New Jersey Audubon Society devoted an entire issue of its monthly magazine to a review of the report, and Elmer Rowley, the society's active spokesman for Pine Barrens protection, saw that all state legislators and congressmen received copies. Rowley also arranged numerous public meetings at which Jack Hauptmann of the BOR gave slide presentations summarizing the federal recommendations.

The Interior Department's report was important for several reasons. First, it restated fundamental environmental facts that had been underscored by McCormick's work in the 1950s, but ignored in the planning processes of the Pinelands Environmental Council and the Pinelands Regional Planning Board as well as in the enabling legislation establishing both planning groups. These facts are that the Pine Barrens constitutes an ecosystem of almost one million acres and that the integrity of this total ecosystem must be protected in order to preserve each of the system's individual components; moreover, not only are the individual attributes of the ecosystem nationally significant, but also the very proximity of the resource to large urban centers must be considered as significant.

Using these concepts, the BOR report then identified a need to redelineate the boundaries of the present-day Pine Barrens, and to devise and implement a plan for protection of the total area. To accomplish this, the planning forum "must recognize State and National interests in protecting the Pine Barrens as a whole." The report also said that there would be a need for a moratorium on growth-stimulating programs during the planning period.[24] The report suggested that state enabling legislation would be required to establish an authority to develop, administer, and enforce water and land-use controls. These recommendations—to consider the total Pine Barrens as one ecosystem, to have statewide and federal representation in the planning process, to place a moratorium on development pressures during the planning period, and to continue regional land-use controls—fueled acrimonious debates about the next actions to be taken to protect the Pine Barrens.

The 1976 BOR report was important for another reason. It emphasized that, while there were several options for the sharing of state and federal responsibilities with respect to the acquisition and management of public lands in the Pine Barrens, before the federal government would assume any role it needed assurance that appropriate land and water policies would be developed and enforced by the state. Clearly, the Department of the Interior was passing the ball to the state; establishment of a Pine Barrens National Ecological Reserve would rest on state initiative.

Interior's National Park Service, which was vying with the Heritage, Conservation and Recreation Service for management responsibility of reserves, followed up the 1976 report by forming a committee within its North Atlantic Regional Office to develop a plan by which the Pine Barrens could be included in the national park system. The Rutgers University Center for Coastal and Environmental Studies assisted the National Park Service in its planning effort, and in 1978 issued a report entitled "A Plan for a Pinelands National Preserve," which suggested the strategies by which protection of the Pine Barrens could be accomplished. These recommendations were to be useful in the development of the federal Pinelands legislation.

State Response to the Federal Challenge. The federal challenge for a state commitment to protect the Pine Barrens was timely. Governor Brendan Byrne, who later would list his Pinelands work as his most notable achievement, had already been prodded on this subject by a good friend, author John McPhee. In his compelling book, *The Pine Barrens*, McPhee described the beauty of the Pines in words that would be paraphrased many times by the governor: "The picture of New Jersey most people hold in their minds is so different from this one that, considered beside it, the Pine Barrens, as they are called, become as incongruous as they are beautiful."[25]

During the summer and fall of 1976 members of the governor's staff framed a "Save the Barrens Program" out of which came a November meeting with Democratic mayors, freeholders, and state legislators to explore potential support for protection legislation.[26] This was quickly followed by a day-long governor's conference on the Pine Barrens held in

Princeton, primarily for leaders of environmental groups and state and local officials who were advocates of stronger protection measures. The governor's address highlighted the conference, as Byrne for the first time endorsed publicly many of the proposals that had been advanced earlier, including the need for a new comprehensive land-use plan prepared by representatives of regional, state, and national interests. He emphasized preservation as a primary goal, and called for more effective mechanisms to ensure proper implementation of the plan. Acknowledging that these goals would require legislative action, the governor outlined interim steps that he proposed to take. These included the implementation of up-graded water quality standards for the Pine Barrens and the creation of a cabinet-level group—a Pinelands Review Committee—to coordinate state programs in the region.

Upgrading of Water Quality Standards. In January 1977 DEP Commis-sioner Bardin issued proposed standards for point-source discharges of effluents "to prevent degradation of the unusual, high quality waters in the Pine Barrens." These standards were to apply to a 760-square-mile core of the central Pine Barrens. Effluent limitations were defined for pa-rameters such as pH, alkalinity, dissolved oxygen, and nitrate-nitrogen. The latter value was of particular interest because nitrate-nitrogen is only minimally removed in sandy soils, and therefore its presence becomes a good indicator of water degradation. The proposed standards called for a limit of two parts per million (or two milligrams per liter of water) of nitrate-nitrogen. Outside the designated core area, effluent could have a nitrate-nitrogen value of 10 ppm (or 10mg/liter), the statewide standard. Both standards allowed a considerably higher nitrate concentration than found in undisturbed streams of the Pine Barrens (see Chapter 1).

The proposed water standards precipitated tumultuous hearings, a pre-cursor of what would come later with the water quality standards promul-gated by the Pinelands Commission. Those who thought the standards were too strict complained that they amounted to a "taking" of land with-out compensation, that they would destroy the value of land, cause ero-sion of home rule and local tax bases, and that they would "regulate many blueberry and truck farms out of business."[27] Environmentalists dis-agreed. Finally, backed by strong support from environmental groups and some local officials and legislators, DEP adopted the standards in January 1978 and at the same time designated the central Pine Barrens as a critical area. This designation gave DEP the authority to review and approve all proposed septic and other sewage disposal systems. No building permit could be issued in the absence of such approval.

The New Jersey Builders Association, claiming that the regulations were "unreasonable, arbitrary, and capricious" and would cause losses as high as $1.6 billion, challenged the legality of the DEP standards.[28] The Appellate Division of the Superior Court rejected this claim, as well as a similar one made by Hammonton Township. Senator Joseph Maressa of Camden County, supported by Burlington County Senator Barry Parker, then introduced legislation to rescind DEP's authority to impose the water quality standards. Environmental groups and the press were quick to charge both legislators with conflict of interest. Maressa, though he first denied it, had land holdings in the Pine Barrens and Parker, an attorney, represented several land developers in the Pines area. No action was taken on the Maressa bill.

Appointment of the Pinelands Review Committee. Because 1977 was an election year and Byrne's chance of re-election to a second term appeared slim, the governor delayed until May 24, 1977, the issuance of his Executive Order 56, which created the Pinelands Review Committee (PRC). As expected, the action provoked a sharp political battle because the new PRC was assigned responsibilities that overlapped those of the Pinelands Environmental Council (PEC), dominated by Republican Burlington and Ocean counties. The PRC, with staff support from the Department of Community Affairs, was directed to coordinate state agency actions and programs in the Pine Barrens in order to ensure consistency with the goal of protecting the area's resources. It was also charged with delineation of the Pine Barrens boundaries and with preparation of a plan for guidance of state decision-making. The objectives of this plan were to be preservation of the unique resources; promotion of agriculture, forestry, and recreation; encouragement of needed development compatible with resource preservation; and discouragement of scattered and piecemeal development.

Unlike that of the PEC, the PRC membership included persons who lived outside the Pine Barrens. Among the sixteen public members appointed to the committee were representatives of agricultural interests, local government, the home building industry, and conservation and environmental interests; in numbers, the latter group dominated. The three state cabinet departments represented were Agriculture, Community Affairs, and Environmental Protection. Community Affairs played the lead role since its chief of regional planning, Richard Binetsky, also served as executive secretary of the committee. Byrne named as chairman, Craig W. Yates, an industrialist and the brother of Burlington Democratic Assemblyman Charles B. Yates. Gary Patterson, a professor of environmental studies at Glassboro State College, was elected vice-chairman and also headed one of two working subcommittees that helped mold the committee's recommendations. The other influential subcommittee was headed by another active advocate of Pine Barrens protection, John Hiros, who at the time was executive director of the Milford Reservation.

Although the final report of the PRC did not appear until 1979—after the federal legislation had been enacted and just before state legislative action was taken—PRC work proved to be an invaluable antecedent to legislative efforts. As one of its first actions, the PRC delineated the boundaries of the Pinelands to include about 1.1 million acres. Within that total area was a core Pinelands Preservation Area—an "extensive and contiguous undeveloped land mass" in its natural state, to be preserved for its "unique ecological features, which have distinguished the Pinelands."[29] This core was surrounded by an outer ring, the Pinelands Protection Area, where the aim was "to afford people the opportunity to live in a Pinelands setting." Specific land-use goals for each area were prescribed.

On July 12, 1978, a South Jersey newspaper leaked a copy of the draft map of the proposed boundaries and a summary of the basic conclusions of the PRC report. It also reported that the PRC was calling for a new regional agency that would exercise zoning authority over the Pinelands until municipal master plans were revised to conform with the regional plan. Ten days later (July 22), Governor Byrne expressed his agreement that the state should have sweeping zoning authority over the Pinelands region, adding "I campaigned very hard on this issue last year and . . . no negative reaction was reflected at the polls."[30]

Public hearings and the newspaper reports on the PRC's draft proposal generated a great deal of interest and heated debate. Garfield DeMarco, former chairman of the PEC, called the PRC suggestions "pie in the sky"; he predicted that "legislators would not want to give the State far reaching land-use powers over local officials" and added that the very suggestion of it "would hit so many booby traps and ambushes in the Legislature that it would never pass."[31] A few municipal officials agreed with DeMarco, but others felt that strong regional regulations were necessary and called for a moratorium on further development in the Pinelands until such regulations could be adopted. From the work of the PRC came both substantive recommendations for legislative action and increased public understanding of and support for protection measures. The public discussions helped solidify a base for strong legislative measures to protect the Pinelands.

On the day that Byrne issued Executive Order 56, creating the PRC, he also announced that $10 million from the state's Green Acres Fund would be allocated specifically for the acquisition of land in the Pine Barrens. At the time appropriations from this fund had been used primarily for acquisition of open space in urban areas; by this action and by the creation of the PRC, the governor effectively responded to the federal challenge to show a state commitment to protect the Pinelands.

A County Proposal: The Plan for Positive Action.   County officials, however, particularly the Burlington freeholders, did not immediately give up hope of keeping complete local control over the destiny of the Pine Barrens. In 1977 Robert Shinn, a freeholder and a member of the Pinelands Environmental Council, proposed an alternative to the PRC plan and its legislative implementation. Instead, Shinn called for a state bond referendum of $74.5 million to provide funds for the purchase of 84,000 acres in the Pine Barrens and for reimbursement to municipalities for lost real estate taxes caused by the state purchase. The plan also called for upgrading of water quality, improving water sampling programs, and creating a regional agency to preserve the area's natural values. It was the "Positive Plan of Action for the Preservation of the New Jersey Pinelands."

Although opposed by Democratic freeholders, Shinn's plan was approved by the Republican-dominated South Jersey Freeholders Association and, in slightly revised form, by the Pinelands Environmental Council. Shinn's alternative, however, did not meet with success. Ironically, although Shinn strongly opposed both federal and state Pinelands legislation, he was later to serve seven years as the Burlington county appointee to the Pinelands Commission. As vice-chairman of the commission, he not only pushed aggressively and positively to carry out the legislative mandates, but also was of great help in enlisting the cooperation of local and state officials in this effort.

New Leadership in Environmental Interest Groups.   The 1970s brought new faces and new leadership in conservation and environmental groups dedicated to the protection of the Pine Barrens. Although PEC chairman Mort Cooper had effectively welded public support against the plans for a jetport in the Pine Barrens in the 1960s, many environmentalists did not share his belief that the council offered "the best possible compromise and a real means of preserving our beloved Pine Barrens."[32] FOCUS, the Pine Barrens environmental coordination organization that Cooper had founded, ceased publication of its newsletter in the mid-1970s. For several years there was no environmental coordinating mechanism to take its place. Nevertheless, several statewide conservation organizations, a variety of local groups, and key national organizations continued to monitor the Pine Barrens, reporting actions destructive to the resources and pushing aggressively for stronger protection of the region.

The New Jersey Audubon Society played a dominant role in these efforts through its Pine Barrens spokesman, Elmer Rowley, who was retired from business and a resident of the Pine Barrens village of Medford. Rowley was low key but eloquent as he pleaded with congressmen; state legislators; and federal, state, and local officials for stronger protection of the Pine Barrens. The New Jersey Conservation Foundation, led by its executive director, Dave Moore, represented an important public voice on Pine Barrens preservation for all New Jersey residents. Moore, formerly involved with state parks and forests operations and completely familiar with administrative and legislative mechanisms on state and local levels, was active in the drafting of state Pinelands legislation. In addition, the New Jersey Conservation Foundation, acting in concert with The Nature Conservancy, a national land preservation group, launched a $750,000 fund-raising campaign for land acquisition in the Pines.

A wide variety of local conservation groups also played important roles in convincing public officials of the need for stronger protection of the Pines. Some—such as the Pine Barrens Conservationists (whose efforts were described earlier)—had originally been formed to pursue a particular interest in an aspect of the natural history of the Pines; others—the Batona Hiking Club, for example—had been formed to encourage a particular recreational activity. Several groups—for example, the Rancocas Creek and Pompeston Creek watershed associations led by Nan and Rick Walnut and Ruth Allen, respectively—actively represented watershed interests. And still others had been organized to oppose specific development projects in the Pine Barrens. One such group—Concerned Citizens of Woodland Township—had successfully opposed the siting of a retirement community in their sparsely developed township. Whatever their previous commitments, however, all now agreed about the necessity of protecting the Pine Barrens resources. National organizations also joined the effort to gain stronger protection and were of great help in convincing federal officials and legislators of the national significance of the area. Among the more active were the Sierra Club, the Environmental Defense Fund, the National Audubon Society, the Natural Resources Defense Council, and the National Parks and Conservation Association.

The demise of FOCUS had left no mechanism to coordinate actions of these many local, state, and national conservation and environmental organizations. So in the spring of 1977, Carol Barrett, who had organized a West Jersey chapter of the Sierra Club and who was impatient with the governor's delay in appointing the Pinelands Review Committee, suggested formation of a new environmental coalition that could demonstrate the wide public support for preserving the Pines. Thus was born the Pine

Barrens Coalition. Like FOCUS, the coalition kept its members abreast of all local, state, and federal actions that impinged on the Barrens. Letter-writing campaigns were organized and demonstrations staged to influence the decision-makers. Barrett served one year as the coalition's chair- and spokesperson and then resumed leadership of the Sierra Club chapter. Mae Barringer, who had effectively organized the Concerned Citizens of Woodland Township, succeeded Barrett and led the coalition through the challenging years during which the legislation and then the Pinelands Commission's plan were debated.

The coalition became a powerful voice for the Pine Barrens, enlisting as members more than fifty state conservation and environmental groups as well as a handful of influential nationwide organizations. It gained the respect of local, state, and federal officials, and provided the primary conduit through which public support for protection of the Pine Barrens was demonstrated to the decision-makers.

Individuals unaffiliated with organizations also played important roles in influencing the decision-makers. Ted Gordon, a science teacher and an outstanding naturalist, monitored every meeting of the Pinelands Environmental Council and alerted it and interested environmentalists whenever a proposed development threatened critical habitats of rare or endangered species or environmentally critical resources. Mary-Ann Thompson, an attorney whose family has been among the largest cranberry growers in the Pine Barrens for more than one hundred years, left a Wall Street law firm and returned to South Jersey to spend full time fighting for the Pines. Thompson later served as a member of Governor Byrne's staff; she and her father were among the few farmers who actively supported the need for stronger state protection.

The actions of environmental groups and individual conservationists were absolutely necessary to offset the strong development bias that had for many years influenced planning and construction not only in South Jersey but in the entire state as well. This bias reflected the endless quest for more ratables, which was at least partly fueled by the ever-present influence of development interests upon, if not within, local and state government. Builders lobbied hard at the local, state, and national levels through the Home Builders League of South Jersey, the New Jersey Builders Association, and the National Association of Home Builders. Likewise, farmers in the Pine Barrens for the most part opposed strict land-use regulations; their views were actively supported by the state Department of Agriculture and the Farm Bureau, as well as by the blueberry and cranberry growers' associations.[33] Without the significant grassroots support for protection of the Pine Barrens that did manifest itself, neither federal nor state legislative initiatives would have been possible.

The Stage Is Set for Legislative Action. On the eve of legislative action, there was strong local support for protection of the New Jersey Pine Barrens, and national prominence had been given to its resource base. Inappropriate development already had begun to pollute its pristine waters, fragment its unique ecosystem, and destroy its plant and animal populations. Pressures for more development in the region were real and at hand.

Although lip service was widely given to the concept that the Pine Barrens should be saved, there was little agreement on what portion of its more than one million acres should be protected. The need for regional planning had been expressed in the 1960s during the jetport debate, but two decades had brought no concensus about who should do this regional planning. In dispute still were the roles to be played by local, county, and state officials; by the various economic and environmental interests; and by resident and nonresident members of the public.

The experiences of the Pinelands Environmental Council had revealed the shortcomings of a regional planning body with no real authority over development regulation. There was still reluctance to assign zoning authority to a regional body; this ran counter to the existing tradition of home rule, a concept that Governor Brendan Byrne noted was "nothing short of religion" throughout New Jersey.[34]

The stakes were high, and the debate over alternatives for the use of the Pines heated. Conservationists, environmentalists, and recreationists interested in protecting the region's resources were pitted against land speculators, large landowners, developers and builders, farmers, and many local and county officials. John McPhee, in his book on the Pine Barrens, expressed the feelings of many about the outcome of this land-use conflict when he said:

> Given the futilities of that debate, given the sort of attention that is usually paid to plans put forward by conservationists, and given the great numbers and the crossed purposes of all the big and little powers that would have to work together to accomplish *anything* on a major scale in the pines, it would appear that the Pine Barrens are not very likely to be the subject of dramatic decrees or acts of legislation. They seem to be headed slowly toward extinction.[35]

The actions of federal and state legislators would prove John McPhee wrong.

Legislation, the Commission, and Its Plan

3. Federal and State Pinelands Legislation

Emily W. B. Russell

Until the late 1970s, efforts to protect the Pine Barrens focused attention on the value of the area, the threats to it, and the many conflicts to be resolved. Although a consensus had been reached that a regional effort was needed, there remained debate on boundaries and on the appropriate level or mechanism of governmental control.

By the mid-1970s several states had already established regional or statewide management plans to protect natural resources. These plans provided models for efforts to protect New Jersey's Pine Barrens. New York had singled out the Adirondack Mountains and California its coastline for protection on a regional basis. Oregon, Florida, and Vermont had also enacted legislation providing for land-use planning and management at the state level. It was clear from these efforts that adequate funding and coercive powers as well as local support were critical for success in protecting natural resources.

New Jersey by this time had also passed regulatory legislation addressing several specific environmental concerns, such as solid waste disposal, and in its Coastal Area Facility Review Act had created a regional authority to regulate uses of coastal wetlands and shores. The state also had set up a regional commission to prepare and implement a land-use plan for the Hackensack Meadowlands, located in northeastern New Jersey. As its name implies, however, the Hackensack Meadowlands Development Commission was oriented more toward promotion of development than toward resource protection. Finally, the regional agency in the Pine Barrens, the Pinelands Environmental Council, not only had jurisdiction over only a small portion of the Barrens, but also it had no teeth, no authority to enforce its recommendations (see Chapter 2). These existing laws thus did not provide a legal basis for strong coordination of local land-use policies.

Because these existing state laws did not provide adequate protection of Pine Barrens' resources, environmental groups and state officials turned to Congress and the federal bureaucracy, particularly to members of the Department of the Interior, for assistance on the national level. This chapter traces first the federal and then the state legislative initiatives that ultimately led to a legal mandate for protection of the Pine Barrens landscape.

Federal Legislation

Three years of deliberations about alternative legislative actions led to the federal legislation that created the Pinelands National Reserve in 1978. The legislation resulted from intensive lobbying by environmental groups and from compromises reached by legislators, often in the last hours of debate before key votes.

Land Acquisition versus the Greenline Concept.   In October 1976 Congressman Edwin Forsythe, a Republican whose district encompassed much of the Pine Barrens area that was under the jurisdiction of the Pinelands Environmental Council, introduced legislation (H.R. 15826) calling for purchase by the Secretary of the Interior of up to 10,000 acres of Pine Barrens land identified by the PEC as having high ecological value. This legislation also called for reimbursement to municipalities for tax losses resulting from this purchase and gave power to the PEC to oversee development throughout the Pine Barrens. The 94th Congress took no action on this bill, and, although Forsythe reintroduced it in February 1977 (H.R. 3157), it was never reported out of committee.

A year before Forsythe's first introduction of his bill, some members of Congress and the Department of the Interior, in another situation, had recognized the impracticality of using the traditional national park concept to protect large tracts of significant natural and cultural resources in densely populated areas of the country. They felt that fee acquisition of land to be dedicated as a National Park in such densely populated areas would be prohibitively expensive as well as inappropriate. In 1975, in a report for the Senate's Committee on Interior and Insular Affairs (during its study of a then-pending bill for protection of the Santa Monica Mountains in California), Charles E. Little proposed using an alternative approach, the "greenline park." Unlike traditional national parkland, greenline parkland need not be entirely owned by the federal government. Instead, the government would set standards and impose restrictions on use of private land within the boundaries of the "park" to achieve the goals for which the park was established.

Little modeled his concept on the 1971 New York State Adirondack Park legislation, which, in essence, drew a line (a blue line in the Adirondacks) around the area to be protected and used legislation written and administered by a commission to plan and manage land, both private and public, within that line.[1] Another, more distant, model was the English national park system in which a countryside commission oversees the planning and management of parks that consist largely of privately owned properties.

Some congressmen felt, for several reasons, that the greenline park concept would be especially useful in developing a protection strategy for the Pine Barrens. First, numerous reports by the U.S. Department of the Interior had already documented the national significance of the Pine Barrens, both as a recreational area close to two major metropolitan regions and as a valuable scientific and natural resource (see Chapter 2). Second, development of the privately owned interstices between and around parcels of public land was beginning to threaten these important resources. Finally, total acquisition of the land was impractical. As Senator Clifford Case (R–NJ) explained, the Pine Barrens was "too big, too complex, too valuable, and too interwoven with the fabric of existing communities to be protected by the federal government alone."[2]

Three Legislative Proposals.   The debate over how to protect the Pine Barrens region without unduly restricting local development led to a series of legislative proposals.

The Florio Proposal: A Pine Barrens National Ecological Reserve. On April 26, 1977, Representative James Florio (D–NJ), whose district included a portion of the western part of the Pine Barrens, introduced a greenline park bill proposing that 970,000 acres of the Pine Barrens be made a Pine Barrens National Ecological Reserve (H.R. 6625). Florio's bill was quickly embraced by environmental groups and endorsed by the Department of the Interior, which had assisted in drafting it, as well as by the newly appointed Pinelands Review Committee (see Chapter 2) and by New Jersey's Governor Brendan Byrne.

The Forsythe–Hughes Proposal: A Pinelands National Wildlife Refuge. As support grew for Florio's legislation, it became apparent that Forsythe's initial bill, which simply called for limited land acquisition in the Pine Barrens, would not gain adequate backing. Therefore Congressman William Hughes, a Democrat whose district also included a large portion of the Pine Barrens, joined with Forsythe in drafting alternate legislation aimed at retaining local control of land use in the Pine Barrens. In October 1977 he and Forsythe introduced duplicate but separate bills, each labeled the Pinelands Preservation Act (H.R. 9535 and H.R. 9539). Both called for the establishment of a Pinelands National Wildlife Refuge, under the management of the U.S. Fish and Wildlife Service. The Pinelands Refuge was to be no larger than 50,000 acres. In addition, the Secretary of the Interior was to identify other privately owned parcels of Pine Barrens land that should be preserved from overdevelopment through land-use regulation by locally dominated management bodies.

The Case–Williams Proposal: A National Reserve System. The third approach to protection was embodied in a generic bill to establish a national system of greenline parks. This was introduced by New Jersey Senators Clifford Case and Harrison Williams on November 1, 1977 (S. 2306). Part of this bill was the designation of the New Jersey Pine Barrens as the first National Reserve planning area; the region was to be protected by a mix of acquisition and regulation of private land.

Legislative Issues. Thus, by the end of 1977 congressional committees were considering three separate Pinelands bills: (1) Florio's Pine Barrens National Ecological Reserve bill, (2) Forsythe and Hughes's Pinelands National Wildlife Refuge, and (3) Case and Williams's system of national reserves, or greenline parks, that included the Pinelands as the first to be designated. The similarities and differences among these bills highlighted the principal issues that would need to be resolved in final Pine Barrens protection legislation.

All three bills emphasized the national significance of the Pine Barrens in terms of both ecology and recreation. All three also proposed that it was in the national interest to protect the region from threats of encroaching development by assisting state and/or local authorities in their preservation efforts. All advocated a combination of land acquisition and regulatory control over private uses to protect natural resources. All three defined the Pinelands as the 970,000 acres identified by the Bureau of Outdoor Recreation in its 1976 report (see Chapter 2). Here, however, the similarities ended.

Florio's Pine Barrens National Ecological Reserve bill called for federal acquisition of up to 50,000 acres, with federal expenditures of up to $50 million for that acquisition as well as for general land management. The proposal conditioned this federal funding, however, on the establishment of a state commission for planning and management. This commission, of twelve members, was to have at least four who were not residents of the Pinelands, a proviso generally recommended for greenline parks, and it was to have broad powers to set boundaries, formulate a management plan, enforce that plan, and enforce interim land-use regulations.[3] A requirement that the commission consult with a citizen advisory committee offered the only opportunity for local citizen participation.

Although Forsythe and Hughes also proposed acquisition of up to 50,000 acres and an appropriation of almost $50 million, their plan offered, at least initially, more opportunity for local control. Parts of the Pine Barrens deemed critical for maintaining the natural values of the reserve were to be designated as "ecological management units." The municipalities within each unit were to design a management plan to conserve the resources of that unit. Only if the municipalities failed to do so, could the state appoint a regional planning commission (that would be dominated, however, by local officials).

The Case–Williams proposal differed by requiring that a state management plan be developed for an area *before* it could be designated for protection as a National Reserve. Like Florio, Case and Williams proposed to give enforcement powers to a regional agency, but unlike Florio, the senators placed relatively less emphasis on the role of the federal government in planning and implementation and relatively more on the need for local participation. Both the Florio and the Case–Williams proposals (but not the Forsythe–Hughes bill) emphasized the need for interim development regulation during the planning phase.

The three legislative proposals provided differing schemes for balancing land acquisition with land-use regulations and for establishing the relative roles and responsibilities of federal, state, and local authorities in planning, implementation, and enforcement. In arriving at the final legislation establishing the New Jersey Pinelands National Reserve, the legislators had to hammer out many compromises among competing interests.

The Process of Legislative Compromise.   The Department of the Interior supported both the Florio and the Case–Williams proposals, which it had helped to draft.[4] These bills, though differing in detail, offered opportunity for strong state and federal participation in Pinelands protection. Gubernatorial support was expressed by Gary Patterson speaking for the governor's Pinelands Review Committee. Secretary of the Interior Andrus, after a visit to the Pine Barrens arranged by Governor Byrne, also strongly supported "cooperative planning endeavors" of the federal, state, and local governments in the form of the Florio bill.[5]

On the local front, however, the scene was less tranquil and not uniformly favorable. On October 28, 1977, Congressmen Forsythe and Hughes held hearings on their Pinelands legislation at Stockton State College in Atlantic County. About half of those testifying favored the bill. Many of these, mostly local officials, also suggested improvements, such as stricter interim controls on development and creation of a regional planning body in place of or in addition to the local ecological management units. The bill's opponents, mostly representatives of environmental groups, but including two local mayors, suggested a stronger and less politicized regional agency. These speakers encouraged Congressmen Forsythe and Hughes to compromise with Congressman Florio. The three-to-one approval by the voters of Burlington County of a one-million-dollar bond issue for conservation easements in the Pine Barrens finally spurred the three congressmen to work out their differences and propose a single bill in the House of Representatives.[6]

House Action. Protection of the Pine Barrens was included as Section 503 of the omnibus National Parks and Recreation Act (H.R. 12536), passed by the House of Representatives on May 10, 1978. It was weak and vague legislation, but did include $26 million in appropriations for the Pinelands—$1 million for planning and $25 million for land acquisition. Congressman Florio's staff drafted the original version of this section, and then had to compromise with Hughes and Forsythe to get it out of committee. In the process, the state's role in planning was weakened and interim development restrictions were omitted. Section 503 required the Secretary of the Interior to prepare a management plan for the 970,000 acres, with state cooperation if the state so desired. There were few details about how the land-use plan would be implemented.

The Department of the Interior withheld its support from the House version of the Pinelands legislation, because it did not "tend toward a national reserve concept for the Pines."[7] Instead the department decided to wait for completion of a National Park Service report on the Pine Barrens that was being prepared by Rutgers University's Center for Coastal and Environmental Studies. This report was expected to provide guidelines and reasons for establishing the Pine Barrens greenline park. Dr. Paul Buckley of the National Park Service, who was directing the report, strongly supported protection for the Pinelands, including the coastal areas. The report established the basic outline for setting up a National Reserve, including the concept of protection and preservation areas that received different levels of regulation.

Senate Action. Senate hearings on the Pinelands legislation were also held up pending the NPS–Rutgers report. These hearings finally occurred in July and early August of 1978. Out of them came the establishment of the Pinelands National Reserve, again as a part of the omnibus National Parks and Recreation Act.

The Pinelands legislation was technically written by the Senate, but with considerable input by individual congressmen. The House immediately adopted the Senate version in place of its own with no further changes. The late Congressman Philip Burton (R–California), chairman of the House Interior Committee and interested in designation of the Santa Monica Mountains as a National Reserve, has been credited by the Sierra Club with a major role in shaping the whole National Parks and Recreation Act,[8] although it was the united support of Representatives Florio,

Forsythe, and Hughes, and Senators Case and Williams, that got Pinelands protection included in the final version; any one of them could have stopped it from moving out of committee.

To get the legislation passed, the members of the New Jersey delegation had pledged to set aside their differences and work together in a bipartisan, bicameral effort. Their united front indicated the commitment of all five. Witness comments made early in the hearings, on August 4—Forsythe: "The actual legislative language is still being developed with all of us and the administration. We are in harmony in terms of objectives here." Forsythe also warned, however, that there must be local support for any management plan. Hughes, while supporting protection, also expressed his concern over the proposed freeze on federally sponsored projects in part of the area. Case assured the committee that the delegation would "work it out, so there is no difference at all among us on this thing."[9]

The proposal that was modified to win the approval of the Senate and the House was prepared by Deputy Assistant Secretary of the Interior David Hales, with the assistance of the entire New Jersey delegation (particularly of Florio) and members of Governor Byrne's staff. This proposal called for a planning entity of undesignated size that was to be (with the exception of one Interior Department representative) composed entirely of gubernatorial appointees. The boundary of the reserve encompassed about one million acres and roughly followed the boundary suggested in the National Park Service report prepared by Rutgers. The Senate proposal also provided for an immediate freeze on federal projects in the core of the Pinelands (the so-called Federal Project Review Area) until a management plan could be prepared for the entire area, a clause Hales insisted on. It appropriated up to $26 million for use by the Department of the Interior during the planning period for acquisition of critically sensitive land threatened by development.

Reactions, More Compromises, and Final Passage.   By September, a draft of the Senate's Pinelands National Reserve legislation was available to the public. Feelings ran high. Section 502 (which had been numbered 503 in early versions) was strongly preservationist; environmentalists generally favored it, but many local officials opposed it. Vituperative letters in the South Jersey edition of the Philadelphia *Evening Bulletin* highlighted differences among the factions. It appeared that Clifford Hansen (R–Wyoming), a member of the Senate committee that was considering Section 502, was almost right when he remarked that the Pine Barrens proposal was too controversial to be passed as part of the omnibus parks bill.[10] Back in New Jersey, away from Washington and the pressures to compromise, Hughes and Forsythe accused the Department of the Interior of trying to take over the Pinelands and pointed with pride at their House bill, which had kept most control at the local level.[11] "Local control," however, clearly meant different things to different people. The Pine Barrens Coalition, a coalition of environmental organizations led by Mae Barringer, charged that the "locals" referred to by Hughes and Forsythe were pawns of speculators and developers whose interests were something other than preservation; they, the Pine Barrens Coalition, represented the true local interest.[12]

Another aspect of this problem, and the issue that caused the greatest political stir, was the question of local representation on the "planning entity." Between October 5 and October 12, this portion of the federal legislation was amended three times. Through the amendment process and in an atmosphere of intense lobbying by local interests the composition of the planning body gradually became more specific. First, the number of members was defined; it was changed from undesignated, to twenty-one members, to fifteen members. At the same time, specific categories of membership were worked out. The final version, drafted on the very eve of the full Senate vote, called for a fifteen-member group composed of one federal representative, seven local county representatives (one from each of the seven counties in the Pinelands Reserve), and seven gubernatorial appointees, who had to include representatives of both regional economic interests (for example, Pinelands agriculture) and statewide conservation interests.

At the same time as these compromises on membership were being hammered out, Congressman Hughes continued his opposition to any development moratorium in the Pinelands. The federal bill, of course, could limit only projects requiring federal permits. Support for the restriction on development, however, remained strong. Environmentalists, Department of the Interior staff members, and even proponents of the Forsythe–Hughes proposal all worked together to stop last-minute attempts to remove building restrictions from the Senate bill. In the end, the freeze on building was restricted to a limited "Federal Project Review Area."

The Senate vote on the National Parks and Recreation Act, which included the designation of the Pinelands National Reserve as Section 502, took place in the last hours of the 95th Congress, under pressure of time. The bill was approved by the House of Representatives in its Senate form, and thus never went to a conference committee. It was signed into law by President Carter on November 10, 1978.

Provisions of the Federal Legislation. The federal legislation established that the approximately one million acres of the "Pine Barrens Area, New Jersey" was a resource of national significance and that it was appropriate for the federal government to assist the state and municipalities in their efforts to protect it. The legislation also provided federal funds of up to $26 million for land acquisition in the area.

To protect the reserve, the legislation required that the Secretary of the Interior call on the governor of New Jersey to set up a fifteen-member planning entity, as discussed above. This entity was directed to prepare a comprehensive management plan for the area as well as to administer during the planning phase a moratorium on federal projects within a 486,000-acre Federal Project Review Area in the core of the Pinelands. The act also specified that the comprehensive management plan must include, among other things, a resource assessment; maps of boundaries, critical areas, and land-use capability; and details of how the resources were to be protected using state and local regulatory and zoning powers. The plan was to recognize existing activities and encourage those that were consistent with protecting the resource.

During the planning period, the secretary could make grants to the state for acquisition of immediately threatened land, as determined by the planning entity. These lands would be conveyed to the state or local authorities after federal approval of the final management plan. Further acquisition as called for by the findings of the comprehensive management plan was also allowed. Federal approval of the management plan was to be based on a list of criteria including adequate public participation in planning and the assurance of the governor's continuing effective oversight of implementation of the plan.

State Response to the Federal Legislation

The state quickly moved to implement the federal legislation, first with the issuance of an executive order and then with the introduction of legislation. Much of the preliminary work had already been done, or at least set into motion.

At a meeting on November 6, 1978, four days before President Carter signed the new law in Washington, members of the New Jersey Department of Environmental Protection (Commissioner Daniel O'Hern, Deputy Commissioner Betty Wilson, and Pinelands Coordinator Sean Reilly) met with members of the state Department of Community Affairs (Director of the Division of State and Regional Planning Richard Ginman and the Bureau of Regional Planning Head Richard Binetsky) to recommend procedures for implementation of the federal act. These included presentation of the nearly completed Pinelands Review Committee report on Pine Barrens protection and drafting of "strong state legislation."

The departments pointed out that, while the federal law had specified the composition of the Pinelands planning entity, its powers and functions had been left open. State legislation would need to clarify these. They also suggested that "a movement . . . by some special interest groups to gain control of the planning body by deciding on the chairman and hiring PEC as staff [should be] nipped in the bud" by gubernatorial appointment of both chairman and executive director of the future planning commission. [13]

Pinelands Review Committee Report.   The Pinelands Review Committee's report on protection of the Pine Barrens was prepared under an executive order by Governor Byrne (see Chapter 2). After some last-minute changes to bring it into conformance with the new federal legislation, it was brought out in early February 1979. In a sense, this report put the state's imprimatur on the creation of the Pinelands National Reserve. The report also strongly influenced the substance of both Executive Order 71 and the state Pinelands protection legislation.

This influence was especially important in the establishment of boundaries and development controls. The PRC recommended, and the state later mandated, that the Pinelands be divided into two areas. The northern, 339,000-acre, Preservation Area corresponded roughly with DEP's Critical Area for water quality control (see Chapter 2) and the Federal Project Review Area established by the federal law. This core area was slated for the most stringent protection. The rest of the region was recommended for a Protection Area where some controlled development would be allowed. (See Figure 3–1.)

Executive Order 71.   The federal legislation directed the Secretary of the Interior to request the Governor of New Jersey to designate a "planning entity" for the Pinelands. On February 8, 1979, Governor Brendan Byrne responded by issuing Executive Order 71, which established a Pinelands Planning Commission and imposed temporary controls on development during the period in which a Pinelands management plan was being prepared. The executive order filled the gap until the legislature could act. The Secretary of the Interior called this order an "absolutely right" action, and a former New Jersey Deputy Attorney General has since remarked that it was "perhaps the broadest use of executive power ever seen" in the state. [14]

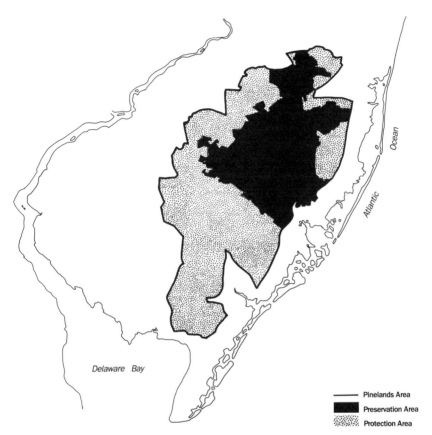

Figure 3–1. Boundaries of the Pinelands Preservation Area and of the Pinelands Protection Area. Map by Tina Campbell.

Although the earliest drafts of the executive order (as well as of the Pinelands legislation, which was proposed only five days later) did not include interim building restrictions, Governor Byrne's office wanted stringent controls and eventually got them.[15] Some local officials as well as conservationists also supported the imposition of interim development controls, at least in the core area.[16] Both the departments of Environmental Protection (DEP) and Community Affairs (DCA) recommended that the executive order "suspend issuing approvals for commencing capital construction in the Pine Barrens Critical Area and . . . institute a review process in the rest of the area."[17] The governor's executive order went beyond this recommendation by imposing interim regulations on the entire Pinelands Area.

In establishing the Pinelands Commission, the governor took the advice of the DEP and the DCA in principle, although he did not follow their specific suggestions that the chairman of the commission be a member of the governor's staff nor that its executive director be the DEP Pinelands coordinator. In fact, the governor appointed to the first commission no representative from either the DEP or the DCA. Instead, the independence of the commission from previously existing bureaucracies was carefully guarded. He did, however, take DEP's advice to appoint both the executive director and the chairman of the commission, thus strengthening his role with relation to the counties by denying them a say in choosing the leadership of the new planning body.[18]

The Legislative Proposal.   Only five days after Executive Order 71 was issued, on February 13, 1979, New Jersey Senate President Joseph Merlino (D–Mercer) and Senator Charles Yates (D–Burlington) introduced the Pinelands Protection Act (S. 3091). Similarities between this bill and the executive order were not coincidental. They had been drafted together; both aimed at implementing the new federal legislation and both were strongly influenced by the Pinelands Review Committee's report.

The legislation set the boundaries of the Pinelands as recommended by the PRC. The proposal also included interim development controls for the entire Pinelands Area, although exemptions from the building restrictions were to be more easily obtained in the Protection Area than in the core Preservation Area. The legislation also spelled out in some detail the role of the Pinelands Commission, which was both to prepare and to implement the management plan. The proposal gave the governor sole responsibility for appointing seven members of the commission as well as veto power over the commission's minutes. This latter power meant that the governor could veto any action of the commission.

Reactions to the Executive Order and the Senate Proposal.   Negative reactions to the executive order and the proposed legislation were swift. The New Jersey Builders Association filed a lawsuit in the Appellate Division of the New Jersey Superior Court to suspend the moratorium and to get a ruling on the constitutionality of the executive order, charging that the moratorium would cost New Jersey 3,000 jobs and $900 million.[19] Others argued that the moratorium should apply only to the Preservation Area. Builders' organizations supported this concept, or at least they indicated that they could live with it.[20]

Indeed, the moratorium remained a critical issue throughout the planning process. It was at the heart of the debate about where the "real" boundaries of the Pinelands were. At hearings held on the Pinelands Protection Act in February 1979, even some who were critical of the act were shifting their criticism of the building restrictions from the Preservation Area to the Protection Area (for example, Hazel Gluck's remarks at the hearings before the Senate Energy and Environment Committee on February 22).[21] At least in the Preservation Area environmental evidence for preservation was very strong, while pressure for development was relatively weak. In the Protection Area, however, residential growth threatened from the north, the east, and the west. Left unchecked, as Senator Merlino and the Pine Barrens Coalition both pointed out, such development in the Protection Area would ultimately threaten the integrity of the Preservation Area itself.[22] As a result, neither Senator Merlino nor Senator Yates was willing to consider limiting the building restrictions to just the Preservation Area, and so the final state legislation, like the executive order, imposed the development limitations on the entire Pinelands Area.

Another important area of discussion and conflict was gubernatorial power. Not only was the governor to appoint the chairman of the commission and its executive director, but also he had veto power over the minutes of commission meetings and made his appointments to the commission with no legislative oversight. The Department of the Interior supported the governor's veto power over the actions of the commission as an effective vehicle for executive oversight. In fact, Hales of that Department indicated that without it his department would not approve any eventual management plan. Finally, the proposed requirement for a two-thirds vote to grant an exemption from the building moratorium was, to many builders and local politicians, another distasteful, though indirect, manifestation of the governor's control over "local" affairs. The two-thirds vote meant, of course, that the governor's appointees voting as a bloc could effectively block any exemption request.

The lines of battle were clear. Affiliations tended to be predictive of reactions to the proposal: builders and many local politicians opposed it as written; those representing conservation groups supported it. Typically, the opposition argued that "preservation has got to be kept to a fair minimum"—meaning that preservation was fine so long as it had only minor economic impact.[23] Sometimes merely the name of an organization indicated its position—a builders' group called the Coalition for the Sensible Preservation of the Pinelands, for example.

On the other hand, environmentalists pointed out that the loss of the Pine Barrens would be irreparable. They argued that it would be better to err, if at all, in the direction of protection. The New Jersey Conservation Foundation called for quick action on the senate bill, "while we still have the chance to preserve the last remaining open area along the mid-Atlantic coast."[24] A poll of 367 Burlington County residents found that 70 percent favored the moratorium, and that 60 percent supported the moratorium for one of three reasons: that the "ecology should be saved," that recreational needs demanded it, or that the area was "too built up already."[25]

Legislative Alternatives to the Merlino–Yates Proposal.   Three more bills were introduced into the New Jersey legislature in the spring of 1979 as alternatives to the Merlino–Yates proposal. Two of these (one introduced into the senate by John Russo [D–Burlington] and three cosponsors on February 26 and one into the assembly by Assemblyman James Hurley [R–Cumberland] and five cosponsors on April 26) restricted the building limitations to the Preservation Area, removed the governor's power to veto the commission's minutes, and required senate advice and consent for original appointees to the Pinelands Commission. Assemblyman Michael Matthews (D–Atlantic) and three cosponsors introduced a third bill on May 3 with no building restrictions at all and no gubernatorial oversight over the actions of the commission. All three bills died in committee.

Three issues dominated legislative criticism of the Merlino–Yates bill: (1) the conflict between preserving open space and encouraging economic growth; (2) provision of adequate local participation in the planning and management processes; and (3) limitation of the governor's power. Out of these concerns came a variety of amendments. The interim building regulations as originally proposed were weakened as a concession to economic interests: agricultural and horticultural uses, for example, were exempted from the regulations throughout the Pinelands and some construction of single-family houses in the Protection Area was to be allowed. Moreover, in the final legislation, exemptions from the regulations could be granted by a majority, rather than a two-thirds, vote of the commission. To encourage local participation, a mayors' council was set up to offer advice and comment on the management plan. To limit the power of the governor, appointments required the advice and consent of the senate for gubernatorial appointments and gave the commission the power to choose its own executive director.

Passage of the New Jersey Pinelands Protection Act.   The amended bill was passed by the New Jersey Senate on May 21, 1979, by an overwhelming 33–2 vote. It was passed by the Assembly at 3 a.m. on June 21 by a vote of 48–16, after a marathon debate. The governor signed the legislation at a public ceremony on June 28.

Overall, the bill remained strongly preservationist in spite of attempts to modify it, and the governor retained tight control through his powers of appointment and veto. Compromises did, however, indicate a willingness to deal fairly with the economic and home-rule interests of the local residents. The shifting position of Senator Lee Laskin (R–Burlington) characterized legislative reaction to the compromise process. On March 1 the *Central Record* of Medford (Burlington County) reported his opposition to the building moratorium in the Protection Area; by May 17, after three public hearings and 60 to 70 hours of committee discussion, the same paper reported that Laskin now supported the bill, because the hearings and the committee discussions had cleared up his difficulties with it.

Summary of the State Pinelands Legislation.   The state Pinelands Protection Act was designed, first, "to implement the . . . Federal Act and insure the realization of pinelands protection through the establishment of a regional planning and management commission to prepare and oversee the implementation of a comprehensive management plan for the pinelands area." Second, it singled out an "especially vulnerable" Preservation Area, where restrictions on development should be more stringent than elsewhere and acquisition should be concentrated. Finally, the legislation created interim limitations on the issuance of permits for construction throughout the Pinelands in order to protect the region from the immediate threat of random and uncoordinated growth. The details and procedures of the act directed how these three aims were to be carried out.

Membership of the Pinelands Commission as established by the state legislation followed the federal mandate. In addition, the governor was given the power to appoint the chairman and to veto any commission action. The commission itself had three charges—(1) to write the Comprehensive Management Plan, (2) to administer the interim building restrictions, and (3) to recommend sites for acquisition.

Specific legislative directions for preparation of the Comprehensive Management Plan were similar to those in the federal act; in most cases, they were identical. Once this management plan had won approval, the state legislation, unlike the federal, also required that all municipalities and counties within the Pinelands Area bring their local master plans and zoning ordinances into conformance with it. Municipalities that failed to do so would forfeit their right to review development applications before Pinelands Commission approval.

After adoption of the plan, the commission had review authority over "any final municipal or county approval . . . of any application for development in the pinelands area." Moreover, the commission's vote on applications was to be binding and to supersede municipal approval; it was subject only to judicial review.

Comparison of Federal and State Legislation

Boundaries.   The area included in both the National Pinelands Reserve and the state Pinelands Area was defined more or less by the Cohansey Formation outcrop (see Chapter 1). This scientific basis for protection, however, did not mean that the boundaries of the national and the state protected zones were identical (see Figure 3–2). Various other influences also entered into the process of setting boundaries.

The National Park Service–Rutgers study had recommended the exclusion of heavily developed areas from the protected zone. The reasoning behind this was similar to the reasoning that had led to the exclusion of heavily developed areas from the English national park system. As a consequence, both state and federal legislation excluded finger-shaped areas of potential heavy development covering more than 30,000 acres extending westward into the Pine Barrens from Atlantic City. The federal legislation also excluded from the National Reserve a total of about 20,000 acres in three other areas with development potential, the largest in Atlantic County, one in Cumberland County, and another across the Atlantic-Cumberland County boundary. The state legislation excluded no other acreage from the Pinelands Area on grounds of existing or potential heavy development. It is for this reason that the oddly shaped area west of Atlantic City, part of the district of state Senator Stephen Perskie, an outspoken critic of Pinelands legislation (who did, however, vote for it) became known as Perskie's Thumb and Forefinger, in reference to his suspected influence in the drawing of these particular boundary lines.

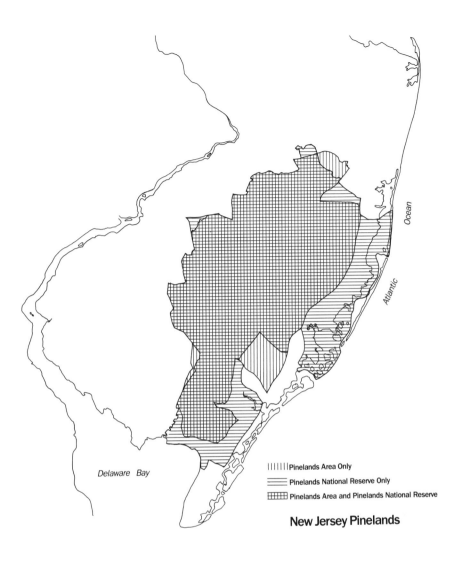

Figure 3–2. Details of the Boundaries of the Pinelands National Reserve and of the Pinelands Area. Map by Tina Campbell.

The Pinelands National Reserve included 1,083,000 acres; the state Pinelands Area was almost 180,000 acres smaller. The principal reason for this was the inclusion of 150,000 acres along the Atlantic and Delaware coasts in the National Reserve but not in the state Pinelands Area. The state reasoned that this area was already regulated under the provisions of the Coastal Area Facility Review Act (CAFRA), which included directions for coordinating development of the region under its comprehensive management plan; thus its inclusion in the Pinelands Area would have been redundant. Also included in the reserve but not in the state Pinelands Area were approximately 20,000 acres in western Burlington and northern Ocean counties. Michael Catania, who drafted the state legislation, attributed most differences in the northern boundaries to inadequacies in the federal maps.[26]

Both federal and state legislation recognized the special nature of the core of the Pine Barrens (about 340,000 acres), and their designations of the internal boundaries for this area generally coincide. The federal legislation called this core the Federal Project Review Area, while the state legislation, as we have seen, divided the Pinelands Area into a Preservation Area (the core) and the Protection Area. The special protections given the core area by both state and federal acts did not, however, exclude the larger region from the jurisdiction of the regional planning body or from strict development controls.

In general, most boundaries of the protected regions follow cultural features, such as roads, rather than natural features, since these were easier to define in an area of low relief and where interbasin transfer of water in aquifers rendered the concept of watershed rather vague. All boundaries were based, in large part, on those suggested by the NPS–Rutgers report and the PRC report (see Chapter 2). Although these reports did vary in some details, both used major ecosystem and landscape features to determine the area that needed protection. More important, both emphasized the necessity for preserving the entire Pine Barrens, not just a part of it.

Protection of the Ecological Resources.   The natural resources of the Pine Barrens provided the basis for protection. Both state and federal legislation cited the expanse of forest, pristine water and air, and rare species as features of the Pine Barrens worthy of preservation. The state bill also emphasized the habitats of rare and endangered species as critical features. The principal threat to these natural resources was viewed as disorderly, uncoordinated, random, scattered development, both public and private. Not viewed as a threat was agriculture, especially the culture of indigenous cranberries and blueberries; indeed, cranberry and blueberry culture was actually viewed as a natural resource to be preserved. Fire was another prominent feature of the environment of the Pine Barrens mentioned by both bills; neither bill, however, specifically defined fire as either a resource or a threat, thus neatly side-stepping any possible conflict between the double role of fire as preserver of the ecosystem and destroyer of life and property.

Although protection of the valued natural resources from threats was the central aim of both bills, both left the means of protection up to the planning entity, with broad latitude. Acquisition was to be limited to those areas determined to be most critical and immediately threatened. Federal and state funds were to be appropriated for this purpose and all lands so acquired would eventually fall under state jurisdiction. Protection of the remaining privately owned land (estimated to be about two-thirds of the total area) would depend on a variety of methods to be detailed in the Comprehensive Management Plan, including conservation easements; purchase, resale, or leaseback; and zoning. Both bills explicitly required the planning entity to direct growth; there was no specific commitment to *limit* growth. Both pieces of legislation appeared to agree that orderly, well-planned growth could be accommodated within the Pinelands Area, even though both bills also made clear that their primary aim was preservation. Neither made any clear distinction between "preservation" and "protection." In fact, the name proposed by the NPS–Rutgers study was "National Preserve" not "Reserve," and no explanation was ever offered concerning what the National Reserve was being reserved for. The lack of clear definitions for such terms continued to muddy discussions throughout planning.

Protection of Social, Cultural, and Historical Resources. Both bills placed a high value on recreational resources. Other social, cultural, and historical resources were mentioned but given short shrift: they were to be "assessed with a determination of policies necessary to maintain them." This emphasis on recreation harked back to the concept of greenline parks, for which recreation was a major goal. Both acts required the protection and enhancement of recreational facilities, and neither suggested that recreation might be a serious threat to the natural resources. The state act further required consideration of both state acquisition of more public recreation sites and greater public access to private land for recreational use. Added in committee was a strong clause that "nothing in this act shall be construed to authorize any regulation of hunting, fishing, trapping, or possession of wildlife, or other recreational activities in the pinelands area, except as otherwise provided." Thus was acknowledged the great popularity in the Pine Barrens of hunting, a traditional activity. The one recognition of recreation's possible negative impact on natural resources was the prohibition of "power vessels" in certain areas and of motor vehicles on public land in the Pinelands Area, except on public highways and areas designated by the Pinelands Commission.

Economic Activities.   The Pinelands legislation, both federal and state, sought to maintain the economic viability of the Pine Barrens, an aim also vital to the greenline park concept. At the same time, the overriding concern of both federal and state legislation was that all economic activities be compatible with maintenance of the unique ecology of the Pine Barrens. Both acts recognized some economic activities to be encouraged, especially agriculture, horticulture, and recreation, by requiring the "protection and enhancement" of "those indigenous industries and commercial and residential development which are consistent with . . . the purposes and provisions" of the act [state wording]. The state legislation also recognized "pressures for residential, commercial, and industrial development" as threats to the natural resources. Interpretation of these statements and the relative emphasis given to "protection and enhancement" of industry and development versus protection of the natural resources provided a major challenge in writing the management plan.

The state legislation, in response to much testimony at hearings, made special allowances to those who owned land prior to February 7, 1979, for construction of single-family residences meeting certain criteria under the interim development restrictions; thus the act recognized the right of individuals to use their land, within guidelines, for their own purposes. On the other hand, both federal and state legislation required all major developments (residential and commercial) to be planned in an orderly way compatible with the maintenance of "ecological values." In all cases ecological values, not economic returns, were to receive first consideration.

Funding.   The federal legislation divided allocations for the National Reserve into three categories: planning funds, operating funds after the original planning document was completed, and acquisition. It authorized an appropriation of not more than $26 million, including up to $3 million for planning and the remainder for acquisition. The federal monies had a string attached, however: If at any time the Secretary of the Interior determined that the state was not properly carrying out the purposes of the federal act, he could demand reimbursement from the state for all previously granted funds.

The state legislation authorized no funds specifically for acquisition. Instead, it directed that money from Green Acres bond issues or other sources should be used to purchase land. All funding for Pinelands protection, moreover, was to be funneled through the state's Department of Environmental Protection.

Both federal and state acts required that the management plan include a financial component that would outline sources of revenue and costs of implementing the plan, including operating funds and payments in lieu of taxes to municipalities. Further details of financial management were left to the planning body.

Allocation of Political Roles.   Both federal and state acts were marked by a complexity of interrelated political roles, an inevitable consequence of the greenline park concept. In fact, clarifying these interrelationships was a major task of implementing that concept. The federal act provided a framework, but because of statutory limitations of federal authority when dealing with the internal workings of a state, it was the state legislation that was most expansive on this topic, especially on questions related to the roles of the commission and the municipalities.

Role of the Federal Government. The federal legislation gave the Department of the Interior a congressional mandate to carry out the law, although it singled out no one agency within the department to be lead agency. The Secretary of the Interior was to request the Governor of New Jersey to set up a planning entity for the Pinelands National Reserve. The secretary was also directed to appoint one member of the planning entity and, during the planning process, to provide technical and financial assistance. Once the plan was written, the secretary was directed to evaluate it according to a specific list of criteria and then to approve or disapprove the plan. If the plan was approved, the secretary was to exercise continuing oversight, especially when changes to the plan were proposed.

Role of the State Government. The state executive order complied with the federal mandate by creating the Pinelands Commission. In addition, the state legislation gave the governor both direct (the veto) and indirect (appointments) powers over this commission. The state legislation also gave the governor discretionary power to appoint a citizens' committee. All gubernatorial appointments were to be made with the advice and consent of the senate, and the legislature as a whole retained the right to review, but not to veto, the final management plan.

Four principal duties were specifically allocated to the state Department of Environmental Protection: (1) to provide technical advice to the commission, (2) to acquire land, (3) to administer development review in the coastal zone area, and (4) to manage state-owned lands. In addition, the DEP commissioner had to be notified of any private property transfer of more than ten acres in the Preservation Area, when that property was to be passed outside the owner's immediate family. (This was an unpopular provision among local citizens.) The Pinelands Commission was located technically within the DEP, but was independent of its control. This provision led to some strain between the commission and the DEP, as they tried to define their changing roles during development of the comprehensive management plan and when reviewing applications for development.

Role of Local Governments. Local governments and the Pinelands Commission were both to be involved in the day-to-day implementation of the legislative mandates. Counties appointed members to the commission, and performed some regulatory and planning functions, such as formulating solid-waste management plans. Municipalities could offer advice through the Municipal Council, and, most important, they administered the Pinelands Comprehensive Management Plan at the local level. It was, in the end, to be local implementation that would make or break the plan, for, although the commission retained oversight, a lack of cooperation from municipalities could create an impossible burden for the commission. By requiring the commission to seek advice from the Municipal Council and to consult with local officials, the drafters of both federal and state legislation hoped to ensure some degree of local support for the management plan.

Role of the Pinelands Commission. Congressman Florio's original proposal for a Pine Barrens National Ecological Reserve had called for a commission to "oversee the regulation of land uses and the control of developments of areawide significance" as well as to formulate a management plan.[27] The Case–Williams bill had also included as a requirement for establishing any National Reserve that "a state or local planning and management agency . . . [be] established . . . to carry out land use and conservation planning in the area of the prospective National Reserve [and] . . . establish and enforce development standards." Thus, it appeared to have been the intention of at least three of the principals that the planning agency would also serve as the management body for the Pinelands. The final federal legislation, however, did not specifically state that the planning entity should both prepare the plan and then continue on as the implementing and management agency. It stated only that the planning entity should plan and that it should administer the building moratorium during the planning phase.

The definition of this continuing role for the commission was left instead to the state legislation. After considerable controversy, the state act directed that the commission should prepare the management plan, administer the interim development controls, and then implement and carry out the approved plan.

A regional commission that planned and managed development was implicit in the greenline park concept. As yet another layer of government, the regional commission involved, even if only indirectly, both federal and state governments in what had been heretofore local decision-making. Both federal and state legislation recognized this novel situation and responded by creating a framework for intergovernmental relationships and by giving the commission the task of coordinating federal, state, and municipal actions and policies.

Legal Issues. The Pinelands legislation raised at least two important legal issues: that of "taking" of private property and that of due process. Neither issue was treated explicitly in the federal law.

The greenline park concept relied, except for limited acquisition, on the regulation of the use of private land. Thus it directly raised the question of how far public regulation could impinge on private property rights. Although the Bill of Rights prohibits the "taking" of private property for public use without adequate compensation, it fails to clarify exactly what constitutes a "taking" for which compensation is required. State and municipal governments traditionally have retained the power to restrict certain uses of private land in the public interest, although they may not restrict the use of land such as to render it valueless, thus "taking" it. An amendment to the state Pinelands bill addressed this issue by requiring the commission to identify those lands whose use would be so adversely affected by restrictions imposed as a result of the legislation that compensation was necessary.

Questions of due process were raised by interim development controls and by the requirement that municipalities bring local master plans into conformance with the Comprehensive Management Plan. The state act addressed this issue by setting up criteria and procedures both for requesting exemptions from the moratorium and for bringing local master plans into conformance.

Conclusion

The salient feature of both the federal and the state legislation was the strong preservationist stance. Economic interests were accommodated, but only insofar as they were consistent with preservation of the natural resources of the Pine Barrens.

Strong commitments by Governor Byrne, by the Department of the Interior, and by many legislators were prerequisites for passage of both federal and state legislation. Effective lobbying by environmental organizations, both national and local, was crucial. Local support (for example, Byrne's re-election, passage of conservation bond issues, testimony at hearings, and public-opinion polls) also helped get the federal and state legislation passed. Overall, success depended on a willingness to compromise while holding firm on critical issues.

4. The Pinelands Commission: Startup and Interim Development Regulation

Beryl Robichaud Collins

Emily W. B. Russell

The Pinelands Commission is the critical element for carrying out both federal and state legislative mandates to protect the resources of the Pine Barrens. The first step toward achieving this overall goal was to get organized and begin to write the Comprehensive Management Plan. During this initial phase, the commission had also to administer the building moratorium. The commission's experiences with the moratorium not only gave the commissioners and staff important training and background, but it also directly affected the ultimate shape of the final management plan. This chapter traces the development of the commission and its activities during this interim period before final adoption of the comprehensive management plan.

Establishment of the Commission

The Pinelands Planning Commission was created in February 1979 when Governor Byrne issued his Executive Order 71. The commission was charged, first, with preparing a comprehensive management plan for the new Pinelands National Reserve and, second, with administering temporary controls on development during the interim planning period. In June 1979 state legislation added implementation of the plan to the commission's roster of responsibilities and, appropriately, renamed it simply the Pinelands Commission.

Membership. The fifteen members of the commission, as mandated by the federal legislation, ensured a degree of local, state, and federal participation both in planning the Pinelands National Reserve and in implementing the law. The seven county appointees were assumed to represent local interests or county governments, while the seven gubernatorial appointees represented state interests, and the Secretary of the Interior's single appointee represented those of the federal government.

The governor could strongly influence the direction of the commission's planning through his appointment powers. His seven appointees represented one fewer than a majority on the commission, but more members

87

than any other person or county could individually appoint. He also selected the chairman of the commission. The governor's power was at its greatest during the startup phase, since his first appointments were exempt from the advice and consent of the New Jersey Senate.

County appointees, chosen by their respective freeholder boards, represented a variety of local and county interests. They could not be expected to vote as a bloc. Indeed, the composition of the first Pinelands Planning Commission proved the point—it included both vociferous opponents of the Pinelands protection legislation and strong supporters of the commission's activities.

The federal appointee played a vital role in linking the state commission with the federal government and thus reinforcing the national importance of the Pinelands. This member served and voted as any other commissioner, but could also communicate messages from the Secretary of the Interior to the commission. This function was of critical importance in winning the secretary's approval of the final management plan. The federal appointee also had access to the Department of the Interior's many resources, which he could then make available to the commission.

Both federal and state legislation required that the membership of the commission include both residents of the Pinelands National Reserve, who would represent local economic activities such as agriculture, and residents from other parts of New Jersey, who would represent statewide conservation interests. Commissioners, who were unpaid, served for three-year terms, staggered initially to ensure continuity. The legislation provided for no representation from the two state departments that had actively worked to get strong Pinelands protection—the Department of Environmental Protection and the Department of Community Affairs. Although administratively classed within the DEP, the commission was independent of any supervision or control by that department. The commission's actions may, however, be vetoed by the governor.

The First Commission.   Because the governor's first appointments to the commission were made prior to passage of the state Pinelands Protection Act, his initial appointees did not require approval by the senate. Four of these appointees were residents of the Pinelands and three had already been involved in Pinelands preservation efforts. Tom Darlington, a berry farmer whose family had strong ties to the Pine Barrens, and Gary Patterson, director of environmental education programs at Glassboro State College, had both served on the governor's Pinelands Review Committee; Floyd West, mayor of Bass River Township, had been on the Pinelands Environmental Council. Both Patterson and West had spoken at hearings in favor of strong protectionist legislation. The fourth local resident, Peter Burke, Jr., treasurer of a real-estate management company and Bill Bradley's campaign finance manager, was appointed apparently as a favor to the senator.

Two other gubernatorial appointees, Candace Ashmun and Chairman Franklin Parker, were from northern New Jersey, and represented state-wide and national conservation interests. Ashmun was executive director of the Association of New Jersey Environmental Commissions and Parker, a lawyer, was chairman of the board of the New Jersey Conservation Foundation and a trustee of the Natural Resources Defense Council. The final gubernatorial appointee, B. Budd Chavooshian of Trenton, a planner and former director of state and regional planning in New Jersey, was an extension specialist in land-use and resource management in the Department of Environmental Resources at Rutgers University's Cook College.

The governor had assembled an impressive group. Among its important attributes were familiarity with the myriad of existing New Jersey environmental regulations and a thorough knowledge of municipal and county planning processes, as well as involvement in previous Pinelands planning efforts. Also, most of the appointees, Ashmun and Chavooshian in particular, had close working relationships with many state officials. The governor appointed Parker as chairman, apparently on the recommendation of Laurence Rockefeller, who had been very active in the development of the Adirondack Park.[1]

The original county appointees included three county freeholders—Robert Shinn (Burlington), Hazel Gluck (Ocean), and Donald Wagner (Gloucester)—and two mayors—Russell Clark (Hammonton, Atlantic County) and Patrick Fiorilli (Vineland, Cumberland County). Three of these appointees had testified either against the state legislation (Shinn and Gluck) or for the Forsythe–Hughes bill (Shinn, Fiorilli). In addition, Clark had been generally outspoken against the state legislation. The appointee from Cape May, Lester Germanio, was a farmer and developer, and Joan Batory, from Camden (home of James Florio) headed the Camden County environmental agency.

At the outset, Batory was the only one of the county group who favored the federal and state Pinelands legislation. Although Shinn had convinced both the Pinelands Environmental Council, of which he was a member, and the freeholders of South Jersey to endorse an alternative federal proposal that emphasized local control over the Pinelands (see Chapter 2), he had earned the respect of some as a champion of conservation interests when he successfully promoted county bond authorizations for conservation easements and farmland preservation. Though environmentalists initially were suspicious of Shinn, he turned out to be one of the commission's most effective members.

The initial federal appointee to the commission was David Hales, Deputy Assistant Secretary for Fish, Wildlife, and Parks in the Department of the Interior. Hales had helped draft the federal Pinelands legislation. He soon found, however, that the commission's work involved too much time, and so in late 1979 Donald Kennard, a former Texas legislator and consultant to the Department of the Interior, was selected as his replacement.

The early tone and priorities of the commission were set primarily by its strong, committed, conservation-oriented members—the governor's seven appointees and two county members, Shinn and Batory. Commission Chairman Parker was a low-key individual with an unusual ability to defuse highly politicized situations and to steer group deliberations constructively on complex issues. Shinn, who was elected vice-chairman, worked well with Chairman Parker to moderate debates between differing factions.

Initial Activities.   The Pinelands Planning Commission was responsible for ruling on requests for waivers and exemptions from the building restrictions, but had no staff or standards ready at hand for making judgments. It also needed to develop a strategy for writing the Comprehensive Management Plan within the tight schedule set by the state legislation. The DEP loaned its Pinelands Coordinator Sean Reilly to assist with these preliminary activities. As a first step, the commission established four subcommittees early in April—Search, Work Plan, Review Standards, and Bylaws.

The Search Committee's first task was to recruit an executive director for the commission. It compiled a list of potential candidates for the position, all but one of whom were state residents as required by the governor. The whole commission then narrowed the list to four and interviewed and ranked them. The short list included two planners, one former member of the governor's Pinelands Review Board, and the executive director of the Newark Watershed Conservation and Development Corporation. The commission forwarded this list to the governor, who rejected the commission's unanimous first choice, a planner, in favor of Terrence Moore of the Newark Watershed. The governor, using his powers under Executive Order 71, appointed Moore; then he signed the state legislation, which gave the commission the power to select its own executive director.

The commission and its new executive director faced a formidable task. In only a little over a year they had to write the Comprehensive Management Plan for the Pinelands, but when Moore took up his position as executive director on July 13, 1979, he had no independent budget and a staff on loan from DEP.

Funding.   One of the executive director's first actions, then, was to seek independent funding. This led to a memorandum of agreement between DEP and the commission, which was signed in early September, granting the commission $500,000 from DEP's Green Acres funds, for personnel and operations (including planning). An additional $75,000 was allocated from the governor's account for staffing costs. Moore also received from the private, New Jersey Geraldine R. Dodge Foundation a grant of $200,000 to support development review activities.

The federal legislation had allocated up to $3 million for planning, but these funds were not immediately available; nor were they to be used to administer interim development review, even in the Federal Project Review Area. It was not until January 18, 1980, that any federal funds came to the commission. On that day Secretary Andrus presented a check for $100,000 to the governor in a public ceremony at the State House. According to Andrus, it was the first time the secretary's contingency reserves from the Land and Water Conservation Funds had been used for planning. The money was the first of a promised $500,000 from that source.

The acquisition funding vital to the preservation effort, however, was soon to be affected by federal budget cuts. In Section 502 of the Parks and Recreation Act (the section dealing with Pinelands preservation) Congress had authorized $23 million for land acquisition in the Pinelands, most to become available after the secretary had signed the final management plan, but some to be used immediately to acquire currently threatened properties. In February 1980, the initial September 1979 allocation of $12 million was cut in half. Senators Williams and Bradley and Representative Florio pledged their support for reinstatement of these funds,[2] while Representatives Hughes and Forsythe supported the cut in order to force changes on the Pinelands Commission. In May 1980 the cut was postponed and the $12 million became available, $800,000 for planning and $11.2 million for acquisition.

Staff.   Executive Director Moore quickly began recruiting staff, making his first appointments, with commission approval, in July 1979. He appointed William Harrison, a staff attorney for DEP who was already working on the interim development review process, as assistant director for development review. For the time being, Moore kept planning operations under his own direction, not appointing an assistant director for planning until late February 1980. The original commission staff included three natural scientists, two planners (one each for development review and planning), and one public involvement coordinator. A third planner, the coordinator for special projects, had also served on the staff of the Pinelands Review Committee. Further appointments in 1980 brought the staff total, including clerical staff, up to thirty full-time members, ten of whom were involved in development review activities.

The staff operated from an historic, three-story house on the northern fringes of the Pinelands. The commission leased the building from a state agency in September 1979 and moved in in October. The building was adequate as an office, but contained no room large enough for the commission meetings, so these had to be held in public buildings elsewhere in the Pinelands. This procession of meetings somewhat mitigated complaints that the office was far from many areas of the Pinelands (up to two hours by car), but made organizing meetings rather more awkward than it would have been had they been held at the office.

The commission's staff was young and energetic. Executive Director Terry Moore, in his late thirties and once an environmental fellow at Harvard University, was a soft-spoken individual who did not often display reaction to criticism, however severe. Critics viewed this as indifference to outside suggestions, while supporters claimed that an unflustered manner was essential for his work. Both, however, acknowledged his mastery of commission affairs and his organizational skill.

Younger staff members tended to have lower thresholds of tolerance for criticism, and did not always react well to comments on their work. A few were accused of being brash and arrogant, especially by applicants denied in the development review process and by municipal officials who resented the intrusion into local government affairs. At least initially, the relative youth and aggressiveness of the commission staff, combined with their inexperience, made acceptance of the commission and its plan more difficult.

Control over Development during the Planning Period

During the almost two years between the signing of the state legislation and the effective date of the Pinelands Comprehensive Management Plan—that is, during the so-called moratorium on building—the commission approved applications for more than 11,000 housing units; it denied, however, nearly all proposals for large developments, particularly those sited in undeveloped areas. During this interim period members of the

Pinelands Commission and representatives of various public-interest groups became increasingly aware of those policies and procedural mechanisms that would have to be addressed in the provisions of the Pinelands Comprehensive Management Plan.

Legal Basis for Interim Development Regulation.   In New Jersey, building permits and occupancy certificates are issued through a municipal regulatory process. Under the governor's executive order the commission was given no power over this process. Development control during the interim planning period initially was exercised by placing limitations on permits issued by state departments or agencies. This control mechanism could be effective in the Pinelands, where public water and sewer systems were few and far between. Septic systems required state permits, as did projects involving stream encroachment, water diversion, road impact, relocation of utility poles, and a variety of other situations, and thus could be brought under commission review.

Under Executive Order 71 a state agency or department could grant permit approval for construction or development in the Pinelands Preservation Area only if a compelling public need could be demonstrated or if denial of the approval would result in extraordinary hardship for the applicant. Any development permitted in this area had to be consistent with the intent, goals, and objectives of both the executive order and the federal legislation. Moreover, a development project could not be approved in either the Preservation or the Protection Area if it would result in a substantial impairment of the natural resources. The executive order gave no guidelines, however, for defining "compelling public need," "extraordinary hardship," "consistency," or "substantial impairment."

Pinelands Development Review Board.   Between the issuance of the governor's executive order and the actual formation of the Pinelands Planning Commission, the governor gave the Department of Environmental Protection authority to coordinate the permit review process. After three weeks of meetings, the DEP and affected state departments decided to establish a single, independent permit review body—a three-member Pinelands Development Review Board comprising representatives from the departments of Agriculture, Community Affairs, and Environmental Protection—the latter to serve as chairman.

No operating funds were made available to this review board, but by the end of the first week of its operation, it had recruited a staff of six employees on a loan basis from various state agencies. This staff was headed by Sean Reilly.

Initially, the board received about fifty applications each week, mostly requests for residential development. The board met weekly in open session to act on these applications, permitting members of the public to comment on applications under consideration. Environmentalists frequently questioned the impact of proposed projects on water quality.

Although there were no specific guidelines for the evaluation of proposed development projects, adherence to the existing Pine Barrens critical water quality standards was a prime objective of the board, as was location with relation to existing development. Any applicant dissatisfied with the findings of the review board could request a hearing before the three departmental commissioners whose representatives served on the review board. The Office of Administrative Law (OAL) later became involved in the appeal process.

During its short life of just less than five months, the Pinelands Development Review Board received about 600 applications and acted on more than 400, a large proportion of which requested approval for construction of one single-family home.[3] The board was very generous in its handling of these, approving 87 percent. On the other hand, of the 11,799 housing units requested in 82 subdivision applications, the board approved only 14 percent; applications for 10,036 units were denied. All the larger subdivision applications were denied, including a request for a 4,500-unit retirement community in Manchester (Ocean County), another for a planned unit development of 3,700 homes in Evesham (Burlington County), and a third for a 1,456-unit project in Berkeley Township (Ocean County). The review board approved only three projects of 100 units or more, the largest of which was for 360 units in an already-developed area in Winslow (Camden County). The board approved all but two of the applications for projects classified as commercial or industrial development; all were for small retail construction or campgrounds.

Almost all of the approvals were for projects located in the Pinelands Protection Area, and in 81 percent of these cases, the review board justified its action on the basis of consistency with the legislation. Another 18 percent of the approvals were granted on the basis of extraordinary hardship. The small number of remaining approvals were found to satisfy a compelling public need such as road or sewer work or construction of public buildings.

Interim Regulation under the Pinelands Protection Act.   The life of the Pinelands Development Review Board officially ended on June 28, 1979, when the Pinelands Protection Act was passed. In that act, despite strong opposition from the construction industry, the legislature sanctioned the continuation of temporary development restrictions during the period in which the management plan was being prepared. Thus the legislature showed its agreement with the governor's concern that "the current pace of random and uncoordinated development and construction in the Pinelands Area poses an immediate threat to the resources thereof" (PPA: Section 13).

The provisions of the Pinelands Protection Act for temporary control over development superseded those laid down by the governor's executive order. At the request of the Pinelands Commission, however, the review board (now legally defunct) continued its review function for several more weeks, forwarding its recommendations to the Pinelands Commission for final action. In addition, the development review staff on loan from state agencies remained on duty until the commission completed recruitment of replacements.

Unlike the executive order, the Pinelands Protection Act excluded development for agricultural or horticultural structures from regulation by the commission. In addition, any individual who owned property in the Protection Area as of February 7, 1979 (the day prior to the executive order), was allowed under certain circumstances to build a single-family home for his own occupancy. If an on-site septic system was to be used, the lot had to be larger than one acre; if the home was to be served by sewers (with sufficient capacity), the lot could be any size. The legislature also instructed the commission to adopt standards within ninety days to define "extraordinary hardship," "compelling public need," "substantial impairment," and "consistency" as these criteria were being used in the development review process.

The Pinelands Act strengthened interim development control by extending the commission's power of review to cover municipal and county permits as well as those of state agencies. In the Preservation Area no development permits could be issued without Pinelands Commission approval; in the Protection Area municipal or county permits for major development (that is, the building of five or more residential units, commercial development on more than three acres, or any clearing of more than 5,000 square feet of land) also required commission approval.

Interim Development Review Standards. The expressed purpose of the interim standards adopted in July 1979 was to promote greater consistency and to minimize subjectivity in the development review process until a Pinelands management plan could be completed. These standards were based on four criteria—compelling public need, extraordinary hardship, consistency with the goals of the legislation, and no substantial impairment of the environment.[4]

To prove a compelling public need, the applicant had to obtain government verification that this project, and no other, was necessary to preserve the public health, safety, and welfare. The definition of extraordinary hardship provoked severe criticism from the construction industry. An approval to construct a single-family dwelling for use by the property owner's family would be given based on extraordinary hardship only if the property had been purchased prior to February 8, 1979, and if a delay in construction would cause either significant financial harm or endangerment of health or safety. Other approvals based on extraordinary hardship could be obtained only if the applicant had already received local approval prior to February 8, 1979, and if a substantial commitment toward physical improvement of land had already been made or if money had already been borrowed that could not be paid back unless development proceeded. Much to the dismay of developers, preconstruction expenditures for legal and other professional services associated with a development project were not to be considered in the hardship evaluation.

To judge whether or not a development proposal was consistent with the intent of the legislation and whether or not it would result in substantial impairment of the resources, the commission delineated twelve environmental standards against which each application would be reviewed "on its own merits." Violation of any one of these standards created a presumption of substantial impairment, and each violation was an individual and independent reason for denial of the application.

Three key standards dealt with the protection of water quality and wetlands. Development was discouraged (1) when on-site waste disposal systems were proposed in areas with a seasonal high water table of less than five feet, (2) when a site showed a percolation rate of less than five to eight minutes per inch, or (3) when a building was located within 300 feet of wetlands. The percolation rate standard was subsequently replaced by a statement discouraging any development in violation of state surface or ground water quality standards. The commission also required that a DEP dilution model test be made to insure that residential development using on-site waste disposal systems met state standards.

Piecemeal and scattered development was also discouraged, although these terms were not defined in the legislation. Commission judgments of appropriateness of location were based on the legislative statement that "random and uncoordinated development poses an immediate threat to the resources." For example, projects that required new sewage or water facilities or other off-tract improvements that, in turn, might themselves encourage additional development were usually denied.

With the exception of the standard that discouraged projects that created fire hazards or hindered the use of controlled burning when necessary for the maintenance of the Pinelands ecological system, the remaining standards were designed to protect threatened and endangered species, registered specimen trees, wild and scenic river areas, and culturally significant sites. They also preserved buffer areas adjacent to public land as well as the ambient air quality as measured by state and federal standards.

Interim Development Review Process. By September 1979 the commission had in place its own development review staff. Applications for development in the Pinelands had to be accompanied by a statement from local authorities attesting that the project was consistent with local land-use laws. No application was required for projects exempt from the interim regulations, although the commission requested that local officials report monthly on any such exempt projects they had approved. Also, at this time, applicants unhappy with earlier decisions by the Pinelands Development Review Board (active from January to June 1979) could reapply under the new development standards and interim regulations.

The review process included both public and staff participation. On the basis of staff findings, the executive director recommended approval, approval with conditions, or denial of the application. A copy of his recommendation was then forwarded to the applicant, who if dissatisfied had fifteen days to request a hearing before an administrative law judge. If an approval was recommended or if the applicant did not request a hearing, the executive director then forwarded the application and its supporting documentation to the commission. For applications involving a hearing, the record of that hearing and the nonbinding recommendation of the judge were also sent to the commission. The commission made the final decision, which could be appealed to the Appellate Division of the New Jersey Superior Court.

Between June 29, 1979, and January 14, 1981, the Pinelands Commission acted on about 1,700 applications, including several hundred that had been denied by the Pinelands Development Review Board. Applications for industrial and commercial projects remained minor both in number and in development impact; the approval rate for these, as well as for public projects, continued at about 90 percent. The commission's greatest concern was with subdivision projects, which called for almost 18,000 new units.

The commission was much more generous than the review board in its review of subdivision applications, approving 50 percent (representing more than 8,900 units) versus the 17 percent approved by the review board. Approval was given for 15 subdivisions with more than 100 units; the two largest of these were in Hamilton Township (Atlantic County)— up to 2,534 units and 1,104 units, respectively. On the other hand, the interim standards adopted by the Pinelands Commission resulted in a higher denial rate (40 percent) for applications for single-family residences than had been experienced under the review board (13 percent).[5]

Fewer than 1 percent of the housing units approved by either the review board or the commission were to be located in the Preservation Area. In the Protection Area, Hamilton Township accounted for 38 percent of the units approved, and Medford and Winslow townships together accounted for another 16 percent of the total units. All told, 10 of the 52 Pinelands townships accounted for 84 percent of the residential units approved during the interim period.

The reasons given by the commission for its approval of interim applications paralleled those given by the review board. Eighty-eight percent were based on "consistency with the legislation"; another 9 percent were based on "hardship"; and 3 percent satisfied "a compelling public need." In many cases, approvals were conditioned upon a reduction in the number of units or upon locating buildings in more appropriate positions on sites.

The commission denied original applications for slightly more than 9,000 units; it also confirmed denials by the review board on resubmitted applications for another 9,000 units. The majority of this second group of 9,000 units came from the three large developments referred to earlier—the 4,500-unit project known as ROC in Manchester Township (Ocean County), the 3,700-unit Kings Grant project in Evesham (Burlington County), and the 1,456-unit Hovson project in Berkeley Township (Ocean County); these developments were turned down by both the review board and the commission.

Just over half the denials during the interim period stemmed from failure to meet water quality standards; 16 percent more were deemed to represent scattered and piecemeal development; and 5 percent posed fire management problems. The rest of the applications were denied for failure to meet other standards.

Two of the commission's denials were challenged in court, with important results in favor of the commission. One was the case of Hanada Development Corporation, which wanted to build a 208-unit residential development in Galloway Township (Atlantic County). The site for this proposed development was almost entirely bordered by vacant land. The commission denied the application because the proposed development in the area was not "compatible in scale or use" with other development. The applicant appealed. The Appellate Division of the New Jersey Superior Court rejected the appeal and at the same time affirmed the constitutionality of both the Pinelands Protection Act and the interim restrictions on development, specifying in particular the standards discouraging scattered and piecemeal development and no substantial environmental impairment.[6] Another ruling by the appellate division dismissed claims by Orleans Builders and Developers that denial of its application to construct 955 apartments and townhouses in Evesham Township (Burlington County) constituted a "taking" of property. Orleans had planned to build a total of 1,523 units adjacent to Barton Run Creek; 568 of these had already been built prior to February 8, 1979, the effective date of the governor's moratorium. The Pinelands Development Review Board then denied Orleans' application for sections of the remaining 955 units on the grounds of high water table, the presence of endangered species, and projected water runoff into Barton Run Creek. When the application was resubmitted to the Pinelands Commission for consideration under its interim regulations, the application was again denied on grounds of "substantial impairment to the natural resources," despite the recommendation of an Administrative Law Judge that approval be given for part of the development. The applicant then appealed to superior court. This court found the term "substantial impairment" sufficiently precise to withstand constitutional attack and, moreover, rejected an argument that the real test should be whether or not development would "substantially impair" the resources of the entire Pinelands Area, not just the project site.[7]

The building moratorium during the interim planning period came to an end on January 14, 1981, the effective date of the Pinelands Comprehensive Management Plan (CMP). Most of the applications for subdivisions that had been denied by the Pinelands Development Review Board and/or the Pinelands Commission were later resubmitted for evaluation under the CMP.

Impacts of the Building Moratorium.   In retrospect, the experiences of the two-year Pinelands moratorium period supported the governor's concerns, voiced in 1979, that without interim restraints on development, further destruction of the natural resources would have occurred. If all the applications for large-scale subdivision development denied during the interim had been allowed to proceed, critical resources would have been damaged and the landscape fragmented in such a way as to limit future planning options.

It is also apparent that an executive order was an effective initial mechanism to implement a moratorium. The swiftness with which the moratorium was imposed contrasted markedly with the slowness of legislative action—although the Pinelands Protection Act was introduced the same week as the governor's executive order was promulgated, the law was not enacted for almost five more months.

The building moratorium did, however, have some negative economic impact, though not of the magnitude predicted by representatives of the building industry. When announcement of the moratorium was made, the president of the Home Builders League asserted that New Jersey would lose $900 million worth of development and 3,000 jobs; another industry representative predicted that it "could lead to the worst crisis New Jersey has ever had."[8] Obviously, the true economic impact of the interim regulations can never be measured accurately; however, the commission's staff economist did find, as might be expected, that in 1979 and 1980 (the moratorium years) both building activity and land sales in the Pinelands showed a downward shift in most areas. Although it is possible that other factors, such as recession or high interest rates, contributed to this downward trend, the controls instituted during the moratorium were the most likely cause.[9]

There were at least two other effects of the moratorium whose significance had not been wholly anticipated. First, for the commission staff, involvement in the task of processing development applications during the two-year interim period meant that an experienced team was in place on the effective date of the Comprehensive Management Plan. And second, while processing interim applications, the staff encountered a variety of issues and procedural problems that would have to be addressed if an effective management plan were to be prepared. For example, the commission came to realize that, while a very strict interpretation of hardship might have been justifiable during the interim period, permanent controls would have to be more flexible, providing consideration for such items as preconstruction costs. It also gave the planners firsthand insight into the actual pattern of development pressures that existed in the Pinelands. In terms of procedures, the interim experience was very helpful in illustrating the time that development review decision-making required; in so doing, it clarified thinking as to desirable roles of commission vis-à-vis staff under permanent regulations.

Finally, the activities of the commission during the moratorium period attracted the attention of more and more New Jersey residents across the state. Because of it, citizens became much more aware of both the area itself and of the issues involved in protecting it. Ultimately this awareness proved to be a benefit for the planning process, although it did not always produce an easy or a pleasant situation for those officials immediately involved in implementing the moratorium. As one angry assemblyman said shortly after the governor issued his executive order, "He's got more people mad than I've ever seen in my twenty years of government."[10] Not everyone was angry, however; in fact, a poll conducted by Congressman Edwin Forsythe in July 1979, found that 83 percent of his constituents in the sixth district, which included three Pinelands counties, favored the building moratorium.[11] Whether one favored the interim regulations or opposed them, one had to admit that the moratorium created a great stir of interest, and this stir was itself of great help in identifying the issues that had to be faced as the Comprehensive Management Plan was prepared and the procedures for implementing it laid down.

5. Preparation of the Comprehensive Management Plan: Issues and Procedures

Emily W. B. Russell

The state Pinelands Protection Act required that the Pinelands Commission prepare and adopt a Comprehensive Management Plan (CMP) for the Pinelands on or before August 8, 1980. An amendment to the legislation passed in June 1980, however, delayed adoption of that part of the plan covering the Protection Area until between November 14 and December 15, 1980. Although the commissioners had begun outlining their work on the management plan under the authority of Executive Order 71, it was not until the legislation had been signed into law and Terrence Moore had been appointed executive director (June 1979) that they could begin work in earnest. They thus had very tight time constraints for preparing the plan.

The commission released a draft of the CMP for comment on June 6, 1980. The final plan for the Preservation Area was adopted on August 8; the plan for the Protection Area was adopted on November 21. The whole plan went into effect on January 14, 1981. To write the plan the commission had to deal with a variety of issues and find solutions for conflicts, especially those between preservation of the natural resources and protection of private rights as well as those generated by the sometimes contradictory aims of the legislation itself.

The Workplan

Preparation of the Comprehensive Management Plan began with development of a workplan that detailed the steps to be followed. Within two months of his appointment, Executive Director Moore had in hand a commission-approved workplan and had begun hiring staff. The quick pace of activity during these initial months as well as the organization of the staff and the workplan itself established a pattern that would be followed throughout the writing of the CMP.

When Moore became executive director of the commission in July 1979, he inherited a tentative workplan that had been drawn up by the

Workplan Subcommittee of the Pinelands Planning Commission, assisted by Sean Reilly of the New Jersey Department of Environmental Protection. Although this plan itself was not used, it helped the commissioners focus on some of the issues to be resolved, and helped pave the way for Moore and the subcommittee, using their borrowed DEP staff, to produce quickly an outline of the final workplan for public comment. More than a hundred individuals representing a wide variety of interests participated in a workshop on this proposal. Many of their recommendations were incorporated in the workplan, especially those regarding expansion of the public information and involvement sections, analyses of ground water quantity, and determination of critical areas and of criteria for establishing land carrying capacities. Land-use and zoning specialists as well as commission members also reviewed the workplan before its final approval. They made suggestions about both the scopes of consultant services, which would be used for much of the work on the CMP, and the budget, which included as much money for consultants as for the commission's own planning staff. The commission approved the workplan on September 21, with no dissenting votes.

The workplan consisted of nine components to be developed sequentially. The first four of these, natural resources, historical and archeological resources, sociocultural factors, and physical resources (primarily human-built structures), provided for collection and analysis of existing data as well as for additional surveys. Next, the plan called for a "growth-factor analysis" to determine "existing and future development pressures in the Pinelands." The next three components (land-management techniques, intergovernmental coordination, and finances) would result in an analysis of options and recommendations for how to protect the resources given the growth pressures. The final component concerned public information and participation and resulted from a recognition by the commission that "the public involvement process is an integral element of the planning process."

Ecological Issues and Options

The first step in the development of the management plan was to identify the ecological issues and the options for protection, since these were the principal concerns of the legislation. The Pinelands National Reserve had been established "to protect, preserve and enhance the significant values of the land and water resources of the Pinelands." To define this central goal more clearly, both federal and state legislation added subordinate goals, which the commission itself further refined and organized. In the end, the commission's stated goal for natural resources was to "pre-serve, protect, and enhance the overall ecological values of the Pinelands, including its large forested area, its essential character, and its potential to recover from disturbance."

In its efforts to fulfill this goal, the commission established numerous specific and quantifiable standards, designed to protect the "essential character" of the Pinelands. Although all these standards were justified by scientific studies, none was completely unassailable, because, in the end, the choice of which precise value to assign as the standard was al-ways a subjective one.

Defining the Essential Character of the Pinelands.   The commission committed much time and effort to defining the so-called "essential char-acter" of the Pinelands and to mapping land-use capabilities. Half the budget for consultant services was allocated to the natural resource as-sessments, indicating that the emphasis was to be placed there. The com-mission produced thousands of pages of reports on the natural resources of the entire Pine Barrens area. It also produced the required land-use map delineating "major areas within the [Pinelands National Reserve] which are of critical ecological importance."

On February 22, 1980, Executive Director Moore unveiled a map illus-trating those areas of the Pinelands most sensitive to degradation. This map was said to epitomize the "essential character" of the Pinelands. It was made using overlays of seven criteria of environmental sensitivity: ecologically critical areas; undisturbed watersheds; wetlands; cranberry cultivation areas and the areas draining into them; areas of deep aquifer recharge; "unique resources," such as the Pine Plains; and public lands managed for resource protection or recreation.[1]

The same method was used to produce each of the overlay maps for the seven main criteria. To produce the map of the ecologically critical areas, for example, the staff consolidated various factor maps based on aerial photographs. These maps took into account seventeen different factors that had been weighted by consultants and by the public at three public meetings. Though ranking such criteria as linkage corridors and migratory stopovers was obviously a subjective process, the large number of factors and the analysis of a large database resulted in strong support for the final product.

The map unveiled on February 22 showed that the most sensitive area of the Pine Barrens clearly included southern parts of the Pinelands Re-serve, the northern Preservation Area, and a corridor, crossing the major east-west highways, between these two sections. This sensitive area included 790,000 acres, about three-fourths of the Pinelands National Reserve. Of this, one-third was in public ownership. About half the total was in the Preservation Area and was already slated for strict controls; almost half of this land was publicly owned.

Protecting the Large Contiguous Area.   The features deemed essential to the character of the Pinelands could be found throughout the region in undeveloped areas, but the continuity of these undeveloped areas was somewhat interrupted by scattered strip development along the major east-west highways between Philadelphia and Atlantic City. Ecological theories derived from island biogeography suggest that isolating parts of a landscape decreases diversity by limiting genetic interchange between the isolated portions, and thus may change the character of a region. This theoretical consideration, as well as the strongly preservationist sense of the legislation, provided the basis for including in the sensitive area some of the partly developed east-west Philadelphia-to-Atlantic City corridor.

In the final Comprehensive Management Plan the most sensitive lands were included within the Preservation Area and the Forest Areas (which included the corridor section); both districts were then subjected to strict limitations on growth.

Protecting Water Quality and Quantity.   Degradation of the water quality was viewed as the most insidious threat to the essential character of the Pinelands. Thus, protecting water quality became the single most important consideration in establishing guidelines for development in the entire Pinelands Area.

There is no simple way to measure water quality. After considerable debate, the commission accepted its consultants' recommendations that the standard for water quality should be based on the character of undisturbed Pinelands streams, which included a nitrate-nitrogen content (measured as milligrams of nitrate per liter, or parts per million, ppm) of 0.17, phosphorus content (measured as ppm phosphate) of 0.02, and pH (acidity) of less than 5, as well as other chemical characterizations. The DEP's critical area standards, which were then being enforced for part of the Pinelands, were higher: 2.0 ppm nitrate-nitrogen, 0.7 ppm phosphate-phosphorus, and a pH of 3.5–5.5. Although the original version of the Comprehensive Management Plan used the stricter commission values for nitrate-nitrogen and phosphate-phosphorus as standards for water quality in the Preservation and Forest areas, during the review process the commission agreed to adopt the DEP critical area standards. Most of DEP's standards outside the Pinelands critical areas were set primarily to protect human health. The commission, however, was charged also with protecting the essential natural character of the Pinelands, making more strict standards appropriate for certain areas; therefore it extended these standards to include the whole Pinelands Area and set additional ones for other minerals and contaminants.[2] This resulted in a certain amount of public confusion and criticism, particularly since these water quality standards formed the basis for land-use designations.

The minimum allowable size of building lots was based on a variety of factors, the most important of which was maintenance of water quality. For example, for homes on lots not served by sewers, the commission established a minimum size of 3.2 acres, based on the need to dilute nitrates from septic system discharge.[3] According to the commission model this would result in the permitted concentration of 2 ppm of nitrate-nitrogen in the groundwater at the property boundary.

Consideration of water quality also resulted in the suggestion that the density of new housing in the Forest Area be limited to seventeen new units per square mile. This was the approximate concentration of housing in this region in 1980. An assumption was made, however, that doubling this density would have no serious impact on habitat or water quality. This proposal stimulated much opposition, but remained essentially unchanged in the CMP.

The Coalition for the Sensible Preservation of the Pinelands, a builders' organization, opposed the 3.2-acre minimum lot size and attacked the water quality standards that were its basis. The coalition argued that the Pinelands commission had not used appropriate data, had not analyzed its data according to proper statistical procedures, and had not been fair in its selection of data. They also contended that the dilution model used by the commission was inadequate. The coalition's own report, however, was no more objective than the commission's, for neither was dealing with easily quantifiable values. For example, the coalition criticized the water quality index developed for the Pinelands Commission; the index prepared for them was better, they said, because it had "the closest correspondence with the *judgmental* consensus of water quality experts" [italics mine] and "*appears* to be more sensitive to field conditions" [italics mine].[4] Their argument, which they eventually lost, merely highlighted the subjective aspect of setting standards.

Wetlands are a characteristic feature of the Pinelands, and measures to protect them overlapped with those to protect water quality in general. In particular, the commission decided that the 300-foot undisturbed buffer zone, established as an interim standard for development, must be kept around all areas defined as wetlands. When the staff presented this proposal on April 25, Executive Director Moore explained that the basis for the zone was the consultants' reports, which indicated that this distance would adequately protect wetlands from both stormwater runoff and the impact of septic systems. Further discussion established no better, simpler, or more objective justification of the standard, so it was left at what appeared to be a reasonable distance.

Descriptions of the resources of the Pine Barrens almost invariably refer to the huge amount of water in aquifers under the area. The commissioners, the public, and local officials all were adamant that the Comprehensive Management Plan should ban the shipment of water out of the Pinelands. The threat of tapping aquifers in the Pinelands to supply water for other parts of the state seemed at this time very pertinent. Northern New Jersey had experienced water shortages in the 1970s and some officials were eyeing supplies in the Pinelands. Residents felt that not only would South Jersey lose a precious resource if the water were pumped out of the region, but also local water tables would be lowered, thus changing habitats, increasing fire hazards, and allowing more saltwater intrusion at the eastern edge of the aquifers. In response to these concerns, language forbidding export of water from the Pinelands counties was strengthened in the final form of the Comprehensive Management Plan.

Social, Cultural, and Historical Considerations

Both federal and state legislation called for "an assessment of scenic, aesthetic, cultural, open space, and outdoor recreational resources of the area, together with a determination of overall policies required to maintain and enhance these resources." For this assessment the commission used a study unit approach that had been developed by the Heritage, Conservation, and Recreation Service (HCRS) of the U.S. Department of the Interior to survey prehistoric and historic sites. In addition, because of the unique cultural heritage and nature of the National Reserve, the commission also concerned itself with traditional lifestyles and ethnic settlements and conducted a series of interviews with 200 residents.

Presentation of the findings of these assessments at a workshop on February 16, 1980, and a conference on March 21 and 22 encouraged the public to help evaluate these resources. At these meetings the consultants pointed out many prehistoric and historic sites that were of considerable local as well as, perhaps, national interest. They also identified a variety of cultural subregions within the National Reserve. Because the commission's staff was small and the Pinelands Area was large and included much privately owned property, local cooperation was vital in making the assessment; to get this necessary local cooperation, the commission had to take seriously the different issues in each subregion and to plan accordingly.

Policy goals for cultural issues were vague: for example, to maintain "opportunities for traditional lifestyles" and to "maintain the social and cultural integrity of traditional Pinelands communities." The "traditional," or "Piney," lifestyle consisted primarily of being left alone to live a life of hunting, gathering, and getting seasonal employment.[5] It required large areas of open space, and generally involved trespassing. In their discussions of it, the commissioners suggested that education and economic pressure were eroding this lifestyle; the situation exemplified a comment made by a consultant to the commission that in many areas the most picturesque farmers were the poorest.[6] The plan reflected the observation made by Commissioner Darlington that vagueness would probably be the best way to deal with this lifestyle; that way the commission would not be accused of encouraging trespassing.

On the other hand, the plan did try, indirectly, to encourage traditional lifestyles by "grandfathering" small lots for building and offering special exemptions for lots possessed by an applicant who could "demonstrate a cultural, social or economic link to the essential character of the Pinelands" either through family connections with the Pinelands for at least twenty years or through economic dependency on Pinelands resources (see Chapter 6), and by keeping open space available. In addition, the CMP recognized fifty-nine villages (fourteen had been added during the revision process), which would be permitted to expand within strict limits in ways compatible with their existing character. Six towns were also designated for growth based on the availability of sewerage and/or public water supply. One of these was Egg Harbor City, the only sizable German community in the Pine Barrens. Otherwise the Comprehensive Management Plan generally ignored traditional communities; instead it emphasized protection of historic resources, but did not clearly explain details of preserving even these. Little else resulted from the cultural survey.

Historical and archeological surveys revealed 532 prehistoric sites, the majority of which (75 percent) were located near rivers. Twenty-five sites on either the national or the state register of historic places or buildings, as well as many more potentially eligible sites, were found scattered throughout the Pinelands, also along rivers. The commission established a procedure for designation and preservation of such sites, strongly encouraging local or state action. The future role of the commission was expected to be further study, including development of a predictive model for finding even more prehistoric sites, and oversight of the preservation process.

Accommodating Growth

Predicting growth and deciding how to accommodate it formed the next major series of considerations for the commission. By "accommodating growth" the commission meant directing it toward sites less sensitive to degradation through a mix of incentives and restrictions.

Population Projections.   Analysis of population trends highlighted several characteristics directly relevant to planning in the Pinelands National Reserve. The reserve itself occupied about 20 percent of the land area of the state of New Jersey, but it contained less than 5 percent of the state's population. In the 1970s the Pinelands' population was increasing at a rate of 3.5 to 5 percent annually, with most of this increase occurring in three regions: the Philadelphia/Camden metropolitan area, northern Ocean County, and near Atlantic City. Furthermore, most land transactions in the Pinelands were at this time concentrated in a few very active municipalities on the edges of the reserve; most of these involved lots or small acreage, not large land deals.

The Pinelands Commission, therefore, decided to accommodate projected growth by directing development to these active areas. This decision to direct rather than restrict growth resulted from the commission's view that the greatest threat to the integrity of the Pinelands was not so much growth itself as disorderly growth. The decision was further supported by the legislative mandate to encourage "appropriate patterns of compatible residential, commercial and industrial development . . . in order to accommodate regional growth influences in an orderly way" in the Protection Area.

The "Taking" Issue.   During the writing of the plan much debate centered on the issue of "taking" (see Chapter 3). The commission's stated policy in the beginning was that "no provision of the Comprehensive Management Plan shall deprive an owner of property without due process of law, nor shall private property be taken for public use without just compensation." Although this provision repeated the law of the land as laid down in the fifth amendment to the Constitution of the United States, the commission had hoped that its repetition might serve to allay people's fears.

The debate over whether or not to include the guarantee of just compensation in the plan itself for less than a total taking was highly polarized and led to much bitterness on both sides. Those opposed to including it insisted that they were not precluding just compensation, while those who favored inclusion felt that the others were trying to ride roughshod over private property rights. The final decision not to include the guarantee of just compensation in the CMP for less than a total taking had repercussions later in the discussions of the development credit program.

Pinelands Development Credit Program. The Pinelands Development Credit Program was the commission's novel system of making amends to owners for less than a total restriction on the use of their land, especially of farmland. It was based on the idea of transfer of development rights. Under this concept a landowner may sell his right to develop his land to someone else; he thus removes the right to develop from one portion of land and transfers it to land more appropriate for development.[7] Such systems had been used successfully elsewhere to direct growth on a limited scale, but the Pinelands National Reserve represented the largest application of the concept yet attempted. Some commissioners viewed the system basically as a bonus; others saw it as the cornerstone of fairness in the plan, the restrictions of which would decrease the value of some land and increase the value of land elsewhere. (See Chapter 6.)

Impact on Municipalities of Directed Growth. Much municipal criticism of the draft plan focused on its potential for eroding the tax base. Local concerns were primarily three: first, rezoning land to a more restricted use might prompt landowners to appeal their current tax assessments; second, use of Pinelands development credits for land outside the original municipality might lead to tax losses through lower assessments; and, finally, public acquisition of land would remove that land from the tax rolls. In general, municipal officials argued that the commission had inadequately considered the potential economic impact of the plan on municipalities.

In response, the Comprehensive Management Plan included an economic analysis of the potential tax loss if all vacant land were to be removed from the tax rolls. It found that the tax loss to most communities would be inconsequential, as would be the tax increases needed to offset any potential loss. Several citizens also pointed out that the loss in tax revenue should be offset by savings in projected expenditures for new municipal services, since less intense use of land and clustering of development costs a community less than unplanned suburban sprawl. Of course, municipalities that were slated for growth could anticipate large expenditures for extending services such as water and sewers to new developments, although many hoped that formal designation as a growth area by the plan would make them eligible to receive federal assistance for these projects. Finally, the commission's own financial consultant recommended that the state pay full taxes on any public land acquired in the future.

Other issues arose concerning very small and very large development. From the governor's office down to local public meetings, many worried about restricting the building expectations of owners of small lots. The Comprehensive Management Plan responded to these worries by permitting owners of lots larger than one acre in the Protection Area to build a house for their own use within one year of the effective date of the CMP, under certain conditions. Thus the plan was made fairer to owners of some lots smaller than 3.2 acres, but at an undetermined cost in environmental degradation.

For large-scale developments, the commission made three modifications in the original draft plan, all allowing more development. First, the commission granted waivers from the new requirements for certain developments already under way, especially those that had already received final subdivision approval. Second, it allowed municipalities to earmark for future growth certain areas called "Municipal Reserves." These would be outside land designated in the original proposal as high-density growth areas. And, finally, the revision encouraged clustering of development in the Forest Area. A proposal for more concentrated development (a so-called "new town" provision) was not adopted. Environmentalists vigorously opposed all these proposals.[8]

The compromise reached during the revision of the plan certainly allowed more development than the draft plan had envisioned, but they also made the final CMP more acceptable both to those who had to live in the Pinelands and to those who had to administer the plan's regulations.

Affordable Housing Opportunities. In the Mount Laurel decision, the Supreme Court of New Jersey ruled that a developing community must make provision for housing of low and moderate cost. By limiting development in some areas of the Pinelands and encouraging it in others, the Pinelands Commission influenced housing prices and zoning in developing regions and thus placed communities under the strictures of the Mount Laurel ruling. While there was some debate in a commission meeting in October 1980 about whether or not the commission needed to address this problem directly, the New Jersey Public Advocate's Office insisted on its responsibility to take positive, affirmative action. The Attorney General's Office concurred. Governor Byrne also emphasized the importance of commission support for low-cost housing. The plan thus explicitly required that builders of subdivisions of certain sizes include at least a certain percentage of low- and moderate-cost housing. The commission also recommended that the Atlantic City Casino Control Commission earmark certain tax revenues for so-called "least-cost" housing.

Accommodating Local Economic Activities

The federal legislation required the commission to "recognize existing economic activities within the area and provide for the protection and enhancement of such activities as farming, forestry, proprietary recreational facilities, and those indigenous industries and commercial and residential developments which are consistent with . . . this section." The Comprehensive Management Plan singled out agriculture and recreation for special treatment, but restricted most other economic activities that could be damaging to the natural resources.

Encouraging Agriculture.   Both the Pinelands legislation and the CMP favored agriculture. The federal legislation required that the resource assessment "determine the amount and type of human development and activity [that] the ecosystem can sustain while still maintaining the overall ecological values . . . with special reference to . . . the protection and enhancement of blueberry and cranberry production and other agricultural activity." The state Pinelands legislation included similar clauses; it also called for promotion of certain other categories of agriculture and horticulture, including "indigenous" activities in the Protection Area and "compatible" activities in the Preservation Area. The Pinelands legislation did not, however, say explicitly that agriculture and horticulture should be promoted regardless of their effects on water quality and quantity, air quality, or other natural resources of the Pinelands. The Pinelands Protection Act did exempt agricultural and horticultural development from the interim building restrictions, and the CMP, by its definitions, exempted agricultural uses from having to apply for development permits, thus implicitly exempting these uses from the standards to be met for permits.

The question of how to protect and enhance agriculture without degrading the ecosystem stimulated much discussion and several written comments, but no real answers. Environmentalists pointed out that farm operations can degrade water quality through leaching of chemicals applied to crops. Farmers, however, resisted restraints on their "normal" operations. The conflicts were essentially resolved by exempting agriculture from many of the regulations, by setting up special agricultural districts where agriculture would be the favored use of the land, and by requiring that farmers use "recommended management practices." The general consensus was that agriculture was a positive force in the Pinelands; the few lone voices among the environmentalists objecting that agriculture could be destructive were generally overruled.

Although the Agricultural Production Districts were created to help farmers while preserving farmland, they nevertheless led to serious disputes with the farm community, which viewed the agricultural zones as a threat to the economic viability of agriculture.[9] To preserve extant agricultural lands or land with good potential for farming, the commission placed strict building limitations on the land. Some claimed that the commission decreased the value of the land. Those who wanted to sell or develop agricultural land were, therefore, irritated. But so too were some farmers who wanted to use their land as collateral for farming loans. These farmers claimed that the building limitations unfairly lowered their credit base and thus actually worked toward the destruction, rather than the preservation, of agriculture.

Not everyone agreed and rebuttals were heard. Some representatives of lending institutions as well as some farmers argued that responsible lending was actually based on the potential productivity of the farm, not on the nonagricultural development value of the land.[10] The commission tried to compromise by encouraging lending institutions to grant so-called "chattel" mortgages, which used the projected value of crops and the value of Pinelands development credits as collateral.

Thus the commission attempted to protect agriculture from nuisance ordinances as well as from encroaching development. It did not, however, help the farmer who hoped to sell his farmland for other uses. And it was most probably this category of farmer who joined with developers in hiring a law firm to oppose the Comprehensive Management Plan. Their effort, however, failed to weaken restrictions on using farmland in agricultural zones for development.

Encouraging and Controlling Recreation.   Both federal and state legislation recognized recreational resources as an important asset of the Pinelands. There were, however, serious conflicts between recreational use and protection of the fragile ecosystem of the Pine Barrens. Overuse for recreation could be as harmful as too much development; both would pollute the water and impinge on open space. Conflicts between kinds of recreation, between active and passive recreation, or between motorized and nonmotorized activities also had to be recognized and dealt with. For example, when dealing with parking trailers in campgrounds, where did recreation stop and development begin? In the end, the commission decided to limit recreation in the interests of maintenance of natural resources. Thus, the plan permitted limited expansion of existing intensive recreational uses in the Preservation and Forest areas, and low-intensity recreational use in both areas.

Restrictions on Landfills and Resource Extraction.   Landfills and resource extraction were the most serious other local economic issue. Both activities were historically important uses of land in the Pinelands—landfills, because the land had been cheap and sparsely inhabited; and resource extraction, because of the good quality and large quantity of sand and gravel. Highly visible and extremely dangerous to water supplies, landfills received much public and commission attention. In a sense, building restrictions were easier to deal with than trash restrictions, even though both threatened the integrity of Pine Barrens resources, partly because of state-mandated solid-waste management programs. The problem was the relationship with the state's solid-waste administration.[11] The final compromise allowed new landfills in the Pinelands Protection Area only where they were the "significantly preferable" option with no other alternative available and where the waste they accepted came from counties with more than 50 percent of their land in the Pinelands; all landfills were to be closed by 1990. The regulations also forbade the dumping of hazardous wastes in the Pinelands. This widespread and very serious problem was not amenable to a simple solution, since much of the dumping is done illegally anyway.

The resource extraction industry effectively lobbied for better treatment than had been originally proposed, although they did not get all the changes that they wanted. At conferences with the commission staff and commissioners, for example, industry representatives achieved compromises allowing more area to be mined to greater depths than had been proposed. Lack of clear data on damage to the groundwater and the ecosystem by extensive mining permitted such a change.[12]

Land Management Techniques

Once ecological, economic, and cultural goals had been set, the plan next had to address the complex management problems of implementing them in a large reserve with a unique character and a multiplicity of local jurisdictions.

Both federal and state legislation left most of the critical details of management technique unspecified, although the state legislation did clearly require municipalities to bring their local zoning into conformance with the Comprehensive Management Plan; it also authorized the commission to review municipal development permits. Several management options were available to the commission, from traditional zoning techniques to the establishment of performance standards. Under either option the commission could also choose to retain close review of all local permitting decisions or to provide general oversight. In the end the commission selected management techniques that were stricter and more explicitly detailed than those used by some other regional planning groups—for example, the Adirondacks Park Commission.[13] The management plan of the Pinelands Commission relied more heavily on traditional zoning and review practices than on newer, more flexible and goal-oriented techniques like the use of performance standards, and established the commission as a reviewing body for all local development permits as authorized by the act.

Land-Use Areas.   The land-use map first proposed on April 18, 1980, divided the entire Pinelands Area into six "land capability" districts, or zones, based primarily on the sensitivity of the natural environment to degradation.[14] The description of these districts, as well as their boundaries, raised several issues during the review process. This debate led to modifications (including the addition of two new districts) but not to a total rejection of the basic concept.

The plan listed permitted uses for each district. It also set minimum performance standards for the entire Pinelands Area, relating to such items as water quality and stream setbacks. The land-use map, the minimum standards, and some administrative procedures were all to be incorporated into the master plans of the individual Pinelands municipalities.

Boundaries of the districts for the most part followed watershed lines, although the management plan did allow municipalities to modify them subject to commission approval. Consultation with the municipalities during drafting was extensive, but, because of the magnitude of the job, the recalcitrance of some municipalities, and the insensitivity of both sides to the needs of the other, disagreements remained. Although Shinn of Burlington County was particularly helpful in dealing with these problems, most county representatives were ineffective in bridging the gap between commission staff and local officials. This lack of communication created much ill will, and probably contributed to heavy workloads in reconciling the local master plans with the CMP.

It was at this point that the commission's strict planning techniques received much criticism. Some wanted the commission to devise performance standards and then let the municipalities decide how they might best be met. The commission, however, repeatedly voted against relying solely on performance standards on the grounds that they were difficult to enforce and often ineffective in controlling development, and allowed, or even promoted, scattered development on good upland sites.

Preservation Area. The land-use area to be most strictly controlled, with virtually no development allowed, was the 339,000-acre Preservation Area. Although opposition to strict land-use controls here had been extremely vigorous in the past, it had lessened by the time the commission came to prepare its Comprehensive Management Plan as much opposition shifted to the Protection Area.

Forest Area. The next most restricted area, the Forest Area, included 420,000 acres, more than half the remaining land. The Preservation and the Forest areas together included about 70 percent of the total land in the Pinelands National Reserve. Because three-fourths of the Forest Area was privately owned, this district in particular stimulated vociferous opposition at commission meetings, workshops, and hearings. The original draft plan had allowed Forest Area development credits to be sold outside the district, but after debate, an internal credit plan was devised so that development on more sensitive lands would be redirected within the district to areas designated as "less sensitive."

Rural Development Area. The next category was the 145,000-acre Rural Development Area. Criteria for separating this zone from the Forest Area indicated that the crucial consideration was not so much environmental sensitivity as prior development. To be classed as rural development, a district had to be more than 5 percent developed. It could also have some cropland, some point sources of pollution, and landfills. Overall, population in the Rural Development Area was more dense than that in the Forest Area. Staff and land-use consultants referred to this land in the Rural Development Area as a "spongy area," meaning that it could support either more or less development than proposed depending on population pressure or future findings of environmental sensitivity. Indeed, pressure from development interests did lead to a revision of the draft plan that allowed municipalities to designate parts of the Rural Development Area as "Municipal [Growth] Reserves" for future high-density development. This designation permitted the commission to respond to criticism, especially from developers, that the plan did not allow adequately for future growth.

Agricultural Production Area and Special Agricultural Production Area. The Agricultural districts (78,000 acres) contained large blocks of land in active agriculture or with prime agricultural soils. In response to criticism that many such areas had been missed on the first mapping, the commission revised the Comprehensive Management Plan to allow municipalities to designate more land as Agricultural Area where appropriate. In addition, the municipalities within the Preservation Area could designate Special Agricultural Production districts to encourage cranberry and blueberry growing. In these districts strict limitations were imposed on uses other than berry growing.

Pinelands Villages and Towns. Because the character of the Pinelands included discrete, established settlements even within the Preservation, Forest, Agricultural Production, and Rural Development areas, these settlements received a special designation as Pinelands Villages, or Pinelands Towns (if they had public sewerage and/or water supplies). There was considerable debate about how to set boundaries for these. As a result, the commission established only rough guidelines for designating boundaries, to be adjusted in the conformance process for each municipality. In addition, fourteen villages were added to the list during review of the draft Comprehensive Management Plan, as the commission was convinced that these villages also fit criteria of size, density of existing development, and availability of commercial and community services.

Regional Growth Area. With the exception of military installations, any remaining land was included in the Regional Growth Areas. Debate on whether or not this land was actually less sensitive to environmental degradation than land in the more protected districts was inconclusive. This was largely because the definition of "sensitivity" used by the commission automatically excluded developed land (with one exception—the corridor linking the northern and southern parts of the Forest Area). During the discussions it also became clear that the commission would force growth regions to accept high-density development. For this reason, several communities in the Regional Growth Area opposed the designation.

Military and Federal Installation Area. This category was created during the revision process to give official recognition to established military and federal installations, including Fort Dix Military Reservation, McGuire Air Force Base, the naval Air Engineering Center at Lakehurst, and the Federal Aviation Administration's Technical Center. At that time about 5 percent of the land in the Pinelands could be included in this designation.

Continuing Oversight of Development. The Comprehensive Management Plan also set forth the procedure for reviewing development applications after municipalities had brought their local master plans into conformance with the CMP. Once again, the commission followed procedures that were stricter than those used by most other regional planning bodies. The Adirondacks Commission, for example, reviewed only regional development applications of a certain size or location (e.g., in wetlands).[15]

The Pinelands legislation, however, authorized the Pinelands Commission "to commence a review within fifteen days after any final municipal or county approval thereof, of any application in the Pinelands Area." The commission decided to meet the decision date for all applicants by requiring them to prefile with the commission every application for development in the Pinelands. This allowed the executive director and the commission to judge which projects, even small ones, posed a threat to the Pinelands. It was hoped that, with time, the number of projects needing review by the commission would decline as municipalities and the commission agreed on approval criteria. This detailed review function placed a large burden on the commission and continually kept it in an adversarial position via-à-vis some municipalities.

Reviewing the Draft Comprehensive Management Plan

The commission underestimated interest in the Comprehensive Management Plan. It ran out of copies (three thousand in the first printing) within one month of the release of the draft plan. Although the CMP underwent months of scrutiny, comment, and revision during the review process, its basic shape remained intact.

The commission released the draft CMP for public comment on June 6, 1980. The commission staff had written the first part of the plan, drawing heavily on analytical consultants' reports. The second part, detailing procedures and regulations, was written by the land-use consultants with staff input. Opponents, shocked that the commission had actually produced the plan so quickly, insisted that there was inadequate time to review it and continued their efforts to pass legislation to delay the mandated adoption deadline.

An attempt to delay the release of the draft had failed, but support was growing for a movement to put off the final adoption of the plan by the commission. Some argued that more time was needed for careful consideration of the data base and the potential impact of the plan on residents, municipalities, and businesses. Others said that even more data had to be collected. Opponents of the delay action considered the tactic simply an attempt to sabotage the whole planning effort. Those who favored the delay won a partial victory, however, when on June 26, 1980, the New Jersey State Legislature approved a modification of the Pinelands Act that (1) allowed the governor thirty days rather than ten days in which to make a decision on adoption of the plan, and (2) delayed adoption of the CMP for the Protection Area to no earlier than November 14, 1980, but not later than December 15 of the same year. Lobbying for this change had been intense, with many individuals who owned small lots in the Pinelands brought to Trenton on buses to protest restrictions on their land.

Governor Byrne did not oppose this delay movement, not because he favored the delay but because he needed legislative support to get his new state budget passed. He had been losing some of his support on the Pinelands among legislators, and he felt he could regain it and get his budget approved by compromising on the adoption date of the CMP for the Protection Area.[16] Support for protecting the Preservation Area, however, was strong enough by this time that approval of that part of the plan was not delayed.

The Protection Area delay created many potential problems. For example, the split between Preservation and Protection areas jeopardized several concepts basic to the entire plan, such as the transfer of development rights within the entire area; landowners in the Preservation Area would for a time have no receiving area for their credits. The delay also put off the time when the municipalities could once again be in charge of their own development reviews, since until the plan was adopted, the building moratorium continued in effect, even in areas slated by the plan for growth.

Debate on delaying adoption of the plan had also distracted attention from the real issues, without really satisfying those who opposed the plan. No time schedule, however long, would really please them, although the delay did gain opponents more time to press for modifications of the plan. Indeed, few or no changes were made between August 8 and November 21 that strengthened the plan environmentally; all changes during this period were in the direction of allowing more growth and more local control over planning and zoning. However, in view of the hard work by staff and commissioners and the many hours of meetings between August 8 and November 21, it is difficult to see how the plan could have been as thoroughly thought out if it had been adopted in its entirety in August.

The Pinelands Commission met weekly from June 6 to November 21 for a total of twenty-three regular day-long meetings, plus five additional Saturday sessions. Every other week the commission spent several hours on reviewing applications for development, but most of its meeting time was spent discussing the Comprehensive Management Plan, its data base, the minimum standards, and specific zoning proposals.

On many issues there was real debate needing the expertise of the consultants and staff—for example, on water quality standards and the plight of the farmers. These efforts by the commission led to a thoroughly researched and equitable plan. It is to the credit of the commission, especially Chairman Parker, also that the discussions were generally unpolitical and constructive, although they did tend to be long and often very tedious.

Intergovernmental Participation in Preparing the Plan

All levels of government from federal to municipal participated in preparation of the Comprehensive Management Plan for the national reserve. In turn the plan described the roles each level would play when the time came for implementation.

Federal Involvement. Those members of Congress who had worked on the legislation continued to watch over the actions of the Pinelands Commission during the planning phase. Their support or opposition to federal funding for Pinelands protection was the principal vehicle for expressing their concerns. (See Chapter 4.)

Allocation of funds for acquisition and oversight of the administration of the Pinelands National Reserve fell primarily under the jurisdiction of the Department of the Interior. The various activities of the federal government and the Pinelands Commission required coordination; therefore, in December 1979, the department set up a federal Advisory Task Force primarily to assess potential conflicts between the state and federal legislation. The task force provided an important link between the two levels of government and effectively ironed out many potential problems. In addition, representatives of two Interior Department agencies, Edward Hay of the National Park Service and Bernard Fagan of the Heritage, Conservation, and Recreation Service (HCRS), attended commission meetings. Because the federal government was involved in a process with potential environmental impact, it was required to prepare an Environmental Impact Statement for the National Reserve's CMP. Although this voluminous report prepared by the HCRS recommended less development than allowed under the CMP as the preferable option for preservation, it concluded that the CMP was acceptable.

Coordination between the Department of Defense (DOD) and the Pinelands Commission was necessary for management of the Military and Federal Installation Area. Although the commission made recommendations and required that a land-use plan be prepared, it had no power of enforcement over the DOD except where state permits were required for development. In addition, the U.S. Air Force and Air National Guard proposed expanding their bombing range in Warren Grove to 40,000 acres, including much land in the Pine Plains. This proposal led to considerable discussion of the conflict in land use for this very special ecosystem.

The Environmental Protection Agency commented on the plan and participated in the Federal Advisory Task Force. Its most significant recommendation was that the Cohansey Aquifer be designated a sole source aquifer.

State Involvement.   The governor exercised his influence over the commission at least twice during the planning process. First, he opposed most bills in the legislature designed to amend and thereby weaken the legislation. Second, late in the planning process, he sent a letter to the commission making specific recommendations for revisions of the proposed plan; he was particularly interested in allowing owners of small lots to build on them for their own use and in requiring the commission to take affirmative action regarding affordable housing. In both cases, he got what he wanted. In general, there was close cooperation between his office and the commission.

The legislature, too, was interested in the activities of the commission. Although it considered many bills that would have weakened the original act, it rejected all of them except the four-month delay discussed above. In addition, members of the Senate Energy and Environment Committee exercised their rights to legislative oversight by holding hearings and by attending briefings by the commission staff. On February 6, 1980, for example, the committee's chairman, Senator Frank Dodd, held a public hearing on the complaint that individual landowners were being hurt by restrictions on building. At that meeting the senators heard from builders and local municipal officials; no individual spoke up on his or her own behalf. In fact Mayor Steve Corcoran of Medford Township, in response to a question from Senator Dodd as to whether he knew of any specific complaints by individuals about the commission's activities, said that, on the contrary, the commission was very fair, and approvals far outweighed denials. It appeared from this hearing, at any rate, that builders were more bothered by the regulations than were residents. The committee concluded that the plan was being developed in a manner consistent with the legislative intent.

The plan itself made numerous recommendations for future state legislative action to ensure the effectiveness of, or even the application of, some of its most important provisions. These included recommendations both for specific actions directly related only to the Pinelands and for more general actions related to the entire state. On the other hand, the original legislation had been written to make the CMP law as soon as the governor signed it, with no further legislative considerations. It was partly this reason that prompted the spate of bills aimed at changing the original legislation.

During the early planning stages, the Pinelands Commission worked closely with the Department of Environmental Protection, of which it was technically a part. Before the governor had signed the Pinelands legislation, the DEP's Division of Water Resources staff had done most of the development review of septic systems for the commission. After the legislation was adopted, this authority devolved to the new Pinelands Commission and the Division of Water Resources felt slighted. Strains developed as new lines of authority for review, land acquisition, and other areas were worked out.[17] In addition, although the DEP had no formal coordinator for its Pinelands affairs after the signing of the state legislation, it was asked to provide information or interagency reports on fire, forest management, and fish and wildlife, and to administer land acquisitions. Coastal areas of the Pinelands National Reserve that were not included in the state Pinelands Area were also administered by DEP's Coastal Area Facility Review Act. DEP appointed a coordinator in July 1980 to work on these issues and coordinate review of the draft plan.

The tensions between the Pinelands Commission and other state agencies arose from the powerful mandate under which the commission worked. Standards set by the commission would affect other agencies' activities. The governor, however, assumed that if he heard no major complaints from the directors of these agencies, they were not seriously bothered by the decisions of the commission.[18] Therefore, little was done to ease a problem that had not even been officially recognized.

County and Municipal Involvement.   By statute, the counties exerted their main influence on the commission through their commission representatives. For Camden and Burlington counties, represented by Joan Batory and Robert Shinn, this worked fairly well. The interests of the other counties, especially Ocean and Cape May, were less well served. Ocean County suffered from several changes of representative (it went for periods of several weeks with no appointee) and from the high absentee rate of its representative early in the planning phase (she missed about half the meetings before release of the draft plan). Cape May's representative, Lester Germanio, was effective primarily in his opposition to landfills. And because of high absenteeism, Atlantic County too was not well represented until Philip Nanzetta's appointment at the end of February 1980.

Ocean and Atlantic counties both presented written criticisms of the draft plan, but none of their substantive proposals was accepted. Although the commission did accept a request by Ocean County to change housing density in some southern areas of the county from 3.5 to 2 units per acre, the county was still dissatisfied and passed a resolution, addressed to the governor, the state legislators, and other public officials within the Pinelands, calling for a 120-day delay in adoption of the CMP. In September, Atlantic County launched a publicity campaign to "galvanize voters against the plan." [19] Given the strength of the opposition by the Atlantic, Cape May, and Ocean county representatives, it is likely that more effort by the commission to involve them in the planning process would have been to no avail.

During preparation of the plan, the interests of the municipalities were formally represented by the Municipal Council, which had been set up by state legislation at the request of the mayors. Their first meeting had an attendance of ten and the second of twelve, out of the fifty-two municipalities in the Pinelands Area. Twenty-nine attended the third meeting on May 18, the first time that the council had a quorum. Mayor Garnett (Evesham Township) had testified at a senate committee hearing in early February that the mayors were not participating in the Municipal Council, which had been included in the legislation expressly at their request. One possible reason for this, according to the mayor of Eagleswood Township John Hendrickson (who was later to serve on the commission), was that the mayors felt that whatever they said would not matter, that the environmentalists had usurped the municipal prerogatives. Whatever the reason, however, the mayors were passing up an opportunity to be heard, and undoubtedly this lost them some credibility with Senator Dodd, who was reported as being "shocked" by the lack of interest. [20]

The lack of participation was not due to a want of issues. The mayors' greatest concern was the lack of time and resources to review properly the soon-to-appear draft CMP. They got the delay of adoption of part of the plan in response to this concern. They were also bothered about the possibility of water being shipped out of the Pinelands and about the loss of tax revenues on land acquired for the Pinelands National Reserve. Both these issues were treated in the CMP. Also, the municipalities were to bear most of the responsibility for implementing the CMP. It would be impossible for the commission to review formally all applications for development after the conformance process was completed; thus the burden of review was designed to fall to the municipalities.

Although some mayors, such as John Garnett of Evesham, were willing to work with the commission, more were not—for example, Dominic Maise of Winslow Township. Two commissioners were also mayors, although they differed in their opinions of the work of the commission. One of these was Floyd West of Bass River (Burlington), who was very supportive of a strong plan even though his community could expect to have some of the most severe tax-revenue losses. The other was John Hendrickson of Eagleswood (Ocean), who opposed the plan because he said that the legislation had already encouraged people to stop paying their property taxes and that the plan would make matters worse. Indeed, resistance by many mayors to the authority of the commission and an unwillingness to take part in the planning process hindered a productive interchange of ideas. For its part the commission, which was on a tight schedule and itself convinced of the value of its work, often appeared to have neither the time nor the patience to nurture good relationships with recalcitrant municipal officials.

The Commissioners. As might be expected, the contributions of individual commissioners to the planning process reflected their varied interests and experiences. Two of the more influential commissioners were Chairman Parker and Vice-chairman Shinn, who mediated among groups when discussions threatened to divide the commission. Shinn and Chavooshian were particularly active in supporting the development credit plan, and Commissioners Ashmun and Batory helped to make programs direct and workable, as well as fair, by keeping an eye on both communication with municipalities and the practical side of implementation. The point of view of farmers and landowners was voiced by Commissioner Darlington, who was also very concerned to protect open space. Moreover, his careful consideration of issues such as compensation helped clarify them for all. Commissioner Nanzetta (appointed in late February) contributed critical appraisals of staff proposals, insisting on detailed, though often overly lengthy, justifications of each program. Commissioners West and Patterson were the most outspoken environmentalists; they kept attention focused on protection of the landscape, while, according to Terrence Moore, Commissioner Burke worked behind the scenes with Senator Bradley and Representative Florio to get acquisition money. Commissioner Germanio concentrated on the issue of landfills. In all, the group functioned well together, a critical element in preparing the plan well and quickly.

Public Involvement in the Planning Process

In addition to local representation on the commission, the public was offered the opportunity to participate in all stages of the planning. This was felt to be a crucial factor in gaining local support. To marshall regional academic talent, John Cooney of Rutgers, The State University, convened the Technical Advisory Committee, composed of faculty members from local colleges and universities. At their first meeting, on May 4, 1979, this committee noted that public involvement would be a highly volatile issue, because of the impact of the plan on local communities. Already, in pre-legislative debates and hearings, divisive issues such as the right of the state to regulate the use of private land had arisen, and it was clear that even with compromises no real consensus between developers and environmentalists would be likely.

Program for Public Participation. The commission initiated a formal system of public participation through workshops, hearings, and commission meetings. Staff members arranged and ran public meetings organized around a theme, such as current progress in writing the plan, or specific issues related to special groups, such as municipal planning boards or the agricultural community. Meetings with municipal officials or special-interest groups were arranged upon request. In addition, the commission held public hearings on the draft plan and the public was invited to comment at all commission meetings.

A handful of individuals, each representing a special interest, provided the bulk of the public's input. Mae Barringer, for example, represented the Pine Barrens Coalition of environmental groups; Sean Reilly, formerly DEP's Pinelands Coordinator, had shifted his allegiance (probably in reaction to not being appointed executive director of the commission), and he and Frank Brill represented the builders; and Mayor John Garnett of Evesham Township and Peter Murphy of Dennis Township represented at least some of the mayors. A few concerned citizens, especially Isabelle Dietz, were also faithful followers of commission activities and helped point out concerns of general interest. Many local citizens, however, felt left out of the process; as environmentalists debated builders, they saw their wishes for compromise ignored.

Input at public workshops for data collection and decision-making was uneven in quality and quantity. At some meetings, especially those on designation of critical areas, residents contributed many suggestions and ideas. On the other hand, at meetings on goals and policies most comments were unrelated to the issues. In general, people wanted to talk about specifics, such as the designation of a place with which they were familiar, rather than about philosophical issues.

These public meetings did, however, give the public a chance to speak out about their concerns, particularly about their opposition to the state legislation. Some were concerned about loss of property value and the effect of the Pinelands National Reserve on property taxes. At one meeting on goals and policies on March 28, 1980, at Chatsworth, in the "heart of the Pines," all the questions were directed to such issues; none was directed toward goals and policies. One exchange near the end of the meeting summed up this attitude:

> RESIDENT: [Paraphrased] Anybody who has lived here a long time is something of an environmentalist. Anybody who builds a house now is a capitalist. This Pinelands National Reserve has been shoved down our throats. You will get cooperation from us only because we don't want lots of development.

> EXECUTIVE DIRECTOR MOORE: [Also paraphrased] The problem is that individually you may not be able to prevent development. We will set standards, etc., for the town to use in planning. The big developer you don't want can be stopped by recourse to the Pinelands Commission.

This was the message that needed to be communicated to more of the public to win local support for the commission.

Special-Interest Groups.   The Pinelands Commission appointed an Agricultural Task Force, chaired by the New Jersey Secretary of Agriculture, to represent the agricultural interests in the area. Twenty-five to thirty builders' organizations formed the Coalition for the Sensible Preservation of the Pinelands. The Pine Barrens Coalition (formed in 1977, see Chapter 2) by 1980 represented fifty or more local and national environmental organizations.[21] During preparation of the plan, each of these special-interest groups presented at least one position paper making specific recommendations to the commission.

The most limited and specific were the April 1, 1980, comments of the builders (the Coalition for the Sensible Preservation of the Pinelands) on goals and policies of the commission. Of their fourteen suggestions for change, only one was partly accepted, a recommendation that subdivisions with preliminary or final approvals by the effective date of the CMP be allowed.

The Agricultural Task Force, on the other hand, made a number of substantive suggestions, almost all of which were incorporated into the plan and some of which influenced other decisions. For example, the task force requested and got protections from nuisance ordinances, strengthening of trespass laws, allowances for the construction of processing plants, and permission to use pesticides according to state and federal guidelines.

Also in accordance with their suggestions, the CMP recommended that the state legislature expand coverage of farmland assessments for land in the Agricultural Districts. To help mitigate decreases in property values on land in these districts, which was no longer developable, the Pinelands Development Credit System gave farmers in these districts more credits than landowners outside them.

Recommendations by the Pine Barrens Coalition fared better than those made by the builders, but not as well as those made by the Agricultural Task Force. The coalition's request for strict regulation of pesticide use and limits on clearing for agriculture, for example, were resolved in favor of the farmers. On the other hand, their recommendation that "the bulk of development [to] take place within the Pines. . . . [be] clustered and restricted to the outer fringe of the protection zone only" was accepted.[22] The revised plan also incorporated some of their thirteen other recommendations, such as those suggesting continuation of payments in lieu of taxes for land acquired by the state as well as restrictions on landfills and clearcutting. The coalition's general recommendations that growth, low-growth, and no-growth areas be identified and that strict environmental standards be developed became major provisions of the Comprehensive Management Plan. They also strongly supported the provisions of the Pinelands Protection Act that required municipal master plans and ordinances to conform with the CMP and that continued the commission's call-up rights over local development permits.

Public Reaction to the Draft CMP.   The volume of comments grew rapidly once the draft became available to the public. Between the release of the draft plan on June 6 and its final adoption on November 21, the commission received thousands of written comments and heard many oral statements at regular commission meetings. The range of viewpoints may be indicated by two reports. The three-volume *Report to the Pinelands Commission on the Protection Area* prepared by the Coalition for the Sensible Preservation of the Pinelands recommended using only performance standards and a flexible, annually-set, housing-allocation-per-municipality figure in conjunction with maps of land suitability for development, while the Department of the Interior's Environmental Impact Statement preferred allowing less development than the CMP.

Overall, environmentalists discounted local pressures for development, while the builders generally ignored the importance to the ecosystem of maintaining a large, contiguous, uninterrupted forest area. Local residents testified both favorably and unfavorably. Some of the many concrete suggestions and criticisms that were offered during the comment period led to changes in details of the CMP; none of the revisions, however, changed the basic philosophy behind the plan.

During this period, the focus of major criticism shifted from the state legislation not carrying out the mandate of the federal legislation to the CMP not carrying out the mandate of the state legislation. In addition, by the time of the hearings on the draft CMP in July, many opponents had retreated from fighting the plan in the Preservation Area. As Assemblyman John Doyle remarked, the need to protect this core region was no longer an issue. Even the legislation that was being proposed at the time to weaken the law directed itself either toward removing the Protection Area from the jurisdiction of the commission or toward making the commission's activities merely advisory; no bill attempted to undermine protections in the Preservation Area (see Chapter 11).

Two comments illustrate the wide gulf separating critics and supporters of the CMP: First, there was the remark of a lawyer representing "members of [his] law firm, and several property owners and businessmen, too numerous to mention":

> The plan can only be characterized as "diabolic" in nature . . . It indicates a moral and ethical bankruptcy to coincidentally accompany the financial bankruptcies likely to be occasioned by its imposition.[23]

On the other hand, there were the observations of the solicitor for the Atlantic City Planning Board:

> The draft Comprehensive Management Plan represents an enlightened and courageous response to the challenge posed by the pressures of urban sprawl upon a unique and fragile environment unsuited for intense development. . . . Imprudent development of the Pinelands could result in an ecological disaster, detrimental not only to the environment but also to man and his investments.[24]

Adoption and Approval of the CMP

The Comprehensive Management Plan was adopted by the Pinelands Commission on November 21, 1980. It represented a compromise between environmentalists and local economic concerns. Some environmental groups labelled it a development plan while builders said that it would put them out of business. If the builders had not been critical of it, one might have doubted that it would have had the desired effect of preserving the landscape, since indiscriminate location of development was the principal direct threat to the integrity of the landscape.

The commissioners voted eleven to four to approve the plan. All the governor's appointees, the federal appointee, and three of the county representatives voted in favor. The three county representatives who approved the plan (Batory, Shinn, and Wagner) were the only county representatives who had served on the commission since its inception. Two who opposed it had been on the commission only one month. The approval by the three county representatives who had the longest connection with the commission's activities indicated that at least in these three counties the representatives knew the plan well and were convinced that it did not ignore local rights. Governor Byrne signed the plan soon after its approval, and Secretary of the Interior Cecil Andrus signed it on January 16, 1981.

The Comprehensive Management Plan provided a strong basis for preservation of the natural resources in the Pinelands. The existence of an excellent resource database even before work began and the zeal and dedication of the commission and its staff had allowed the plan to be prepared and written quickly. The fast pace of activity had also kept opposition to the plan off balance, thus blunting the effectiveness of attacks. Although the lack of individual contact between commission staff and residents of the Pinelands had sometimes led to local antagonisms and misunderstandings, the public comments, solicited throughout the planning period, had generally received careful attention and in many cases had resulted in significant revisions in the details of the plan.[25] Support for the commission's work throughout the planning phase continued to come from the governor's office, the state legislature, the federal bureaucracy, and the general public. All these factors, as well as a contemporary political climate favoring environmental protection, enabled the commission to interpret its legislative mandate liberally and so to produce a strong management plan.

6. Pinelands Comprehensive Management Plan

Beryl Robichaud Collins

Emily W. B. Russell

In an impressive 474-page document the Pinelands Commission sets forth a land-use strategy and implementing policies and programs that have been called "the most stringent environmental regulations in the United States."[1] Provisions of the Pinelands Comprehensive Management Plan, which became effective January 14, 1981, encourage agricultural and recreational use of the land and accommodate compatible residential, commercial, and industrial patterns of development but emphasize that the overall ecological values and historic and cultural resources are to be protected.

As described earlier, the CMP evolved from assessments of Pinelands natural and sociocultural resources within a context of past and present human use of these resources as well as the demands of future population growth. As a preface to presentation of the plan's goals and management policies and programs, the first third of the CMP document summarizes these assessments in narrative and illustrative form.

Resource Assessments and CMP Goals

Starting with geologic history, the natural resource assessments treat hydrology, soils, vegetation, aquatic communities, wildlife, climate, and air quality. This organization permits evaluation of the interrelationships of these elements at each stage—for example, the impacts of water quality on aquatic communities. Overall, the data re-emphasize the uniqueness of the Pinelands landscape and its susceptibility to degradation by human activity. The long-standing human use of resources is recognized, but the CMP also suggests that heretofore the ecosystem has been resilient in the face of these severe but transient activities, such as the cutting of forests for charcoal. New threats, however, having virtually irreversible impact on natural resources, presently endanger the stability of the Pine Barrens ecosystem. Water quality assessments formed a critical basis for many of the decisions regarding protection of the natural environment (see Chapter 5).

The CMP considers prehistoric and historic sites and unique cultural groups and activities to be positive resources of the Pinelands. Invento-

130

ries revealed abundant prehistoric sites in the Pine Barrens, despite earlier theories of very sparse habitation. In the past, the desire to exploit resources dominated human attitudes toward the natural resources of the Barrens; thus those cultural sites sought out and designated for preservation by the CMP are mostly the remains of former resource-based industrial activities, such as iron manufacture and glass-making, and of early settlements associated with berry culture (see Chapter 1).

In keeping with the goal of the Pinelands legislation—"to protect, preserve and enhance the significant values of the land and water resources"—it is only after discussion of the natural and sociocultural resources that the CMP document assesses present and future demands for resource use. This sequential treatment emphasizes that the legislative goals are to accommodate human populations at the least risk to the natural environment. Studies of past and anticipated (to the year 2000) patterns and rates of population growth are analyzed, and graphic projections made of development alternatives under three scenarios: unconstrained growth at moderately high levels, unconstrained growth at high levels, and growth at high levels constrained by the CMP growth-management strategy. Under the constrained scenario, settlement is concentrated primarily in peripheral areas of the Pinelands with little development spilling over into undeveloped areas especially in the east-west, Philadelphia-to-Atlantic City corridor region. Within the growth area, however, the plan does provide substantial potential for increased development, particularly at higher densities in or adjoining already-developed regions.

Within the framework of the legislative mandate, the Pinelands Commission translated the resource availability and demand analyses into a set of five goals for the CMP (CMP, Part I, p. 193–194):

Natural Resources Goal: Preserve, protect, and enhance the overall ecological values of the Pinelands, including its large forested areas, its essential character, and its potential to recover from disturbance.

Historic and Cultural Goal: Maintain and enhance the historic and cultural resources of the Pinelands.

Agricultural and Horticultural Goal: Preserve and enhance agricultural and horticultural uses that are compatible with the preservation and protection of the overall ecological values of the Pinelands.

Development Goal: Accommodate residential, commercial, and industrial development in a way that is compatible with the preservation and protection of the overall ecological and cultural values of the Pinelands.

Table 6–1. Building Restrictions in Land-Use Management Areas of the Pinelands National Reserve

Management Area	Acreage	No. of Permitted Residential Units[c]	Minimum Lot Size (Acres) Waste Water System[a]		
			Sewer	St. Sept.	Inn. Alt.
Preservation Area	339,144[b]	None except by exemption[c]	No Sewer	3.2	1[d]
Forest Area	420,220	Max.:1 unit per 15.8 acres of privately owned, undeveloped uplands[e]	No Sewer	3.2	1[d]
Agricultural Production Area	77,520	Only for farm owner or employee at density of 10 acres per dwelling[e]	No Sewer	3.2	1[d]
Rural Development Area	145,000	Max.:1 unit per 3.2 acres of privately owned, undeveloped uplands[f]	3.2	3.2	1[d]
Pinelands Towns[g]	15,080	Limited only by compatibility with existing patterns of settlement	No Std.[h]	3.2	1
Regional Growth Areas	119,050	Min.: 1.5–3.5 units per acre of privately owned, undeveloped uplands based on existing character and infrastructure	No Std.	3.2	1
Military & Federal Installations	48,011[b]	No restrictions except development in Preservation or Forest Areas only if it requires no infrastructure	No Std.	No Std.	No Std.

[a] St. Sept=Standard septic wastewater system; Inn. Alt=Innovative/Alternative wastewater system.
[b] A total of 29,656 Preservation acres are included as part of the Military & Federal Installation acreage. Preservation total includes Special Agricultural and Agricultural Production areas identified in the conformance process.
[c] Sociocultural (Piney) exemption permitted in the Preservation Area.
[d] Permitted only with hardship waiver approval.
[e] Sociocultural and grandfathered lot exemptions permitted.
[f] Grandfathered lot exemptions permitted.
[g] Pinelands Village acreage determined in conformance process.
[h] No Std.=No Standard.
Data compiled from an analysis of the Pinelands Comprehensive Management Plan.

Recreation Goal: Protect and enhance outdoor recreational uses and the natural resources on which they depend.

Each goal is supported by three or more policy statements, twenty-five in total; these statements serve as the basis for the CMP management strategy and its supporting regulatory mechanisms.

CMP Land-Use Management Strategy

The management strategy used to achieve the Pinelands goals is presented in two ways. Part I of the CMP document explains in narrative form the substantive programs for protecting and managing land-use, and Part II presents the substantive provisions of the programs and procedural mechanisms as enforceable regulations for use by the commission and by local and state governmental agencies.

With minor exceptions, all activities that alter land and water in the Pinelands or that change uses of structures or land are subject to regulation under the CMP. Exemptions are allowed only for agricultural or horticultural construction or for the improvement, expansion, or rebuilding of an existing single-family dwelling. Construction of structures accessory to single-family residences and utility installations that serve existing or approved development also are exempted. No permit is required either for the clearing of less than 1,500 square feet of land not located in a wetland or within 300 feet of a scenic corridor, or for the construction, repair, or removal of any sign.

The Pinelands land-use strategy is built around three cornerstones: a zoning system of land-use management areas, project performance standards, and use of Pinelands development credits. This basic framework is then supported by a variety of supplementary programs.

Land-Use Management Areas. The Comprehensive Management Plan divides the Pinelands National Reserve, about 1.1 million acres in size, into eight management areas within which specified land uses of varying intensities are permitted (frontispiece). The purposes of the land area designations are (1) to protect undisturbed, or minimally disturbed, areas by directing development away from the more sensitive resources and toward areas near existing settlements; and (2) to encourage agricultural and recreational uses of appropriate lands. Acreage totals for each management area are listed on Table 6–1.

Preservation Area. State legislation established boundaries for the

Preservation Area to encompass an extensive and contiguous area of land in its natural state, which, according to the CMP, includes "significant environmental and economic values that are especially vulnerable to degradation." (CMP, Part II, Sec. 5–203A.) Just more than half of the Preservation Area was in public ownership at the time the CMP was prepared. The only permitted uses of importance in the Preservation Area are culture of berries and native plants, forestry, operation of recreational facilities such as campgrounds, resource extraction, and canoe rental operations already authorized at the time that the CMP became effective. Residential development is prohibited except for one exemption, described later.

Forest Areas. Within the Protection Area, the most restricted lands are designated as Forest Areas, and about one-quarter of these are public lands. Forest Areas include ecologically sensitive coastal wetlands and expanses of undisturbed forest adjoining the Preservation Area or stretching as a corridor from it into the southern section of the Pinelands. Agriculture, forestry, low-intensity recreation, resource extraction, and limited, local, commercial service activities are the permitted uses. Within any Forest Area, the number of new residential housing units allowed is limited to a maximum of one dwelling unit for each 15.8 acres of the total privately owned, undeveloped upland acreage in the area. Within that allowance, there is a minimum lot size of 3.2 acres per residential unit.

Agricultural Production Areas. Active farmlands and adjoining lands having suitable agricultural soils are designated as Agricultural Production Areas; with few exceptions, all this land lies within the Protection Area. The term "Special Agricultural Production Area" is used to designate an eighth management area, land within the Preservation Area that is dedicated to berry culture or to native horticultural activities. Boundaries for these lands are established in the conformance process. In addition to farming, commercial agricultural activities (including processing facilities), forestry, resource extraction, and campgrounds and other recreational uses are also permitted in this zone. Only residential housing for farmowners or their employees can be built in this area, and then each residential unit requires a 10-acre parcel.

Rural Development Areas. Lands separating less-developed Protection Areas from settlements generally are designated as Rural Development Areas; these serve as buffers and potential reserves for future development. The permitted uses are less restrictive than those in Agricultural Production Areas. Allowance is made for new residential development in each Rural Development Area up to a maximum of one residential unit for each 3.2 acres of the total privately owned, undeveloped uplands. Within that allowance, a minimum lot size of 3.2 acres per dwelling unit is required.

Pinelands Towns and Villages. The CMP identifies boundaries of six towns and names fifty-nine Pinelands villages within the national reserve, distinguishing the former from the latter by their larger size and by the availability of public sewer and/or water facilities. Municipalities have the task of defining within given criteria the boundaries of their Villages. Residential, commercial, and industrial infill development compatible with the existing character of the settlement is permitted in both Towns and Villages.

Regional Growth Areas. Future growth is directed primarily to Regional Growth Areas, which generally are situated adjacent to existing development; for the most part these areas are also areas now experiencing development pressures. Commercial, industrial, and all other uses may be permitted in each Growth Area, which also must provide for a minimum number of new residential units. This minimum ranges from 1.0 to 3.5 dwellings for each acre of privately owned, undeveloped upland in the Growth Area, depending upon the existing character of the development and available infrastructure. The allocation of new residential units in the reserve was determined using commission analyses of population growth and estimates of new housing needs until the year 2000. About 70 percent of this total demand for new housing is to be satisfied by construction in Regional Growth Areas.[2] Within each Growth Area, municipalities may provide for zoning districts encompassing a range of permitted uses and residential densities varying from 0.5 dwelling units per acre to 12 or more units for each acre. Municipalities, under strict conditions, also may designate Municipal Reserves in adjacent Rural Development Areas; within these reserves development at densities specified for Regional Growth Areas will be permitted after a municipality's Regional Growth Areas have become saturated.

Military and Federal Installation Areas. There are four major federal landholdings classified as Military and Federal Installation Areas: Fort Dix Military Reservation, McGuire Air Force Base, the Naval Air Engineering Center at Lakehurst, and the Federal Aviation Administration Technical Center in Atlantic County. This category includes land in both the Preservation and the Protection areas. With the exception of banning uses in the Preservation and Forest areas that would need additional infrastructure, no other land-use prohibition is placed on these federal lands except to require that all development must "substantially meet" the performance standards (described later).

Exemptions from Management Area Restrictions. Two types of exemptions from management area restrictions are written into the CMP. (As described later, other exemptions for different reasons may be granted in the permitting process.) One is the controversial sociocultural exemption, commonly called the "Piney exemption"; this allows an individual who can demonstrate a cultural, social, or economic link to the Pinelands to build for his own use a primary residential dwelling on 3.2 acres in the Preservation, Forest, or Agricultural areas, without regard for the prescribed residential density allowances. To receive this exemption, an applicant may not have built another residence under this exemption provision within the last five years and the applicant must satisfy these tests:

1. The parcel of land for the proposed dwelling must have been owned by the applicant or a family member on February 7, 1979; and either

a. The applicant is a member of a two-generation family that has resided in the Pinelands for at least twenty years, *or*

b. The primary source of the applicant's income is employment or participation in a Pinelands resource-related activity.

A second exemption, called the "grandfather lot clause," deals with substandard-sized lots. In this provision lots of one acre or more that are located in a Forest, Agricultural Production, or Rural Development area but not in the Preservation Area may be exempted from lot-size minimums, if (1) lot ownership dates back to February 7, 1979; (2) no contiguous land is owned; and (3) the dwelling unit will be the primary residence of the owner or a member of the immediate family. As a CMP provision, the grandfather exemption clause expired one year after the effective date of the plan; however, many certified municipalities incorporated the exemption provision into their ordinances. Development qualifying for both types of exemption must still meet CMP performance standards.

Performance Standards. Regardless of its location, every development project subject to regulation under the provisions of the Comprehensive Management Plan must meet a set of performance standards that are established to protect natural resources, such as water quality, and sociocultural values, such as preservation of historic sites. These performance standards, described as "programs" in Part I of the CMP and as "enforceable regulations" in Part II, are as follows:

Water Quality. Ground water leaving a parcel of land used for commercial, industrial, or residential development or discharging into surface water cannot exceed two parts per million nitrate-nitrogen. Since much of the Pinelands is unsewered, this standard often serves as the controlling factor when determining minimum lot-size requirements, even in management areas in which growth is to be encouraged. To meet the standards no residential dwelling may be located on a parcel of less than 3.2 acres, if served by a conventional on-site septic wastewater system. In Regional Growth Areas and Pinelands Towns and Villages a parcel of one acre may be used, if the development is served by an alternative or innovative on-site wastewater system (a waterless toilet, for example).

Standards are given for control of stormwater runoff and wastewater treatment facilities, and prohibitions are placed on nondomestic discharges, use of septic tank cleansers, and on the disposal of other toxic chemicals and materials anywhere in the Pinelands. To avoid the danger of groundwater pollution, landfills are prohibited in the Preservation Area and severely restricted in the Protection Area; in the latter, existing facilities may be operated only until 1990 and new facilities established only if there are not practical, alternative disposal sites available outside the Pinelands. To ensure maintenance of the ecosystem and protection of groundwater supplies, exportation of water out of counties of the Pinelands is prohibited. After adoption of the CMP, legislation was passed prohibiting exportation of surface or groundwater more than ten miles beyond the boundaries of the Pinelands National Reserve.

Wetlands. Delineation of coastal and inland wetlands within the reserve is based on vegetation and soils; in wetlands, only berry culture, native-plant horticulture, forestry, specified public improvements, and low-intensity or water-based recreational activities are permitted. In addition, a buffer zone of 300 feet is established around all wetlands to minimize impacts from upland development. No development is allowed in this buffer unless the applicant demonstrates, according to set criteria, that the proposed project will not result in "a significant adverse impact" on the wetland, criteria for which are defined.

Vegetation and Wildlife. The CMP attempts to protect populations of native plants and animals from two threats: destruction of populations of endangered or threatened species by human activity, and displacement of native species by new species introduced by humans. Development is therefore prohibited unless it is designed to avoid irreversible adverse impacts on habitats or populations of identified threatened and endangered plant and animal species. In addition, clearing of more than 1500 square feet of vegetation is permitted only under certain conditions, and landscaping materials must be compatible with native vegetation.

Fire Management. To protect life and property from damage by forest fire, development projects not only must meet certain materials specifications but also must maintain firebreak widths in keeping with the area's fire hazard rating. Concerned about maintenance of the Pinelands fire-dependent vegetation, the CMP also recommends use of controlled burning programs.

Air Quality. CMP air quality standards follow exactly state and federal regulations, requiring developments that generate substantial vehicular traffic or space-heating emissions to take appropriate measures to maintain the ambient air quality.

Historic, Archaeological, and Cultural Preservation. Nine structures and sites are designated by the commission as worthy of protection. The CMP also encourages counties and municipalities to identify additional areas or sites of special historic and archaeological interest or which reflect significant elements of Pinelands architecture, culture, and social or economic activities. Cultural site surveys are required before major development projects may proceed, and once a structure or site is found to be of historic or prehistoric significance, demolition, new construction, or alterations may not be undertaken without approval.

Other provisions protect scenic resources through special setback requirements and height restrictions in designated scenic corridors—highways, lakes, ponds, and rivers. The use of signs is restricted, especially in the Preservation Area.

The CMP also recognizes the New Jersey court mandate (known as the Mount Laurel decision) to provide affordable housing for a variety of income classes in the Pinelands, and initially required that at least 10 percent of the housing units in larger developments in Regional Growth Areas be for low-income households, with an additional 10 percent for moderate-income families and 5 percent for middle-income households. Following the second Mount Laurel decision, which was handed down after issuance of the CMP, the commission modified these requirements to conform with the court's mandate.

Pinelands Development Credit Program.   The third cornerstone of the Comprehensive Management Plan is the Pinelands Development Credit Program, which is based on the transferable development rights (TDR) concept. Pinelands development credits (PDCs) provide "an alternative use to property owners" in the most restrictive management areas—the Preservation Area and the Agricultural Production Areas (CMP, Part I, p. 210). The idea is that by selling his development credits a landowner can, for example, continue to farm without losing the financial benefit of increasing land values realized in the growth areas. Thus, the commission reasoned, PDCs provide a way to encourage agriculture and protect the resources and yet mitigate the negative economic impact of restrictions on development.

The basis for allocating PDCs varies by management area. In the Preservation Area, one PDC is allocated for each 39 acres of uplands and 0.2 PDCs for each 39 wetland acres. Property owners in Agricultural Production Areas (and Special Agricultural Production Areas) receive two PDCs for each 39 acres of uplands and also two PDCs for each 39 acres of actively farmed wetlands in berry culture. Other wetlands in the agricultural areas are given only 0.2 PDCs per 39 acres. Below the 39-acre threshold fractional credits are allotted, with a minimum of 0.25 PDCs allocated to lots of 0.1 or more acres, if the parcel is undeveloped, owned as of February 9, 1979, and not contiguous with other land under the same ownership. PDCs may be sold on the open market to developers, who then have the right to build four bonus housing units for each purchased PDC. An owner wishing to sell a PDC is required only to record its sale as a property deed restriction.

Supporting CMP Programs. A variety of other programs make up the remainder of the substantive provisions of the Comprehensive Management Plan. Three of these deal with resource use activities—agriculture, forestry, and resource extraction.

Resource Use Programs. Agricultural activities are highly encouraged by the CMP, as witnessed by the provision exempting agricultural development from the water-quality performance standards imposed on other forms of development. Instead, it is expected that the recommended management practices established by the N.J. Department of Agriculture, the Soil Conservation Service, and the State University Agricultural Experiment Station will be followed.

Landowners whose property is not included in established Agricultural Production Areas may petition local municipalities or the commission for inclusion; if successful, they gain an allocation of PDCs. Additional encouragement for farming is provided in the requirement that municipalities exempt farm operations from so-called "nuisance ordinances" (working time limits, for example), which inhibit production.

Forestry operations also are encouraged under the CMP, which initially contained very simple application requirements for permission to cut timber. Within a short time, however, these proved inadequate, having led to a number of illegal wood-harvesting operations. Tighter controls over permitting activities were later imposed.

Resource extraction operations are recognized for their important role in the Pinelands economy. The program, aimed primarily at sand and gravel mining operations, emphasizes restoration standards, requires minimum buffers from property lines, and restricts excavation below the water table, which might cause pollution of ground water.

Recreation. This program acknowledges potential conflicts between recreational activities and resource protection and identifies which low-intensity recreational activities are appropriate for undeveloped areas and which more-intensive activities are suitable for developed areas. Power boats are limited to the lower reaches of the Pinelands rivers; motorized vehicles are permitted only on designated sand roads. Guidelines are given for recreational facilities in major residential development projects.

Nonregulatory Programs. Several nonregulatory programs deal with critical issues. A land acquisition program is outlined, and recommendations made to encourage growth-generating capital improvement projects in Regional Growth Areas. Another program identifies the many interrelationships among local, state, and federal agencies and the Pinelands Commission that must be coordinated to achieve effective implementation of the CMP. This program highlights in particular the need for cooperation with the state Department of Environmental Protection, which through its coastal management program (CAFRA) has responsibility for implementing the CMP in that part of the National Reserve not included in the Pinelands Area.

A financial program details the costs of implementing the Comprehensive Management Plan and identifies sources of revenue for covering these costs. Discussion of the economic impact of the CMP on the regional economy—land values, property taxes, and municipal revenues—suggests legislative action to compensate municipalities for loss of property tax revenues resulting from public land acquisition.

A separate chapter of the CMP addresses the need for public participation by summarizing how the public had been involved during the preparation of the plan and by outlining the ongoing public information, education, and involvement programs that are planned for the implementation period. Finally, recognizing that "many questions still exist about the complex natural and human relationships in the region," the Pinelands Commission identifies a number of issues that require further research and study to determine whether or not the CMP management program is dealing effectively with environmental, cultural, and economic impacts and implications (CMP, Part I, p. 264).

CMP Procedural Mechanisms

The state Pinelands Protection Act created an organizational framework for division of regulatory functions. Each Pinelands municipality and county is given the opportunity to exercise primary responsibility for development regulation within its jurisdictional authority, if it revises its master plan and land-use ordinances to conform with the provisions of the CMP. The Pinelands Commission is also authorized to review development approved by the local governments to assure consistency with the plan. If a local government fails to revise its master plan and ordinances, and thus fails to be certified for regulatory consistency with the CMP, the commission is ordered to adopt and enforce such rules and regulations as necessary to implement CMP minimum standards.

Part II of the CMP sets forth both the procedures by which municipalities and counties may gain certification of their master plans and ordinances and also the development-permitting mechanisms for both certified and uncertified local governments. In addition, the CMP defines its amendment process.

Certification of Municipal and County Plans.   Following the legislative mandate, the Comprehensive Management Plan allows local governments one year to submit master plans and ordinances that conform with the plan's provisions. The task is not simple. Municipalities are required to incorporate into their planning documents (1) comprehensive natural resource inventories and analyses, (2) the substantive land-use standards and policies described above, and (3) procedures that are in keeping with the CMP-prescribed mechanisms for processing development applications. This means that a municipality must adopt zoning ordinances that recognize CMP management area boundaries within its jurisdiction and that establish permitted uses, residential zoning densities, and minimum lot-size restrictions for each area as described in the plan. Municipalities with Regional Growth Areas must allow for the minimum residential build-out specified by the CMP and must provide opportunity for developers to use PDCs to achieve bonus densities. Municipalities have more zoning latitude in Growth Areas than in the more highly restricted, environmentally sensitive areas.

Counties have a somewhat simpler task, since they do not deal with zoning. Conformance with the CMP can be achieved by including in the county land-use regulations: (1) current and complete natural resource inventories and analyses, (2) development regulatory standards and procedures consistent with the CMP, (3) solid- and liquid-waste management programs that meet water quality standards, and (4) a capital improvements program to serve permitted development.

Once local regulations are revised to be consistent with CMP provisions, the mechanics of gaining certification are quite simple. Master plans and ordinances are submitted to the commission's executive director, who holds a public hearing to consider the application for certification. The executive director then submits a recommendation to the Pinelands Commission, which issues the order certifying, certifying with conditions, or disapproving the master plan and land-use ordinances. If the submitted documents are certified with conditions or disapproved, local governments have 120 days to make the specified changes that would lead to certification.

In retrospect, one of the most helpful provisions of the CMP is this statement: "It is a policy of this Plan to allow municipalities the greatest degree of flexibility and discretion in the preparation of local plans and ordinances, so long as . . . [these] do not conflict with the ultimate objectives and minimum requirements of this Plan" (CMP, Part II, Sec. 3–101). Flexibility in interpretation was necessary for successful implementation of the certification process (see Chapter 7).

Certification of Federal Installation Plans.   The CMP required that each federal installation adopt, within one year after approval of the plan, a master plan in substantial conformance with the CMP. This provision, however, was later amended and revisions have softened the requirements to eliminate mandatory certification of federal master plans, though the installations are still required to submit master plans simply for commission review. In addition, federal installations are subject to the CMP development regulatory process.

Development Review Procedures.   The CMP outlines three development review procedures: the procedure to be followed during the first year of plan implementation (the conformance period), the postconformance procedure for certified municipalities and counties, and the postconformance procedure for uncertified local governments. Detailed distinctions among these three processes are made in Chapter 8, which also describes procedural modifications made since the CMP was initially issued. Overall, the permitting authority in certified municipalities and counties is quite different from that in jurisdictions not yet certified by the commission.

Permitting Authority: Certified versus Noncertified Jurisdictions. Certified municipalities and counties have authority to make initial development review decisions and to issue or deny permits on the basis of their CMP-certified ordinances. The Pinelands Commission exercises a right to review (call-up) any development approval, and if it finds that the local approval is inconsistent with the provisions of the CMP, that local government must either modify or revoke its approval to conform with the commission findings. This process allows local governments to retain their jurisdictional authority and at the same time does not require multiple permitting by local government and the regional agency.

If a local government does not gain certification of its master plan and land-use ordinances, no development in its jurisdiction may be carried out without the commission's approval. In addition, the commission may approve development that has been denied by local government. Initially, the development review process in uncertified municipalities called for a double permitting process; developers had to secure permits from both the local government and from the Pinelands Commission. In 1985, however, this procedure was changed to eliminate the duplicate permitting by instituting a commission call-up review of local approval and denial actions.

Exemptions Waiving Compliance to CMP Provisions. Built into the development review procedures is a mechanism known as the waiver process, under which exemptions can be granted by the commission to provide relief if strict compliance with CMP provisions will create an extraordinary hardship or if the exemption is necessary to serve a "compelling public need." In neither case, however, may a waiver be granted if the proposed project will result in substantial impairment to the resources or is inconsistent with either the legislation or the plan. By legislative mandate, only the commission has the authority to grant these waivers. The CMP originally defined three tests of eligibility for hardship waivers, two of which have expired. By 1985, relief could be granted only to property owners for whom the plan does not provide a beneficial use of their property; as such, this clause was intended to avoid the "taking" issue. The criteria used by the commission staff to judge eligibility under this clause are described in Chapter 8.

Two of the hardship tests were designed to recognize the vested rights of applicants who had obtained municipal development approvals prior to the effective date of the CMP. One test, which had a life of two years, permitted granting of a hardship waiver to an applicant who had a valid final subdivision approval as of February 8, 1979, provided that the development would conform with the CMP performance standards. If sewers were not available, residential building was restricted to lots of one acre or more. A second hardship test, which expired on January 14, 1984, provided that a waiver could be granted to an individual who, relying on a valid municipal development approval, had made expenditures on which he now was unable to secure a minimum reasonable rate of return unless granted a waiver of compliance from CMP standards. The commission believed that this latter test was a necessary sequel to the interim period of development regulation (see Chapter 4). During the moratorium, the tests for hardship exemptions were very strict, since it had been understood that once the CMP became effective, applicants would be permitted to resubmit development applications under more flexible and lenient hardship provisions.[3] For example, in determining a reasonable return the CMP provides for consideration of certain "soft" costs, such as legal and professional costs related to project design and construction, that had been excluded from interim evaluations.

Interpretation of CMP Provisions. Recognizing that the Comprehensive Management Plan could not anticipate all possible situations, the Pinelands Commission wisely provided that any individual or organization (private or governmental) could request clarification of the meaning of specific CMP policies or an interpretation of any given regulation within the context of a proposed development project. The executive director was authorized to respond to such a written request for a policy interpretation by issuing a Letter of Interpretation.

Since adoption, a variety of CMP policies have been clarified, as illustrated by these examples: a township planning board was advised that depth of seasonal high water table should be measured from natural (unfilled) ground surface; the state Division of Water Resources was told that it did not have to file applications for monitoring wells to evaluate approved developments; a resource extraction company was given an enumeration of the information necessary to demonstrate that extraction activities sixty-five feet below the surface would not result in significant adverse impact; and the Environmental Defense Fund was given an explanation of the type of costs considered by the commission in a hardship case, as well as the calculations used to determine a reasonable rate of return, and the basis for claiming a valid municipal development approval.[4] Altogether the letter of interpretation process has provided the commission with an invaluable means of adapting the CMP to unforeseen situations.

Amendments to the CMP.   State legislators recognized a need for periodic revision of the Comprehensive Management Plan, and so the Pinelands Commission (to its later regret) provided in the CMP that "at least every three years after the adoption of this Plan, the Executive Director shall comprehensively review the Plan and all actions taken by the Commission or the Executive Director . . . and submit a report to the Commission detailing any recommended amendments to the Plan" (Part II, Sec. 7–111). Prior to adopting a proposed amendment, the commission, at its option, may hold a public hearing; all amendment proposals must be submitted to the Pinelands Municipal Council for review and recommendations at least sixty days before commission action. Once an amendment is adopted by the commission, it then must be approved by the governor, the state legislature, and the Secretary of the Department of the Interior.

No provision in the CMP clarifies exactly when a refinement or adjustment of management area boundaries, as permitted in the conformance process, should be considered as an amendment to the plan. Several times the issue has been raised (see Chapter 7), and in early 1986 an environmental group filed suit against the commission charging that its agreement with an adjustment of management boundaries in Berkeley Township was illegal, since the change had not been handled as an amendment.[5]

About one year after adoption of the CMP, seventeen amendments were approved. Most of these were technical clarifications; a few provided greater flexibility in the conformance process and in handling development applications. Minor corrections were also made in the designation of the Preservation and the Protection area boundaries. None of these amendments provoked any criticism from public or special-interest groups. In late 1985, as a result of a court decision, the development review procedures, particularly those used in uncertified municipalities, were also amended (see Chapter 8).

In December 1982, shortly before the second anniversary of the effective date of the CMP, the Pinelands Commission set into action a process, known as the triennial review, by which it would fulfill its obligation for a comprehensive three-year plan review. A commission subcommittee on plan review was appointed to oversee the process and to develop a final set of recommended actions for the full commission. Extensive staff work was undertaken to prepare a progress report on the implementation of the CMP, and an active public involvement program was developed to solicit comments from municipal, county, and state officials, as well as state and national environmental groups, industry groups (including developers and realtors), various civic and cultural organizations, and any others who had expressed interest in the Pinelands.[6] Hearings were held, recommendations screened, and more public hearings held. It was not until January 1986 that the commission finally acted on a selected group of CMP and administrative procedural changes. The approved changes then had to be translated into regulatory language, reviewed again in public hearings, reapproved (or rejected) by the commission, and then forwarded to the governor and the Secretary of the Interior. It is not likely that this process will be completed before late 1987, the time at which the second triennial review is due. Understandably, among the recommended changes is one that calls for extending the plan review interval from three to five years. (The significant issues that were raised in the first triennial review and their likely impact on the Pinelands are discussed in Chapter 12.)

Summary

In its topical coverage of issues, the Comprehensive Management Plan meets the specific requirements of both state and federal legislation. In addition, opportunity for meaningful local involvement in the implementation of the plan is provided by institutionalizing CMP standards, programs, and mechanisms within existing regulatory and enforcement responsibilities. This design is intended to minimize ongoing commission intrusion in the local development regulatory process; also, by certification, double permitting is avoided. At the same time comprehensive substantive standards and programs limit ad hoc regulatory decision-making by local governments, and, to a lesser extent, by the Pinelands Commission.

Before arguing whether or not CMP substantive provisions and implementation mechanisms also provide an effective means of achieving protection of the Pinelands natural resources and cultural values while accommodating economic growth, we will examine in the next four chapters, six years of implementation experiences. A fifth chapter examines how well the plan has withstood legal and legislative challenges, and Chapter 12 then provides an overall assessment of the Pinelands program.

Making the Pinelands
Plan Work

PART III

7. Management of the Pinelands: An Intergovernmental Partnership

Beryl Robichaud Collins

Congress, when enacting the legislation that created the Pinelands National Reserve, called for a management program that "combines the capabilities and resources of the local, State and Federal governments . . . [and thus] provides an alternative to direct Federal acquisition and management." New Jersey legislators emphasized that the program was "to provide for the maximum feasible local government [and public] participation." The result is an intergovernmental sharing of responsibilities for implementing the Comprehensive Management Plan, with five levels of government participating in the partnership.

Municipalities and counties are given the opportunity to exercise primary responsibility for development regulation within the range of their normal jurisdictional authority. Various state agencies—the Department of Environmental Protection, in particular—have important assignments for implementation of specific programs in the Pinelands Comprehensive Management Plan, including, for example, enforcement of water and air quality programs and management of state-owned lands. The federal government participates in the intergovernmental partnership by virtue of its representation on the Pinelands Commission. Overall responsibility for assuring effective implementation of the Comprehensive Management Plan, however, is vested largely in the Pinelands Commission, the state-created regional agency that prepared the plan.

The Pinelands Commission acknowledges that ultimate success in protecting the Pinelands hinges on its ability to make this intergovernmental partnership work effectively, particularly on the local level. As Executive Director Terrence Moore puts it, "The key is acceptance and application of the CMP by local governments."[1] Winning cooperation from local and state governmental units, however, has been a slow process.

Municipal Role: Partnership through Conformance

In New Jersey, the primary responsibility for control of land-use activities is delegated by the legislature to municipal governments. Under the 1976 Municipal Land Use Law each of the state's 567 municipalities is required to adopt a master plan as a prerequisite to establishing zoning ordinances (NJSA 40:55 D–1 et seq.). The 1979 Pinelands Protection Act provides that a municipality having land in the Pinelands Area earns the right to exercise primary responsibility for development regulation within the area of its jurisdiction by revising its master plan and land use ordinances to make them consistent with the objectives and standards prescribed in the Pinelands CMP. Consistency is achieved through the conformance process. When a local government has satisfactorily completed the process, it is said to be "in conformance" and its master plan and ordinances are then "certified." No changes may be made in certified master plans or ordinances without the approval of the Pinelands Commission.

Believing that this conformance process could be completed within a time span of one year, state legislators ordered the commission to enforce the minimum standards of the management plan in those municipalities and counties whose master plans and ordinances were not certified by January 14, 1982 (one year after adoption of the CMP).

Initial Impediments to the Conformance Process.   The conformance process, however, turned out to be far more complex and time-consuming than had been originally anticipated: By the end of the first year of plan implementation, only three municipalities were in conformance. First among many reasons for the delay is that, although the Pinelands municipalities share the region's resources, each has its own individuality and presents a distinctive set of issues to the conformance process.

Mix of Pinelands Municipalities. Among the fifty-two municipalities that are managed under the provisions of the Comprehensive Management Plan is the largest township in the state—Hamilton, encompassing 113 square miles—and one of the smallest—Lakehurst, which is less than one square mile in area. (See Appendix Table A–2). On average, Pinelands municipalities are about forty-one square miles in size. Political boundaries, however, are not always coincident with those delineating the Pinelands Area. Only eleven municipalities lie wholly within the Pinelands Area (Figure 7–1). An additional twenty-four townships have more than 50 percent of their land in the Area, while some of the remaining municipalities include only small amounts of Pinelands land within their boundaries: One, Corbin City, includes only sixty-four acres of Pinelands and seven others have less than one square mile. Altogether, about 31 percent of the total land in the fifty-two Pinelands municipalities lies outside the boundaries of the state-designated Pinelands Area, although much of this land is included in the federally designated Pinelands National Reserve. Municipalities are not, however, required to have their

Figure 7–1. Political Jurisdictions in the Pinelands Area. The Pinelands Area encompasses all, or part, of fifty-two New Jersey municipalities and seven counties. Map by Tina Campbell.

development regulations for reserve acreage certified as consistent with the CMP; indeed, only three have done so at this writing.

Demographic characteristics of the Pinelands municipalities vary widely. According to 1980 census data, population densities per square mile ranged from a low of 8 people per square mile in Washington Township (the second largest township in the state and the least populated) to a high of 3,966 people per square mile in Medford Lakes Boro. In 1980, thirteen of the fifty-two Pinelands municipalities had fewer than one hundred people per square mile, and thirty-one were populated with fewer than two hundred per square mile. At the other extreme were several municipalities—Lakehurst, for example, which at the time that the CMP became effective had few vacant lots to be developed. A 1980 commission staff study classifies eleven of the fifty-two municipalities as almost fully developed, another fourteen were in the stage of being actively developed, thirteen more were in an early stage of development and the remaining fourteen municipalities had yet to experience significant development pressure.[2]

Some of the difficulties of the municipal conformance process could have been foretold by looking at studies of land-use controls in Pinelands municipalities made prior to preparation of the CMP. Master plans and ordinances often reflected "fiscal zoning," a common practice in New Jersey where property taxes are the major source of municipal revenue and zoning powers are frequently used to maximize tax revenues rather than to satisfy long-range planning goals.[3] For the most part, pre-CMP Pinelands zoning restricted residential development to detached single-family housing, often allowing these units to be built on small-sized lots (some less than one-quarter acre) even though sewers were not available. In one township, Beachwood Boro, subdivisions created lots as small as twenty feet by one hundred feet. Few local master plans gave any real consideration to conservation and resource protection issues or were even backed by adequate environmental data.[4] A Rutgers land-use specialist found that many of the pre-CMP Pinelands ordinances permitted "tremendous amounts" of potential residential and commercial development, and that there generally was a poor fit between the zoning ordinances of adjacent municipalities.[5] The sizable gap that remained between existing municipal land-use regulations and those that would be necessary if the Pinelands resources were to be protected had to be bridged by the conformance process.

Politics and Conformance. Local antagonisms against both the Pinelands Commission and the Comprehensive Management Plan were strong initial impediments to the conformance process. Officials of Atlantic, Cape May, and Ocean counties refused to conform with CMP regulations, and urged that their municipalities join the boycott. As Atlantic County Executive Charles Worthington said, "We must rise up and tell the administration this plan is not going to work and we want to see some changes made."[6]

Commission staff members worked hard to overcome the initial resistance of many local officials to meet for discussion of the conformance issues. Nevertheless, as a result of several political events, foot-dragging on conformance work continued for more than a year.

Shortly after the CMP became effective, influential Atlantic County Senator Steven Perskie announced his intention to introduce a bill that would greatly curtail the Pinelands Commission's authority in the Protection Area and thus reduce the need for municipalities to revise their existing ordinances (see Chapter 11). The threat of Perskie's action hung over the conformance process until July 1981, when Governor Brendan Byrne indicated his opposition to the bill; it then finally died in committee. But Democratic Governor Byrne's final term of office was about to expire, and attention quickly focused on the possibility that the Republican gubernatorial candidate, if elected, might be disposed to weaken the Pinelands Commission's authority. In November 1981, by a very slim margin, Republican Thomas Kean defeated South Jersey's James Florio, a champion of strong Pinelands protection. Unexpected support for Kean had come from the state's southern counties, especially Atlantic, and many believed that in partial payment of this debt to the politicians who had turned out the favorable vote, the new governor might support efforts to weaken the CMP. In March 1982 the New Jersey Conservation Foundation observed that these expectations were indeed having a negative effect on the conformance process: "Many towns seem to be slowing down their work in anticipation of a change in the rules. After all, why should they waste time and money on an effort which may prove useless?"[7] Only by mid-1982 did it become apparent that the new administration was not going to approve any drastic changes in the CMP regulations, and at about the same time, municipalities were faced with the penalty for nonconformance—loss of development approval authority. Together these events provided the stimulus needed to get the conformance process rolling.

Mechanics of the Conformance Process.   The Pinelands Commission organized itself for the conformance process by establishing a subcommittee to act as a liaison between the full commission, the commission staff, and municipal and county officials. Although the full commission retains sole authority to certify (with or without conditions) or to reject municipal and county master plans and ordinances that are inconsistent with the CMP, the Conformance Subcommittee serves as a sounding board and guide for commission staff members involved in the conformance process. The committee meets with municipal and county officials and their consultants to discuss and endorse policy strategies by which consistency with the CMP can be achieved, and it advises the full commission on certification actions. After master plans and ordinances are certified, the subcommittee evaluates whether or not any requested changes to certified ordinances are consistent with the CMP. Though the decision to establish the Conformance Subcommittee was not unanimous, in retrospect it has been an invaluable mechanism for facilitating the work of conformance.[8]

During the first five years of CMP implementation, commission staff work on conformance was delegated to three staff planners, all licensed by the state but young and relatively inexperienced. Each planner was assigned two or three of the Pinelands counties and given responsibility for shepherding through the certification process both the counties themselves and all municipalities within them. Staff resource scientists assisted the planners, and the commission's executive director and the two assistant directors, acting as a working committee, carefully guided the conformance work, and participated in the hundreds of meetings and hearings that were held with local officials. In late 1985, when only three counties and ten municipalities had yet to complete the conformance process, staff activities were reorganized. Conformance responsibilities are now vested in a newly established planning and research function reporting to one of the commission's two assistant directors.

Soon after the CMP took effect, the commission staff forwarded to each municipality and county a packet of materials to aid them in the conformance process. This packet included resource inventory data and maps, information about the type of revision that would have to be made in local master plans and ordinances, and an outline of the procedural steps in the conformance process. This packet was quickly followed by a series of workshops held by the staff for all municipalities in each county, and then by staff meetings with individual local governing bodies. The purpose was to review the CMP requirements and the procedural steps involved in conformance. The commission also retained the consulting firm that had previously played an important role in preparation of the CMP to draft sample ordinances and to review from a legal standpoint proposed ordinance changes in the context of the CMP requirements.

Within the municipalities, local political structures determine which of the various local officials—whether members of the governing body, the planning board, or an ad hoc committee—would act as liaison with the Pinelands staff. Usually the details of master plan and ordinance revisions have been worked out by planning and/or legal consultants engaged by the local government on a part-time basis. Often one consultant has served several municipalities in the Pinelands. Over a two-year period the legislature provided the commission with a budget of $600,000 to reimburse municipalities and counties for the costs of conformance work.

An additional $300,000 was requested in the third year, but subsequently was eliminated in a statewide cost-reduction program. There continues to be a sizable shortfall between the appropriated funds and actual costs of conformance work. The commission staff today believes that a larger appropriation (about $1.8 million) would have expedited the process.[9]

Overall, the mechanics of the conformance process as prescribed in the CMP are straightforward. A municipality or county revises its master plan and land-use ordinances to meet the objectives and minimum provisions of the CMP; it gains local approval of such changes; and then it submits the revised and approved master plan and ordinances to the executive director of the Pinelands Commission for certification. All of this was supposed to have been done within one year after adoption of the CMP. Within sixty days of receipt of a set of completed municipal conformance documents (within thirty days for county applications), the executive director holds a public hearing to consider the application for certification; following this hearing he makes a nonbinding recommendation for full certification, certification with conditions, or disapproval of the master plan and ordinances as submitted. The commission reviews the findings and recommendations of the executive director and issues the final order certifying, certifying with condition, or disapproving the master plan and land-use ordinances. If the master plan and/or ordinances are certified with conditions or disapproved, the commission must specify what changes are necessary to gain approval; municipalities and counties then have 120 days to modify their master plans or ordinances.

In practice, conformance turned out to be a three-step negotiating process: (1) gain agreement on the delineation of management area boundaries; (2) zone for permitted uses and residential densities; and (3) incorporate in ordinances the CMP standards, programs, and procedural elements. Significant issues raised in each step have tested the commission's promise to "allow municipalities the greatest degree of flexibility and discretion in the preparation of local plans and ordinances, so long as . . . [these] do not conflict with ultimate objectives and minimum requirements" of the plan.

CMP Management Area Boundary Issues. The Comprehensive Management Plan delineates on a map the boundaries for seven types of land-use areas—Preservation, Forest, Agricultural Production, Rural Development, Regional Growth, Military and Federal Installations, and Towns (see Chapter 6). The boundaries for an eighth category—Villages (communities smaller than towns and without public water and/or sewage facilities)—are not established in the CMP but are negotiated in the conformance process, as are designations of Special Agricultural Areas within the Preservation Area and Municipal Growth Reserves within the Rural Development Areas. To achieve certification a municipality must incorporate into its local master plan and ordinances the boundaries for any of the management areas that fall within its jurisdiction. The boundaries laid down in the CMP are drawn on the basis of knowledge about the regional distribution of natural resources and development patterns; however, they "may be refined and/or adjusted . . . provided that the commission determines that the goals and objectives of the Plan will be implemented by the proposed master plan or land use ordinance." To a municipality, the area delineations are critical because they control permitted uses of land and growth potential.

As a starting point for negotiation, simple adjustments are sometimes made so that boundary lines coincide with block or lot ownership patterns or with landscape features such as streams and roads. Such changes are now readily accepted by the commission, though in the early months of the conformance process they were less so.[10] For a number of municipalities (twelve in the first five years), certification was achieved with no further changes in management areas. This was not true, however, for the remaining townships, most of which had to deal with a complex of three or more Pinelands management area designations; ten include acreage in six or more of the CMP areas.

Designation of Village Boundaries. Negotiation of Village boundaries usually is the first real test of commission flexibility. The CMP classifies fifty-nine settlements within various Pinelands municipalities as being potential "Villages" and sets forth rules to restrict their future size. The most important of these rules is that the quantity of vacant land within the boundaries of a designated Village cannot be greater than the quantity of already developed land nor can it provide for more structures than exist at the time of designation. A supplemental guideline suggests that Village boundaries should encompass no more than one square mile. Many municipal officials have found it difficult within this restriction to provide adequate growth potential while still maintaining the "existing character" of the Village, another CMP objective. To accommodate a doubling of the number of dwelling units and yet retain the large lot sizes (often five acres)—a common Village characteristic—frequently requires more than one square mile. Taking perhaps an extreme position, Manchester Township officials initially proposed that the Village of Whiting should encompass eleven square miles; they finally won approval for a Village size of about seven square miles. Commission approvals of larger Village sizes as well as of several new Village designations, such as Jenkins in rural

Washington Township, have been of concern to environmentalists because more than half of the 25,000-plus acres (about forty square miles) of Village land designated by the end of 1986 has been carved out of the Preservation and Forest areas. The commission staff, however, is quick to point out that this allocation is not unreasonable, considering that the Preservation and Forest areas together make up 65 percent of the Pinelands Area. In addition, many Villages are considerably smaller than the one square mile limit—often because of environmental building restraints, such as the presence of wetlands, for example; moreover, not only is the average size of Villages (excluding Whiting) in the forty-two municipalities certified by the end of 1986 just under one square mile, but also the total number of Villages in these municipalities is less than anticipated in the CMP.

Infill Development Areas. An associated issue has been the designation of "infill" settlement zones in the Preservation Area, the boundaries of which are set by the Pinelands Preservation Act and cannot be altered in the conformance process. The concept of infill zones was developed as a commission response to complaints about the lack of adequate development opportunities in municipalities with large land holdings in the Preservation Area. Using this concept—subject to defined criteria and approval of the Commission—these municipalities may now designate nodes of settlement too small for even Village status as infill development areas within which vacant land may be developed. By the end of 1985 about 1,700 such infill development acres had been approved, providing potential for development of 120 homes and 20 commercial activities that could not have been permitted under the normal land-use regulations for the Preservation Area except by waiver. Although municipal officials have applauded this commission action as an opportunity for additional ratables, others have accused the commission of fostering "scattered and piecemeal development" through the infill development concept.[11]

Management Area Changes to Increase Growth Potential. The commission decided that it did not have authority to approve Corbin City's (Atlantic County) request to alter management area boundaries to exclude from the Pinelands Area its holding of sixty-four acres in the Forest Area. The commision has, however, been responsive to a number of other requests for changes in management area boundaries. A few of these have been settled by negotiating exchanges from one management area designation to another. Such exchanges of almost equal-sized land parcels do not significantly change the total acreage in a management area. Medford Lakes Boro, for example, switched the designation on golf course acreage classed as Regional Growth to Rural Development, and at the same time changed the designation on an equal acreage of sewered land from Rural Development to Regional Growth Area. In another variation of this, Monroe Township was permitted to reclassify a section of its Rural Development land as Regional Growth Area to allow extension of a sewer system that was needed to alleviate a particular septic problem; the municipality offset this reclassification by changing an equal acreage located in a river headwaters area from Rural Development to Forest.

Most requests for management area boundary changes arise because municipal officials find the permitted growth potential under a particular CMP management area delineation to be inadequate. The most frequent outcome of these municipal requests has been to increase Regional Growth Areas at the expense of Rural Development Areas—which, in turn, have been enlarged by reclassification of Agricultural Production or Forest acreage to Rural Development. By the end of 1986 six municipalities had received approvals to increase their Regional Growth Areas by more than 15 percent—Winslow, Waterford, and Monroe on the western edge of the Pinelands, Southampton in the northwest, and Jackson and Berkeley in the northeast. Officials of Franklin Township, adjacent to Monroe, convinced the commission that almost half of its wooded Agricultural Production Area would be more appropriately classed as Rural Development. Plumsted was able to transfer Forest Area land along a major highway to Rural Development, thus permitting a land use more compatible with the use of the non-Pinelands Area land across the road. Although several Burlington County townships did increase their Agricultural Production land, the total acreage in this management class has dropped by about 6 percent since 1980; this may be attributed in great part to the reclassification of more than 3,500 acres of Hammonton farmland as Town Area. Overall the Forest Area has had an even a greater reduction (8 percent), but most of the decrease represents acreage incorporated into Villages or designated as Agricultural Production. Attempts to reclassify one large tract of Forest Area for higher intensity use in Ocean County's Berkeley Township brought a storm of protest from environmental groups, and the failure of the attempt produced a deep rift between county planning officials and the Pinelands Commission staff.

For two decades prior to the implementation of the Comprehensive Management Plan, Berkeley Township, in the northeast of the Pinelands, has been one of the focal points of Ocean's County's boom in retirement communities. That portion of Berkeley (38 percent) included in the Pinelands Area, however, is relatively undeveloped and is, therefore, classed for the most part as Forest land. Not only does this part of Berkeley Township serve as an important ecological buffer between heavily settled areas to the north and the Preservation Area to the south, but also it encompasses several undisturbed watersheds and habitats for two threatened snake species. Ocean County planning officials, however, saw the Berkeley Pinelands Area as the logical location for potential growth, and so suggested the reclassification of 4,000 acres of Forest and Rural Development land to Regional Growth. Berkeley Township officials, seeking more ratables in the form of senior citizen housing, favored the county's proposal and delayed their application for certification until it could be considered.

The Ocean County proposal caused such an uproar among environmental groups that the federal representative on the commission requested a legal opinion as to whether or not the proposed reclassification of land would be considered a modification of the CMP, and thus require approval by the Secretary of the Interior. The answer was that a change of the magnitude proposed would indeed represent an amendment to the plan. It took two years of negotiation before Berkeley municipal officials and the commission could agree on a compromise, which in the end pleased neither the Ocean County planners nor the environmentalists. As a result of this compromise Berkeley's certified ordinances provide development opportunity for 3,425 more dwelling units (5,138 if Pinelands Development Credits are used) than had been allocated in the CMP. (This figure includes 1,411 dwelling units granted on a waiver independent of the management change.) This additional development is to be accommodated by reclassifying Forest and Rural Development land in order to create a Regional Growth Area of 687 acres and a Rural Development Municipal Reserve of 283 acres. Although the county planners agreed to the number of dwelling units worked out in the compromise, they wanted the development to extend over several hundred more acres. When commission Executive Director Terrence Moore suggested that the county wanted the larger development area so builders would help pay for the construction of a much needed road extension, Ocean County Planner Stephen Pollack denied the charges and bitterly accused Moore of negotiating in bad faith.[12]

The Berkeley compromise reduces the municipality's Forest Area by more than 10 percent. This reduction, together with commission approval of several development projects in the vicinity, led one environmentalist to accuse the commission of "failing to assure adequate protection for the Pine Barrens . . . [and] acting beyond any reason expected from the CMP or the federal and state legislation."[13] Several Sierra Club members requested the governor to veto the commission's certification action. When the governor failed to respond to this request, these individuals filed suit against the commission in the Appellate Court in early 1986. In December 1986 the Court ruled that the Pinelands Commission should not have reclassified the Berkeley Forest Area without proceeding through the formal process to amend the boundaries in the CMP. In its January 1987 meeting, the commission voted not to appeal the court decision, making it necessary to renegotiate the management area boundaries with Berkeley Township.[14]

Management Area Changes to Decrease Growth Potential. Equally controversial was the commission's flexibility toward management area boundary changes in Hamilton Township. In this situation, the building industry was first a supporter and then an opponent of the commission. Hamilton is not only the largest municipality in the Pinelands Area, but in 1981 it also encompassed almost 17 percent of the original CMP Regional Growth Area. Another 15,500 acres in the township was initially classed as Rural Development land. Clearly, the CMP had pinpointed Hamilton, as well as neighboring Egg Harbor Township, as the key areas to accommodate much of the housing demand created by the casino-hotel growth in nearby Atlantic City. As such, both municipalities are also important large potential receivers of Pinelands development credits (PDCs).

Initially, Hamilton Township officials criticized the CMP because it did not allow enough growth potential, but a new municipal administration took a different stance, strongly opposing the development that the CMP would have imposed on the township. At the time (1980) Hamilton had in its entire 113 square miles a total population of under 10,000, with only about 3,500 housing units. The CMP, however, would have allowed at least 15,000 more residences to be built (22,500 residences with the use of PDCs), yielding a population increase of about 50,000 in the Regional Growth Area alone. The newly elected township officials wanted a cutback in the allowed density assigned to Hamilton, claiming that the demand for housing growth "is not progressing as fast as anticipated" by the CMP.[15]

Pressed by the building industry, which was desirous of more opportunity for development, and by agricultural interests and supporters of the plan who saw the need for a more active market for PDCs, the commission was eager to complete Hamilton's conformance process.[16] The commission therefore engaged a consultant who, through the use of computer modelling, tested alternative ordinances within a context of the CMP's growth potential goals. But the Hamilton conformance process remained stalemated until the fall of 1984, when the penalty for nonconformance became objectionable enough to stimulate the township to seek a way to gain certification.

To get negotiations restarted, Hamilton officials and the Pinelands Commission agreed to charge two individuals, Peter Karabashian (Hamilton Township's planner) and John Stokes (the assistant director of the commission), with the responsibility for coming up with a joint recommendation for achieving conformance. If these two could not agree on a particular issue, that issue was to be referred for arbitration to another consultant, selected by both parties. This, however, was never necessary and the team developed recommendations that, after lengthy discussions, were approved by the township; the master plan and ordinances of Hamilton were fully certified in March 1985. During the negotiation, the commission agreed to downzone 2,514 acres of unsewered Regional Growth land, reclassifying it as a Municipal Reserve district within a Rural Development Area. This reclassification reduced the potential number of new development units in the Regional Growth Area to about 11,590 (17,385 with PDCs). Moreover, according to the agreement, heavy development would be withheld in the Reserve Growth district until 1991, at which time the area will automatically be treated as Regional Growth unless the township gains commission approval to delay the growth designation.

Representatives of the building industry and several developers objected strenuously to some of the development standards worked out in the compromise, accusing the commission of "making a deal with Hamilton behind closed doors" and charging that the new ordinances were "unworkable."[17] In designing its now-certified ordinances Hamilton officials attempted to retain as far as possible the pattern of single-family detached housing that characterizes the township by specifying minimums for housing types and mix in each of the zoning districts. Developers charged that the requirements for wetland buffers and minimum percentages for single-family housing barred them from achieving the zoning potential, particularly where the needs for low- and moderate-cost housing also had to be satisfied. Failing to convince the commission that the Hamilton ordinances should not be certified, developers filed suit against both the township and the commission. Subsequently Hamilton, with the approval of the commission, revised its ordinances making more specific the forms of relief that the planning board can grant developers when requirements for wetland buffers and minimums for housing types do not permit them to achieve the assigned densities for Planned Unit Residential Development. Developers today, however, remain skeptical about ever achieving the development potential that is authorized by the certified ordinances.

Zoning Issues: Permitted Uses and Densities.   Agreement on management area boundaries provides the basis for the next step in conformance—the definition of permitted uses and the development of density standards within zoning districts in each management area. To do this, local officials use a formula established in the Comprehensive Management Plan to translate the number of privately owned, undeveloped, upland acres in the Rural Development and Forest areas into the maximum allowable number of new dwelling units for these areas, and to translate the number of undeveloped acres in the Regional Growth Areas into a minimum number of new dwelling units (see Chapter 6). Then they designate where and how this new development should be accommodated, using as their guide CMP provisions covering permitted and optional uses, minimum lot sizes, environmental standards, and use of PDCs for bonus density. Finally, within each management area, they establish zoning districts to group permitted uses and densities that are consistent with existing patterns of development and local planning objectives.

In this phase of the conformance negotiation, the Pinelands Commission has exhibited a great deal of flexibility on a variety of matters. There has been negotiation, for example, of the total number of residential units permitted in the Protection Areas, usually ending with modest increases in density. The requirement to provide for the use of PDCs in each Regional Growth Area has been waived in instances where there are so few lots available for development that use of the bonus density system would be an "overkill."[18] Several municipalities have been permitted to recognize existing development patterns by creating commercial zones within the Preservation and Forest areas, and some others have been allowed to provide for agricultural-related housing in the Preservation Special Agriculture Area, not a permitted use under the CMP. On the other hand, Hamilton Township has not been allowed to designate an Adult Bookstore District in its Forest Area nor has Ocean Township been permitted to site a landfill on Forest acreage. Except for grandfathered exemptions (see below), nonagricultural housing has not been permitted in Agricultural Production Areas, though this use was strongly pressed by agricultural interests. (A pending CMP amendment will change this policy.)

Various clustering options have been proposed by municipalities with land in Rural Development and Forest areas, and generally the commission has allowed the clustering of units on undersized lots, if the density requirements on the total parcel are not exceeded. In the Rural Development Areas objections to clustering on lots as small as one acre have not been raised. In the Forest Area, however, environmentalists (in their effort to protect water quality) have vigorously opposed reductions in the minimum lot size to less than 3.2 acres. On the other hand, environmentalists have raised no challenge to the use of clustering on smaller lots in a Forest Area to protect the ecologically valuable Pine Plains.

A number of municipalities have objected to CMP provisions granting certain exemptions to the density limitations—notably the substandard, grandfathered lot exemption and the so-called cultural, or "Piney," exemption (see Chapter 6). Estell Manor City officials, for example, have reported that a great deal of hostility toward the Pinelands Commission came from owners of substandard lots who wanted to sell their lots rather than develop them for their own use.[19] In this case local officials agreed with the owners; moreover, they also wanted no part of the Piney exemption provision, which they declared was discriminatory and unconstitutional. The issue was resolved when the local officials identified each substandard lot, and reduced the total management area density by the substandard lot count, thus permitting these lots to be developed without regard for previous ownership and without exceeding the CMP's allowed density. Several municipalities copied Estell Manor's handling of these exemption provisions, while commission officials did not require municipalities to adopt the Piney exemption provision.

Performance Standards, Programs, and Procedural Elements. The final step toward conformance is acceptance of the CMP performance standards and programs dealing with environmental, scenic, social, and cultural issues. The commission and the municipality must also agree on procedural mechanisms covering development review and ordinance amendment.

Water quality standards and wetland buffers have been the chief environmental issues during the conformance process. Four municipalities, for example, all served by the same planner, were unable to get commission approval for ordinances that failed to recognize the two parts per million nitrate-nitrogen standard and the need for septic system maintenance and testing. The commission has been more flexible about modifications of the 300-foot wetland buffer provision and has approved in several townships the establishment of reduced buffers on the basis of existing patterns of development and the inferior quality of the wetlands.

Certification of Stafford Township's ordinances was delayed by the sign provision of the CMP's scenic program, which calls for all nonconforming signs to be removed by 1991. Stafford's Mayor Wesley K. Block, who also owned the Wes Outdoor Advertising Company, charged that the CMP sign provisions were "unconstitutional."[20] After months of dispute, Stafford municipal officials, with the mayor as the lone dissenter, finally voted to comply with the commission's sign requirements. In subsequent legal suits, the courts have upheld the sign provisions.

The CMP housing program also created problems, because state policies concerning municipal obligations to provide affordable housing have changed several times since implementation of the CMP began. In January 1983, the New Jersey Supreme Court handed down its famed Mount Laurel II decision, which sets forth policies by which present and prospective low- and moderate-income housing needs in New Jersey are to be met.[21] Acting on advice from the attorney general, the commission amended the original housing proram in the CMP, which had requirements for low-, moderate-, and middle-income housing. The revised program requires that residential development projects of twenty-five or more dwelling units in Regional Growth Areas provide at least 10 percent of the units to meet low-income housing needs and another 10 percent for moderate-income households. An exception to this requirement was granted to Tabernacle, a township that did not have a sewered Regional Growth Area. Here the high-density requirement was coupled to sewered development. In mid-1985 the state legislature enacted the Fair Housing Act, which required Pinelands municipalities to accommodate in growth areas their "fair shares" of regional affordable housing needs.

Usually the last subjects for negotiation are the procedures for development review and for amendment of certified ordinances. To some, these procedural steps appear less important than the discussions of particular programs and standards; however, as one commission planner explained, this work can still be critical, since "it is done at a stage when hard feelings can easily develop because . . . [municipal officials] have gone through tough decisions and now trivial, tedious points must be worked on."[22] The commission has shown some flexibility in this phase of the work when responding to complaints about the cumbersome procedure for development review. It has agreed, for example, to a simplification of the process by "duplicate filing" of development applications. (See Chapter 8 for a description of the duplicate filing process.)

Certification of Revised Plans and Ordinances. After negotiation, ordinances are rewritten to include the myriad changes that have been worked out to gain consistency with the Comprehensive Management Plan. The sample ordinances prepared by the commission's consultant turned out to be of no help here, because each municipality's needs are different. Some townships that have land both within and without the Pinelands Area elect to have separate codes for the CMP regulations, while others integrate the CMP regulations directly into their ordinances.

On balance, municipalities with unified ordinances combining zoning districts, development standards, and procedural requirements into a single ordinance have had a less complicated task than those townships having multiple ordinance articles.

Revised ordinances must gain local approval before being submitted to the commission, and this often takes much longer than expected. Moreover, sometimes the commission staff does not see the ordinances in their final form before they are introduced locally; then later they find technical misinterpretations or oversights in the locally approved documents, which, though usually of minor nature, have to be corrected and reapproved. More often, administrative slipups cause delay. Witness the events in one municipality: In November 1982 the township adopted ordinances that qualified it for certification; in December the township clerk realized that the planning board had inadvertently neglected to adopt formally the parallel revisions to the master plan; then because of a lack of a quorum or improper public notification, the township's planning board could not act again until April 1983, at which time it duly adopted all the necessary amendments even though somewhat behind schedule.[23]

Amendment of Certified Ordinances. A certified municipality may not effect changes in its ordinances without approval by the Pinelands Commission. The process calls for the commission's executive director to review each proposed ordinance change and to determine whether or not it raises a substantial issue with respect to conformance with the Comprehensive Master Plan. If it does not, no further commission action is necessary. If the director does determine that a substantial issue is raised, the ordinance amendment is passed on to the full commission for its approval or denial. In practice, all proposals for changes in management area boundaries are classed as substantial issues.

In the first six years of plan implementation, most requests for ordinance amendment did not raise substantial issues; many have been introduced only to correct oversights in the original certified ordinances. Other minor changes have altered permitted uses in a management area. Chesilhurst, for example, added acid manufacturing as a prohibited use in its commercial area. Several townships have strengthened ordinances to provide stronger enforcement of the forestry provisions. Municipalities have sought only minor adjustments in certified management area boundaries; for example, Winslow petitioned successfully to change eight acres classed as Agricultural Production land to Village and to redesignate nine Village acres as Agricultural land.

Penalties For Nonconformance.   In January 1982, the penalty for non-conformance (loss of development review authority) came into play. The commission, however, delayed imposition of this penalty for up to six months for those municipalities that were showing progress on conformance. In nonconforming municipalities, individuals seeking approval for development projects had to receive a Pinelands Development Approval from the Pinelands Commission before applying for local approvals. Municipal authorities cannot approve development that the commission has denied, or deny on the basis of CMP standards a project that has been approved by the commission. Though the procedure for handling development review in uncertified municipalities was changed in late 1985 to permit a municipality to conduct an initial review of development applications, final authority for approval or denial of development applications in nonconforming towns remains in the hands of the commission. (See Chapter 8 for a full description of the development review and approval process.)

Commission review of development applications from nonconforming municipalities is done without the benefits that come from conformance negotiation. Acceptability of development is judged solely within the context of the management areas as delineated in the CMP and without designation of either Village areas or other boundary modifications. CMP minimum standards for permitted uses and allotted densities are the guides, with no consideration given to possible zoning districts within management areas. Thus, standards are applied in each area without regard for existing differentiation of residential, commercial, and industrial patterns of use. The result is that the commission has denied some projects that would have been approved had the municipality been in conformance, and has approved projects that would have been denied by the municipality. For example, the commission staff could not approve construction of a single-family dwelling on a ten-acre site in Lacey Township, although it acknowledged that the project would very likely have been permitted if Lacey Township had been in conformance. The denial decision stemmed from the site's location in the Forest Area, where the CMP calls for a minimum fifteen-acre lot size. If Lacey had been certified, the proposed development site would probably have been included in a Village where zoning would have permitted construction on a less than ten-acre lot. In another case, the commission was required by CMP regulations to approve a request for a garbage transfer station in a residential area, because such development is a permitted use in a Regional Growth Management Area, the location of the project; however, if the municipality had been in conformance, this use probably would not have been permitted in a residential section of the Growth Area. Commission actions such as these caused a bitter conflict over the rights of uncertified municipalities, which came to a head in 1984.

Rights of Uncertified Municipalities. In 1983 Egg Harbor Township appealed to the Office of Administrative Law (OAL) for reconsideration of two Pinelands development approvals that permitted storage trailers on private property and for reconsideration of a Letter of Interpretation that stated that a nursing home was a permitted use in a Regional Growth Area, the intended location of the project. In its appeal Egg Harbor held that it sought "to protect what it believes is its right to impose its own land use standards in addition to the minimum requirements used by the commission."[24] The administrative law judge disagreed with Egg Harbor and ruled that if a municipality chooses not to go through the conformance process, it loses the right to approve applications for development, unless it is considering regulations not included in the CMP. Despite this decision, Egg Harbor (as well as Hamilton Township, where development activity was also high) continued to appeal commission approvals of development projects within its borders.

By the spring of 1984 more than thirty appeals of commission actions on development in uncertified municipalities had been filed, and representatives of the building industry several times complained at commission meetings that these appeals were delaying approved development projects for three to six months, thus adding significant costs to the projects. They requested that the commission "take the position" that an uncertified municipality has "no status" to challenge a Pinelands Development Approval. The commission's executive director also objected to the appeals, since they tied up his staff with preparing defenses. In April 1984, after a very hot debate, the commission voted 11 to 3 to pass Resolution 84–20, stating that the appeal actions were "thwarting the goals of the Pinelands Protection Act and the CMP." The three dissenting commissioners represented the uncertified counties—Atlantic, Cape May, and Ocean.

The passage of Resolution 84–20 caused an uproar. Even the *New York Times* (April 13, 1984) carried a headline reading "Appeals Ban Angers Pinelands Towns." The article quoted powerful state Senator William L. Gormley (R–Absecon) as saying, "The commission's barring the right to appeal is very inappropriate, and I am reviewing several alternatives to have it set aside." Officials of the three municipalities most affected by the ruling—Egg Harbor, Galloway, and Hamilton townships—sent a mailgram to Governor Thomas Kean calling the Pinelands resolution "undemocratic and unAmerican."[25] The criticisms carried weight with the governor, who at the time was planning a second-term race and needed support from South Jersey. Word was passed from the governor's office to the commission that unless it modified its action, gubernatorial veto authority (never before exercised) might be used to nullify Resolution 84–20.

At its next meeting, the commission qualified its previous action by passing another resolution (84–32) requesting the OAL to conduct a quasi-judicial investigation on past appeals from uncertified municipalities to determine if these had raised valid and substantive issues and to make recommendations about how future requests for reconsideration should be handled.

The OAL accepted the request and did review the appeals. As a result of this review, the administrative law judge (ALJ) agreed with representatives of the New Jersey Builders Association that the effect of twenty-seven appeals was "largely to delay the builder from beginning construction, with all of the financial and practical difficulties that attend such delay" and that there were no "reasonably supported arguments" made by the municipalities for modification of the staff approvals.[26] Although the ALJ finding was subsequently appealed to the Appellate Court, which decided in favor of the uncertified townships, the issue more or less disappeared when Hamilton Township became certified and when the commission revised its development review procedures to permit uncertified municipalities to conduct an initial review of development projects (see Chapter 8).

Other Incentives for Conformance. Two legislative actions have provided additional stimulus for local governments to seek Pinelands Commission certification. The Pinelands Municipal Property Tax Stabilization Act, which took effect in January 1984, provides state payments to offset municipal losses of revenue caused by lowered assessments on vacant land; municipalities that have not conformed, however, are not eligible to receive payments. In November 1985, Mayor Waskovich of Lacey Township (Ocean County) after three years of rebellion against the commission announced:

> The Township can no longer afford to defy the state because of thousands of dollars it may be losing in funding. . . . I think we're fighting a losing battle . . . and its time we sit down and talk to them [Pinelands Commission] to see if the mutual differences can be resolved.[27]

Further incentive came in 1985 when New Jersey voters approved a $30 million bond fund for infrastructure improvement in the Pinelands growth areas with a condition that funding be limited to projects located in certified municipalities and counties.

This mix of incentives stimulated nonconforming municipalities to seek certification. By the sixth anniversary of the plan (January 14, 1987) only eight of the fifty-two municipalities remained uncertified, and all these were actively meeting with the commission staff to identify revisions in local master plans and ordinances necessary to gain certification.

Outcomes of Municipal Conformance. Compared with other regional agencies that require or encourage local governments to bring their zoning regulations into conformity with regional programs, the Pinelands Commission has been extraordinarily successful. In seven years the Adirondack Park Agency certified only seven out of one hundred seven local government plans and in five years the California Coast Commission gained conformance of only one of sixty-eight local plans.[28] The numbers themselves are important because the conformance decreases the development review workload. Success, however, cannot be measured in numbers alone. There are at least two other considerations—the extent to which certified plans and ordinances reflect the goals of the CMP, and the acceptance by municipal officials of both the CMP and the Pinelands Commission.

Substantive Changes Resulting from Conformance. Environmentalists have argued that the concessions made during the conformance process have weakened the Comprehensive Management Plan to the extent that it may not "fulfill the legislative mandate to protect, preserve and enhance the Pinelands."[29] Without question, the conformance negotiations described above have increased development opportunities on the western and northeastern fringes of the Pinelands Area and have allowed more potential for growth in the Preservation Area. On the other hand, the growth potential for the areas bordering Atlantic City has been tempered. Overall, changes in management area boundaries (see Table 7–1) and in permitted uses and allotted densities appear to favor more development; but quantification of how much of this development will actually occur is difficult and therefore a precise description of how development will impact the Pinelands resources is not possible. Estimates of growth under the original CMP provisions included consideration of the entire Pinelands National Reserve, including the 221,000 acres not under the jurisdiction of the Pinelands Commission, most of which is not being brought into conformance. The commission staff feels that with the growth potential that exists in noncertified Pinelands and Reserve Areas, the total housing potential is about the same as originally estimated but the ratio of zoning

Table 7–1. Changes in Management Areas Made During Conformance, January 14, 1981, to January 14, 1987

Management Area	Under CMP	Certified Municipalities[a]	Not Change
Preservation Area			
Special Agricultural	0	35,333	+35,333
Infill Development	0	1,665	+ 1,665
Pinelands Villages	0	4,402	+ 4,402
All Other	337,554	295,929	−41,625
Total	337,554	337,329	− 225[b]
Protection Area			
Forest	284,501	264,790	−19,711
Agricultural Production	78,870	74,170	− 4,700
Rural Development	126,056	116,769	− 9,287
Regional Growth	75,546	81,686	+ 6,140
Pinelands Towns	12,116	16,536	+ 4,420
Military & Federal	46,331	46,286	− 45
Pinelands Villages	0	23,408	+23,408
Total	623,420	623,645	+ 225[b]
Total Pinelands Area	960,974	960,974	0

Source: Data compiled from Pinelands Commission conformance records, 14 January 1987.

[a] Figures include changes made in forty-four municipalities certified as of 14 January, 1987. Uncertified municipalities are included as unchanged from CMP allocations.

[b] A total of 225 acres classed as Preservation Area was certified as Agricultural Production land.

capacity for PDCs to allocated credits has decreased from 2.3:1 to 2:1, reflecting a reduced market potential for PDCs. Chapter 12 discusses the lack of adequate scientific data to assess the aggregate ecological impact of increases in development permitted by conformance changes or permit waivers.

Although Executive Director Moore is surprised that municipalities have not asked for more changes in management areas, he believes that the changes that have been negotiated during the conformance process will provide a plan for the protection of the Pinelands that is much more workable than the CMP before certification.[30] Planners agree that municipal planning activities have benefited from participation in the conformance process. Adequate resource data are now available for land-use decision-making, and the negotiating process itself has reoriented local planning perspectives to longer-range objectives (so-called "growth management") and to various regional considerations, especially those involving solid-waste management issues, infrastructure plans, and water supplies. Even Hamilton Township officials admit that the growth imposed on them by the CMP, which they thought too much, is no larger than what would have been permitted by their pre-CMP ordinances.

Municipalities that want to protect their critical resources or rural environments appreciate the support offered by the CMP. Evesham's mayor, for example, considers the CMP regulations "a special asset [allowing the township] to preserve open space areas of great beauty."[31] Nevertheless, the reality is that municipalities have lost much of their local autonomy over land-use regulations. As one major said in a statewide planning conference: "We have lost control of our own destiny, and reorienting ourselves to accept this is difficult."[32]

Attitudinal Changes Resulting from Conformance. At the conclusion of a conformance negotiation process it has not been unusual for township representatives to express their appreciation for the commission's and the staff's flexibility and helpfulness in solving the issues faced by the municipality. In fact, the Conformance Subcommittee meetings with municipal officials for the most part have been conducted in a very congenial atmosphere in which commission members have conveyed a real interest in reaching satisfactory solutions. To many, the Pinelands Commission and the Comprehensive Management Plan turned out to be not quite so bad as expected. As the Washington Township engineer put it,

> Our initial reaction to the Pinelands legislation and the CMP was volcanic . . . and as a municipal planner and engineer for a good number of years, I admit to being pleasantly surprised by the efforts of the Pinelands Commission staff in truly taking an interest in the welfare and needs of a community, listening to our concerns and working together to develop two fine land use documents that will guide the Township in its future development.[33]

Of course, not all municipalities came out of conformance with the same attitude. Officials of several townships submitted requests for certification with statements of objections. For example, Upper Township (Cape May County) said:

> The Planning Board was applying for certification under protest because township officials felt that the Pinelands plan represented (a) an action of northern New Jersey to protect the groundwater for its own use in the future, (b) an opportunity for politicians to lower the value of land by regulation and then "grab" the land for their own gain and (c) an action that prevented mainland landowners from

capitalizing on profits from speculation on their land as had beach owners.[34]

The fact that only three municipalities have voluntarily elected to seek certification for non-Pinelands Area acreage in the National Reserve indicates a less-than-complete acceptance of the CMP land-use regulations. Several townships, however, have adopted various CMP standards for use in that part of the reserve outside commission jurisdiction. On balance, the process of conformance negotiation seems to have defused much of the initial, intense hostility directed toward the commission and the CMP. The remark by Hamilton Township's planning board chairman after a bitter conformance conflict sums up both the process and its outcomes: "I honestly think it is a true compromise. Both sides gave."[35]

Public Involvement in Conformance.   There has been little public involvement in the conformance process as compared with public participation in the planning period. Conformance Subcommittee meetings are held during the daytime, on weekdays, sometimes as often as three times a month. Few members of the public attend these meetings, although one regular attendee since the initial meeting has been the Pinelands coordinator for the New Jersey Conservation Foundation, Michele Byers. Byers alerts representatives of other environmental groups to particular issues that deserve their attention or possible defensive action. Her help was especially useful during the Ocean County and Berkeley Township negotiations. Representatives of the building industry have also shown interest in conformance meetings, primarily those on Hamilton Township. Hearings held by local officials and by the commission's executive director offer other opportunities for public participation in the process, but most of these, too, have been sparsely attended. Of the few questions that have been raised in the hearings, most concern the permitted uses of a particular land parcel, usually one owned by the questioner.

Environmental groups have had little success in persuading municipal officials to get on with conformance; instead, their influence has come largely through the commission itself. Spokesmen for the New Jersey Conservation Foundation, the Pine Barrens Coalition, the Environmental Defense Fund, and the Sierra Club have all helped make commission members aware of the environmental consequences of their decisions and of any strong public reactions to these. Building interests and developers, on the other hand, appear to be a much more powerful influence at the local level. Often, municipal officials (and state legislators) who serve on a part-time, paid or unpaid, basis are concurrently engaged in some phase of land speculation or development activities.

County Role in the Management Partnership

In New Jersey, counties play only a minor role in land-use regulation, their authority being limited to approval of subdivision and site plans for traffic impacts on county roads and drainage impacts on county facilities. New Jersey's County and Regional Planning Act permits wide latitude in county master plans; thus counties may choose from a range of planning structures and staff support services. A few counties operate without any planning staffs (for example, Burlington and Camden counties), while others have large active staffs that develop countywide land-use plans (for example, Ocean County). Under the Comprehensive Management Plan, Pinelands counties, like municipalities, gain the right to exercise their authorized responsibilities for development regulation by bringing their master plans and supporting land-use programs and development review regulations into conformance with the CMP.

Of the seven counties with land in the Pinelands Area, three account for 82 percent of its total area. Burlington County, with 84 percent of its land in the Pinelands, has the largest share, almost one-third of the total. Atlantic and Ocean counties each accounts for about one-fifth of the Pinelands Area; of the remaining four counties—Camden, Cape May, Cumberland, and Gloucester—each has less than a 6 percent share. Although all seven counties are considerably less densely populated than the rest of the state, in the 1960s Ocean County became the fastest-growing county in the state, while Atlantic County now faces a potentially large future-growth associated with casino development. Interpretation of population trends for both of these counties has created major issues in the conformance process.

County Conformance Process. The county conformance process is less complicated than the municipal process. Generally, it means only ensuring that the standards and procedures for development review, solid-waste management, and capital improvements programs are consistent with those in the Comprehensive Management Plan. If a county has a master land-use plan, it also means ensuring that county land-use designations are consistent with uses in the CMP management areas. Counties, therefore, may vary in the type of documentation presented and in the scope of their conformance negotiations.

Backed by strong support from their representatives serving on the Pinelands Commission, the counties of Burlington, Camden, and Gloucester were certified by the end of 1982, and Cumberland, in early 1983. Atlantic, Cape May, and Ocean counties at the outset of the process announced a boycott of conformance, and by mid-1987, only Ocean County had been certified.

Uncertified counties cannot take actions on development applications that are inconsistent with either the ordinances of certified county municipalities or with the CMP itself. For example, subdivision drainage must be considered within the context of CMP provisions rather than according to existing county standards, because drainage is an issue in the CMP. Items not covered by the CMP, however, such as traffic impact, remain a county review function. Although forfeiture of county review authority by nonconformance actually has slight effect on the regulation of development, the failure of remaining counties to gain certification has been an irritant to the commission, as county officials continue to pass along to state legislators and the governor their discontent with the Pinelands legislation and the CMP. Also, votes by individual county representatives on the Pinelands Commission on broad issues have sometimes been influenced by county positions on narrower conformance issues.[36]

Issues of County Nonconformance.   Generally, county opposition to conformance may well be the result, at least partly, of natural resistance by (local) county planning staffs to the perceived invasion of their "turf" by the (regional) Pinelands Commission. Other reasons for county noncompliance, however, result from specific, individual situations.

Atlantic County's posture on nonconformance up to 1984, for example, was set by its powerful county executive, Charles Worthington, who, according to press reports, was speculating in Pinelands land at the time he was condemning the CMP.[37] In 1980 the county spent $30,000 in public money to fight the Pinelands legislation and the CMP, and Worthington vociferously opposed actions by the county's municipalities to seek certification. Richard Squires, Worthington's successor, tempered the county's position, and a spokesman for his administration announced in late 1985 that the county would seek approval of its master plan—an action triggered by approval of the Pinelands Infrastructure Bond Fund. The obstacles to be overcome in Atlantic County's conformance negotiations were few in number, but included a need to agree on the extent to which a high-technology area near the Atlantic City airport can be expanded.

The conditioned eligibility for infrastructure funding also led Ocean County planners to reopen their conformance negotiations with the commission in early 1986, after an almost three-year break over the question of permitted growth in Berkeley Township (discussed earlier under the municipal conformance process). The commission had refused to certify the county master plan in 1983, because it called for more growth in western Berkeley than the CMP permitted. Also needing resolution was the issue of further development of the county's airpark in Berkeley and its adjoining industrial park. Both issues were resolved in 1987.

As of early 1987 Cape May, the southernmost county in the state, had still not reopened conformance negotiations; it probably will be the last county to conform, even though its three Pinelands municipalities already have been certified. The resentment of the planning board toward the intrusion of a regional agency seems stronger here than anywhere else, and because there are no Growth Areas in the county the infrastructure bond fund offers no incentive for compliance. In early 1982 the county submitted its existing master plan and land-development regulations to the commission, even though county officials knew that these did not comply with CMP guidelines, particularly with respect to water quality and drainage standards. The commission gave Cape May a conditional certification, but by a 5 to 4 vote the county planning board decided not to comply with the conditions; no further negotiations have occurred.

State Role in the Management Partnership

Although local governments are more important in the continuing management of the Pinelands than are the state agencies, the state nevertheless does have several significant functions. Most of these state responsibilities for implementation of the Comprehensive Management Plan rest with the Department of Environmental Protection.

DEP's Managerial Role. Through its various operating divisions, DEP exercises authority in four areas of prime concern to the Pinelands Commission:

> First, as part of its statewide authority, DEP establishes regulations and administers regulatory programs covering Pinelands water quality, air quality, and the handling of solid and hazardous wastes;
>
> Second, acting as steward of all state parks, forests and wildlife areas, DEP establishes programs for resource management and recreational use for the more than 275,000 acres of state-owned lands in the Pinelands;
>
> Third, DEP acts as the purchasing agent for acquisition of Pinelands land; and

Fourth, DEP regulates development in the Pinelands coastal area—212,000 acres of the National Reserve not under the authority of the Pinelands Commission;

At the present time, lack of effective coordination between DEP and the Pinelands Commission weakens the intergovernmental partnership. One reason for this lack undoubtedly stems from turf rivalry. DEP sees itself as the protector of New Jersey's total environment, including the Pinelands. The Pinelands Commission, though administratively classified as being within DEP, is completely independent of DEP's authority, and attempts to enforce in the Pinelands environmental standards (water quality, for example) that are more restrictive than those promulgated for the rest of the state.

The friction between these two bodies has led to many problems. State regulations and permits inconsistent with CMP standards have been issued by DEP's Division of Water Resources (DWR) without consultation with the Pinelands Commission. Getting DWR to recognize and effectively enforce the stricter CMP water-quality programs and standards has been a slow process (see Chapter 8). Managers in the Division of Parks and Forestry have proposed recreational and resource management plans for state-owned land in the Pinelands that are in violation of CMP provisions, and Green Acres' execution time on land acquisition proposals has appeared unjustifiably long (see Chapter 9). Lack of effective cooperative effort between the Pinelands Commission staff and DEP's Division of Coastal Resources (DCR) has permitted development inconsistent with the CMP in the 212,000 coastal acres of the National Reserve that are not under the jurisdiction of the Pinelands Commission. This action appears to violate the Pinelands Protection Act, which calls for the Division of Coastal Resources, in consultation with the Pinelands Commission, to "review the environmental design for the coastal area which is also within the boundaries of the Pinelands National Reserve, [and] make any necessary revisions to such environmental design as may be necessary in order to effectuate the purposes of this act and the Federal Act." In response to this mandate, DCR and the commission staff identified the principal differences between proposed CMP development standards and the existing coastal regulations. But without making any real attempt to reconcile them, DEP, immediately after adoption of the CMP, formally transmitted a one-page declaration that coastal area policies were consistent with the Pinelands plan.[38] Also, although DEP and the commission agreed in 1980 to enter into a Memorandum of Agreement to make their policies more consistent, this has yet to be done. The actual working relationship between the two agencies, however, appeared to improve in 1985, when new discussions about ways to reconcile the two programs got underway.

Actions to Improve Interagency Coordination. Although DEP is the principal state agency involved in the Pinelands, it is not the only state agency with which the commission has had problems of coordination. Local building inspectors employed by the Department of Community Affairs have sometimes issued permits inconsistent with the CMP (see Chapter 8), and the Department of Agriculture has been a continuing antagonist of the CMP and the Pinelands Commission.

During the three years of CMP review meetings, members of the public commented on the need to improve intergovernmental relationships on the state level. The commission's executive director agrees, saying that in the first five years of plan implementation staff efforts were concentrated on conformance; they gave little time to improving interagency relationships. In late 1985 completion of the major portion of conformance work provided opportunity for a staff reorganization. A new function was established to concentrate on intergovernmental coordination and enforcement problems. In addition, in early 1986, the commission approved several administrative actions that may improve the situation: The commission's Intergovernmental Affairs Subcommittee will work with DEP to resolve issues in conflict, including reconciliation of inconsistencies in coastal regulations; the commission itself will work to ensure the compatibility of statewide and Pinelands agricultural programs, and evaluate with the help of the Department of Agriculture the PDC program; and the commission will form an interagency task force to coordinate more effectively enforcement of Pinelands regulations.

Federal Role in the Management Partnership

The federal government, which put up $26 million for planning and land acquisition in the Pinelands National Reserve, reserves for itself a rather weak managerial role. Land purchased with federal funds is placed in state ownership, and only one of the fifteen commission members represents the federal government. The federal legislation emphasizes that implementation of the CMP rests with state and local government, with "effective and continuing oversight" to be exercised by the governor. However, the Secretary of the Interior must pass on all revisions of the CMP, and if the state fails to gain the secretary's approval for plan amendments, it runs the risk of having to reimburse the federal government for all funds previously disbursed for the reserve. Administratively, the

Department of the Interior, through the National Park Service, handles federal grants for land acquisition, provides technical assistance to the commission, and is mandated to "monitor at periodic intervals the implementation of the approved plan."

The CMP became effective a week before President Reagan's inauguration. The president's program calling for a "new federalism" and James Watt's policy and management changes within the Department of the Interior have changed the federal government's role in the Pinelands.

Weakening Ties with Washington.   The first two federal appointees to the commission had close ties with the Secretary of the Interior (see Chapter 4); a third appointee (Ray Bateman of New Jersey) served only a few months before being replaced by Watt's representative, Ric Davidge, a special assistant to the Assistant Secretary for Fish and Wildlife and the National Park Service. Davidge gave early warning that gaining additional financial assistance for the Pinelands would be difficult,[39] and throughout 1986 this indeed was true. Cutbacks in federal funding to state and local governments have also meant lack of funding for the construction of much-needed infrastructure, especially sewers, in Regional Growth Areas.

While serving as a commissioner, Davidge pulled together a committee of federal agencies to coordinate their Pinelands programs, but since the federal government was concurrently bailing out of most of these programs, the coordinating effort was superfluous. With minor exceptions, however, the commission staff has not experienced as many problems in working with federal agencies as with state agencies. The one recalcitrant federal agency is the Department of Defense, which has secured commission endorsement of management plans for only two of its five installations, which total more than 55,000 acres. Additionally, the Pinelands Commission has been concerned about poor management at Pinelands federal installations of hazardous and toxic wastes, which have threatened to contaminate local water supplies.

Davidge also labored to assert a federal presence by insisting (to the annoyance of other commissioners) that extension of the conformance period required the secretary's approval as a plan modification, but his attendance at commission meetings was spotty. In 1983 Davidge was reassigned to a post in Alaska, and was succeeded by James Coleman, Jr., regional director of the National Park Service's Mid-Atlantic Region. Coleman's attendance at meetings has been good, and he has been very supportive of the Pinelands Reserve. Still, as a NPS Regional Director he faces competing demands for funding and staff resources at a time that total funding for the NPS has been reduced. Although representation of the Department of the Interior by a regional- rather than a national-level bureaucrat has brought more active federal participation in management decision-making, it has also meant a loss of influence in Washington and thus less access to funds. In the long run, when the current political environment (which emphasizes program reductions) has changed this trade-off may turn out to have been detrimental.

Federal Monitoring of the CMP.   Through the National Park Service's Mid-Atlantic regional office, technical assistance has been given to the commission in a variety of areas: staff help and/or funding assistance for the development of a management information system, a Pinelands interpretative program, and a cultural resource management plan. Comprehensive studies of Pinelands sand and mining activities and their impacts have been conducted. NPS also processes all funding applications for the land acquisition program. As yet, however, no acceptable program has been developed to fulfill the federal obligation to monitor the implementation of the Pinelands CMP to ensure that federal legislative goals are being achieved.

Pinelands Commission: Overseer of the CMP

To oversee implementation of the Comprehensive Management Plan as directed by the state legislature, the Pinelands Commission is endowed with strong powers: "to prepare, promulgate, adopt, amend, or repeal . . . such rules and regulations as are necessary in order to implement the provisions of the [Pinelands Protection Act]." Its authority, however, is confined to the Pinelands Area. Excluded from commission jurisdiction are 221,000 acres of Pinelands National Reserve, all but 8,700 of which are regulated by DEP's Division of Coastal Resources. The problems caused by this split jurisdiction are described in Chapter 8.

The role of overseer in the Pinelands Area encompasses a host of managerial functions. The commission must be satisfied that development approved by certified local governments is consistent with the plan. In municipalities and counties not in conformance, the commission must endorse both permit approvals and denials. Commission implementation responsibility extends to many other program areas: economic support, land acquisition, resource management, public involvement, and research. The chapters that follow describe commission activities in these various fields.

New Jersey's governor may veto commission actions. Although this power has yet to be exercised, as described earlier a threat to do so tempered the commission's action against uncertified municipalities. The appointive powers of the governor, and to a lesser extent of the seven Pinelands counties, are another rein on the commission.

Turnover in commission membership has been high, primarily among county and federal representatives. By the sixth anniversary of the CMP, only four of the original fifteen commissioners remained, and none was a county representative. The federal government and Ocean and Atlantic counties each has had five representatives on the commission, Burlington and Camden two apiece, and each of the remaining three counties has had three appointees. 1985 was a year of significant change. Burlington's Bob Shinn, who had served as the commission's vice-chairman from the outset, left to assume a seat in the New Jersey Assembly; Charles Newcomb of Gloucester left to join the governor's office and had to be replaced; and Camden's commissioner, Joan Batory, moved out-of-state.

Much to the dismay of environmentalists, Governor Kean in 1983 failed to reappoint two of the most outspoken, pro-regulation members of the commission, Gary Patterson and Floyd West. The replacements for these two and for a third initial appointee, Peter Burke, are, in the words of the N.J. Builders Association, individuals "of more moderate position."[40] Garfield DeMarco, a large landowner and berry farmer prominent in Burlington County politics and one of the most vigorous opponents of the Pinelands legislation and the CMP, said about the Kean appointments: "Some of the appointments are excellent. The composition now is more reasonable, and the commission more flexible and sympathetic to local people."[41]

Changes in the composition of the commission bring a change in decision-making attitudes. As one Ocean County planner observed, chances for approval of their growth plans were brighter in 1986 than in 1983 because "membership on the Pinelands Commission has changed faces." The significance of a potential shift in commission direction is discussed in Chapter 12.

8. Development Regulation: Processes and Outcomes

Beryl Robichaud Collins

A s previously noted, regulatory responsibility over development in the Pinelands National Reserve is divided between two state agencies. The Pinelands Commission has jurisdiction over the approximately 940,000 acres that is designated as the Pinelands Area. Another 212,000 acres in the coastal portion of the Pineland National Reserve (but not in the state Pinelands Area) is regulated by the Division of Coastal Resources, an agency of New Jersey's Department of Environmental Protection. A remaining 8,700 acres of the Pinelands National Reserve, orphaned from any regional control, is regulated only under normal New Jersey municipal, county, and state land-use rules. The boundaries of these three jurisdictional areas are depicted in Figure 3–2.

Within the Pinelands Area itself, responsibilities for development review have changed through time. On January 14, 1981, the effective date of the Pinelands Comprehensive Management Plan, the interim (or "moratorium") development controls, which had been in effect since February 8, 1979, were replaced by another temporary development review process, which by legislative mandate was to be in effect only one year. During this "conformance period," municipalities were to make their master plans and ordinances consistent with the CMP, and while they were doing this, the Pinelands Commission shared municipal development review authority in the Protection Area but retained permitting power in the Preservation Area.

Since the expiration of the conformance period in 1982, municipalities and counties whose master plans and ordinances have been certified as consistent with the CMP have been allowed to exercise primary development review authority in both the Protection and Preservation areas. In uncertified municipalities development cannot be authorized without commission authorization, and a project approved by the commission can be denied by local government only on the basis of ordinances governing matters not regulated by the CMP. Development regulation differs widely under these various jurisdictional alternatives.

181

Development Regulation in Certified Municipalities

As described in Chapter 7, a municipality achieves certification by revising its master plan and ordinances to conform with the Comprehensive Management Plan. In the process, a local government incorporates both substantive provisions governing project evaluation and procedural mechanisms for development review. Any local activity that alters land or water or changes uses of structures or land requires permitting unless exempted from CMP development regulations (see Chapter 6).

Project Review Process.   Initially, applicants seeking approvals for development projects were encouraged as a first step to request a Pre–Application ("Pre-Ap") conference with a member of the Pinelands Development Review staff. In the early years of plan implementation, a Pre–Ap conference was helpful because development review standards were unfamiliar to many local reviewing agencies as well as to the applicants. With the passage of time, as more municipalities gained certification of their ordinances and became familiar with the review standards, the Pre–Ap conference with the commission staff served less purpose, and led to some confusion in the minds of applicants about the division of authority between local government and the commission. For this reason, the staff now, with certain exceptions, encourages applicants in certified municipalities to discuss their projects with local officials. In the case of a very large project, a conference provides an informal discussion of the strengths and weaknesses of the proposal and of possible alterations that might increase the likelihood of project approval. A conference may also clarify an applicant's need to seek a Letter of Interpretation or a Waiver of Strict Compliance prior to filing an application for development approval. The process for obtaining either of these is described later.

Application Filing.   An applicant proposing a major development (defined as a lot subdivision or a construction of five or more units, commercial or industrial development of a site of more than three acres, or any land clearing in excess of 5,000 square feet) must first file a development application with the Pinelands Commission. Within thirty days of receiving a completed application, the staff issues to both the applicant and the local planning board a Certificate of Filing, which does not indicate approval of the project but simply notes that the application information is complete. The applicant may then file a request for development with the municipality in which the project is located.

A certified municipality may elect to have the Certificate of Filing requirement eliminated in the case of minor development (defined as any development not classed as major), and most have. In such a case, the first step in the process is the filing of the application with the municipality, with a duplicate copy sent to the commission. The duplicate filing process may save almost a month in the development review process. Municipal officials and representatives of the building industry have urged the commission to eliminate the Certificate of Filing requirement for major development as well, but the commission's staff is reluctant, claiming that it is necessary to ensure completeness of application data before the time clock for commission review and approval action starts.

Project Review. The local municipality and the Pinelands development review staff concurrently, and independently, review and evaluate the development application. In some cases there may be joint site inspections, and members of the Pinelands staff may attend local planning board meetings and hearings. The staff review work is handled by one of six environmental specialists, each of whom has responsibility for specific Pineland municipalities within which he or she acts as a liaison on development regulatory matters. Initially, three resource staff members—a soil scientist, a biologist, and a cultural resource specialist—were available for advice on technical aspects of a project. In certified municipalities a project site visit is not compulsory, though it usually is done except where the land characteristics are well known to the staff member through previous site inspections in nearby locations.

Acceptability of a proposed project depends, first, on its location with respect to the CMP management areas and, second, on its conformance with CMP performance standards and programs (see Chapter 6). For all projects, evaluators must be able to answer at least such questions as:

> Is the project compatible with the permitted uses and density maximums in the designated zone of the management area?

> Will the development impinge on wetlands? And, what are the minimum buffer requirements and what is the appropriate site location for the structure and septic system, if required? (The commission staff uses a decision-table model to assess appropriate buffer widths.)

> If there is no sewer system to service the development, what constraints do lot size, soils, and depth to seasonal high water table place on the type of wastewater system that can be used to achieve the nitrate-nitrogen standard of no more than two parts per million at property boundaries? (A computer model is used by the staff to determine if a given parcel proposed for residential, commercial, or industrial development served by a septic system is large enough

to dilute nitrate-nitrogen to the level required by the CMP. To use a standard septic system on most Pinelands soils a single-family residence requires a lot size of at least 3.2 acres. Depending on soils, a pressure dosing septic system and flush toilets may be used on lots as small as 1.6 acres. Permission has been granted for use of a limited number of the newly designed RUCK systems with flush toilets on building lots between 1.6 and 1.0 acres in size. Except for these alternatives, a waterless toilet must be used on lots smaller than 3.2 acres.)

Will the development pose a danger to threatened or endangered species, and give adequate protection to native vegetation?

What are the fire hazards surrounding the development?

Will the development threaten historic, archeological, or other cultural resources? Should a cultural resource survey (at developer's expense) be required?

For major development projects a host of other considerations must be taken into account, including allowances for affordable housing, recreational facilities, traffic, scenic resources, and air quality.

Obviously in the review process, especially for major development projects, there is some duplication between commission staff work and the effort of local officials. Often, however, staff expertise supplements local efforts, particularly for the collection and assessment of environmental data; moreover, in the very process of information exchange, staff concerns can be transmitted to planning officials. A few staff members feel that the certification of municipalities has not (as was promised) significantly reduced their development review workload. Bill Harrison, the head of development review, acknowledges that it has taken longer than expected to make the certified review process work as expected, but he believes that in certified municipalities more staff time is now being spent constructively in discussions with local officials.

Project Approval Process. The commission has fifteen days after a local agency has given a final development approval, and thirty days after issuance of a preliminary approval, to decide whether the local approval action may be inconsistent with the policies of the Comprehensive Management Plan. If no substantial issue is raised by the approval, the local action stands. If there are substantial issues, the approval action is called up for review. The commission has no authority to call up municipal denial actions in certified municipalities; the only recourse for applicants denied is through New Jersey's courts.

If the local action being called up is a preliminary approval, the applicant requesting the development may have his case heard by an administrative law judge in the Office of Administrative Law. If a final approval is called up, the applicant has the choice of having the hearing conducted by the OAL or by the Pinelands executive director, the former usually taking a much longer time. The OAL recommendation, the findings of the executive director, and the record of any hearing are then forwarded to the Pinelands Commission. The commission has forty-five days to take action to approve, approve with conditions, or deny the ALJ recommendation or to remand the case back to the OAL for further consideration. All actions of the commission require a majority vote of its authorized membership (eight votes). If no action is taken by the commission within the allowed time period, the decision handed down by the Office of Administrative Law stands. Further recourse is available to an applicant only through appeal to the Appellate Division of the Superior Court.

Surprisingly few development approvals in certified municipalities have been called up in the postconformance period. In six years only sixty-six out of 2,263 local approval actions (about 2.9 percent) have been called up and only ten of these (nineteen housing units) were denied. One of the call-ups was approved after commission review; another sixteen were approved with conditions, many of which involved relocation of development with respect to wetlands or redesign of wastewater systems; and final dispositions are still pending on the remaining call-ups.

Development Review Process for Public Projects.   The commission retains sole review authority on public projects, even in certified municipalities. Agencies file requests for developments, not exempt from the Comprehensive Management Plan, directly with the Pinelands Commission. If the application is for a major development, the agency is required to give public notice of the filing.[1] The executive director then has thirty days after receipt of the complete application to issue a report recommending approval, approval with conditions, or denial of the proposed project. Copies of the findings and recommendations are forwarded to the commission, the applicant, and any interested parties, any of whom may request reconsideration of these findings by the Office of Administrative Law. If the OAL becomes involved, its recommendation is also forwarded to the commission. In both instances, however, the recommendations are nonbinding and the Pinelands Commission has final authority to approve, approve with conditions, or deny a proposal, or, as in the case of local call-ups, to remand OAL findings. If the commission fails to take action, the recommendation of the executive director, or of the OAL, which supersedes it, stands. No public agency may carry out development that has been denied by the commission.

In the first six years of CMP implementation, applications for 330 public development projects were received. Only one was denied, although some had to be redesigned to gain commission approval. Almost half of the public development projects were sponsored by local governments and most of these consisted of road, sidewalk, bridge, and dam work or expansion or construction of schools or other public buildings in Towns, Villages, or Regional Growth Areas. Much state activity is associated with forestry or facility maintenance projects in state-owned parks and forests.

Public development applications (excluding landfill waiver requests) have caused little problem except for Burlington County's proposed Pemberton bypass highway project, which came to a halt when its proposed route was found to cross the site of one of the last known state populations of the endangered climbing fern. Environmentalists, demanding that the fern be protected, were opposed by residents who wanted the bypass built to reduce traffic on the township's main street. The county finally rerouted the bypass to avoid the fern site, after debate had delayed the project almost a year.

Letters of Interpretation.   The use of Letters of Interpretation to clarify CMP policies is explained in Chapter 6. Any individual or organization or private or government agency also may request a written clarification of the interpretation of a given regulation within the context of a planned development project. The executive director is authorized to respond to such written requests without the approval of the commission, but a report of all pending requests for such letters must be made to the commission at its monthly meeting. Reconsideration of an interpretation can be requested from the OAL, whose findings are then subject to commission approval or denial.

By the end of 1986, 379 Letters of Interpretation had been issued. In the initial implementation years, questions focused on permitted land uses in particular management areas or on specific sites. For example, two requests concerned uses in the Forest Area—one, Could a church be built? (answer: yes); the other, Could an owner's professional engineering office be located in a new single-family dwelling? (answer: no).[2] As more municipalities were certified and local officials became familiar with management area boundaries and permitted uses, the content of the requests shifted to questions about site acceptability, development in wetlands, and buffer requirements. The executive director has also responded to questions from property owners or developers about whether the presence of archeological remains or habitats of threatened or endangered species would interfere with development plans, as well as requests for designation of the number of Pinelands Development Credits attributable to a specific land parcel. In none of these cases does a Letter of Interpretation serve as authorization for a development project; rather, it provides clarification of specific development requirements in the early stages of project planning. Once issued, however, the letter becomes a binding determination guiding the courts as well as landowners, developers, and members of the public concerned with a particular development review.

Waivers of Strict Compliance.   Only the Pinelands Commission is authorized by state legislation to grant exemptions from the CMP provisions, and the issuance of Waivers of Strict Compliance has been one of the most controversial activities of the commission. The waiver process is important even though a waiver in itself is not a development authorization. An individual with an approved waiver must still go through the regular development application and review process, and so must apply for a variance from the certified ordinances. With few exceptions these have been granted when requested. As will be described later, Stafford Township was reluctant to give a variance to a developer who had received waiver approval from the commission.

Waiver Review Process. To request an exemption from CMP provisions, an applicant must first file with the Pinelands Commission and give public notice of his request. The executive director then has ninety days from receipt of the completed application to decide whether the applicant is eligible for relief, and if so, the type of relief that is appropriate. A copy of this finding is then sent to the commission, the applicant, and any interested parties. Again, any recipient (including the commission) may request reconsideration of the recommended action from the OAL. Experience has shown that applicants tend to request hearings on denials or on approvals qualified by conditions, and environmental groups, to request reconsideration of what they deem to be erroneous approval actions.

If an OAL hearing has been held, the commission may approve, approve with condition, deny, or remand the OAL opinion. If the commission takes no action, the recommendation of the OAL will stand. If an OAL hearing has not been requested, the commission may either approve the executive director's recommendation or refer it to the OAL for a hearing. Further reconsideration of the final decision is done by appeal to the Appellate Division of the Superior Court.

A waiver from CMP requirements may be granted for one of two reasons: first, to provide the minimum relief necessary to ease an extraordinary hardship, or, second, to satisfy a compelling public need. In neither case, however, is a waiver to be granted if the proposed project will result in substantial impairment to Pinelands resources or is inconsistent with the legislation or the plan. Both environmental groups and representatives of the building industry have complained about the lack of any formal delineation of the criteria used to judge substantial impairment. Executive Director Moore responded, "If you try to publish a complete list of criteria, you will miss some that will come back to haunt you on future applications."[3] Examination of waivers denied because of substantial impairment indicates that development on undisturbed wetlands that are a part of a larger wetland complex is usually considered to be substantial impairment.

Waivers for Extraordinary Hardship. Currently, there is only one test of eligibility for a Pinelands hardship waiver, and this was placed in the Comprehensive Management Plan to provide relief for property owners for whom the plan does not provide a beneficial use of their property. It is intended to safeguard constitutional rights. This waiver may be granted only if the CMP's land-use requirements prevent an applicant's property from yielding a reasonable return, providing that this inability arises from "unique circumstances peculiar to the subject property" that do not apply to surrounding properties and do not result from any action of the owner or relate to his personal situation.[4] In testing for waiver eligibility, the staff must consider whether the purchase of adjacent land would make a combined parcel that can be of beneficial use. Most of those applying for this type of hardship waiver have been owners of small parcels that do not meet the minimum residential lot-size requirements. To qualify for a hardship, therefore, these individuals must document that the tract in question is truly landlocked—that there is no adjacent vacant land or no land "reasonably available" whose purchase might allow the applicant to meet the minimum requirement. An adjacent parcel is considered "reasonably available" if its owner is willing to sell it at a fair market value. Conversely, the applicant must also consider whether the adjoining property owner would be willing to purchase the undersized lot in question at a fair market value, for this sale would be considered by the commission a "reasonable return." If an adjacent property owner refuses to sell vacant property to an applicant at a reasonable price (or refuses to purchase the vacant undersized property at a reasonable price), an exemption from the lot-size minimums may be granted to the applicant; at the same time, the staff reminds the adjoining land owner that his refusal to sell or purchase will be remembered should he himself ever apply for a similar waiver on his own parcel. Another test of eligibility is whether the applicant's property is in an area where there are other, similar undersized lots; if it is, the parcel will not meet the criterion of "unique circumstances" and thus will not qualify for the hardship waiver.

Typical of these waiver requests was one received from an owner of a 0.5-acre parcel in a Rural Development Area in Medford Township.[5] This applicant requested exemption from the requirements for minimum lot size for construction of a single-family home. The lot was bordered on two sides by roads, there was an existing dwelling on the third side, and the owners of the vacant lot bordering the fourth side of the applicant's property refused to sell their parcel to the applicant. The waiver was granted, conditioned on the use of an alternative wastewater system (waterless toilet, for example) to avoid substantial impairment of the resources. In another common situation, the staff conditioned an exemption from the wetlands buffer standards with a requirement that the proposed residence be sited in a certain location to minimize its impact on a cedar swamp.[6] Moreover, OAL opinions have consistently upheld both waiver denials and approvals conditioned on use of waterless toilets or the siting of structures in particular locations.

The hardship criterion based on the reasonable return test has been a consideration in about 75 percent of all waiver applications, although it accounts for only 2 percent of the residential units in waiver applications. Two other CMP provisions that have since expired were the basis of all waiver requests so far received from large developers. These provisions were designed to recognize the vested rights of applicants who had obtained municipal approvals prior to the effective date of the CMP (see Chapter 6).

Waivers for Compelling Public Need. Fewer than one percent of all the waiver applications have been for reasons of compelling public need. Approvals for such requests are granted only if it can be demonstrated that public health or safety requires a proposed project, and that public benefits from a project override the importance of protecting the Pinelands, and that a proposed development will serve an essential health or safety need in the community of its location or will serve the needs of existing Pinelands residents. Waiver approval will be given only if no equal or better alternative for satisfying the described need exists outside or inside the Pinelands and no better alternative exists within the Pinelands Area.

An example of a waiver given to satisfy a compelling need was the approval of the construction of a firehouse in the Preservation Area, a use not permitted under the plan. Waiver approval was justified on the grounds that the project would provide an essential safety service for local residents.[7] On the other hand, the commission turned down a request from a state agency to construct in the Preservation Area a 48-bed temporary minimum-security correctional facility, citing as its reasons the lack of consideration given to alternatives for housing the additional prisoners, and the lack of direct benefit to residents' health and safety.[8]

One waiver granted to satisfy a compelling public need provoked public reaction; this was approval of a request by the Cape May County Municipal Utilities Authority (CMCMUA) to waive provisions in the plan prohibiting the siting of a new sanitary landfill within 2,500 feet of any existing residence.[9] In this situation, although there were eight existing dwellings located within 2,500 feet of the proposed landfill's border, the commission granted the waiver to alleviate the pollution being caused by existing unlined landfills in the county, and it agreed with CMCMUA that there were no practical alternate sites. The commission's unanimous approval was qualified by seventeen conditions to ensure that the landfill would not adversely affect nearby wetlands or water quality. The decision was not well accepted by a number of Cape May residents, who testified at the commission meeting. Some opposed the choice of the landfill site: Those who lived within the 2,500-foot buffer complained that the landfill would lower the value of their properties (county authorities were willing to "buy out" only one residential property). Although the commission did attach to the waiver a condition that required the CMCMUA to negotiate with the residents to reach a settlement, the residents were not satisfied and appealed the approval to the OAL.

Five months later in a meeting hall packed with Cape May residents, the commission reviewed the OAL decision, which recommended waiver approval with the condition that the CMCMUA purchase all residences within 2,500 feet of the landfill. This would cost the authority $700,000 and was not an acceptable condition to the CMCMUA. The commission, despite a show of objection by residents, in an eight to two vote rejected the OAL recommendation, thereby allowing the original waiver approval to stand. At the same time, however, it reiterated the need for the landfill authority to negotiate a settlement with the property owners. Construction of a new landfill started in early 1984, picketed by the still-unhappy property owners. In August 1986 the landfill authority finally satisfied the residents by agreeing to purchase all properties within 2,500 feet of the landfill boundary. Subsequently, the commission would deny requests for county landfill waivers in Atlantic and Camden counties.

Outcomes from the Waiver Process. In the first six years of management under CMP regulations, the commission's staff acted on almost 1,200 waiver applications, many of which came from applicants who had been denied development approval under the interim regulations. More than 50 percent of the filings requested exemption from lot-size minimums; 48 percent asked for exemption from the provisions dealing with seasonal high water table, wetlands, or wetland buffers; and a remaining 2 percent wanted to use the property in a way not permitted in the regulations.[10] Most waiver requests have been associated with residential development. Nonresidential waiver requests (only 4 percent of the total) have requested exemptions for relatively small commercial projects or campgrounds. None of the waivers filed for public development has created substantive issues except those for county landfills (Cape May's, for example).

A little more than half (54 percent) of the requests for waivers have been approved. These authorize exemptions for the construction of about 12,600 housing units, and have included some very large developments, facts decried by environmentalists. Denials have been issued for about 7,000 units requested on waiver applications, and not all units requested on approved waivers have been permitted. Three developments denied under the interim regulations were able to qualify for waivers under the CMP extraordinary hardship tests that recognized valid municipal approvals issued prior to the CMP and expenses incurred by applicants who were relying on these approvals. These included the Kings Grant Project of 4,500 units to be built in Evesham (Burlington County), the Leisure-towne project of 2,559 units in Southampton (Burlington County), and the Hovson's-Davenport project of 1,411 units in Berkeley (Ocean County). Together the three projects make up 67 percent of the approved waiver units. The developer of a fourth large housing complex, the ROC project, was unable to get waiver approval.

The complexities and pressures entailed in the evaluation of waiver applications for exemptions from CMP regulations are well illustrated by two cases: The first, the Oxly project, was approved over the strong objections of environmental groups, and the second project, the ROC development, was denied despite loud protests from the developers.

Waiver Approval for the Oxly Project. The New Jersey Conservation Foundation and the Environmental Defense Fund together challenged a staff decision to grant Oxly, Inc., exemption from the CMP's minimum lot-size requirements so they might develop 483 residential units on 483 acres in Stafford Township (Ocean County). The development site was part of a larger 2,343-acre tract and included wetlands, the headwaters of Mill Creek, and a good representation of upland Pinelands vegetation. The entire site is located within a large unbroken expanse of undeveloped land and within 1.5 miles of the highly valued Pinelands dwarf forest area.

In its waiver application Oxly proposed clustering the 483 dwellings on 200 acres of uplands and deed-restricting the use of an adjoining 283 acres. This meant lot sizes smaller than the CMP minimum for the Forest Area where the proposed development was to be located. The developer claimed that on the basis of having received a valid final subdivision approval prior to February 8, 1979, he also qualified for an extraordinary hardship waiver.

Oxly had first sought development approval as early as 1975. In December of 1976 the Stafford Township Planning Board passed a resolution approving the project conditioned on the applicant's fulfillment of bonding requirements, receipt of necessary permits from other governmental agencies, and review of the project by the Pinelands Environmental Council. These conditions were not completed by the day on which the Pinelands building moratorium became effective (February 8, 1979). All bonding agreements had not been executed and project development maps had not been signed by municipal officials, though the mayor at the time later testified that he had considered the project to have been officially approved.

Oxly did not apply for development approval of its project under the interim regulations but waited to file under the waiver provisions of the Comprehensive Management Plan. The staff found that the applicant had secured a valid final municipal subdivision approval as of February 7, 1979; that Oxly was eligible for a hardship waiver; and that the development as it had been approved would not cause substantial impairment to the Pinelands resources and was consistent with other provisions of the CMP. Although their approval required use of alternate septic systems, by its decision the staff acknowledged its policy to allow the average concentration of nitrate-nitrogen at individual property lines to be as high as 10 ppm if the concentration could be reduced to the required 2 ppm at the project boundaries.

Claiming that the applicant's original municipal approval had expired and that the project would indeed result in substantial impairment to the resources, the New Jersey Conservation Foundation and the Environmental Defense Fund filed for reconsideration of the waiver approval and were joined in their suit by other environmental groups. This appeal effort was more successful than that of the Pine Barrens Coalition to reverse a waiver approval given for development of a campground on a wetland or that of the Sierra Club to negate the approval given for the 1,411-unit Hovson's development in Berkeley Township. In the Oxly case, an administrative law judge did rule in favor of the environmentalists, holding that the applicant did not have a valid subdivision approval. Although the ALJ was not persuaded on the evidence of substantial impairment, the decision stated "the waiver should be amended to provide that Oxly has to prepare an environmental assessment of the development and submit it as part of its application for development approval."[11]

On the day that the Pinelands Commission was to render its final decision on the Oxly waiver in light of the ALJ decision, a busload of Stafford Township residents, holding handmade signs protesting the waiver, appeared at the meeting. Much to the protestors' dismay, the commission, by a twelve to two vote, rejected the OAL's finding and reaffirmed the staff waiver approval. Environmental groups did not have the funding needed to appeal this decision to the appellate court, but Stafford Township officials delayed issuance of the variance needed to permit development to proceed. Finally, in early 1986, an agreement was negotiated; the project could be undertaken as planned but future development on 2,000 adjoining acres owned by the applicant would be restricted. Oxly, however, failed to start work on the development prior to May 29, 1986, the expiration date of its waiver. When the staff denied a request for an extension of the waiver, Oxly appealed the decision to the OAL. As of August 15, 1987, no decision on the appeal had been rendered.

Waiver Denial for the ROC Project. One project alone accounted for about 65 percent of all the residential units denied in waivers through 1985. Known as the ROC project (sponsored by the ROC Investment Corporation), the proposed development called for a 4,500-unit planned retirement community on a 1,106-acre parcel in Manchester Township (Ocean County).

In 1978 ROC had received from the Manchester Township Planning Board conceptual approval for its project, subject to twenty-three conditions, one of which required an informal review of the project by the Pinelands Environmental Council. The ninety-day PEC review period was to start upon the receipt of an environmental impact statement. ROC did not, however, submit its EIS prior to February 8, 1979 (the date on which the Pinelands moratorium began), and thus had to restart the application process with a submission to the Pinelands Development Review Board. This new application was denied in March 1979, and the developer submitted it again for consideration by the newly formed Pinelands Commission, under its interim regulations. The commission also denied the project in 1980. After the Comprehensive Management Plan became effective, ROC applied for waiver approval to obtain exemptions from the lot-size minimums and from the permitted use requirements of the Forest Area in which the project site was located. In 1982 the commission staff denied the waiver on the basis that the applicant had not received a municipal development approval that would have entitled ROC to qualify for a hardship waiver.

At the request of ROC, the OAL reviewed the staff's decision and concurred with the denial of the waiver. The commission unanimously affirmed the OAL decision in June 1983, but the case did not end there. ROC appealed the decision to the Appellate Division of the Superior Court. In 1984 the court ruled that ROC was not eligible for an exemption from the CMP regulations, agreeing that it did not have a valid approval when the interim development control took effect in the Pinelands on February 8, 1979.[12] The decision was important because it reaffirmed the validity of the eligibility tests for extraordinary-hardship exemptions from the CMP regulations.

Development Regulation in Uncertified Municipalities

In late 1985 an appellate court decision prompted the Pinelands commission to make a significant change in the process for handling regulation of development in uncertified municipalities. This procedural change, however, has not affected the final decision-making authority. Where municipal ordinances are not certified by the commission, no development can take place without commission authorization, nor can an uncertified municipality deny a development permit for any project that is consistent with the CMP unless that denial is based solely on local issues not regulated by the CMP.

Project Review Process as Originally Designed. After the initial conformance period expired in 1982, every applicant seeking approval for development in an uncertified municipality had to obtain from the Pinelands Commission an approved Pinelands Development Application before applying to local authorities for approval. Unless the staff was completely familiar with the site of the proposed project, a site inspection and soil tests, as necessary, had to be made. The acceptability of a development project in an uncertified township was judged by the commission staff within the context of management area boundaries as delineated in the CMP, without consideration of Village or other Area modifications that might have been made as part of the conformance negotiation. CMP minimum standards were used as evaluation criteria for both permitted uses and housing densities, without regard for differentiation of residential, commercial, or industrial zones; moreover, residential density was considered to be uniform throughout each management area. The result of such a review might have been the opposite of what would have occurred if the municipality had completed the conformance process. (See Chapter 7.)

By the end of the ninety-day review period, the Pinelands executive director had to notify the applicant that his application was approved, approved with conditions, or denied. Any applicant or interested person dissatisfied with the staff decision or with the conditions of the approval could request reconsideration in a hearing before an administrative law judge. The ALJ recommendations together with the staff findings were sent to the Pinelands Commission, which had forty-five days to approve, approve with condition, deny, or remand the decision back to the ALJ for further consideration. If no action was taken by the commission, the recommendation of the ALJ stood. Applicants with approved Pinelands Development applications could then apply for local permits, with municipal and county review limited to matters not covered by CMP standards. An applicant who had been denied by the commission could not be granted local permits for the development.

Current Project Review Process. The battle between uncertified municipalities and the commission over local rights to challenge Pinelands development decisions is described in Chapter 7. The conflict ended in May 1985 when an Appellate Court upheld the right of Egg Harbor and Hamilton townships to raise objections to a huge housing, hotel, office, and shopping center complex, the first phase of which the commission had approved. The commission had held that neither township had the right to question the approval action because they had not abided by the Pinelands plan. Although the Pinelands Commission appealed the appellate court decision to the New Jersey Supreme Court, it immediately revised its procedure for handling development review in uncertified municipalities. As a result, the appeal was dismissed as moot.

Under the revised procedures an applicant in an uncertified municipality starts a development request by filing an application with the Pinelands Commission. When the application is complete, it is evaluated by the commission staff, which then issues a Certificate of Compliance, stating whether the project should be approved, approved with conditions, or denied. Copies of the certificate are then sent to the applicant, the commission, and interested persons; the certificate serves as a document to authorize other agencies to review and take action on the development request. Local action, whether it be an approval or a denial of the development request, is then subject to review by the commission.

The staff determines whether the municipal action conforms with CMP

Table 8–1. Development Review Approvals, January 1, 1981, to December 31, 1986.

Type of Approved Development	Applications Approved			Residential Units Approved		
	Total	Protection Area	Preservation Area	Total	Protection Area	Preservation Area
Residential Housing						
Single-family	1,555	1,485	70	1,555	1,485	70
Subdivisions						
1–9 units	639	615	24	1,735	1,662	73
10–99 units	66	65	1	2,049	2,025	24
100–499 units	17	17	—	3,097	3,097	—
500–999 units	4	4	—	2,632	2,632	—
Over 1,000 units	3	3	—	6,346	6,346	—
Total	2,284	2,189	95	17,414	17,247	167
Commercial, Industrial, and Other						
Commercial and Industrial	769	744	25			
Utility Development	13	12	1			
Recreation Facilities	14	13	1			
Other	276	253	23			
Total	1,072	1,022	50			
Public Development						
Schools and Institutions	53	48	5			
Government Facilities	67	61	6			
Roads and Other Infrastructure	108	88	20			
Forestry	21	3	18			
Recreation Facilities	16	16	—			
Other	64	53	11			
Total	329	269	60			
Other Approvals						
Resource Extraction Permits	40					
Forestry Permits	51					
Total	91					

Source: Data compiled from William Harrison's report to the Pinelands Commission: *Development Review Actions under the Comprehen-

requirements. If it does, the action is allowed to stand; otherwise, the action is called up for review by the commission. The applicant, an interested party, the municipality, or the commission may request a hearing by the OAL, following which a staff recommendation is issued. If the municipal action is a final approval and no OAL hearing is requested, the executive director must conduct a public hearing and issue a report on the meeting. In all cases, the recommendations of the executive director and any related OAL opinions are reviewed by the commission, which takes action to approve, approve with conditions, deny, or remand OAL opinions; or, if there is no OAL hearing, to approve, approve with conditions, or to deny the recommendations of the executive director. Further reconsideration is through the appellate courts.

There has been too little time to judge the effectiveness of this new review process, although it appears more cumbersome for an applicant than the original process. This, however, seems not to be crucial, since there were only eight uncertified municipalities by mid-1987, and most of these were at that time actively seeking conformance.

Development Review Outcomes for the Pinelands Area

The outcomes of the development review decision-making processes in the Pinelands Area for the six-year period starting January 14, 1981, are summarized in Table 8–1. These results include decisions made during the earlier transitional conformance period as well as during the post-conformance period under the ongoing development review process in certified and uncertified townships. More than 3,500 development applications were approved during this time, with home-building being the most important development activity.

Patterns of Approved Residential Development.   From January 14, 1981, through December 31, 1986, approval was given for the construction of more than 17,000 housing units in certified and noncertified municipalities. This figure excludes approvals for 11,500 other housing units given during the moratorium period (February 8, 1979, to January 13, 1981) and also does not include waiver approvals still "in the pipeline," which by the end of 1986 had not been translated into development approvals.

Unfortunately there are no available data on numbers of application denials. This is because the commission does not now review development applications denied by certified municipalities nor did it review denials made by municipalities during the eighteen-month conformance period.

The commission's assumption is that there are only a small number of denials, resulting in an extremely high approval rate. This conclusion merits some qualification, however. First, in denying waivers for 7,000 housing units, the commission precluded development approvals for these projects; one of these waiver denials involved a 4,500-unit planned retirement development in the Forest Area of Manchester Township (the ROC project). Second, the necessity of having to conform with CMP regulations, and the availability of preapplication conferences result in many unacceptable elements being dropped from development projects before formal applications are filed. Often, the number of units requested are reduced in the process. Finally, about 30 percent of the filed applications are withdrawn before approval (or denial) action can be taken. These withdrawals, which result primarily from anticipation of project denial, in the aggregate could add considerably to the commission's denial rate. For example, one particularly significant withdrawn application started as a request to build a 4,400-unit retirement community on a 1,000-acre tract of environmentally sensitive land in Woodland's Preservation Area.[13]

Although more than two-thirds of the approved residential applications called for the building of only one single-family home, these actually accounted for only 9 percent of the total number of approved housing units. Subdivisions thus constituted the bulk of the building volume, and twenty-four projects involving a hundred units or more accounted for about 70 percent of this total. The largest project was the 3,600-unit Kings Grant development approved during the conformance period in Evesham (Burlington County). As described in Chapter 6, a concerted effort is made in the CMP to direct development to designated Pinelands Growth Areas, thereby avoiding threats to more environmentally sensitive lands. In actuality this is being accomplished. During the first six years of the plan's implementation, only 167 housing units were permitted in the Preservation Area, mostly in Village Areas. Because computerization of development review actions was not initiated until 1984, more precise information on the location of all approved projects is not available for the full period. For purposes of the three-year plan review effort, the commission staff analyzed applications handled in the first two and one-half years. Their study reveals two distinct locational patterns.[14] First, most of the approved residential development is indeed sited in those CMP management areas that were intended to accommodate growth. Of the total number of units approved, 85 percent are in Regional Growth Areas, another 5 percent in Towns and Villages, and still another 5 percent in Rural Development Areas. Only 1 percent of the home units are located in Forest and Agricultural Production areas.

A second distinctive characteristic of the approved residential development is the concentration of building in two clusters of municipalities. Three Atlantic County townships—Egg Harbor, Galloway, and Hamilton—located in the southeastern part of the Pinelands close to Atlantic City, account for 60 percent of the total approved development units. Hamilton Township alone accounts for 46 percent of the total. A second concentration of residential development occurs on the western fringes of the Pinelands, in municipalities that are sharing the growth of the Philadelphia Standard Metropolitan Statistical Area (SMSA), particularly Medford, Pemberton, and Evesham townships (Burlington County), Winslow (Camden County), and Monroe (Gloucester County). Almost half of the fifty-two Pinelands municipalities have had very little, if any, residential development activity in the Pinelands portion of their jurisdiction. Some of these municipalities were substantially developed before the Pinelands plan was adopted; others have relatively small land areas within the Pinelands; and still others, because of their location, have not yet become a focus of growth demand. Finally there are those townships that would have had more residential growth but for the Pinelands development regulations. Representatives of the building industry, who from the outset had been critical of the CMP development regulations, five years later were to be found complaining that the management plan "has forced development to spread up and down the Garden State Parkway and then leapfrog across the Pinelands" to the western fringe, whereas the "normal and logical path of development would have been across the state" along the east-west highways; "that belt would have had a huge burst of economic activity because the land was very cheap and . . . [casino] workers would have moved if housing had been affordable."[15] It is, of course, just this type of solid east-west development belt that the CMP is designed to prevent in order to maintain an undeveloped forest corridor connecting the southern Pinelands with the Preservation Area in the north.

Nonresidential Development. Nonresidential development activity in the first six years of plan implementation accounted for about one-third of the applications, but for the most part the projects have not been of significant impact.

Commerial, Industrial, and Other Private Development. In six years slightly more than 1,000 applications classed as requests for commercial, industrial, or miscellaneous development were approved. About half of these involved retail stores, restaurants, shopping centers, or office buildings. The largest of the commercial projects involved shopping-center construction, primarily in the Hamilton-Egg Harbor growth area, and about another 100 were classed as industrial development. The remaining projects included construction work on churches, private schools and medical facilities, campground sites, and firehouses, and utility work regulated by the Comprehensive Management Plan. Many applications involved only requests for expansion or structural or use changes in existing buildings. Locational patterns for these approved projects parallel those described for residential projects.

Public Development. Only one of the 330 applications filed for public development projects in the first six years of plan implementation not requiring waivers was denied by the commission. This was a request for a firing range in the Preservation Area. Permission was given for the construction or alteration of schools, park facilities, and buildings to accommodate municipal or county activities and project work on roads, dams, bridges, sewers, and landfills. Almost one-quarter of these projects involved work in the Preservation Area where there are extensive public land holdings.

Resource Extraction. No applications for resource extraction permits were denied by the commission in six years of plan implementation. All the permitted activities were for sand and gravel mining, one of the indigenous Pinelands economic activities that by legislative mandate is to be encouraged. When a natural-gas company proposed to store thousands of cubic feet of natural gas in porous rock underneath the sandy soils in the Warren Grove area of Stafford Township, the commission discovered that the township did not require site plan approval for such activities, and therefore the commission itself had no authority to either approve or deny the exploratory drilling activity. The drilling efforts were subsequently abandoned, and the commission has since taken action to prohibit any mining that will adversely affect significant natural resources.

About half of the 7,000 acres approved for sand and gravel mining are located in the Preservation Area. Operators who had state mining permits prior to the CMP are allowed to continue, but no new operations are permitted here. The approved mining operations are heavily concentrated in two Ocean County municipalities, Lacey and Barnegat, which along with five additional municipalities account for 88 percent of permitted mining acreage.

Forestry. There are virtually no provisions in the CMP for denial of a properly executed forestry application. Indeed, in the first six years of implementation only one of the fifty-two applications was denied; the exception proposed cutting on land which fell within the boundaries of Wharton State Forest.

Forestry activities are permitted in all management areas, and under the state's farmland assessment act, which allows reduced assessments on lands actively timbered, private owners of wooded tracts larger than five acres are encouraged to harvest trees. Almost one-half of the acreage approved for cutting is Preservation land, a concern to environmental groups, who have urged tightening of forestry permit application requirements.

Development Regulation in the Pinelands Coastal Area

New Jersey's Division of Coastal Resources has development regulatory authority in the 212,000 coastal acres of the Pinelands National Reserve that are not within the jurisdiction of the Pinelands commission. DCR, an agency of the Department of Environmental Protection, regulates this coastal land under a regional management program known as CAFRA, the name being derived from its enabling legislation, the Coastal Area Facility Review Act, enacted by New Jersey in 1973 as the state participation in the federal coastal-zone management program.[16]

Exemptions from CAFRA's development authority do not necessarily coincide with Pinelands exemptions. For example, residential development projects that involve fewer than twenty-five dwelling units do not require CAFRA permitting. Small retail stores or shopping centers, warehousing facilities, professional offices, service stations, and public facilities and buildings (all common in the Pinelands Area where they must be in conformance with CMP provisions) also do not require CAFRA permitting unless the project involves the construction of 300 or more parking spaces or the construction of 1,200 or more linear feet of roadway or pipeline in a single municipality during one year. All agricultural and forestry activities also are exempt from CAFRA regulation.

CAFRA Development Review Process. Unlike the Pinelands Commission, the Division of Coastal Resources does not share its development review authority with local governments nor does it have any provision requiring local ordinances to conform with CAFRA regulations. Instead, the CAFRA review process is superimposed on existing permitting systems. An applicant seeking permit approval for a project in CAFRA's jurisdiction submits an application to DCR accompanied by an environmental impact statement. Within sixty days after the application information is complete, a Staff Preliminary Analysis is issued and a public hearing held, although an allowance for securing additional information is given, if needed. The Director of Coastal Resources usually makes the final decision on the project. An applicant may appeal a policy decision to the cabinet-level Coastal Area Review Board, or facts or findings to the Office of Administrative Law, or final agency action to the Appellate Division of the Superior Court. Though a developer may secure local approval for a project, work cannot proceed without a CAFRA permit; conversely, although CAFRA approval may have been gained, a developer may not proceed without all other necessary local and state permits.

CAFRA Criteria for Project Acceptability. In establishing the CAFRA management program, the legislature wished to "encourage the development of compatible land uses in order to improve the overall economic position of the inhabitants of that area within the framework of a comprehensive environmental design strategy which preserves the most ecologically sensitive and fragile area from inappropriate development." This goal explains why the management policies and regulations set forth by the Division of Coastal Resources are more development oriented than those promulgated by the Pinelands Commission.

Using its Coastal Location Acceptability Method (CLAM) DCR determines the acceptability of a proposed development by matching the project location with a set of general and special land and water types, each of which has a designated range of possible uses.[17] For example, general land areas are divided into three growth regions, ranging in capacity from highest to lowest—the Development Region, the Extension Region, and the Limited Growth Region, respectively. Within a given region the acceptable development intensity depends upon the environmental sensitivity of the project site (as judged by its vegetation and soils) and the site development potential (as judged by the availability of sewers and roads and infill development potential). A second set of policies—the so-called "use policies"—sets forth regulations for particular types of development projects such as housing, recreation, energy, public facilities, and industry-commerce. One use policy permits approval of large-scale development projects in areas that have been designated for low growth. This is one reason why the results of the CLAM review process are not easily predictable. Resource policies serve as standards to control the effect of a development on various manmade and natural resources.

Conflicts: CAFRA and CMP Development Regulations. The handling of development, both regulated and unregulated, under the CAFRA program is producing outcomes significantly different from those that would occur if the provisions of the CMP were to prevail in the coastal region.

CAFRA-Regulated Development Outcomes. An analysis by the author of each application for development in the Pinelands National Reserve on which the Division of Coastal Resources rendered a decision between

1981 and 1983 clearly demonstrates the differing outcomes of the CAFRA and CMP permitting regulations.[18] Under CMP regulations it is likely that at least seven of the twenty-one applications approved by DCR would have been denied, representing roughly one-quarter of the 7,194 authorized housing units. Although the commission would probably have approved fourteen of the remaining residential applications, some of its approvals might have carried conditions calling for reduction in the number of residential units, adjustment of wetland buffers, use of waterless toilets, and changes in stormwater management systems. In all likelihood, the CMP regulations also would have called for a denial of an application for a new nursing home and reduced the number of campsites approved on another application. The commission would probably have denied all the projects denied by DCR in this three-year period, but a project in a Regional Growth Area denied by DCR in 1984 might well have been approved by the commission.

These inconsistencies in probable outcomes under the CAFRA and CMP permitting processes stem primarily from differences not only in the designation of growth areas but also in water quality standards. DCR seeks maintenance of the statewide 10 ppm nitrate-nitrogen standard at a development property line; the CMP, of course, calls for a more strict 2 ppm standard.

The Problem of Unregulated Development. The Bureau of Coastal Planning and Development has found that the statutory limitation that exempts residential developments of fewer than twenty-five units from CAFRA regulation means that about 37 percent of residential development escapes CAFRA regulation and that in all probability about an equal percentage of nonresidential development is also unregulated.[19] The bureau also notes that development exempt from the CAFRA program is regulated primarily through municipalities, which for the most part have zoning ordinances less stringent than the state's coastal standards, not to mention the Pinelands CMP standards.

The analysis by the author of the unregulated residential development between 1981 and 1983 in the Pinelands National Reserve portion of three townships in CAFRA's jurisdiction again demonstrates the divergent outcomes between the CAFRA and the CMP programs. When approved building permits in these townships were tested against the CMP regulations for project acceptability, the results indicated that development unacceptable by CMP standards occurred at a very high rate. Permits were granted for large numbers of residential units on nonsewered lots too small to meet even the statewide standard of 10 ppm nitrate-nitrogen. Only 22 percent of the building permits issued in this three-year period would have been approved under the Pinelands CMP permitting process without a waiver, and about half of these would have required use of a waterless toilet. The study, moreover, confirmed a tendency to scale down residential building projects to gain exemption from the CAFRA program. There was a concentration of subdivisions at the 23/24 unit level, and of the total unregulated development in the three townships studied, 40 percent of the building permits were for subdivisions of twenty to twenty-four units.

The incompatibility of coastal permitting outcomes with CMP provisions raises the question of whether the legislative mandate is being completely met in that portion of the Pinelands National Reserve that is not under the authority of the Pinelands Commission. This issue is discussed further in Chapter 12.

Enforcement of Development Regulations

Short shrift is given to the enforcement issue in the Pinelands Protection Act. Although penalties are specified for disposal of litter and for certain unauthorized uses of motor vehicles and power boats within the Pinelands Area, the commission is not given any authority to impose fines or to issue stop-work orders for violations of development regulations. Responsibility for ensuring compliance with Comprehensive Management Plan standards and permit conditions rests primarily with the certified municipalities. State agencies, of course, have enforcement authority over the handling of waste management, testing of alternative technologies for wastewater disposal, prevention of stream encroachment, and protection of state lands. The role of the Pinelands Commission, however, is one of oversight to ensure effective implementation of the plan.

Effectiveness of Enforcement Mechanisms.   On the township level, building inspectors (or construction code officials) and code enforcement officers are responsible for enforcement of development ordinances. In many Pinelands municipalities one individual may perform both functions, on a part-time or a full-time basis. Municipalities with a heavier development load may employ more than one code enforcement officer to ensure compliance with building materials specifications, plumbing and electrical work, setbacks, and so forth. In a few townships, environmental commissions take an active role in monitoring for compliance with local ordinances. For the most part municipalities and counties have already in place, or can adopt adequate enforcement mechanisms to ensure compliance with the CMP regulations and permit conditions. Indeed, several municipalities have reinforced the CMP forestry provisions by adopting stronger ordinances to allow local authorities to issue stop-work orders and impose fines for illegal wood-cutting.

There is disparity, however, in the results of compliance-monitoring efforts. Municipal and county officials vary in their degree of enthusiasm for enforcing CMP ordinances. Police often are unwilling to search out illegal cutters in the backwoods, for example, and some commission staff members also express dissatisfaction with lax enforcement by the Department of Environmental Protection, when stream encroachment violations are referred to its Division of Water Resources.

To identify the types of violations that are occurring and the reasons for noncompliance with CMP regulations, the author initiated a research project which included a series of interviews with local and state officials and members of the public and of the commission staff. The material that follows is drawn from the research findings.[20]

Residential and Commercial Development Violations. One kind of residential or commercial development violation occurs when an individual starts construction or land development before obtaining a valid permit under the CMP development review process. One person, for example, placed a mobile home on a lot without a permit, another started a house foundation, and a third, the construction of a commercial-use garage (housing a school bus service). A staff member estimates that 95 percent of the violators who are building without the appropriate permits are detected. Only those building "way out in the boondocks"—the peripheral areas of the Pinelands, in Cape May and Cumberland counties—escape detection.

Another type of violation occurs when an individual obtains a permit but does not follow the permit conditions. The building's structure and/or its use may not be the same as what was authorized. For example, a duplex may be built instead of the single-family residence that was approved; the location of a structure and/or waste disposal system with respect to wetlands may not follow permit provisions; or a waterless toilet may not be installed as called for in the development approval. Or, if an original owner sells a property, a subsequent owner may fail to comply with the original permit conditions; for example, the new owner may disconnect the alternative waste system and use a regular flush toilet.

In some cases, the violator and the local officials are both ignorant of the CMP approval requirements. In most cases, however, the violator is aware of the requirements, but chooses not to follow them, believing that "The CMP restrictions are not legal" or "What I do on my land [wetlands, in this case] will hurt nothing" or "There is little risk of detection or of punishment." Waterless toilets are extremely unpopular; they are thought to be "unpleasant to use" and there are complaints that it is difficult to secure financing to buy homes with waterless toilets and that "It's hard to sell houses with them." Several individuals offered the information that waterless toilets can be, and are, rented for purposes of passing the building inspection to obtain the Certificate of Occupancy. Once the inspection is made, however, the unit is removed and a flush toilet is connected to the grey-water system. Because of lax inspection efforts individuals may well be unconcerned about being penalized for their violation.

Initially, a lack of cooperation from a few (municipal and Department of Community Affairs) building inspectors and code enforcement officers (both municipal and state) meant that occasionally local approvals were given to projects that had been denied by the commission. In one case a DCA inspector overlooked the construction of a garage apartment when the commission had denied a waiver to allow the construction. In another case, local approval was given for occupancy even though a developer had not located the septic leach field as called for by the commission permit.

Forestry Violations. More than half the calls on violations received from the public at the commission's office report illegal wood-cutting. Most of these violations involve relatively small acreages, but one planning board member in Maurice River Township (Cumberland County) estimated that in one year as much as $50,000 worth of cedar may have been cut illegally in that community. A ranger in Bass River State Forest believes that "five or six locals" equipped with mufflered chainsaws regularly cut there without permit. He and others in the Department of Parks and Forests estimate that perhaps only 25 to 33 percent of those who are cutting illegally for their own use may be caught, but that 90 percent of those who cut illegally for commercial sale of the wood are caught.

The more serious violations, from an environmental point of view, occur when a forestry permit is obtained, but permit conditions are not followed. Tree trunks may not be cut to ground level, slash may not be removed, or cutting may be done in unapproved locations. Usually the latter type of violation occurs in timber operations when a contractor arranges for others to cut on the owner's property primarily to gain the benefit of farmland assessment. Under CMP regulations such a timber contractor may obtain the forestry permit and then sell his cutting rights to independent wood-cutters. Frequently, however, cutters under contract have been found guilty of cutting on property not covered by permit. When caught, the cutters fault the contractor for giving poor instructions on property boundaries, while, needless to say, the contractor blames the cutters. The largest timber contractor in the Pinelands, who had been faced with numerous charges of illegal cutting including one incident involving the cutting of several hundred cords of wood on property almost a mile away from the permitted area, excused these violations with a shrug—"We're not dealing with an industry of PhD's."

Obviously, much illegal cutting is stimulated by economics. The energy crisis, for example, caused a significant increase in violations throughout the state, which peaked in 1981 and since has dropped off. Thus far, except for cedar cutting, state foresters do not believe that illegal cutting is extensive enough to be considered a long-term problem for the Pinelands forests, although they admit that the violators often take the wrong wood—the healthy and not the diseased trees. Members of the public, however, have expressed in commission meetings deep concerns about these forestry violations.

Resource Extraction Violations. There are about fifty active sand and gravel mines operating under CMP permits, and several have been charged with failure to meet permit conditions regarding observance of mining boundaries, reclamation, and landscaping requirements as well as stream encroachment restrictions. Many of these violations are reported by neighbors of mining sites, who are concerned about safety hazards, soil erosion, truck traffic, and the lack of adequate buffers and landscaping.

Violations of permit conditions appear to stem largely from a strong economic incentive to avoid the cost of compliance. Environmentalists suggest that this motivation is reinforced by the common knowledge that present mechanisms do not provide adequate monitoring to detect noncompliance. Also, in resource extraction permitting, as in that for forestry, the escrow provisions meant to ensure site restoration do not always offer an adequate incentive to gain conformance by the permit holder. The assistant director for development review believes that the practice of requiring mining operators to correct current violations before renewing their permits will improve the situation.

Illegal Dumping. Because the soils in the Pine Barrens permit fast infiltration to groundwater, illegal dumping of liquid or solid waste materials poses one of the most serious threats to the region. Long before the Pinelands Commission came into being, illegal disposal of waste materials, including toxic substances, was a problem. The Pinelands' large, remote, unpatrolled areas and sandy roads make such illegal disposal of toxic and nontoxic waste materials relatively easy.

In the mid-1980s, as landfills throughout the state were forced to close and as counties and municipalities failed to develop alternative sites, the numbers of "midnight dumpers" in the Pinelands increased. Acting in concert with other local and state agencies, the commission has initiated a public awareness campaign to alert residents to the dangers of illegal dumping and to solicit their help in reporting possible violations. The commission also has taken vigorous action against operators of authorized landfills who violate the conditions under which their activities are allowed. The Southern Ocean County Landfill in Waretown, for example, was stopped from accepting sludge when not authorized to do so; Big Hill landfill in Southampton (Burlington County) was prevented from expanding its operation beyond the authorized limits; and the Department of Defense was pressured to clean up toxic contamination emanating from the Fort Dix landfill.

Commission Enforcement Activities.   To prevent violations in any location, the Pinelands development review staff visits sites to monitor construction activity. This monitoring is said to have been done on a hit-or-miss basis prior to the reduction in the staff workload that resulted from certification of a majority of the municipalities. Currently, however, a staff site visit is required whenever a compliance issue is raised. This allows verification, for example, of the correct location of an approved structure or septic field on a site, or of the installation of alternative and innovative wastewater systems, such as the pressure dosing and the Ruck systems. Confirmation of a permanent installation of a waterless toilet is more difficult. A recently implemented step calls for a member of the development review staff to accompany the local construction code official in the final inspection to verify the installation of a waterless toilet prior to the issuance of a Certificate of Occupancy.

As a matter of experience, the staff has learned which builders may give trouble and in which townships they will need to do more monitoring for compliance. Public monitoring for compliance is encouraged and each reported violation is investigated. If a violation occurs, the first step in the commission enforcement process is to contact the violator to urge that the violation be corrected. If, however, voluntary compliance is not secured in the initial contact, written notification of the violation of CMP regulations or permit conditions is sent to the offender by the assistant director for development review. Continued lack of corrective action leads to a second, stronger letter, which states that legal action will be taken to ensure correction of the violation. If the violator still does not cooperate, the staff refers the case to the New Jersey Attorney General's Office, which first will seek settlement. If voluntary compliance still cannot be obtained, the attorney general's office will request, with commission approval, the superior court to issue a stop-work order until the violation is corrected. The staff reports that fewer than ten violations have been referred for court action; the remaining have been settled by negotiation. None has involved a large developer. The assistant director for development review feels comfortable with the competence and thoroughness of staff monitoring efforts on large projects.[21] Moreover, if any violation does occur, the developer must correct the wrongdoing before any amendments to the project will be considered.

The lack of commission authority to impose fines and the lack of funding for adequate staffing to monitor compliance are the two most serious enforcement problems. Initially, follow-up of violations was done as a half-time assignment of one staff member. In late 1985, when most of the conformance work was completed, three full-time staff positions were established to handle enforcement (and intergovernmental coordinating) work. Still, with almost one million acres to police, the commission must realistically rely on the enforcement efforts of local and state officials, aided by the volunteer monitoring network of citizens.

Development Regulatory Issues

Enforcement problems and problems resulting from the split in regulatory authority between the Pinelands Commission and the Division of Coastal Resources aside—how well has the regulation of development by the Pinelands Commission really worked? Judging by administrative law judge opinions on appeals, the Pinelands CMP decision-making process is working well. Few of these findings have disagreed with staff recommendations, and only one commission decision has been overturned by appeal to higher courts. Sharing of permit review authority with municipalities is working remarkably well, too, when judged in the context of the few numbers of local decisions called up for commission review. But the initial years of development regulation under the Comprehensive Management Plan were not nearly so tranquil. Michele Byers, Pinelands Coordinator for the New Jersey Conservation Foundation, described the commission's early predicament: "They've got the developers yelling at them; they've got the environmentalists yelling at them. And the politicians hear from everybody and then yell at them."[22]

As development regulation has become institutionalized at the local level through the conformance process, the heat on the commission has been greatly reduced. Nevertheless, complaints about the regulatory processes continued to surface in the triennial review process. Representatives of the building industry complain that permit requirements are cumbersome and commission interpretations too rigid. Disappointed applicants agree with them. At the other extreme environmentalists say that there is not enough public involvement in the regulatory process and that the commission has been too lenient, particularly when granting waivers from CMP provisions.

Burdensome Administrative Requirements.   Unnecessary CMP administrative requirements are recognized by the staff as a problem. As a result they have recommended reduction in information requirements for major development projects and formation of a task force to suggest ways of streamlining the regulatory process.[23] In particular, the need for a Certificate of Filing on a major development will be evaluated. The staff agrees that forestry permitting requirements should be severely tightened, as suggested by the Natural Resources Defense Council, but disagrees with the president of the New Jersey Builders Association, who claims that the cultural resource requirement for major development is the "type of regulatory overkill that unnecessarily adds to the cost of housing."[24] On only one point is there any unanimity: staff, developers, and environmental groups all see the benefit of a computerized application tracking system to ensure proper recording and follow-up of review actions and to provide a much-needed database for analyses of application processing times and decision actions. Such a system was installed in late 1986.

No consideration has been given yet to eliminating the two-track permitting procedure, which contributes much to the complexity of the regulatory process. Certified municipalities have primary responsibility for development permit approval, but, by legislative mandate, only the commission may grant exemptions from CMP regulations. As a result, an applicant may have to go first through the commission waiver approval process to obtain an exemption from a plan requirement and then start all over again with a second review process on the local level to gain the actual development permit.

Though the number of call-ups on local development approval actions is extremely low, some municipalities and counties feel that there still is too much commission staff involvement in the permitting process. An exceptional few—those without adequate staff resources—would like the commission to review all development proposals before the local review takes place. The commission, however, is satisfied with the present division of responsibilities, but notes that more staff aid should be made available to those municipalities that need it.

Considering the relatively young age of the development review staff and the eagerness with which each staff member pursues compliance with CMP regulations, surprisingly few complaints about staff performance have been registered publicly. For example, suggestions at commission meetings that a botanist and a civil engineer be added to the development review team reflect concern about the adequacy of staff numbers rather than criticism of their professional expertise. That staff efforts and decisions have been accepted as well as they have been is a tribute to the capabilities of Assistant Director for Development Review Bill Harrison, who personally oversees the preparation of findings of fact and staff recommendations on all decision actions. One seasoned township attorney suggests that it is Harrison's phenomenal memory for details that has given such consistency to the commission's decision-making process, and another lawyer who has represented many large developers in South Jersey volunteered that the commission's development review staff is "one of the best agency groups to work with—it's small and pretty well managed, and they are a bunch of hard-working people." [25]

Adequacy of Public Involvement.   Environmental groups have not been satisfied with the opportunities for public involvement in development review decision-making, and in this respect the CMP regulatory process has been compared unfavorably with that used for CAFRA permitting. [26] Although the commission issues to subscription holders a biweekly list of all applications and development review actions, environmental groups have not found this a helpful instrument for tracking action on the more important development projects. [27] The 1985 procedural revision requiring public notice of all applications for waivers, major public development, and major private development in uncertified townships partially fills the information gap. But the core of the problem is that the commission staff does not hold public hearings on all large development actions prior to the issuance of its findings. Thus, the only real opportunity for members of the public to take issue with staff findings is to request reconsideration of the decision by an administrative law judge. The time, effort, and cost of assembling a case, including expert testimony, for a hearing in the Office of Administrative Law is sufficiently large to dissuade many potential appeals.

Members of the public also have reason to quarrel with the process. Often, after taking time to attend a meeting in which the commission is to act on a controversial ALJ recommendation, individuals have learned that because of a legal restriction no public input introducing new evidence is permitted prior to commission action.

Social Costs of Development Regulation.   Six years of regulatory experience under the CMP has revealed some of the costs associated with the Pinelands protection program. Many owners of lots smaller than the permitted minimum sizes find that to develop their property, they must invest additional funds to acquire vacant adjoining property to enlarge their parcels.[28] Others, who years before the passage of Pinelands legislation purchased large-sized (or several adjoining) lots in the expectation of later selling off portions, find that the minimum lot sizes will not permit this.[29] There have been heart-rending tales—one of an elderly couple who, in 1977, paid about four times the going price for a five-acre lot on which they expected to erect four residential dwellings, but the CMP placed their land in a Rural Development Area; even with a hardship waiver, the couple's property was suitable for at most two residential units.[30] Another is the plight of a couple who in 1973, with expectations of building a retirement home sometime in the future, bought a 1.4-acre lot in what turned out to be the Pinelands Preservation Area; the CMP became effective before these owners applied for their building permit, and because neither individual qualifies under the "Piney" exemption criteria, by CMP regulations they cannot build a residence on their property. (They are, however, eligible for a fractional unit of a Pinelands Development Credit.)[31]

In a few other cases, individuals qualify for hardship waivers but then find they still cannot build on their property because building would cause "substantial impairment" of the resources, usually by disturbing water quality.[32] In one situation, the commission has allowed an owner to exercise his waiver right on another land parcel. In numbers, the most dissatisfaction appears to come from property owners who are not allowed to use standard septic systems, and especially those who are limited to waterless waste systems, which are not nearly as satisfactory as traditional systems. These applicants are particularly galled when there are neighboring property owners with equal-sized lots who have received approval for standard septic systems from the commission.[33] These, of course, were granted in the interim period of development review, when the water quality standard was less rigid.

Even developers have been caught midway in project build-outs. One had completed thirty-six homes with septic systems on substandard lots, approval being granted under the interim regulations; however, he was required to use waterless systems in the remaining twelve units, which were regulated under the CMP.[34] One very frustrating situation for the commission staff is Ocean County's Ocean Acres, an unsewered development of 8,000 home units, typically on lots no larger than 9,000 square feet. To date only about 25 percent of the project has been completed and building has virtually been halted; the problem is the Pine Barrens water quality standards, which first went into effect in 1978. As a result, vacant parcels plummeted in value from a high of between $6,000 and $8,000 to a current average of about $3,000.[35]

That implementation of the Pinelands Comprehensive Management Plan would result in economic hardships for some individuals was not unexpected. The price of landscape protection in an area as large as the reserve has its costs only partly mitigated by the Pinelands economic support programs. These programs and their impacts are discussed in Chapter 10.

9. Acquisition, Management, and Use of Public Lands

Robert A. Zampella

The public acquisition of land in the Pine Barrens as state parks, forests, and wildlife management areas began long before Congress thought of creating a Pinelands National Reserve. By 1979, when the state Pinelands Protection Act was passed, 335,000 acres of the Pinelands (representing more than one-quarter of the reserve) were already in public ownership (Table 9–1). Both federal and state lawmakers recognized, however, that additional acquisitions of "environmentally sensitive areas and recreation sites" would have to be made. Nevertheless, the prior existence of extensive public holdings in the Pinelands provided a compelling reason among many others for these legislators to consider the greenline park concept as an appropriate method for protecting Pinelands resources.

Land Acquisition in the Pinelands before the CMP

Two agencies, operating independently of one another but both within New Jersey's Department of Environmental Protection, administer the state's conservation lands (the divisions of Fish, Game, and Wildlife, and Parks and Forestry). Through the mid-1970s these divisions were also mainly responsible for determining which lands would be acquired by the state. The Division of Fish, Game, and Wildlife purchased lands mainly for use as hunting and fishing areas, while Parks and Forestry acquired land that would satisfy broader conservation and recreation needs.

New Jersey's system of state parks and forests was born in 1905, when the legislature created the New Jersey Board of Forest Park Reservation Commissioners. This board was empowered "to acquire a fee simple estate of any lands to be taken for the purposes of forest park reservations" and was charged with the "care, management and preservation of the forest preserves."[1] In that same year, the board made its first acquisitions (see Table 9–1). The Mays Landing Reserve (Atlantic County) and the Bass River Reserve (Burlington County) were to be managed as demonstration forests. They were also the state's first significant commitment to preserve Pinelands resources through public acquisition.

By 1910 several more Pinelands tracts had been added to state holdings. All these early reserves were demonstration areas, meant to show

Table 9–1. Federal and State Land Holdings in the Pinelands.

Landholding[a]	Acreage[b]	Landholding[a]	Acreage
State Conservation Lands		*State Lands Acquired Under*	
Acquired Prior to 1979		*Pinelands Program*	
Colliers Mills WMA (1941)	12,211	Cedar Creek Watershed	15,400
State Tree Nursery (1981)	290	Upper Wading River Watershed	3,400
Manchester WMA (1954)	2,376	West Plains/Greenwood	
Whiting WMA (1952)	1,200	connector	9,000
Lebanon SF (1908)	29,413	Goose Ponds at Tabernacle	909
Pasadena WMA (1954)	3,100	Friendship Bogs	2,170
Greenwood Forest WMA (1948)	9,000	Oswego River extension	10,250
Double Trouble SP (1964)	1,677	Bass River extension	8,500
State Game Farm (1912)	538	Makepeace Lake	8,000
Island Beach SP (1953)	3,002	Other state land additions	1,000
Sedge Islands WMA (1978)	171	East Plains, Stafford Forge[d]	8,400
Barnegat Light SP (1953)	31		
Wharton SF (1954)	99,672	*State Facilities*	
Penn SF (1910)	3,366	New Lisbon Developmental	
Winslow WMA (1947)	5,940	Center	1,854
Hammonton Lake Natural		Coyle Airfield	550
Area (1960)	98	Ancora Hospital	785
Green Bank SF (1930)	—[c]	Stockton State College	1,500
Bass River SF (1905)	9,100	Leesburg State Prison	1,094
Stafford Forge WMA (1965)	2,788	Woodbine Developmental Center	198
Manahawkin WMA (1933)	965		
Swan Bay WMA (1968)	1,078	*Federal Land and Facilities*	
Port Republic WMA (1962)	755	Edwin B. Forsythe National	
Great Bay WMA (1974)	4,141	Wildlife Refuge	28,000
North Brigantine Natural		Fort Dix Military Reservation	31,992
Area (1967)	678	McGuire Air Force Base	3,490
Absecon WMA (1966)	3,548	Lakehurst Naval Air Station	7,412
Peaslee WMA (1954)	14,276	U.S. Aeronautical Communica-	
Lester G. McNamara WMA (1933)	12,438	tions Station	200
Belleplain SF (1928)	11,270	Warren Grove Weapons Range	8,500
Heislerville WMA (1956)	3,844	Federal Aviation Administra-	
Dennis Creek WMA (1957)	5,109	tion Technical Center	5,055
Beaver Swamp WMA (1964)	2,700		

[a]WMA—Wildlife Management Area; SF—State Forest; SP—State Park.
[b]Acreage figures as recorded in Pinelands Comprehensive Management Plan.
[c]Acreage included in Wharton SF figure.
[d]Acquisition not completed as of August 1, 1987.

that Pine Barrens forests, with proper management (including fire protection), could be economically productive. This effort reflected the findings of an 1895 state geologist's report that had concluded that abuse and neglect had decimated the forest resources of southern New Jersey and that "large areas of waste land" should be reforested by the state.[2] These two objectives—productivity and fire protection—remain a major influence on the policies of today's Division of Parks and Forestry.

In the 1930s, the objectives motivating state land acquisitions began to shift away from forest management and toward providing public recreation opportunities. Moreover, in 1931 State Forester C. P. Wilber identified nearly 267,000 acres in the Pine Barrens, including the Wharton Estate, that he recommended for purchase.[3] Wilber's program was not implemented immediately, although much of the land he identified in that 1931 report has since been bought by the state and has become an important element in the Pinelands protection program of the 1980s.

During the 1930s the Division of Fish, Game, and Wildlife established its first two management units, the Manahawkin and the Lester G. MacNamara wildlife management areas; both are coastal reserves located in the Pinelands. Three more areas were acquired in the 1940s: Colliers Mills and Greenwood Forest, both located in the north-central Pinelands, and Winslow, originally known as Inskip, located along the Great Egg Harbor River.

Additional acquisitions were made in the 1940s and the 1950s, but certainly the most significant state acquisition in the Pine Barrens was the two-part purchase in 1954 and 1955 of nearly 100,000 acres in the heart of the Pines. This was the Wharton tract, which extends into three counties—Burlington, Camden, and Atlantic. It belonged to the heirs of Joseph Wharton, Philadelphia philanthropist and the founder of the Wharton School at the University of Pennsylvania. Wharton had acquired the land between 1873 and his death in 1912; his original intention had been to use it as a source of water for Philadelphia, but this plan was forestalled by the New Jersey Legislature, which passed an injunction against the export of water from the state. Wharton then turned his attention to other forms of development—agriculture and timber.

The state's interest in acquiring the Wharton tract dates back to the earliest days of the acquisition program. In 1912, the New Jersey Water Supply Commission proposed purchasing it, and the Forest Park Reservation Commission was "ready to cooperate."[4] The sale price of the land was set by Wharton's heirs at one million dollars, and the question of purchase was placed on the state ballot in November 1915. Although several large North Jersey counties supported it, surprisingly most South Jersey counties did not, and the question was defeated. South Jersey's opposition may well have stemmed from the prospect of tax revenue losses—one township, for example, stood to lose 40 percent of its tax base if the Wharton estate became state land; other townships and three counties were similarly affected.[5]

Although Wilber recommended purchase of the Wharton tract in 1931, nothing more happened for twenty years. The state's final decision to buy it was based largely on the value of the land as a water supply source, although nature-resource and recreational considerations were also influential. The 56,000-acre eastern portion of the tract was at last transferred to the state in 1954 for $2 million; the next year, 40,000 more acres on the western portion of the tract were acquired for another one million dollars.[6] The Wharton State Forest encompasses about 2.5 percent of the total land area of New Jersey and a significant portion of the Pinelands Area.

In 1961 the state's land acquisition program received a big boost from the passage of the Green Acres bond issue, which provided a sizable new source of funds. Before the Green Acres Program, state purchases had been entirely dependent upon specific state legislative appropriations or funding from the federal government for fish and wildlife conservation, as well as on fees, licenses, and various donations. Earmarked funds from the 1961 Green Acres fund were used to purchase several more important tracts in the Pinelands, including three new wildlife management areas and land for the newly created Double Trouble State Park.

Land Acquisition under the CMP

Land acquisition under the Comprehensive Management Plan is based upon an integrated acquisition program for Pinelands protection that was actually begun in 1977 by Governor Brendan T. Byrne. In that year, the governor specifically designated $10 million of Green Acres funds for land purchases in the Barrens; in 1978 another $13.75 million from Green Acres was earmarked, along with matching monies from the federal Land and Water Conservation Fund. The land acquisition element of Section 502 of the 1978 National Parks and Recreation Act (creating the Pinelands National Reserve), which authorized $23 million for purchase of additional ecologically sensitive areas in the Pinelands, was in fact only a further extension of this state-initiated program.

Thus, when the Pinelands Commission was created, the state Department of Environmental Protection had already begun identifying environmentally sensitive lands for acquisition and had opened negotiations for purchase in some areas. The commission immediately entered the acquisition process, even before the formal presentation of its acquisition program in the CMP. Indeed, several acquisitions were actually approved by the commission before the CMP was adopted in 1981. Thus, the state's early efforts in acquiring Pinelands acreage provided a substantial advantage for scheduling and completion of commission projects.

The CMP Acquisition Program.   The Comprehensive Management Plan recommended purchase of approximately 100,000 acres of land (to be made by 1985 at a cost of $80.8 million), including a priority list of 67,000 acres located in eight target areas, and 30,000 acreas representing extensions of existing state-owned tracts. Consistent with the intent of the state legislation that direct acquisition "be concentrated" in the Preservation Area, seventy-five percent of the priority acreage was located in the Preservation Area, principally within the Wading River and the Cedar Creek watersheds; the rest was within Forest Areas, mainly in the southern Pinelands.

By the end of 1985, state acquisition of 42,000 acres was completed, and negotiations for another 25,000 were in process. Of the originally anticipated acquisition funds, $43.3 million has been authorized and committed. An additional expected $8 million for the East Plains–Stafford Forge project will use up the last of currently available acquisition funds authorized by Section 502 of the federal act; one million dollars remains in Green Acres funds.

Selection of Sites for Acquisition.   Contrary to a suggestion by Ronald A. Foresta, administration and maintenance are not the primary considerations in the commission's acquisition program.[7] Nor, with one exception, has acquisition been used as an instrument to block development in disputed areas (western Berkeley in Ocean County [see Chapter 7], for example) or to promote farmland preservation. Although considerations regarding management, recreation, and preservation of cultural and natural resources are used in designating acquisition areas, ecological factors are paramount, the ultimate goal of the commission's program being to develop a system of ecological reserves that is both self-maintaining and representative of the Pine Barrens.

Initially, the commission relied on the earlier work of other governmental agencies that had been involved with acquisition. All these agencies continue to be committed to a common goal of Pinelands preservation through management and acquisition; however, since the specific land objectives of the separate divisions vary, each agency has developed a separate list of potential acquisition areas.

The Division of Parks and Forestry, for example, emphasizes general educational and recreational values, and thus favors acquisition of natural areas suitable for such human activities as swimming and camping, as well as cultural or historic sites that can serve some educational purpose. The Division of Fish, Game, and Wildlife, on the other hand, favors acquisition of areas that have values oriented toward wildlife—hunting and fishing lands, for example; the division also is predisposed towards acquiring wetlands, which are prime wildlife habitats. Certain administrative considerations have also played a part in agency decisions about land acquisition. The needs for maintenance and patrol of state lands, for example, have limited the enthusiasm of Parks and Forestry for large expansions of territories under their jurisdiction, while the Green Acres Program has shown preference for pursuing large tracts of land in single ownership, primarily because these can be more quickly and easily acquired than subdivided pieces in multiple ownership.

Through the acquisition program, the Pinelands Commission and staff have attempted to translate these differing objectives into one comprehensive strategy whose overall goal is Pinelands preservation and whose principal major criteria are resource diversity, ecosystem maintenance, and recreational opportunity. Today, although there is not always total agreement on specific reasons for acquiring a particular site, all selections represent the collective opinions of all four agencies within the context of a single acquisition program.

Protection of Resource Diversity. Although most of the really outstanding botanical sites in the Pine Barrens—Quaker Bridge, Atsion, and Martha Furnace, for example—were acquired, through a combination of public and private effort, before the commission's coordinated program began, the acquisition of sites possessing specific outstanding natural features that add to the natural diversity of protected lands continues to be an important goal of the CMP. Habitats supporting threatened or endangered plant and animal species, as well as sites such as the Pine Plains or the cedar swamps, exemplify this criterion. Most of the major sites that remained when the CMP was adopted have since been acquired or are scheduled for acquisition under the current program. These include Big and Little Goose ponds (Atlantic County), wetlands along the Oswego River, most of the West Plains, and a southern outlier known as the Little Plains. Efforts also are being made to protect the Spring Hill Plains and the East Plains (outside the Warrens Grove Weapons Range).

Inland and coastal wetlands constitute about 35 percent of the Pinelands and are considered a critical resource. Approximately 50 percent of the region's Atlantic white-cedar swamps, a declining resource worthy of special protection, have been or will be acquired by the state, and about 30 percent of the nearly 80,000 acres of coastal marsh located in the Pinelands is also state owned. (Coastal marshes regulated under DEP and U.S. Army Corps of Engineers programs are not considered as major candidates for acquisition under the CMP.)

Acquisition of undisturbed stream basins is another major objective.

Expansions along the Wading and Batsto rivers and the Westecunk and Cedar creeks, which are among the best representatives of Pinelands aquatic ecosystems, are a focal point of the acquisition program.

Several critical natural areas, however, such as Forked River Mountain, as well as some cultural sites (historic and prehistoric), remain in private hands. Regarding the latter, although some important representatives are state held, few historic sites are scheduled for acquisition under the current program. Nor is active farmland now being pursued for acquisition.

Ecosystem Maintenance. Perhaps the most important long-term measure of the success of the acquisition program is to be found in its contribution to the maintenance of the Pinelands ecosystem. To this end, some scientists have recommended concentrating upon acquisitions of large tracts along the north-south axis in order to preserve ecological diversity, landscape continuity, and hydrologic integrity.[8] They place less importance on the acquisition of smaller, dispersed, isolated pieces in the Pinelands, even those containing special habitats or natural features.

The 8,000-acre Makepeace Lake project, which is located in the still undeveloped, narrow corridor linking the northern and southern regions of the Pinelands, and proposed acquisitions of natural reserves in the southern Pinelands, satisfy this criterion. Acquisitions using watersheds, sub-watersheds, and headwaters as the basic ecological units—including the Cedar Creek, West Plains, and Bass River connector projects—are aimed toward protection and maintenance of the integrity of undisturbed watersheds. Others, including the Lebanon headwaters (a component of the Cedar Creek project), the Friendship Bogs, Goose Pond (Tabernacle Township), and the East Plains–Stafford Forge projects, provide additional protection for existing state-owned lands. Although the Wading River headwaters and the Makepeace Lake acquisition projects were planned around watersheds, existing land uses have prevented complete protection in upstream areas. Most of the significant upstream areas that remain in private ownership however, are located within Special Agricultural Production Areas of the Preservation Area and are therefore afforded some measure of protection. Other areas, such as the upper reaches of the Nescochague Creek, which are important for the ecological integrity of state lands, are poor candidates for acquisition because of established land-use patterns.

Recreational Opportunities. The acquisition program tends to benefit most those recreational activities that do not require specific facilities—in other words, hunting, hiking, nature study, birdwatching, canoeing, and fishing. Each acquisition project area also includes extensive trail systems, providing opportunities for both motorized and nonmotorized use. Several areas encompass land recommended for horse- or foot-trail development by the New Jersey Trails Council as part of a statewide system. Canoe trails on major Pinelands streams on state land have been identified, and more are scheduled, including segments of the Oswego River and Cedar Creek.

Administrative Process. The acquisition program is administered cooperatively by the Pinelands Commission; the divisions of Fish, Game, and Wildlife and Parks and Forestry; and the Green Acres Program. The commission is specifically charged with identifying candidates for acquisition, while authority to purchase rests with the Green Acres Program.

The acquisition process is complex and time consuming, requiring federal funding, surveys, title searches (a lengthy and difficult task), appraisals, and contract negotiations. Environmental groups and even some commissioners, eager to apply for additional federal funding for acquisition, have been critical of the length of time required by the state to execute land purchases. They have also suggested that more staff be hired to expedite matters. With present staffing, the average acquisition rate has been about 6,000 acres per year; the commission's schedule, however, calls for a rate of nearly 10,000 acres per year.

Acquisition Strategies. Historically, fee simple acquisition (outright purchase) has been the principal method used by the state to acquire public conservation land in the Pine Barrens, and with good reason. This strategy is the easiest to administer, and, in the past, land in the Pinelands could be purchased at very low prices. For example, in 1905 the state paid $1.50 per acre for the 597-acre Bass River Reserve, while in 1954/55 it obtained the Wharton tract for only slightly more than $30 per acre. Between 1979 and 1985 the price has gone up, but the cost of land in the Pines remains generally less than that of land elsewhere in the state. During this period the state acquired 42,000 acres for a total cost of about $27.7 million (excluding administrative expenses), approximately $660 per acre.

No purchases have yet been made using the state's right of eminent domain. Nor has the state pursued environmental or conservation easements as an acquisition strategy, not only because the costs of outright purchase have remained relatively low, but also because the retention by various private owners and groups of certain rights on the property in question can create administrative difficulties with easements. Alternatives to fee simple acquisition may be found, however, in the Pinelands Development Credit program and in the actions of the Burlington County Conservation Easement and Pinelands Development Credit Board.

Foreclosure as well as bargain sales of various kinds have also played roles in the acquisition process. Foreclosure, in particular, has the potential for adding enormously to the state's Pinelands holdings, although the state has not often pressed its rights in this area.[9] Gifts and donations of land have also been made and could become more important elements of the land acquisition program in the future. Between 1905 and 1979 approximately 3,000 acres in the Pines were donated to the state by private groups, individuals, or other government agencies. In 1968 the legislature created a Natural Lands Trust, to be administered by the Division of Parks and Forestry; its objective was to seek land donations for open-space preservation. Although the trust was relatively inactive in past years, efforts to re-establish it have begun and small donations have recently occurred—among them a 250-acre parcel that includes Crossley, a critical area known to support important populations of northern pine snake, corn snake, and Pine Barrens treefrog. Altogether, since 1979 several thousand acres have been acquired by the state as gifts or through bargain sales.

Management and Use of State Lands

The state's parks and forests are administered by the Division of Parks and Forestry, and the state's wildlife management areas are administered by the Division of Fish, Game, and Wildlife.[10] Distinct differences exist between these divisions in both style of management and permitted use of public lands. As noted above, Parks and Forestry favors general recreational and educational use, and facilities development is a prominent element of its program. Fish and Game, on the other hand, promotes wildlife-oriented activities and directs its attention toward habitat management and improved conditions for game species.

Public Use.   Each division regulates public use of the land within its respective jurisdiction. In the parks and forests, a wide range of active and passive recreational uses are permitted. Many, such as camping, swimming, and resource interpretation, require facilities development, and substantial efforts have been expended in this direction. The Division of Parks and Forestry, however, as well as members of the public and the commissioners, recognize that currently developed recreational facilities may not be sufficient to meet the growing demand. Although the division does not have a coordinated regional Pinelands interpretive program, some type of educational activity is provided at each of its individual management units. In wildlife management areas, however, which are intended primarily for activities such as hunting, trapping, fishing, bird-watching, nature study, and photography, no formal swimming, picnicking or camping areas are maintained. Nonmotorized boating, canoeing, hunting, and fishing are permitted by both divisions, while motorized vehicles and boats are subject to various restrictions.

Resource Management. Natural resource management in the state's parks and forests includes timber and pulpwood operations, firewood cutting by homeowners, fire control and prescribed burning, and gypsy moth control. All these management programs are controlled, and all are implemented by, state foresters and fire wardens.

Both firewood cutting and commercial timber and pulpwood harvesting are generally directed toward forest stands that have been damaged by some natural or human-caused event—for example, fire, gypsy moths, or windthrow. Recently, the division has also used cutting as a means to upgrade poor or unproductive stands. Controlled burns are periodically conducted by the division to reduce the amount of deadwood and thus to decrease the hazard of wildfire. A secondary objective is to foster continuation of pine-dominated forests. The division has also initiated tree-planting programs, involving pitch pine and other indigenous species.

The cultural-resource management program involves the protection of cultural and historic sites as well as the restoration of significant areas, such as the villages of Double Trouble and Batsto, as interpretive centers. The division has also been assigned the responsibility for administering the state's new Open Lands Management Program, which encourages recreational opportunities on private lands by providing financial and management incentives to landowners.

The resource program of the Division of Fish, Game, and Wildlife is directed primarily toward management of animal populations through regulated harvest (i.e., hunting, trapping, and fishing), protection, species introduction, and manipulation of habitat. Various ongoing survey and research programs monitoring the status of many of the state's animal species are also under the division's administration. In addition, the division promulgates and enforces regulations for both game and nongame species; this authority extends, of course, to all parks, forests, and wildlife management areas. Although in the past the division concerned itself mainly with game species, since the initiation of the Endangered and Nongame Species Program in 1973, habitat management for nongame species has played an increasingly important role. A successful osprey egg transfer and nesting pole program, among others, is a result of this new direction.

Both native and nonnative species have been introduced into wildlife management areas. Two game birds—the native bobwhite and the Old World ring-necked pheasant—are released annually on a "put and take" basis. The native turkey, which had disappeared in the state by the turn of the century because of habitat destruction and overhunting, has also been reintroduced at several locations. The endangered peregrine falcon, which did not previously nest in the Pinelands, now breeds in coastal wildlife management areas thanks to division efforts. Native corn and pine snakes have been released in areas where they had become locally extirpated. Efforts to reintroduce the black bear, however, have met with strong public opposition.

In the past, the Division of Fish, Game, and Wildlife stocked numerous Pinelands lakes and ponds with nonnative game fish. Most efforts to establish populations of these fish in the acid waters of the Pinelands have been unsuccessful and recent stockings have therefore been limited.

Traditional upland habitat management techniques, employed in wildlife management areas, include timber harvesting, establishment and maintenance of food plots and fields, creation of hedgerows, and controlled burning. Such practices generally retard plant succession, provide food and cover, and increase habitat diversity. In aquatic habitats, dam restoration, scraping and aquatic vegetation control, and water-level management are designed to encourage the growth of vegetation that is beneficial to game fish and waterfowl. In coastal areas, open-marsh water management and tidal restoration in salt-hay impoundments are practiced. Overall, however, the level of management varies both from area to area and from year to year.

Regulation of Public Land under the CMP.   In general, habitat modifications and certain recreational uses on public as well as private land must conform with the standards of the Comprehensive Management Plan and must be approved by the Pinelands Commission. This provision applies to the actions of state and local governmental agencies and, to a small degree, to federal landowners.

In 1980 the divisions of Fish, Game, and Wildlife and Parks and Forestry began drafting separate management plans for the lands under their respective administrations. If the commission finds these plans to be consistent with the goals of the CMP and approves them, the divisions will be permitted to operate within a more flexible regulatory framework. In certain instances individual project reviews by the commission will not be required. Such permission has already been granted to the Bureau of Forest Management, a section within Parks and Forestry, for its conduct of harvesting operations. Draft plans indicate that most of the other proposed management programs are consistent with the minimum standards of the CMP, although several unresolved conflicts remain, including certain aquatic habitat management practices proposed by Fish and Game and the development intensity and wetland impact of several recreational facilities planned by Parks and Forestry.

Use and Management Conflicts.   Vehicular use of the Pinelands roads has given rise to a public conflict. The Pinelands Commission designates the areas in the Pinelands that are closed to motorized traffic; it also reviews and approves the routes for organized off-road vehicle events (enduros). The New Jersey Sierra Club has recommended the closure of approximately 70,000 acres in the Preservation Area to all but administrative vehicles in order to provide a "natural wilderness" experience in the region. Local sportsmen and the Pine Barrens Coalition, which represents several environmental organizations, both have objected to these restrictions on what they consider to be a local tradition with little environmental impact. So far no resolution to this conflict has been found, although the commission and the Department of Environmental Protection have initiated a program to address the problem.

Practices such as the liming and fertilizing of off-stream impoundments on state lands to increase water pH and thereby the productivity of nonnative fish species present an obvious conflict with the legislative goal to protect, preserve, and enhance Pinelands resources. Although this practice was begun in the 1960s, it is currently used to maintain fish populations at only one previously established experimental pond. The effects of other practices, such as intensive management of food plots to create wildlife habitat, have not been fully assessed.

Certain aspects of current forest management programs on public lands also raise issues with regard to the protection of the essential character of the Pinelands landscape, as mandated by the state legislature. The mosaic of natural vegetation that exists today reflects a long history of wildfire and past timbering activities (see Chapter 1). Its preservation requires an active management program employing particular burning and timber harvesting practices. Fire suppression programs, which have resulted in a decrease in the frequency and size of fires since the early part of this century, conflict with long-term ecological goals. There is need to develop an acceptable "wildfire" burning strategy in the Pinelands that will not conflict with the parallel social objective to protect life and property from fire.

Forestry programs, too, cause conflicts. Since the time of the Forest Park Reservation Commission, forest productivity goals have been established for the Pinelands. Although productive forest stands are important ecological and cultural features of the Pinelands, a management program that seeks as its primary objective optimum forest productivity could eliminate characteristic elements of the landscape. In this instance, however, the conflict is more in the philosophy than in the practice: timber harvesting methods such as clearcutting and removal of oaks actually contribute to the maintenance of the typical Pinelands landscape (principally by setting back the natural succession of plants). Ironically the general public, including some conservationists, often view these practices as a threat to preservation rather than an aid. Although timber harvesting may also be conducted by wildlife managers to set back succession, clearcutting of large areas and removal of oaks may sometimes conflict with wildlife objectives. Coordination between foresters and wildlife managers may resolve such issues, but the dominant objectives in a particular area are set by the administering state agency.

There are several reasons for these management conflicts. Two are the lack of a comprehensive and coordinated state lands management program, with preservation of the Pinelands ecosystem as its goal, and a tendency for management units in different state agencies to pursue sometimes opposing objectives. These are both policy issues and therefore can be influenced and changed. Practical reasons such as financial constraints and the difficulty or impracticality of implementing alternative strategies, however, are often beyond the control of resource managers and are often overlooked by those who evaluate public programs.

Federal and County Lands

Federal Wildlife Refuges.   The Edwin B. Forsythe National Wildlife Refuge, administered by the U.S. Fish and Wildlife Service, includes two divisions, formerly referred to as Brigantine National Wildlife Refuge and Barnegat National Wildlife Refuge. Both the Barnegat Division (approximately 8,000 acres) and the Brigantine Division (approximately 20,000 acres) were created for the protection and management of waterfowl in the Atlantic flyway. The refuge consists mainly of coastal marsh and bays, but also includes typical upland and lowland Pinelands habitat, barrier beach, fields, and a freshwater impoundment created by diking portions of the salt marsh. The U.S. Fish and Wildlife Service in 1986 released an

acquisition plan calling for adding 11,000 more acres of mostly inland wetland and coastal marsh and bay to the refuge. In addition to monitoring
and regulating wildlife populations and controlling public access within
the refuge, the Fish and Wildlife Service actively manages wildlife habitat through timber stand improvement, water level manipulation, grass-
lands management, and prescribed burning.

Federal Installations.   There are five major federal installations in the
Pinelands—Fort Dix (31,992 acres), McGuire Air Force Base (3,490 acres),
Lakehurst Naval Air Engineering Center (7,412 acres), the Federal Avia-
tion Administration's Technical Center (5,055 acres), and the Warren Grove
Weapons Range (8,500 acres). McGuire and the Technical Center are
highly developed, but there are extensive areas of open space at Fort Dix,
Lakehurst, and Warren Grove.

   Fort Dix and Lakehurst both have ongoing resource conservation programs. Forest management involves timber harvests, timber stand improvement, reforestation, and controlled burning. Wildlife management includes the planting of food and cover plots and stocking. Hunting
and fishing as well as passive recreational activities such as birding, nature study, and camping are also permitted on a limited basis at both
installations.

   There are no active resource conservation or public recreation programs at the FAA Technical Center, but controlled deer hunts have been
permitted on the center's grounds. Maintenance mowing, however, is of
interest, since the establishment of grassland conditions has created suitable habitat for breeding populations of upland sandpiper, vesper sparrow, and grasshopper sparrow, three species listed by the state as threatened or endangered.

   The United States Air Force has recently gained control of approximately 8,500 acres located mainly within the East Plains of Bass River
Township and is in the process of acquiring the area, which has been used
as a weapons range since the early 1940s. In a voluntary cooperative
effort, the National Park Service, the New Jersey Air National Guard, the
Pinelands Commission, and the Department of Environmental Protection
have developed a land management plan for this area whose objectives
are to protect and preserve the unique resources of the East Plains and to
provide research and recreational opportunities while ensuring that the
guard's defense mission continues unimpeded. This plan provides some
access for passive recreation such as birding, botanizing, and hunting; it
regulates the use of motorized vehicles; and it establishes a natural area
for scientific research. A revegetation program, initiated in the spring of

1984, is intended to re-establish characteristic Pine Plains vegetation in areas denuded by range activities. In the spring of 1985, the New Jersey Forestry Service conducted a 60-acre controlled burn in the Weapons Area. Although the principal objective of this burn was to reduce fire hazard, it was also to some degree successful in mimicking the effect of natural wildfire, which is necessary for maintenance of the Pine Plains vegetation.

County Parks.   Atlantic, Camden, and Ocean counties maintain seven separate Pinelands parks encompassing more than 3,000 acres of land. By providing various recreational opportunities and by preserving a wide range of Pinelands habitats, these facilities complement both the ecological and recreational values of state lands.

Ocean County operates three facilities—A. Paul King Park in Stafford Township (60 acres), Tuckerton Park in Tuckerton (17 acres), and Robert Miller Airpark in Berkeley and Lacey townships (944 acres). The county also administers an active recreational and interpretive program at a long list of locations throughout the Pinelands, and in 1985 acquired an additional 650 acres along Oyster Creek at Wells Mills in Ocean Township (an area once considered for acquisition by the state). Although some development of recreational facilities is anticipated in this new park, most of it will be left in a natural state.

Three Atlantic County parks are in the Pinelands—Estell Manor Park in Estell Manor (1,672 acres) and Gaskill and Weymouth parks (both small) in Mays Landing and Weymouth Township, respectively. Estell Manor, located along the South and Great Egg Harbor rivers, supports 250 acres of developed recreational parkland and has a nature center as the focus of its interpretive program. Atlantic County is also in the process of purchasing another extensive tract along the Great Egg Harbor River adjacent to the state's Makepeace Lake project.

New Brooklyn Park, a 600-acre undeveloped tract also located along the Great Egg Harbor River, represents Camden County's only presence in the Pinelands. Boating and fishing are the principal forms of recreation here.

The Role of Private Conservation Groups

Several private, nonprofit organizations have also helped preserve Pinelands resources through land acquisition and management. Among the most active are the New Jersey Conservation Foundation, The Nature

Conservancy, and the Philadelphia Conservationists. The New Jersey Conservation Foundation has had the longest and the closest association with the state's Pinelands acquisition program. In the mid-1970s it was involved with several state projects in the Preservation Area, among them the 909-acre Goose Ponds project, which was acquired by the foundation and then transferred to the state. The foundation has retained title to several other Pinelands parcels, and has assisted the state in the initiation of a tax lien foreclosure program, participated in Burlington County's pilot easement project, and obtained many conservation easements. Recently the foundation was instrumental in the creation and passage of the state's innovative Open Lands Management Program, which encourages private owners to open their lands to public recreation.

The Nature Conservancy is principally interested in acquiring and managing lands with exceptional natural features—wetlands, for example, or habitats supporting endangered species. Like the Conservation Foundation, the Conservancy usually acquires lands and then transfers title to the state. A total of 2,551 acres, including both coastal and inland Pinelands habitats, has been treated in this manner; an additional 3,855 acres of land has been acquired and transferred to the federal Fish and Wildlife Service as part of what used to be called the Barnegat National Wildlife Refuge. With the cooperation of the New Jersey Conservation Foundation, The Nature Conservancy also acquired two small preserves— the Eldora Preserve (Cape May County) and land located along the Manumuskin River (Cumberland County); although both preserves supported critical habitats, neither was a good candidate for state acquisition because of small size or isolated location. The Nature Conservancy recently purchased a unique botanical site in Atlantic County and is pursuing several more large tracts within the Pinelands.

The approach of the Philadelphia Conservationists and its land-holding and planning companion, the Natural Lands Trust, is somewhat different. In addition to direct purchase of land, this group also assists landowners who want both to protect and to use their natural land. The Philadelphia Conservationists worked with the New Jersey Conservation Foundation on the Goose Ponds project, and has itself acquired and transferred to the state or federal government several coastal areas.

The programs of all these conservation groups generally complement and in some ways go beyond the state's acquisition program. As private organizations, they can sometimes work more quickly and use more innovative protection methods than can the state. They can also acquire and manage important parcels that are too small or too separated from existing public lands to be effectively managed by government agencies.

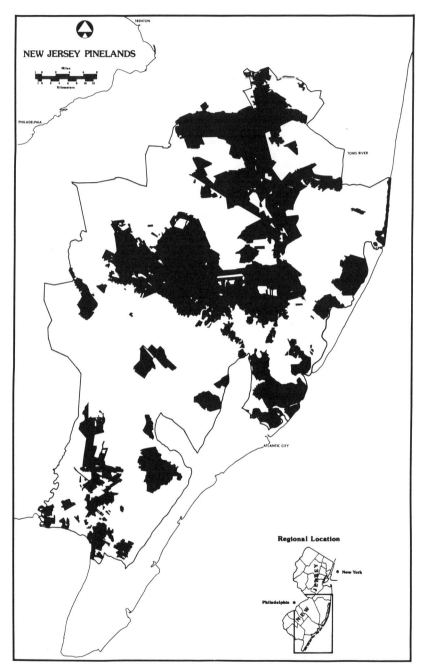

Figure 9–1. Public Land in the Pinelands. Map drawn by Frederick Douthitt.

Summary

Acquisition is certainly the surest way to achieve the preservation of the Pinelands. This fact was recognized early in the twentieth century and today's Pinelands acquisition program is firmly based on the large network of state-owned land that has been built up over the past eighty years. Currently, more than 300,000 acres in the Pinelands is either owned outright by the state or scheduled for purchase under funded projects (Figure 9–1). Continued acquisition of land and implementation of land management strategies, however, are required to ensure the long-term preservation of the entire ecosystem as well as the integrity of the state-land system.

By the end of 1986 the commission had authorized the acquisition of 67,000 acres of environmentally sensitive land. The original $26 million provided by the federal government for land acquisition was fully committed. The outlook for additional federal assistance was not bright until Senator Bill Bradley announced in early 1987 that he would introduce a bill providing $21.2 million for additional land purchases in the Pinelands and $5 million for a much-needed visitors' center. The continued federal support is needed to ensure success of the Pinelands program in preserving many critical natural and cultural resources, in providing recreational opportunities for the public, and in contributing to the long-term maintenance of representative elements of the Pinelands ecosystem.

10. Economic and Fiscal Support Programs

James K. Conant

Peter J. Pizor

The efforts to preserve and protect the Pinelands ignited a political confrontation in New Jersey that Governor Byrne described as the most bitter and emotional conflict during his tenure in the executive office.[1] This political struggle pitted elected officials and interest groups with fundamentally different values and priorities against each other.[2] Among the many factors that contributed to the intensity of this conflict, two were especially important. First, very little was known about the economic and fiscal consequences of land-use planning programs comparable in scope to the one contemplated for the Pinelands. Thus, predictions about what the consequences would be played an important role in the political struggle. Second, many on each side perceived the conflict as a zero-sum game. Proponents of state-imposed development restrictions viewed the increasing pace of development in the region as a serious threat to the ecological viability of the area. Opponents of state intervention predicted that the development restrictions would have disastrous economic and fiscal consequences for the region and its inhabitants.

Although the sponsors and supporters of a strong protection plan for the Pinelands ultimately prevailed in the political struggle, the opponents of state intervention did gain some important concessions through their determined political resistance.[3] Among these concessions were several programs aimed at limiting or ameliorating the predicted negative economic and fiscal consequences of the land-use regulations. The purpose of this chapter is to describe these economic and fiscal support programs and to analyze their effects. As part of this analysis, the predictions each side made about the economic and fiscal consequences of the restrictions are outlined; the actual impact of development restrictions on the regional economy, land markets, and the fiscal condition of the fifty-two Pinelands municipalities is examined; and the extent to which the economic and fiscal support programs cushioned the adverse effects of the development restrictions is assessed.[4]

The Public Debate

Supporters of the Pinelands Protection Act argued that strict land-use controls were needed to deal with the "crisis of random and uncoordinated development," which posed a serious threat to the ecologically sensitive Pines area.[5] Among the primary concerns of those fighting for the act was the belief that increasing numbers of scattered developments would be located within the "core," or the most ecologically sensitive area, of the Pinelands itself. The rapid growth of development activities in areas such as Atlantic City, which bordered the core, was also a concern. Indeed, the large scale of developments planned for the Atlantic City area was one of the considerations that inspired Governor Byrne to stop what he called "unwanted development" in the area through the imposition of an eighteen-month building moratorium in February of 1979.[6]

While Governor Byrne and the environmental groups viewed development as a threat to the ecology of the Pinelands Area, many landowners, farmers, builders, and municipal officials who lived in the Pinelands viewed the moratorium and the protection plan as threats to their economic and political interests. For example, the Coalition for the Sensible Preservation of the Pinelands objected to what it called the "theft" and "confiscation" of private property by the state. The development restrictions, the coalition argued in a full-page newspaper ad, were merely an inexpensive means for the state to acquire private property without paying for it.[7]

In addition to this perceived threat to their property rights, opponents of the Pinelands legislation and the Comprehensive Management Plan predicted that severe economic losses would be suffered as a result of the development restrictions. Some, like the New Jersey Builders Association, argued that the Pinelands Protection Act would "precipitate an economic blight on the entire area of South Jersey."[8] Others, like one representative of the Home Builders League of South Jersey, maintained that the plan restricting development to only 5 percent of the one-million-acre Pinelands region would "spell economic disaster for South Jersey."[9] Among the economic consequences predicted by these interest groups were housing shortages, increased housing prices, increased unemployment, and bankruptcies in construction and related businesses.

The opposition's predictions about the effects that the land-use regulations would have on landowners, like their predictions about the effects on the South Jersey economy, presented a grim scenario. One private consultant employed by opponents of the CMP projected the loss of property value for farm and vacant land at a whopping $653 million.[10] Predictions like this one spurred the South Jersey Chamber of Commerce to oppose the Pinelands plan. "If the people of New Jersey wish to preserve more of the Pinelands than they now own," the chamber argued, "the people of New Jersey should be willing to pay the price. A small group of property owners should not be made to do so."[11]

Also, municipal officials were concerned about the predicted drop in property values, particularly for vacant land. Some argued that the loss in property value would mean a loss in tax base, which in turn would either require spending cutbacks or tax increases. Likewise, municipal officials were concerned about the cost of complying with the new development restrictions, and many objected to the loss of local control over development. The passions aroused on each side by the perceived threat of state action or inaction in the Pinelands Area had dramatic impact on the political arena. Many state legislators from South Jersey felt compelled to respond to their constituents' pleas by opposing the legislation and the CMP. At the same time, Governor Byrne and those legislators who favored a strict protection plan had highly visible, active support from environmental groups and from some citizens and municipal officials within the Pinelands area itself.

Although members of the Byrne administration recognized that the opposition's primary concern over the Pinelands protection efforts was the economic impact it might have, they took the position that the economic effects were not likely to be as dramatic as some of the estimates suggested.[12] Nevertheless, the strong pressure the opposition mounted in the state legislature during the writing of the Comprehensive Management Plan apparently moved Governor Byrne to hold a public hearing on the protection plan in September of 1980. After listening to the fears, concerns, and complaints of Pinelands landowners, farmers, builders, and municipal officials at this hearing, the governor issued a call for a study to assess the plan's possible impacts. The responsibility for conducting this study was given to the Pinelands Commission. Due to lack of staff and in-house resources, the commission hired a consulting firm to do the initial assessment.

Pinelands Commission's Predictions of 1980.   Like the opposition's predictions about the impact the land-use regulations would have, the predictions of the Pinelands Commission became an important part of the debate over the development restrictions. The commission released its predictions about the economic and fiscal effects of the land-use plan in November of 1980. These predictions concerning the impact of the proposed development restrictions were grouped into three main areas: (1) the regional economy, (2) land markets, and (3) municipalities.

In terms of the regional economy, the general conclusion was that, while the Comprehensive Management Plan would bring changes, its effect would not be significant. Only a minimum effect was predicted for construction and manufacturing employment; no negative effects were predicted for agriculture; and gains were predicted for employment in tourism and recreation.[13]

In terms of land values, the general conclusion contained in the report was that the plan's effect would be "highly variable."[14] Vacant land in the Rural Development and Regional Growth areas was expected to increase in price, while values in the Preservation, Forest, and Agricultural areas were expected to fall. The report did note that property values in the Preservation Area could decline by as much as 90 percent owing to the loss of development rights, but the authors maintained that property value depended on a host of factors in addition to land-use restrictions.[15] In order to estimate what the aggregate loss in property values for the Preservation, Forest, and Agricultural areas might be, the authors assumed a loss in property value of 16 to 25 percent. Based on these percentages, the aggregate loss in property value predicted for the restricted area was $6.7 to $83.4 million—a figure far below the $653 million loss predicted by opponents of the land-use regulation plan.[16]

The report published by the Pinelands Commission was also much more optimistic than the opposition's predictions about the plan's impact on the fiscal condition of the Pinelands municipalities. The authors of the report predicted that the plan's impact on property taxes would not be significant. Only three municipalities would lose more than 5 percent of their tax base.[17] These calculations were based on the assumption that the median values for property would rise in the growth areas by 10 percent and fall in the more restricted areas by only 15 percent.[18] The authors of the report also suggested that the cost of changing municipal development rules to comply with the Comprehensive Management Plan would be minimal, ranging from only $12,000 to $20,000.[19] Furthermore, they argued that state aid for assisting with the changeover would be equal to about one-third of these costs.

Reaction and Response.   The initial response by landowners within the Pinelands area to the development moratorium and to the restrictions expected in the Comprehensive Management Plan seemed to confirm some of the predictions made by those who were opposed to the protection plan. Even before the CMP was finalized in November of 1980, tax appeals were being filed by landowners who argued that the land use regulations had significantly reduced the value of their property. In many cases, these appeals were upheld and the assessed value of the property was reduced.

Undoubtedly, the much publicized predictions that the land-use restrictions would sharply reduce property values helped to spur the assessment challenges. By January of 1981, the month the Comprehensive Management Plan was actually implemented, the Ocean County Tax Board had granted 861 assessment appeals, which resulted in a $5.1-million reduction in assessed values for its municipalities. Likewise, the Burlington County Tax Board granted 74 appeals, which reduced the county's property tax base by more than $300,000.[20] In the town of Medford (Burlington County), 65 tax appeals were filed, challenging $5.5 million of the town's $7.0 million of assessed value on those properties.[21]

CMP Economic and Fiscal Support Programs

While the property-tax appeals process was unfolding, the Pinelands Commission was working feverishly to finish the Comprehensive Management Plan by the August 6, 1980, deadline established by Governor Byrne in Executive Order 71. During the spring and summer of that year, the Pinelands commissioners, staff, and consultants had to decide whether to recommend that state assistance be provided to landowners and municipalities adversely affected by the CMP. Specifically, the commission had to decide whether state funds should be made available to a municipality if the CMP had "a significant adverse impact on [that] municipality's tax structure," and whether compensation of some kind should be provided to landowners in the most restricted areas for their loss of development rights.

Support for Municipalities.   The first issue had two elements: whether payments should be made by the state for property taxes lost as a result of property purchased by the state, and whether payments should be made for tax base lost as a result of property devaluation. Compensating local governments for the loss of taxable property as a result of state purchases was not particularly controversial. The precedent for such payments had been established in New Jersey many years before the Pinelands plan was even considered. Furthermore, the state Green Acres Program, already in place, could provide the administration and funding for a reimbursement system. Under New Jersey's Green Acres Program, local governments are reimbursed for taxes lost on land purchased by the state on a declining balance system. The first year, 100 percent of the tax loss is re-imbursed; the second year, 92 percent of the loss is reimbursed, and so on until the reimbursement expires after thirteen years.

Unlike the question of compensation for state land purchases, how-ever, the question of whether to compensate Pinelands municipalities for ratables lost owing to property devaluation was hotly disputed. Moreover, to say that local governments should be compensated for losses of this type would make it very difficult to avoid the conclusion that the property owners themselves ought to be compensated as well. Since there was a strong opposition to compensation for landowners, support for this type of municipal support was only lukewarm. Nevertheless, by the end of the summer of 1980, the commission's policies did include a recommendation that assistance be provided to stabilize tax rates in municipalities which were adversely affected by the development restrictions. Since the com-mission did not have the authority to raise the revenue needed for the program, however, this policy merely remained a recommendation until 1983, when the state legislature finally funded it for a three-year period.

Support Programs for Landowners.   The economic issue that caused the sharpest debate during the development of the Comprehensive Manage-ment Plan was whether compensation of some kind should be provided to property owners for their loss of development rights. Despite what ap-peared to be a growing awareness on the part of the commissioners and staff that their actions might have significant consequences for landowners within the Preservation, Forest, and Agricultural Production manage-ment areas, few were disposed to provide compensation to individual landowners who might suffer economic loss as a result of the development restrictions. Furthermore, some of the environmentalists were adamantly opposed to any kind of compensation for landowners. They insisted that the down-zoning was completely justified on environmental grounds and was legally permissible under the New Jersey Pinelands Protection Act. If the landowners did experience losses, some environmentalists argued, it was a small price to pay for preserving and protecting the "essential char-acter of the Pines," as specified by the state legislature.

The tough stand the environmentalists took toward the compensation issue was reinforced by the legal consultants the commission hired. Rep-resentatives from the Chicago-based law firm of Ross, Hardies, O'Keefe, Babcock, and Parsons argued that there was no legal requirement that compensation be provided to landowners for the loss of development rights. Nevertheless, in contrast to the dominant opinion among the com-missioners, staff, and consultants, at least some commissioners argued that some form of compensation for landowners in the restricted areas was necessary.

B. Budd Chavooshian, viewed by many as the dean of New Jersey land-use planners, maintained that the commission had a responsibility to respond to what he called the "windfall/wipeout" syndrome. Landowners in the Preservation Area, Chavooshian argued, were faced with a wipeout situation, because the loss of development rights would sharply reduce the value of their land. At the same time, he argued, landowners in the areas designated by the CMP as Growth Areas would receive a windfall; both the value of their land and their prospects for selling it would improve dramatically under the CMP. In light of this situation, Chavooshian insisted that some mechanism be included in the Comprehensive Management Plan to reduce the differential between landowners in the windfall and wipeout positions.

At a Pinelands Commission meeting on April 11, 1980, Chavooshian recommended that a program be adopted by the commission that would provide compensation to landowners who might suffer a wipeout as a result of the development restrictions. Generally speaking, the proposal was greeted by hostile responses from other commission members, staff, and environmental groups. Opinions changed over the next several weeks, however, as the matter was discussed further. Eventually, the commission agreed to draft a compromise program that would address the fairness issue, but this program was not supposed to deal exclusively with the issue of compensation.

What finally emerged from the commission's efforts to deal with the fairness issue was an ambitious and relatively new method for dealing with the inequities created by land-use regulation. The program became known as the Pinelands Development Credit Program. In fashioning this program, the commissioners applied a concept, called transfer of development rights, that was keenly debated among land-use experts but virtually unknown outside this small circle of professionals.

In a transfer-of-development-rights (TDR) program, landowners in areas where development is restricted are granted certificates of development rights. These certificiates are transferable and can be sold. The buyer can use the certificate to expand housing densities in the areas designated for development. Thus, at least in theory, landowners in such districts are compensated for their loss of development rights through a market mechanism rather than a fixed government payment. Since sales are uncoerced, the amount of compensation (the sales price of the development credit) is expected to reflect the current market value of additional housing density in the growth zones.

Under the terms of the program established in the Comprehensive Management Plan, landowners in three Pinelands management areas qualify for the development credits. Each development credit can be used to increase residential densities by four single-family units in appropriately zoned areas. Landowners in the Preservation District are eligible for one Pinelands Development Credit (PDC) per thirty-nine acres of upland and 0.2 PDCs for wetlands. Landowners in the Agricultural Production and Special Agricultural Production areas are eligible for two PDCs for each thirty-nine acres of actively farmed land. Wetlands that are not being cultivated qualify for 0.2 PDCs per thirty-nine acres. Landowners whose holdings fall below the thirty-nine-acre threshold receive fractional credits for lots as small as 0.1 acres.

Although the PDC program seemed to provide an effective vehicle for balancing the inequities created by the windfall/wipeout effects of the land-use restrictions, the commission was taking a huge gamble in this pioneering effort. Operational experience with transfer-of-development-rights programs was limited. The technique had been used only in a few areas and it had been used only to preserve historical buildings and farmland. Furthermore, the area affected by these programs had never exceeded one county. Yet in just a few pages of the CMP, the commission outlined a transfer-of-development-rights plan that would affect approximately one million acres of land in seven counties. Furthermore, the plan not only allowed transfer of development rights from one property to another but also allowed transfers across municipal and county boundaries.

Economic and Fiscal Impacts of the CMP

The Commission's Initial Assessment of Effects. In July of 1983, the Pinelands Commission published its first attempt to assess the actual consequences of the Comprehensive Management Plan. The report begins with a statement of the commission's dual goals "to protect and enhance the land and water resources of the Pinelands while providing for economic growth and residential development." To someone familiar with the political collision over environmental and economic values that had taken place during the development of the CMP, this statement of goals might seem somewhat ironic.

The commission's 1983 report is carefully constructed. The basic methodology used for the analysis is "to compare pre-moratorium, moratorium, and post-Plan trends in the Pinelands with trends outside the Pinelands or throughout the seven-county region and state."[22] More specifically, aggregate data on the economic and fiscal consequences of the land-use restrictions are assembled. The primary reason for this type of aggregate, comparative analysis, the authors of the report maintain, is to separate the effects that changes in land-use regulations have from those of other key variables, such as the national and state economies. However, the authors also acknowledge the limitations of their methodology: Significant effects that may have occurred within individual Pinelands municipalities can be lost in the overall trends.

After stating that the political "opposition to the CMP was focused primarily on its perceived negative economic impacts," the commission's initial findings on the economic and fiscal consequences of the CMP are summarized.[23] Based on the economic and fiscal data assembled for the moratorium period (1979–1980) and the postmoratorium period between 1981 and 1982, the commission's report concludes that the development restrictions had very little short-term impact on the regional economy, land markets (individual landowners), or the fiscal condition of the Pinelands municipalities. "No significant shifts in overall employment trends" are identified. "No overall effect on prices per acre in the Protection Area" is found, and "no discernible effect on the overall level of housing sales or on housing prices in the Pinelands" is detected.[24] The data do show that new construction dropped sharply during both the moratorium period and the postmoratorium period from what it was before the CMP; however, "general economic conditions rather than the development restrictions imposed by the Plan" were identified as the principal cause of this decline.[25]

As part of the discussion about the fiscal condition of the Pinelands municipalities, the report notes that a large number of tax appeals on vacant land had been granted and that the state had purchased a substantial amount of land under the Green Acres Program. Yet the report says also that in general, "the effect of this reduction on total assessed valuation has been minor (two percent or less)."[26] The report does acknowledge that property tax rates grew very rapidly in some Pinelands municipalities, but argues that data from a microanalysis of the ten municipalities with the largest tax increases show that spending increases, not reductions in the tax base, have accounted for the rise in property taxes.

The findings contained in the commission's 1983 assessment bear a striking similarity to the commission's 1980 predictions. They also stand in sharp contrast to the disastrous consequences predicted by the opposition to the protection act and the CMP. Furthermore, the findings reported in the initial assessment contrast sharply with contemporary newspaper reports about the plan's adverse economic and fiscal consequences. Perhaps these differences can be explained by varying "levels of analysis." The newspaper stories focus on the effects felt by individual landowners, farmers, developers, and municipalities; the commission's focus is on the aggregate economic and fiscal consequences of the act and the CMP.

The Commission's 1985 Assessment. In 1985, the Pinelands Commission published its second assessment of the CMP's effects. Unlike the first assessment, the CMP's impact on the regional economy is not a major focus for this study. However, the CMP's effects on land markets, housing markets, and municipal finances are systematically examined in the 1985 assessment, just as they were in the 1983 report. In addition, the methodology used for the two reports is similar. Aggregate data are assembled in order to assess the CMP's overall effects.

In contrast to the commission's 1980 predictions and 1983 assessment, the 1985 report concludes that the CMP did have a detectable impact on land markets throughout the Pinelands Area. The report notes that both "the volume of vacant land sales and the number of housing starts in the Pinelands Area" declined.[27] The decline in land transactions, the report says, is most noticable in the Preservation, Forest and Rural Development areas. The decline in housing construction is most visible in the Preservation, Forest, Agricultural Production, and Rural Development areas. The report also notes, however, that despite the drop in housing construction and vacant land transactions, the average price per acre dropped sharply only in the Preservation Area. In all other management areas except the Agricultural Production Area, the report says, increases in price per acre have exceeded those for land outside the Protection Area.

Like the commission's 1980 predictions and 1983 report, the commission's 1985 study found that the CMP's effect on housing prices and the financial condition of municipalities had been minimal. Moreover, the report also says that the CMP did not appear to have had "a significant effect on the value of existing housing in the Pinelands."[28] Only one Pinelands municipality had suffered a significant reduction in its tax base owing to reductions in vacant land assessments resulting fom tax appeals, reassessments, and reevaluations, although twenty-eight other municipalities did lose some property tax base as a result of the CMP.

Current Assessment of the CMP Effects

The following analysis employs the 1985 aggregate statistical data developed by the commission staff to examine in depth the economic and fiscal consequences of the CMP. Of course, the problem with this type of analysis, as the commission noted in its 1983 report, is that hardships suffered by individual landowners, farmers, businesses, and municipalities may not be well documented. In light of this fact, some attempt is made here to identify effects on individual municipalities and Pinelands management areas, but much more research is needed.

Residential Construction and Housing Prices.   Chief among the predictions made by those who opposed the development restrictions was that of a serious adverse effect on the economy of South Jersey. Putting the brakes on residential development, opponents argued, would cause bankruptcies in the construction business, reduce employment, and create a housing shortage that would make housing prices unaffordable. Given the general objecties of the Pinelands legislation and the specific purposes of the CMP to limit development, it seems clear that some reduction in construction was inevitable.

For example, residential development within the Preservation and the Agricultural and Special Agricultural management areas was essentially prohibited, and development within the Forest Area was highly restricted. Since these four management areas account for approximately 64 percent of the land area under the CMP, the prediction that residential construction would be adversely affected does not seem unreasonable. Nevertheless, the commission's 1983 report suggested that the CMP's effect on the overall volume of housing construction was in fact minimal. By stated legislative and commission objectives, the land-use regulations contained in the CMP are intended to channel but not prevent growth. Prior to the CMP, the commission argued, growth had been concentrated in those management areas marked for development under the plan.[29]

When building permits are used as a vehicle to measure the CMP's effect on residential construction, raw data indicate that the CMP has had a significant effect on development. Construction activity as measured by the number of building permits issued peaked in 1978, declined dramatically in the early 1980s, and then rebounded in 1983 and 1984. Before firm conclusions can be drawn about the CMP's effect on residential construction, however, it is important to consider the effect that other factors, such as national and state economic conditions, had on this situation. For example, the high interest rates of the late 1970s and the recession of 1981–1982 had an adverse effect on residential construction nationwide. By putting data for the Pinelands municipalities in a comparative context, the broad effects of these macroeconomic factors can be taken into account. Specifically, it is helpful to compare the data for the Pinelands municipalities with the data for the seven-county region and for the state as a whole.

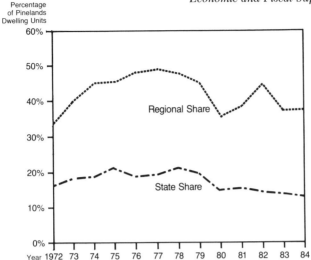

Figure 10–1. Total Residential Dwelling Units Authorized in Fifty-two Pinelands Municipalities as a Percentage Share of Regional and State-Permitted Units, 1972–1984. SOURCE: Chart redrawn by Tina Campbell from Pinelands Commission, *Economic and Fiscal Impacts of the Pinelands Comprehensive Management Plan* (New Lisbon, N.J., November 1985), p. 41.

The data in Figure 10–1 show that the Pinelands municipalities' share of the region's residential construction fell during the moratorium period but moved back up in the first two years of CMP implementation. In 1983 and 1984, the Pineland's share was below the premoratorium level for the region. In contrast, the Pinelands' share of state building permits remained relatively stable after an initial decline in 1979. Nevertheless, despite these somewhat different trends vis-à-vis the regional and state shares, the data do seem to confirm the opposition's prediction that residential construction would be adversely affected by the development restrictions.

What effect did this building slowdown have on housing prices? It had been predicted that the development restrictions would make the price of housing unaffordable, but in fact the data (see Figure 10–2) show that housing prices did not rise in the Pines as fast as they did in the state or the region as a whole. Thus, in this case, the data seem to contradict rather than to confirm the opposition's prediction.

Vacant Land Sales and Values. Predictions that land values would be adversely affected as a result of the development restrictions accompanied predictions about adverse economic effects. The primary focus of the former was an expected decline in the value of vacant and previously un-

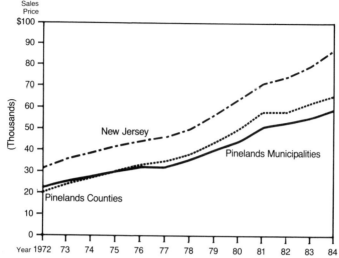

Figure 10–2. Average Sales Price of Residential Units in Fifty-two Pinelands Municipalities as Compared with Average Sales Prices in Seven Pinelands Counties and the State, 1972–1984. SOURCE: Chart redrawn by Tina Campbell from Pinelands Commission, *Economic and Fiscal Impacts of the Pinelands Comprehensive Management Plan* (New Lisbon, N.J., November 1985), p. 52.

developed land. Indeed, some feared that the market for their land would either dry up or would operate only at confiscatory prices.

The data show that a sharp drop in the absolute number of vacant land sales occurred in the Pinelands municipalities between 1979 and 1982. Was this decline caused by the land-use restrictions? Here again, the pattern of decline seems to follow the national and state economies, so it is important to look at the comparative data before drawing hard and fast conclusions. In Figure 10–3, the sales of vacant land in the Pinelands municipalities are compared with similar sales in the seven-county region and the state. These comparative data do seem to confirm the notion that development restrictions were not the only factor that caused the decline in sales of vacant land. The data show that the decline in the Pinelands municipalities' share of vacant land sales actually began in 1976. Thus, the decline began before the recession of 1979–1981, three years before the moratorium and five years before the CMP came into effect. In addition, the data show the Pinelands share of both regional and state sales began to rise again in 1983 and 1984.

This is not to say that the development restrictions had no effect on sales. Rather, the comparative data provide a perspective on the longer-term trend that was in place prior to the time when the land-use restric-

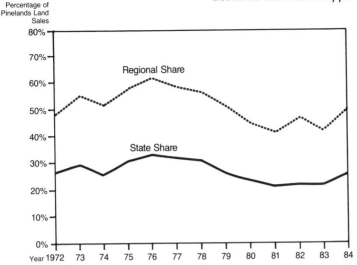

Figure 10–3. Vacant Land Sales in Fifty-two Pinelands Municipalities as a Percentage Share of Regional and State Vacant Land Sales Transactions, 1972–1984. Source: Chart redrawn by Tina Campbell from Pinelands Commission, *Economic and Fiscal Impacts of the Pinelands Comprehensive Management Plan* (New Lisbon, N.J., November 1985), p. 12.

tions were installed. Thus, one might conclude from the data that, while the development restrictions did have an effect, they probably exacerbated rather than caused the downward trend.

In addition to examining the aggregate effects of development restrictions on vacant land sales across all fifty-two Pinelands municipalities, one must also look at the effects of those restrictions in the individual management areas. For example, one might predict that sales volume would decline most in those management areas where development is essentially eliminated, such as the Preservation, Special Agricultural, and Agricultural Production areas, or where it is severely limited, such as the Forest Areas. In general, the data in Table 10–1 confirm that prediction.

Equally important, the data show that land sales are down in all management areas, including those where development is allowed and expected. For example, land sales in the Regional Growth Area were almost 40 percent lower in the post-CMP period than they were in the pre-CMP period. The data also show two other important trends. First, the vacant land sales in the Rural Development Area have declined more than in any other area except the Preservation Area. Second, vacant land sales in the post-CMP period have exceeded those of the pre-CMP period only in land areas outside the Pinelands (but still within the fifty-two Pinelands

Table 10–1. Comparisons of the Number, Average Price, and Parcel Size of Vacant Land Sales in Sixteen Municipalities within and outside the Pinelands

Management Area	Pre-Pinelands (1976–1978)	Post-CMP (1981–1984)	Percent Change
	No. of Land Sales		
Preservation	39	15	−61.5
Forest	235	121	−48.5
Agricultural Production	85	62	−27.1
Rural Development	313	144	−54.0
Regional Growth	190	117	−38.4
Pinelands Towns and Villages	138	105	−23.9
Total Pinelands Area	1000	564	−43.6
Outside Pinelands	348	417	19.8
	Average Price per Acre		
Preservation	$1,643	$ 594	−63.8
Forest	$1,105	$1,777	60.8
Agricultural Production	$2,081	$2,255	8.4
Rural Development	$1,763	$3,380	91.7
Regional Growth	$2,786	$6,166	121.3
Pinelands Towns and Villages	$3,176	$4,252	33.9
Total Pinelands Area	$1,915	$2,588	35.1
Outside Pinelands	$2,634	$3,192	21.2
	Mean No. of Acres per Sale		
Preservation	16.1	123.6	667.7
Forest	12.6	10.0	−20.6
Agricultural Production	9.8	19.2	95.9
Rural Development	7.3	7.1	− 2.7
Regional Growth	12.2	8.3	−32.0
Pinelands Towns and Villages	4.4	4.5	2.3
Total Pinelands Area	9.6	11.9	24.0
Outside Pinelands	8.6	9.7	12.8

SOURCE: Pinelands Commission. November 1985. *Economic & Fiscal Impacts of the Pinelands Comprehensive Management Plan* (New Lisbon, N.J.), pp. 20, 23 and 28.

municipalities). The data confirm that one of the most significant impacts of the development restrictions has been to direct growth away from the Pinelands Area to adjacent areas.

While data on both the total number of vacant land sales and the number of sales by management areas are necessary parts of developing a complete picture of the effects of development restriction, they are not sufficient. Data on the price of the land sold are also needed. For example, it is conceivable that the most dramatic effect of the restrictions has been on the price of the vacant land rather than on sales volume. Indeed, that is what the data in Table 10–1 appear to show.

The average price per acre in the Preservation Area was sharply (63 percent) lower in the post-CMP period than in the pre-CMP period. On the other hand, the price per acre in the Rural Development and Regional Growth areas was much higher (121 percent) than prior to the CMP. Thus the data seem to show that the windfall/wipeout syndrome predicted by Budd Chavooshian was at work. There is, however, one area where the effects do not seem to match up with predictions. Land prices in the heavily restricted Forest and Agricultural Production areas were substantially higher in the post-CMP period rather than lower. Why this trend should occur, particularly in light of declining farmland prices across most of the nation, is not clear.

What factors account for the substantial changes in land prices? Are the development restrictions themselves the key factor? The data suggest that they are, but at least one additional variable needs to be taken into account. The decreases and increases in the average price per acre also seem to be a function of the size of the parcel purchased in each sales transaction. For example, the average (mean) number of acres purchased in the Preservation Area jumped from 16.1 in the pre-CMP period to 123.6 in the post-CMP period. Thus, the development restrictions seem to have resulted in fewer but larger land purchases in the Preservation Area, which resulted in much lower average prices per acre. In the Regional Growth Areas, however, the opposite seems to have occurred: the average number of acres per transaction fell from 12.2 to 8.3.

Municipal Ratables and Tax Rates. Some municipal officials and Pinelands residents opposed the protection plan because they feared it would mean a loss of local tax base, which in turn would mean increased property taxes for homeowners and businesses. This decrease in property tax base was expected to result both from the predicted drop in the value of vacant land and from land purchases by the state.

As with the assessment of other effects, one way to examine the effect of the development restrictions on the municipal tax base is to use aggregate data for all fifty-two Pinelands municipalities. The data in Figure 10–4 show that vacant land did fall as a share of all ratables in the post–CMP period, but the data also show that this decline began in 1975, six years before the CMP was in place and four years before Governor Byrne's development moratorium. Furthermore, no sudden or dramatic drop in municipal tax base occurred in 1979, 1980, or 1981. The slope of the decline seems to have remained relatively constant throughout the ten-year period from 1974 through 1984.

Since aggregate data can mask significant effects that the CMP may

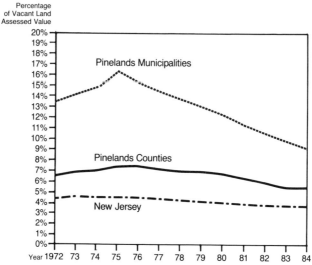

Figure 10–4. Vacant Land Assessed Values as a Percentage of All Ratables in Fifty-two Pinelands Municipalities as Compared with Those in Seven Pinelands Counties and the State, 1972–1984. SOURCE: Chart redrawn by Tina Campbell from Pinelands Commission, *Economic and Fiscal Impacts of the Pinelands Comprehensive Management Plan* (New Lisbon, N.J., November 1985), p. 60.

have had in individual cases, it is important to examine the plan's impact on individual municipalities. Current data show that for most municipalities, the tax base loss was less than 1 percent; however, the restrictions did have a much more significant effect on one municipality and a somewhat more noticeable effect on two others. A decline in vacant land assessment that can be largely attributed to the CMP resulted in a 25.5 percent reduction in the tax base for Woodland (Burlington County). In addition, Washington and Stafford townships (Burlington and Ocean counties, respectively) lost more than 2 percent of their tax base.

Like vacant land assessment, state land purchases did not, in general, have a significant effect on most Pinelands municipalities. However, there are three exceptions to these general findings. Bass River Township's property tax base was reduced 3 percent as a result of state purchases; Woodland Township lost 6 percent of its tax base; and Washington Township lost 5 percent (all townships are in Burlington County). Because of New Jersey's Green Acres tax subsidy program, however, these municipalities felt only a small part of that loss during the first several years.

Of course, the bottom-line issue for many Pinelands residents is whether the CMP has resulted in increased property taxes on their homes. Since only one Pinelands municipality has suffered a significant loss of tax base

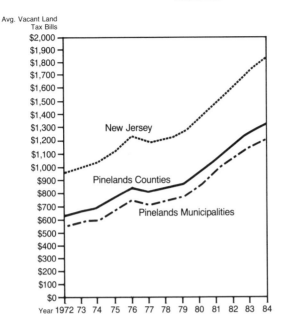

Figure 10–5. Average Vacant Land Tax Bills in Fifty-two Pinelands Municipalities as Compared with Those in Seven Pinelands Counties and the State, 1972–1984. SOURCE: Chart redrawn by Tina Campbell from Pinelands Commission, *Economic and Fiscal Impacts of the Pinelands Comprehensive Management Plan* (New Lisbon, N.J., November 1985), p. 74.

through declines in vacant land assessments and only three have suffered significant losses through state land purchases, it seems safe to predict that the effect on tax rates across the fifty-two municipalities will not be significant. The aggregate data on property taxes seem to confirm that prediction. Average residential property tax rates did increase in Pinelands municipalities between 1978 and 1984, but they did not rise as fast as residential property tax rates for the state as a whole (Figure 10–5). Thus, the overall impact of the CMP on the residential tax bill does not seem to be significant.

Legislative Support Actions

The economic and fiscal analysis contained in the foregoing section presents a relatively complete picture of the aggregate economic and fiscal effects of the Comprehensive Management Plan. Of course this retrospective view was not available to legislators who were being pressured during the years 1981 through 1984 to add new support programs or to fund proposals that were included in the CMP but had not yet been authorized or funded. In those years the legislators had to operate in an environment of uncertainty about what the consequences of the land-use regulations would be. Furthermore, with the exception of the Pinelands Commission's 1983 assessment of the overall effects for 1981 and 1982, the information legislators received about the economic and fiscal consequences generally came from newspaper stories and constituents. The information from these sources generally consisted of stories about the hardships suffered by Pinelands landowners, businesses, and municipalities as a result of the land-use regulations.

In 1983 and again in 1985, the New Jersey Legislature did, therefore, respond to the recommendations of the Pinelands Commision and to some of the individuals and municipalities who had been hurt by the land-use restrictions. Among these legislative responses was the Pinelands Property Tax Stabilization Act, which was approved and signed by Governor Kean in 1983 and implemented in 1984. This act was designed to compensate municipalities for ratables lost as a result of the land-use restrictions. Despite the flurry of tax assessment appeals caused by the land-use restrictions, the anticipated price tag for the program was expected to be relatively modest.

The Pinelands Development Credit Bank, like the Property Tax Stabilization Act, was among the economic and fiscal support programs recommended by the Pinelands Commission in the Comprehensive Management Plan; however, the program was not authorized, funded, and signed by the governor until September of 1985. The legislature actually approved a similar bill earlier in 1983, but Governor Kean objected to several of its provisions and so vetoed it. The purpose of the Pinelands Development Credit Bank was to provide a means to ensure that landowners who wanted or needed to sell their PDCs could do so. In short, the bank was viewed as a key element in making the PDC program workable.

The Pinelands Infrastructure Bond Act, like the Pinelands Development Credit Bank, was passed by the legislature and approved by the governor in 1985. In a referendum later that year New Jersey voters approved the infrastructure bond fund required to implement the act. The purpose of this bill was to provide low-cost state loans and grants to certified Pinelands local governments for the construction, improvement, expansion, or repair of roads, waste treatment facilities, and water supply facilities in Regional Growth Areas. The bond act authorized up to $30 million for these projects.

Assessing the Economic and Fiscal Support Programs

The key issue in any attempt to assess the economic and fiscal support programs for the Pinelands is the extent to which they limit or ameliorate the negative effects of the land-use regulations. However, an evaluation of these programs must also take into account whether the program has been successfully implemented and the length of time the program has been in operation. Only two of the five major support programs established for Pinelands landowners and municipalities—the Pinelands Development Credit Program and the Green Acres program—have been operating since the Comprehensive Management Plan was approved in 1981. The Property Tax Stabilization Act was implemented in 1984. It took longer than expected for the State Commissioner of Banking to establish the Pinelands Development Credit Bank. Although the legislature gave approval in 1985, the bank was still not in operation by August 1987. Funds for infrastructure improvement will begin to flow only in late 1987. Consequently, this assessment should be considered only an initial effort for the first three programs, and exclusively prospective for the latter two programs.

The Pinelands Development Credit Program.   The Pinelands Development Credit program involves landowners, builders, and local government officials in an innovative approach to land-use policy. Because of the effects of the national economic downturn in the early 1980s, the program got off to slow start. A more serious impediment to the program, however, was the delay caused by the conformance process. Each of the fifty-two Pinelands municipalities was required to revise its master plan and its zoning ordinance so that they would be consistent with the CMP. Once the local regulations conform to the CMP, the commission certifies the municipality. Until certification is complete all development, including that with PDCs, must be approved by the Pinelands Commission as well as by the local community. In addition, it is in the conformance process that high-density residential zones are established in Regional Growth Areas, and the receiving districts for PDC transfers designated.

New Jersey is a state with a strong tradition of home rule, and many Pinelands municipalities objected to state review of their planning and zoning ordinances. Opposition was especially intense in those communities designated for additional growth by the CMP. As a result, the conformance process was both longer and more complicated than either the commissioners or the staff expected. The conformance process began in

1981, and six years later, forty-four of the fifty-two municipalities had completed the process.

The interim process required a dual review by the state and the municipality that many developers found cumbersome. Many developers took a wait-and-see approach until the municipal planning and zoning districts were approved. Some were reluctant to propose a project using PDCs, when the rules of the game might change before approvals could be completed. According to one builder in Hamilton Township, "The fact that the township does not conform with the state's wishes because they have other ideas about what's right and wrong, means we're caught in the middle." Developers in uncertified communities were forced to receive approvals from both the local community and the Pinelands Commission. Thus, they were sometimes in the unfortunate position of being trapped between warring parties.

The effect of this situation on the PDC program was magnified since two of the holdout communities in the conformance process, Hamilton and Egg Harbor townships, faced the greatest pressures for residential development in the Pinelands. Because of their proximity to Atlantic City, they accounted for 57 percent of the residential approvals in the entire Pinelands Region during the first eighteen months of the CMP.[30]

Two other factors also delayed the operation of a market for Pinelands Development Credits. The market for housing in the Pinelands softened during the first three years of the 1980s and thus many builders found themselves with larger-than-anticipated inventories of approved but unbuilt projects. The other was the complexity of the program itself. Homebuilders watched as the regulations governing their industry were changed. The earliest projects were slowed at many points as both developers and Pinelands Commission staff went through what some developers perceived to be an endless round of meetings and delays before approvals were granted.

The potential for delay in creating a market for PDCs had prompted the Pineland planners to include in the CMP a plan for a vigorous educational campaign and a request to the legislature for a law establishing a bank to buy and sell PDCs. Although little publicity was given to the PDC program, the bank idea was passed by the legislature, but vetoed by the governor. The Pinelands Development Credit Bank Act did not receive final approval until September, 1985, nearly five years after the PDC program started. Designed to supplement the Pinelands Protection Act, it created a Pinelands Development Credit Bank, which is empowered to buy PDCs from landowners who face a hardship due to the program, and, in addition, which is authorized to buy PDCs when their purchase would further the objectives of the Pinelands Protection Act. The bank can also issue loan guarantees in the amount of $10,000 per credit. It is authorized to sell, exchange, or return any of the credits it acquires, and is capitalized by a $6.5 million appropriation.

The Market for Pinelands Development Credits. Known transfers during the first six and a half years of the program accounted for fewer than one hundred PDCs, slightly below 2 percent of the outstanding credits. The largest purchaser was the Burlington County Conservation Easement and Pinelands Development Credit Exchange Board. Established by the Burlington County Board of Freeholders, the exchange was authorized to purchase credits from Burlington County landowners.

The Burlington County Freeholders authorized the exchange to purchase PDCs at a price of $10,000 per credit, and to sell the credits on the open market, with the proceeds from any sales to be used to buy more PDCs. A May 1978 county bond issue, designed to support conservation easement purchases "in ecologically sensitive and critical areas of the Pinelands located in Burlington County," provided $2 million in working capital. A suit challenging the propriety of the exchange, however, kept it from functioning until the county received a favorable decision.[31]

With the litigation resolved, the first known purchase of rights by the exchange took place October 25, 1982, when Temple Emmanuel of Cherry Hill, agreed to sell 4.5 PDCs originating in Woodland Township to the Burlington County exchange for a total price of $45,000. Since then, the exchange has acquired 82 PDCs, and has subsequently resold 9.5 PDCs to local builders. Because the exchange is the largest PDC purchaser, and under terms of the suit, because it is restricted to purchases originating within Burlington County, landowners outside of Burlington County face a more difficult market, at least until the Pinelands Development Credit Bank becomes operational.

Landowner Response to PDCs. Those who sold PDCs to the Burlington County exchange were delighted to find a market for the rights. All sales to the exchange were voluntary and were initiated at the request of county landowners. After selling PDCs, landowners continue to own and operate their land, although it is permanently restricted from development.

In an effort to identify landowner response to the PDC program, a brief survey was sent to sixty landowners with PDCs. They were selected from those who had applied to the Pinelands commission for a Letter of Interpretation itemizing the number of PDCs they were eligible to sell. (This is the first step in the process of selling a PDC.) Thirty-six responded to the survey and their comments ranged from supportive to critical. One individual called it a "marvelous program to keep land in farming and agriculture." But many found fault with the program, particularly because of what they perceived as inadequate compensation for property losses. The following are representative of these critical comments:

> The concept is good. But our land is being expropriated without proper compensation. The PDC credits are a fraud.

> I feel that the present implementation of the Pinelands protection scheme is tantamount to theft of my property. If protection of the Pinelands was as noble an idea as it was portrayed, the owners of land in the area could have been given fair value for it. As it is, I am left holding the bag for land which I can neither use nor sell, but must pay taxes on.

> I am thoroughly disgusted with the entire Pineland program. I cannot sell my 140 acres because no one is interested if they can't build at least one house. The two people wanting credits would pay only $5,000 each.

The slowness of the market for PDCs was another source of frustration for many landowners.

The Developers' Perspective. Each PDC is worth four additional residential units in a Regional Growth Area. The Burlington County exchange buys and sells PDCs for $10,000 each, or $2,500 per additional building unit. Since a well-developed trade in PDCs has not yet evolved, how can a builder determine the price for PDCs? One young developer who builds in the Pinelands and the Philadelphia suburbs explains that the key questions are two: "What are you paying for the ground now?" and "What is the value of the PDC? If you're paying $4,000 a unit for raw ground, and you're getting PDCs at $2,500 a unit, well, you save $1,500." Or, as the late Robert Meyers, a developer and member of the New Jersey legislature, put it, when asked if the value of a PDC was worth the value of four unfinished building units: "Sure, at $2,500 a unit, that's cheap."

In spite of its drawbacks, the program does, therefore, have a potential attraction for developers. In real estate development, higher densities usually mean increased profits. If zoning allows fifty houses on a given site and that density can be increased by an additional ten units using PDCs, then the total number of houses, and thus the total market value of the development, will rise. This means more units to sell at a lower cost per unit. Increased density means increased value.

Future Viability of the PDC Program. A 1984 Pinelands Commission report reviewing the status of the PDC program acknowledges the delays caused by the conformance process. It also indicates a possible long-range problem if sites presently designated as PDC receiving areas are developed at the lower, non-PDC densities. Should this occur extensively, the number of potential receiving sites could fall below the number needed to accommodate the current supply of PDCs. The report notes that no such problem existed in 1984, however, since there were then redemption opportunities for approximately twice as many PDCs as had been created. Moreover, in a November 1985 referendum, New Jersey voters approved a $30 million bond issue to finance infrastructure in Pinelands Regional Growth Areas. This was important because high-density development, in keeping with CMP provisions, is possible only where sewer lines and other infrastructure have been built. When the outer boundaries of the Pinelands Area were delineated, some sewered areas were deliberately excluded. As a consequence, many of the Pinelands Regional Growth Areas are completely or partially unsewered, making development with PDCs more difficult until infrastructure improvements are made.

After a slow start, interest in selling PDCs has begun to grow. The Letters of Interpretation in response to 131 separate requests from 14 municipalities have allocated nearly 500 PDCs. Given the delays in implementation, it is probably premature to attempt a final evaluation of the PDC program. The program was designed to ease the wipeouts suffered by landowners whose land values may have declined due to Pinelands regulations, but to avoid spending the enormous amounts of public funds necessary to purchase the land. Although the program may yet serve to cushion landowners from the effects of stringent land-use regulation on landowners, it has stimulated very few sales of PDCs, except in Burlington County, and has thus provided little relief to the majority of landowners in the various Preservation and Agricultural districts. The issue was succinctly expressed by one respondent who wrote, "If the people of New Jersey want a playground for their children, they should pay for it." The program's deficiencies have been recognized, and its most severe problems—lack of conformance, lack of infrastructure, and the need for an interim bank—are slowly being addressed. The commission sought and has obtained a $24,000 grant from the Fund for New Jersey, a private philanthropic organization, to develop a program to identify and alleviate developers' objections to the PDC program. This educational program began in late 1986. While many of the key elements in a successful PDC program were not in place when the concept was adopted, it appears that after six years this program is now capable of attaining its early promise: Whether it will do so remains to be seen.

The PDC support program will be strengthened further in 1987 when the bond funds for Pinelands municipal infrastructure improvements are available. Of course, the availability of "free" money for infrastructure development does not ensure that the eligible municipalities will suddenly use it; however, the money should provide a strong incentive for action. Barring another severe economic recession like that of 1980–1981, getting the infrastructure components in place should speed up the pace of residential construction, which in turn should stimulate the market for the sale and use of PDCs.

Municipal Tax Support. As previously shown in the analysis of the CMP's fiscal effects, reassessment of vacant land has reduced the tax base by 2 percent or more in only three communities—Woodland, Washington, and Stafford townships. The development restrictions did have an adverse effect on twenty-eight communities, but in twenty-five, the loss of ratable base was 1.5 percent or less. Consequently, with the possible exception of the three where the tax base loss exceeded 2 percent, most municipal property taxpayers probably would not have noticed the loss. Nevertheless, simply on the grounds of fairness, the property tax stabilization program seems like a necessary element for a state land-use regulation program such as that in the Pinelands. Equally important, at least one Pinelands municipality (Woodland) really would have felt the adverse effects of the restrictions if no state aid had been available. Indeed, that municipality still may be hit hard by the loss of ratables, if the Property Tax Stabilization Act is not renewed before the end of 1987, as currently expected.

Property Tax Stabilization Program. In 1985, the total amount of state aid that could have been distributed under the Property Tax Stabilization Act was a relatively modest $611,287. However, five of the twenty-eight municipalities that were eligible for this aid did not have their local zoning and master plans revised to conform with the CMP. Consequently, they did not qualify for the compensation, and the total amount of state aid actually paid out was $510,799. The largest single distribution for any municipality was $167,571 to Stafford Township, which had lost 2.3 percent of its total $518 million ratable base. The smallest amount of compensation was $13, which went to Chesilhurst. Woodland Township, the municipality most adversely affected by the building restrictions, lost 25.5 percent of its ratable base, and it qualified for $86,367 in state aid. If the property tax stabilization program had not been in place in 1985, the tax-base loss due to the CMP would have cost each of Woodland's 400 taxpayers an additional $218.

In assessing the Property Tax Stabilization Act and its effects, it is important to remember that the act was not authorized until 1983. Consequently, during 1981, 1982, and 1983, the full effects of the ratable losses were felt in a number of communities; however, once the program was established, it seemed to moderate the impact. A key element in the success of the program is that the value of aid distributed is not based exclusively on the amount of ratables lost. The equalized value of the tax property and the local tax rate are included in the calculation of state aid.

Green Acres Program Aid. The Green Acres Program, like the Property Tax Stabilization Act, is a very important program for limiting the adverse effects of state actions on several Pinelands municipalities. State land purchases in three municipalities—Bass River, Woodland, and Washington townships—reduced the property tax base by 5 percent or more. In Lacey and Tabernacle townships, state purchases reduced the property tax base by 1.7 percent and 1.1 percent, respectively. Additional municipalities lost some tax base as a result of state purchases, but in no other municipalities did those purchases exceed 1 percent. Since future state purchases are planned, however, these figures will change somewhat over time.

Particularly in the three communities whose tax base losses exceeded 5 percent, the Green Acres program provided significant short-term relief for local taxpayers. Indeed, since reimbursement during the first year is close to 100 percent of the lost revenue, the adverse impact of the state purchases is effectively hidden; however, as the percentage of reimbursement declines, the adverse fiscal effects of those purchases become more apparent. Nevertheless, such a program, which limits the size of the loss each year, ensures that no sharp increase in tax rates will be caused by state purchases. In addition, it is important to note that the Green Acres Program was in place in 1981 when the CMP was approved. Consequently, the communities affected by state land purchases received state assistance right from the start. The total amount of aid paid out under the Green Acres program in 1985 for Pinelands municipalities was approximately $19 million.

Conclusion

The political struggle over the Pinelands Protection Act and the Comprehensive Management Plan was a bitter, emotional conflict. Opposition to the legislation and the CMP was fueled by predictions that development restrictions would have disastrous consequences for the regional economy, land markets (i.e., individual landowners), and the tax base of Pinelands municipalities. This analysis, however, generally confirms the Pinelands Commission's view that the CMP's overall effects on the regional economy and Pinelands municipalities so far is minimal. This finding does not mean that the land-use regulations had no negative economic or fiscal consequences. Some construction-related businesses were adversely affected, and there were no state-sponsored economic support programs to limit that effect. Some municipalities were also hurt, but the Green Acres Program and the Property Tax Stabilization Act limited these adverse consequences.

In contrast with the CMP's minimal effect on the regional economy and the municipalities, however, its aggregate effect on land markets was more serious and visible. Furthermore, the economic support program established to limit these adverse effects—notably the Pinelands Development Credit Program—did not work well during the first six years. The number of vacant land sales in the post–CMP period declined sharply in all three management areas where development was essentially prohibited, or severely restricted, and prices fell dramatically in the Preservation Area. Clearly, some landowners who needed or wanted to sell their land experienced economic hardships. If the Pinelands Development Credit Program had been fully operational from the time the CMP went into effect in 1981, both the quantity and severity of the hardships suffered probably would have been reduced. Indeed, one of the key lessons to be learned from the Pinelands experience is that the negative economic and fiscal consequences of large land-use plans will be minimized only if support programs are fully operational when the plan is implemented.

The Future: Challenges and Issues

PART IV

11. Legal and Legislative Challenges

Charles L. Siemon

When the New Jersey Pinelands Comprehensive Management Plan was adopted by the New Jersey Pinelands Commission on November 21, 1980, it was generally expected that the plan would be the subject of a variety of legal and legislative challenges. In fact, all during the planning process, landowners and developers decried the confiscation of property that would result from the plan's land-use restrictions and threatened a flood of litigation. Equally strident were promises to have the Pinelands Protection Act repealed. Nevertheless, relatively few lawsuits were actually filed, and legislative initiatives to undo the CMP were given little serious consideration by the legislature.

In order to understand the nature of the challenges that were instituted and to appreciate why the promised challenges did not materialize, it is necessary to explain two aspects of the Comprehensive Management Plan that greatly affected the resolve of those opposed to it.

The first matter of influence was the Pinelands Commission's careful attention to legal detail in the preparation of the CMP. Recognizing that the plan would face challenges from disappointed landowners and developers, the Pinelands Commission's work program called for an in-depth analysis of the taking issue and the question of so-called "vested" rights (the right to complete previously approved development when land-use regulations are changed). The commission's consultant team devoted an entire volume of the commission's five-volume primary background and reference report, *Procedural and Substantive Land Management Techniques of Potential Relevance for New Jersey Pinelands*, to these subjects. As a result, the Pinelands Commission was well versed in these issues and the resulting CMP contains several elements that substantially reduced the probability of litigation.

The first of these elements was a provision authorizing a waiver from strict compliance with the provisions of the plan where "the subject property is not capable of yielding a reasonable return" under the CMP. In other words, the CMP recognized that it is a general proposition of land-use law that a regulation must preserve to a landowner at least a minimum beneficial use of his property and made provision for a process to ensure that the CMP did not have an unlawful effect. If a landowner could demonstrate that the plan's restrictions were "overly restrictive," that is, they denied the owner a minimum beneficial use, then relief was administratively available under the CMP, without recourse to the courts.[1] Since the courts generally defer to available avenues of nonjudicial relief and require that litigants exhaust such avenues prior to initiating a lawsuit, the effect of this provision was to protect the CMP from most litigation in regard to the taking issue.

Another element of the CMP that accounts for the relatively small number of suits filed after its adoption is a provision that provides for a waiver of strict compliance where a landowner can demonstrate a valid claim of vested rights. The Pinelands Commission had learned, as a result of research conducted under criteria established in the CMP during the planning process, that much of the litigation that had been filed in response to other comprehensive planning programs resulted from the conflict between previously approved development and the new regulations—that is, litigation initiated by developers who claimed a vested right to complete a project even in the face of the new regulations. As a result the commission included in the plan a vested-rights procedure whereby a landowner could seek an administrative determination of whether particular development expectations were vested. The CMP provided that a Waiver of Strict Compliance would be granted only where there was extraordinary hardship or compelling public need.[2] Again, the availability of a nonjudicial remedy was a substantial deterrent to court challenges.

The other aspect of the CMP that very likely had a significant deterrent effect was the inclusion of a statutorily mandated acquisition program. Both the federal and the state acts contemplated the inclusion of an acquisition program in the plan for the most sensitive lands in the area, and the CMP itself established criteria for land acquisition and identified approximately 97,000 acres for purchase (almost one-tenth of the entire management area). By the end of 1986 more than $50,000,000 of state and federal funds had been appropriated for the implementation of the acquisition element. Undoubtedly, the acquisition of the most sensitive lands in the Pinelands is a significant reason why the litigation actually filed was less than expected. In other words, the areas that are prone to litigation in most planning situations are the most sensitive and therefore most restrictively regulated; in the CMP these are dealt with in part by acquisition rather than regulation. Nevertheless, there is heavily restricted land, particularly in the Preservation Area that is not slated for acquisition.

The First Legal Challenges

The actual adoption of the Comprehensive Management Plan was challenged in two different forums—state court and federal court. In the state court action, two municipalities within the Pinelands Area, a citizen, and the Coalition to Save Agriculture appealed the adoption of the CMP on procedural and substantive grounds.[3] The appeal, brought under the provisions of New Jersey's administrative procedures act, was limited to a review "on the record" compiled by the Pinelands Commission during its quasi-legislative deliberations (that is, no new evidence could be submitted by the appellants). This circumstance weighed heavily in favor of the CMP because of the detailed factual record that had been established during the planning process. The challenge alleged that the CMP was based on inadequate data and was adopted without adherence to the procedural requirements of the Pinelands Protection Act. The appeal also challenged the so-called "Piney" exemption on the grounds that the preferential housing element that favored long-term Pinelands residents and those gainfully employed in the indigenous Pinelands industries deprived the claimants of equal protection of the laws. The commission's defense, formulated in a lengthy and well written brief prepared by the New Jersey Attorney General's office, stoutly defended the plan:

> In the case of the Pinelands plan, upon review of the numerous reports prepared by the Commission's 21 professional consultants; the many technical studies, treatises and other publications considered by the Commission and most importantly the factual and explanatory narrative contained in the CMP itself, it is obvious that the regulations which implement the CMP are supported by ample technical data. . . . Section 5–302(A) of the CMP is clearly related to a valid public purpose. Since both the federal and State Pinelands legislation recognize and call for the protection of the unique cultural heritage of the Pines, it seems to be hardly debatable whether the objective of the provision, that is, to preserve the cultural heritage of the Pinelands by preserving the opportunity for multi-generation extended families to remain physically intact and ensure the availability of labor for indigenous economic activities, is valid.[4]

The court rejected the appellants' motion to stay the implementation of the CMP and eventually sustained the validity of the CMP, holding that it was supported by the record.

The federal court action, brought by three townships and joined by two Boards of Education (including most of the same parties from the state court action and a euphemistically named developer's group—the Coalition for the Sensible Preservation of the Pinelands) challenged the Secretary of the Interior's decision to approve the CMP, a critical step in the process because under the federal act the release of funds for acquisition was contingent upon such approval. The theory behind the complainant's case was that the Environmental Impact Statement prepared by the Department of the Interior was inadequate and improperly prepared and that therefore the secretary's decision was arbitrary and capricious.

The action was, in large part, a technical challenge to the Environmental Impact Statement (EIS) based on a very strict reading of the National Environmental Policy Act and its implementing regulations. What the plaintiffs claimed was that the draft EIS had been prepared prior to the actual adoption of the CMP (an agreed-upon fact) and was therefore not a fair assessment of the proposed federal action—the approval of the plan. The court held that the EIS had been prepared under exigent circumstances largely because of the tight schedule for plan adoption under the state act, but concluded that the goals and objectives of the EIS process had been satisfied.[5] The court rejected the attack, however, looking to the salutory purposes of the Comprehensive Management Plan and the state and federal acts.

There has been only one other legal challenge that can be considered to be an attack on the CMP itself rather than an action directed to a decision under the plan. In *Orleans Builders Developers v. Byrne*, which was a challenge to the commission's interim regulatory authority under the Pinelands Protection Act, a developer claimed, among other things, that the act was invalid because it depended on a legislative standard of "substantial impairment of resources," a phrase that was alleged to be insufficiently definite and therefore void for vagueness.[6] The court, however, rejected this challenge and sustained the validity of both the act and the Pinelands Commission's actions under the act.

Legal Challenges to Commission Actions Under the CMP

In point of fact there has not been very much litigation challenging specific decisions made under the Comprehensive Management Plan; however, there has been a fair amount of litigation that has "touched on" the plan. For example, in *Matlack v. Board of Chosen Freeholders of the County of Burlington*, a Pinelands landowner (a party in the unsuccessful federal court action) challenged Burlington County's decision to use proceeds from conservation easement bonds to acquire Pinelands Development Credits.[7] The Pinelands Commission was not named as a defendant in the matter; nevertheless, the issue was deemed to be of vital importance to the commission because the plaintiff was attacking the Comprehensive Management Plan's Pinelands Development Credit program—an important part of the plan's overall management strategy. The allegation was *inter alia*, that development credits were securities under the Federal Securities Act and therefore not amenable to the kind of transferable development-rights program contemplated in the Comprehensive Management Plan. The case attracted a substantial amount of interest on both sides of the issue (for example, the Pacific Legal Foundation—a well-known property-rights public-interest group, represented two of the individual plaintiffs and the Environmental Defense Fund intervened on behalf of the conservation interests) and was extensively briefed on motions for summary judgment. The commission, of course, supported the county's position; the attorney general again appeared on behalf of the commission's interests. A complex expert witness case was presented in support of the procedural and substantive aspects of the Pinelands Development Credit program. The court rejected the challenge and upheld the legality of the Pinelands Development Credit program, further deterring potential litigants from challenging this aspect of the CMP.

In *Fine v. Galloway Township* the Pinelands Commission was once again not a principal party to litigation that involved the Comprehensive Management Plan.[8] The plaintiff in *Fine* proposed to develop a ten-acre tract of land in Galloway Township (Atlantic County), a municipality that had not, at the time, had its master plan and land-use regulations certified under the Comprehensive Management Plan. The developer applied for and received development approval from the Pinelands Commission. The township, however, refused to allow development until approval had also been obtained from its planning board. The developer's theory was that the Comprehensive Management Plan was a complete pre-emption of local development review in uncertified jurisdictions. Actually, the plan does provide in pertinent part that "a Pinelands Development Approval shall supersede any local decision if a municipality has not received certification of its master plan and land use ordinances." (Part II, Sec. 3–407). The court examined the challenge by first looking to the intent of the legislature—to ensure that "minimum standards" are established for all development in the Pinelands Protection Area. The court held that, because the act specified these minimum standards, municipalities could adopt and enforce more restrictive regulations provided that the regulations were not "inconsistent with the goals and objectives of the Plan."

Another aspect of the post–CMP litigation that bears review is the number of disputes involving local governments. The planning program was of course alert to the prospects of landowner challenges to the Comprehensive Management Plan because of the substantial down-zonings anticipated in the core areas of the Pinelands forests. The program was not as well prepared to deal with the opposition of local governments in the so-called "growth areas," opposition that stemmed from the designation of particular areas as appropriate for new growth and development. The Pinelands Protection Act contemplated that the Comprehensive Management Plan should "guide" the development of South Jersey away from areas that were environmentally sensitive and toward land that was adjacent to existing development, thus ensuring, among other things, the availability of adequate public facilities. In response to that mandate, the Comprehensive Management Plan undertook to accommodate the full measure of projected regional growth, but it directed that growth away from the central forests of the Pinelands toward the areas adjacent to the Philadelphia-Camden and the Atlantic City areas. Unfortunately, some of the areas that were designated as growth areas were places where local restrictive growth regulations had been prepared as protection from sprawling growth from the Philadelphia metropolitan area and the burgeoning casino development in Atlantic City. The conflict between the commission and these municipalities was often bitter and frequently litigious.

Another case that did not directly involve the Pinelands Comprehensive Management Plan was a challenge to a CAFRA permit requirement that a developer set aside a certain percentage of residential units in a proposed project as low- and moderate-income housing. The court, in reviewing the issue of fair-share housing, quoted with favor the Comprehensive Management Plan's treatment of the housing issue:

> The Legislature established the Pinelands Commission to oversee development of the Pinelands through a management plan and, toward that end, subordinated municipal zoning power to that of the commission. N.J.S.A. 13:18A–10(c). In the management plan for the Pinelands, the Commission has required that municipal master plans, to be certified by the Commission, provide that of all available housing units, 10% be set aside for low income, 10% for moderate income, and 5% for middle income households. New Jersey Pinelands Comprehensive Management Plan §6–1202 at 428 (1980). Generally speaking, in municipalities that have not received certification of their master plan, 25% of the dwelling units shall be affordable in low, moderate and middle income households. *Id.* at §6–1203. Thus, the legislative and executive branches have recognized that protection of the environment and the provision of low and moderate income housing are not only compatible, but essen-

tial. That approach is consistent with our suggestion that "[i]t is desirable that administrative agencies acting under legislative authorization assume the regulation of the housing distribution problem.[9]

The decision had no precedental value, but the court's favorable quotation reinforced the validity of the CMP and provided a further deterrent to litigation.

In 1985 the Appellate Division of the Superior Court of New Jersey once again confirmed judicial deference to actions of the commission in carrying out legislative mandates of the Comprehensive Management Plan.[10] In this case the Centennial Pines Club challenged the commission's approval of a municipal ordinance because it contained a grandfather clause that allowed that municipality to approve applications for development under the provisions of its prior ordinance for a period of six months after "recertification." The Centennial Club contended that the action violated the requirements of the Pinelands Protection Act and lacked legislative authority, because it was inconsistent with the legislative timetable for the implementation of the CMP. The court clearly reiterated what by then had become a consistent position: "In delegation of its authority to the Commission, the Legislature showed its preference for flexibility and fairness over a rigid punitive approach to saving the Pinelands." The court found that the approval of the municipality's ordinance by the commission was clearly within its delegated power.

Challenges through the OAL.   Many challenges to the CMP by developers do not involve litigation but are rather heard by the New Jersey Office of Administrative Law. The commission refers contested cases to the OAL, and the OAL makes a recommended, or "initial," decision. This decision must then be affirmed, modified, or rejected by the Pinelands Commission, which is by law empowered to make a final decision.

The most frequently contested decisions of the Pinelands Commission, and thus the cases most often resolved in an administrative hearing, are denials of a waiver of strict compliance pursuant to the Pinelands Protection Act. If the commission finds that development will cause substantial impairment to the Pinelands, a waiver of strict compliance will be denied. In 1981 a developer submitted an application to the Pinelands Commission for development in a Regional Growth Area of the Pinelands, seeking a waiver of several sections of the CMP so that he could develop forty-six lots. The commission granted the waiver application for thirty-nine lots, but denied it for the additional seven. The developer sought reconsideration of the issue, claiming that he needed the additional seven lots in order to break even on the total project. The administrative law judge, however, did not address the hardship issue, because a preponderance of the evidence showed that substantial impairment of the undisturbed wetlands would result from the development and the petitioner had failed to prove the negative.[11]

In another case, *Brighton Industries v. the Commission*, the administrative law judge did not evaluate the potential damage to the Pinelands but still approved the commission's denial of a Waiver of Strict Compliance because there was no evidence of hardship by the developer.[12] In this case, the developer applied to the Barnegat Township Committee to construct 329 mobile-home sites. Construction was to take place in several stages. Prior to the issuance of Executive Order 71 and the moratorium on construction in the Pinelands, 129 spaces had been built. The developer then applied for and received approval to construct an additional 100 spaces. In this application, the developer (Mo-Park) maintained that he was entitled to seventy-nine to one hundred more sites and contended that the development could not earn a "minimum reasonable rate of return" within the restrictions of the CMP unless these additional sites were approved. In determining the rate of return for such cases, the commission looks only to the amount of actual investment and uses a rate of return correlated to the approximate rate of three-month treasury notes. The commission determined that Mo-Park's rate of return ranged between 10 and 12 percent, well in excess of the minimum reasonable rate as defined by the commission. The hearing officer recommended upholding the staff's determination that the mobile-home park could achieve a minimum rate of return with 229 spaces and thus that the petitioner's application for additional units should be denied.

When a developer can show that there would be hardship if the development is not able to proceed, the commission has shown flexibility and has encouraged creativity to make the property developable while retaining ecological integrity. In *Tordella v. The Pinelands Commission*, the administrative law judge recommended a Waiver of Strict Compliance but restricted the use of the properties involved.[13] The petitioners owned two lots in Medford Township in a designated Rural Development Area. One lot contained 0.747 acres and another, 0.877 acres. In 1982 the owners had applied for permission to develop a single-family dwelling on each of the lots. Under provisions of the CMP no residential dwelling unit shall be located on a lot of less than 3.2 acres in a Rural Development Area (N.J.A.C. 7:50–5:2). At the hearing, the petitioner contended that the development of the lots with approved setbacks and septic systems would not adversely affect the wetlands ecology of the lot or the surrounding area. He also contended that he could not achieve a "reasonable return" on his investment unless he were allowed to develop one unit on each of the lots. The petitioners called two planners, a real estate agent, a CPA, and a biologist as witnesses, and the commission called an economic analyst, an environmental specialist, the commission's Assistant Director, and a staff soil scientist.

The hearing officer agreed with the staff's findings and concluded that the applicant qualified for a waiver on the grounds of extraordinary hardship under the provisions of NJAC 7:50–4:55(a); however, pursuant to NJAC 7:30–4:55(e), the waiver granting the development of one single-family dwelling unit on the combined two lots provided the minimum relief necessary to relieve this extraordinary hardship. The administrative law judge also mandated that the dwelling must be placed on the lot in such a manner as to maintain at least a fifty-foot buffer from the westerly edge of the wetland area and must use an approved-design toilet and septic tank.

Challenges by Uncertified Municipalities. One case that caused concern to those sympathetic to preserving the Pinelands is *In re John Madin.*[14] These consolidated appeals involved challenges by the planning boards of the townships of Egg Harbor and Hamilton to the action of the New Jersey Pinelands Commission that denied them standing and an opportunity to be heard or to object to development approvals granted by the commission's staff in their respective communities. John Madin/Lordland Development International and Castlehard Development International had applied for approval of a Planned Unit Development (PUD) on 528.55 acres that lie in portions of both Hamilton and Egg Harbor townships. The land involved was located in a Regional Growth Area, and neither Egg Harbor nor Hamilton township had been certified by the Pinelands Commission.

The commission approved the developers' application with fourteen conditions on February 17, 1984. The approval letter had a reconsideration provision, which stated that "any person who is aggrieved by this determination may seek reconsideration of the decision by the Pinelands Commission within 18 days of the date of this letter by giving notice, by Certified Mail, of the request for reconsideration to the Pinelands Commission" (N.J.S.A. 7:50–4.17). No public hearing concerning this application was conducted nor does the record indicate that any notice was ever given to the public of such a hearing.

Both Hamilton and Egg Harbor townships filed requests for reconsideration of the development approval. Hamilton contended that approval was not consistent with the Pinelands Protection Act and the Comprehensive Management Plan because, contrary to the commission's assistant director's findings of fact, upon which the decision was at least in part based, there were no existing public sewers, thus the development potentially endangered water quality and the wetlands ecology. The townships also asserted that the air quality and noise standards of the CMP would be exceeded.

In addition, Egg Harbor asserted that it was impossible to determine in the development approval whether the application complied with the density of dwelling units permitted by the CMP. The township also claimed that portions of the property covered by the approval did not meet the water-table standards provided for in the CMP, that the development failed to provide for adequate on-site waste management as required by the CMP, and that there was no provision for minimum middle-income housing as required by the CMP. These requests for hearings were forwarded by the Pinelands Commission's staff to the Office of Administrative Law for hearings as contested cases.

The commission subsequently contacted the state attorney general for advice because of the commission's uncertainty as to whether uncertified municipalities had legal standing to challenge actions on applications for development approval. The attorney general orally opined that uncertified municipalities had no standing to challenge a commission decision. In response, the commission adopted Resolution 84–20 on April 26, 1984, in which it declared that an uncertified municipality can effectively impede the processes of the Pinelands Commission. The commission then wrote the Office of the Administrative Law enclosing a copy of Resolution 84–20 and directing that the challenges by Hamilton and Egg Harbor Planning Boards be returned by the OAL to the commission. The OAL issued a notice of withdrawal on April 17, 1984.

In response, Hamilton and Egg Harbor filed notices of appeal in the New Jersey Superior Court challenging the commission's determination that they were not entitled to reconsideration of staff decisions and that no such request should be referred to the OAL as a contested case. The court found that municipalities do have standing under the circumstances of the case. In its analysis of standing, the court found that municipalities, whether their land-use ordinances are "certified" or "uncertified," do have an interest in commission proceedings, and that this interest mandates that they have standing to be heard or to challenge development. According to the court, development of the sensitive lands and resources of the Pinelands Area requires that those municipalities in which development is proposed to be given opportunity to present relevant information about those portions of the Pinelands about which they have peculiar knowledge. The court concluded that "uncertified municipalities" are "interested persons" entitled to reconsideration of development approvals, pursuant to N.J.A.C. 7:50–4.17. "Certainly a municipality may be 'interested' or even 'aggrieved' when a major development is proposed within its borders by private developers."[15]

The court also found that the public hearings required by N.J.S.A. 13:18–A–15 should be held when the commission reviews development applications in uncertified municipalities. According to the court, the public hearings are necessary to satisfy the requirements of due process of law.

This holding is potentially troubling and could have an impact on the success of the Comprehensive Management Plan which in the past has, at least in part, been attributed to the expeditious manner of approving development while preserving the ecology of the Pinelands. The commission is concerned, probably appropriately, that an uncertified municipality could effectively thwart the goals of the Pinelands Protection Act and the CMP by requesting hearings before the Office of Administrative Law in virtually every case. The decision in *In re John Madin*, could delay the approval process and therefore negatively affect the administration of the CMP in uncertified communities. However, because only eight of the fifty-two municipalities remain uncertified, the potential scope of this problem is somewhat limited.

It is also appropriate to observe at this point another recent case that may indicate how the Office of Administrative Law is becoming less tolerant of the commission's actions. In *Sierra Club v. Pineland Commission and Hovsons, Inc.* the court found that the Sierra Club was entitled to a reconsideration after a waiver had been issued because there was no evidence that it had received notice before that waiver had been granted.[16]

The Confiscation Issue.   Although there were expectations that the "taking" issue would be one of the principal areas of litigation when the CMP was adopted, almost no taking issue cases have actually reached the courts.

One reason for the dearth of this kind of litigation is the somewhat hostile reception one such claim received shortly after the CMP was adopted. In the case of *Orleans Builders and Developers v. Byrne*, the court found that Orleans had no right of inverse condemnation following the negative decision by the Pinelands Commission to its application for major development.[17] Orleans Builders and Developers had been refused permission to develop a total of 332 acres during the Pinelands moratorium. In determining that no compensation was due for a taking of the land, the court relied upon the "prevention of harm" versus the "creation of a public benefit" dichotomy. The court found that the purpose of the development restriction of the CMP was "predominantly to prevent public danger or harm" to the ecology of the Pinelands.

The permanent ban on development in some areas of the Pinelands has not created the rash of attacks on the CMP as predicted. This is a strong indication that the methodical and painstaking creation of the Comprehensive Management Plan resulted in a plan that is a significant deterrent to litigation. The importance of its success is aptly stated by Roger A. Greenbaum:

> Should the plan survive judicial scrutiny, it will serve as a versatile potent tool in land use policy. If an opposite result obtains, then greater public expense is in store for states that would exclude significant urban development from region-scale, ecologically unique "preserves."[18]

Legislative Challenges

Legislative interest in the Pinelands did not end with the Pinelands Protection Act. Since implementation of the Comprehensive Management Plan, a number of bills and resolutions have been introduced in the legislature that also bear directly on the Pinelands Protection Act and the Comprehensive Management Plan. Some of these have attempted to substantially change the CMP; however, frequent reaffirmation of the plan by the governor's office apparently has deterred the legislature from any serious attempts to undo it and thus far all destructive resolutions and bills have been unsuccessful. The following is a description of the most significant amendments to the Protection Act that have been proposed.

In 1981 two bills were filed that proposed amendments to at least forty sections of the Pinelands Protection Act and the Comprehensive Management Plan. The proposed amendments would have:

> reserved the designation of areas for predominant agricultural use as a municipal prerogative;

> required the commission to develop a program to permit "innovative municipal planning areas" or new towns throughout the Pinelands;

> limited the commission's ability to review development proposals; and

modified the Pinelands Development Credit program and created a state bank.

When State Senator Steven P. Perskie introduced S–3335, which would have greatly diluted the authority of the Pinelands Commission, he claimed the support of Daniel O'Hern, the governor's counsel. At the time, however, Governor Brendon Byrne was in Moscow on a trade mission. According to press reports, O'Hern apparently had agreed to recommend that Byrne sign the measure in order to gain the consent of certain congressmen to restore the $8 million appropriation originally budgeted for purchase of critical areas in the Pinelands National Reserve. One week after it was reported that the appropriated funds were released, Byrne returned from the Soviet Union and announced that he would not support legislation to weaken the protection efforts.

The issue of a PDC bank did not die with S–3335, however. The commission continued to push, and in 1984 the legislature passed, and the governor signed, a bill establishing a Pinelands Development Credit Bank. The act authorizes the board of directors of the bank to guarantee no less than $10,000 of the value of a Pinelands Development Credit to secure a loan for any purpose. The board is also authorized to act as a buyer of last resort in the event of economic hardship or to further the purposes of the Pinelands Protection Act. The bill provides for the establishment of County Development Credit Banks and appropriates $5 million to the Pinelands Development Credit Bank, which shall be paid from the proceeds of the sale of credits.

Also passed was the Pinelands Infrastructure Trust Bond Act of 1985. This act aids the implementation of the PDC program by authorizing a bond issue to finance infrastructure improvements in growth areas in the Pinelands (see Chapter 10). The act also authorizes, upon approval of the voters (which has been obtained), a $30 million state bond issue to provide loans and grants to local government units in the Pinelands areas. The loans can be used for infrastructure capital projects that are necessary to accommodate development in Regional Growth Areas. These capital infrastructure projects include roads, water supply systems, and wastewater treatment systems. The projects using these bond monies require the approval of the Department of Environment Protection and the Pinelands Commission.

Some bills introduced but never voted on were designed to alleviate the financial hardships of landowners in the Pinelands. One such bill provided for compensation to certain landowners, another provided in-lieu-of-tax equivalency payments to municipalities on state-owned property in the Pinelands. Actually, the issue of compensation was addressed successfully by the legislature. In January 1984 the Pinelands Municipal Property Tax Stabilization Act was signed into law, which was intended to alleviate local losses caused by the reductions in tax revenues because of declines in land values (see Chapter 10).

Since 1982 there have been unsuccessful legislative attempts to activate the Municipal Council, which was originally formed in the planning period by the commission. Two bills (S–1223 and A–1575) would have resolved the Municipal Council's inability to attain a quorum, and would have allowed it to act on formal resolutions by a majority vote of those members in attendance; however a minimum of ten affirmative votes would have been needed to carry any motion. These bills would also have authorized the council to review proposed regulations, policies, and budgets of the commission prior to adoption. Neither bill got out of committee. Other bills also would have appropriated funds to assist the Municipal Council and clarified the council's function.

There also have been attempts to deplete the acquisition funds available to the commission. In one such effort of 1983 a portion of the funds earmarked in the Pinelands legislation for land acquisition would have been set aside for the establishment of additional cemetery space for New Jersey veterans. Fortunately, since the introduction of these bills, cemetery space has been reserved outside the Pinelands.

Thus, legislative challenges to both the Pinelands Protection Act and the CMP, like legal challenges, have not undone any substantial provisions. In fact, successful legislation has served largely to clarify and strengthen the original intent of the law.

12. How Is the Pinelands Program Working?

Beryl Robichaud Collins

When Congress created the Pinelands National Reserve in 1978, it authorized a radical land-use management experiment for the protection of a treasured landscape, the New Jersey Pine Barrens. At the time, less than one-third of the million acres making up the reserve was publicly owned, and encroaching development threatened irreversible impacts. By creating the reserve, the federal government provided funding for limited acquisition of additional land, and expected New Jersey to protect the Pine Barrens by taking bold actions to control land use on the remaining privately owned lands.

This chapter evaluates six years of operating experience with the Pinelands program by identifying strengths and weaknesses in the ambitious land-use management blueprint and assessing the long-term viability of the protection efforts.

An Inauspicious Beginning

New Jersey, despite a long tradition of home rule, passed remarkably strong preservationist legislation for the Pinelands. As might be expected, however, there was initially a great deal of local hostility both to the reserve concept in general and to the Comprehensive Management Plan in particular. Moreover, the political environment on both the state and the federal level during the early years of the reserve did not augur well for the Pinelands' innovative land-use management program.

The Carter Administration, which late in the president's term had authorized establishment of the reserve and then approved the plan for its management, was almost immediately replaced by the Reagan Administration. Although the concept of a shared local, state, and federal management partnership, which distinguishes the reserve from a national park, might appear consonant with Reagan's "new federalism," widespread cutbacks in the funding of federal programs quickly dampened the Department of the Interior's interest in the reserve experiment.

The political climate on the state level was not much better. Democratic Governor Brendan Byrne, a strong champion of Pine Barrens preservation, was succeeded by Republican Thomas Kean, who, though respected by environmentalists, did not embrace the Pinelands as one of his

275

priorities. Worse, to foster better relationships with South Jersey politicians and officials, Kean distanced himself from the Pinelands Commission, using his initial gubernatorial appointments to weaken its previously strong bias for resource protection. At the same time the reserve lost a well placed ally when state Senate President Joseph Merlino, a chief sponsor of the Pinelands legislation, retired to run for Congress.

Given the traditional hostility of local officials, developers, and landowners to outside intrusion in land-use decision-making, the situation hardly suggested a healthy outcome for the land-use management experiment being conducted in the Pinelands National Reserve. But in the first six years of program implementation, support for the protection efforts grew, despite the faults that environmentalists and others often found with the Pinelands Commission's regulatory actions. Moreover, in six years there were no successful legal or legislative challenges to the Pinelands Protection Act.

By early 1987 forty-four of the fifty-two Pinelands municipalities had their master plans and land-use ordinances certified by the commission as being in conformance with the provisions of the Comprehensive Management Plan and most of the remaining local governments were taking steps to gain conformance. In 1984 and 1985 the state legislature encouraged institutionalizing of CMP provisions by making municipal and county conformance an eligibility test for Pinelands economic support programs. This gave the CMP an aura of permanence and local newspapers began to note that "the rules are settling in," that "the Pinelands Act is working," and that the people of the Pinelands "were learning to live with the Plan."[1] Even some of those who at the outset had been harsh critics of the Pinelands Commission became willing to acknowledge that "the Pinelands Commission is here to stay" and that protection of the significant resources cannot be accomplished without effective regional land-use management.[2] Still, other critics of the Pinelands program remain unconvinced, favoring, at minimum, changes in the CMP either to weaken or strengthen it, depending upon their bias.

Achieving the Primary Goal: Natural Resource Protection

Specific and interrelated natural-resource goals for the Pinelands National Reserve include (1) protection of the high quality and abundant supplies of surface and ground waters; (2) protection of the diversity of plant and animal species, community types, and habitats as well as of extensive unbroken natural forest tracts; and, (3) protection of the integrity of the Pine Barrens ecosystem and its resiliency to recover from disturbance. To accomplish these goals, the commission devised a regional management program based on clustering at macro and micro scales (restrictive land-use management areas and zoning districts within individual areas) and use of strict performance standards in all locations. This strategy is designed to avoid the kind of degradation that comes from the "tyranny of small decisions"—those undesirable, cumulative effects that often characterize unplanned regional decision-making and that have destroyed the ecological integrity of the Long Island Pine Barrens and threaten the Florida Everglades.[3]

Radically diverse opinions about the efficacy of the program and the commission's implementing actions surfaced during the first triennial plan review process, which began in 1983 and continued into 1987. As a judge of itself, the commission claimed that the environment was being effectively protected, citing as proof the fact that 96 percent of all new residential development approved in the first three years occurred outside environmentally sensitive areas. Further, this approved development was subject to stringent performance standards.[4] The commission also held that changes in management area boundaries and permitted use policies made during the conformance process had produced a more balanced and workable plan without resulting in any substantial impairment of the vital resources.

A few environmentalists took strong issue with this judgment, arguing that in consensus building the commission has traded off resource protection for development. Former Pinelands Commissioner Gary Patterson questioned the "ecological validity of the management program as it is being implemented."[5] Floyd West, also a former commissioner, predicted that because of the commission's eagerness to accommodate developers, "in ten years the Pinelands as we know it will be gone."[6] At the other extreme, critics in the building industry, though finding regional development standards advantageous, continued to accuse the commission of "overprotecting" the environment: water quality and wetland standards are too restrictive; stormwater requirements impractical; and wetland buffer sizes unnecessarily large.[7] Disagreeing with the courts as well as the commission, they also argued that the eligibility test for a waiver of exemption should rest on whether a proposed development would "substantially impair" the resources of the *entire* Pinelands, not just of the project site.

The record of development within the state-designated Pinelands Area clearly shows that the commission has been successful in channeling growth away from ecologically sensitive areas. Almost no development has taken place in the Preservation Area (only 167 residential units were approved in six years' time), and very little in the highly restricted Forest and Agricultural Production areas (about one percent of the total number of approved units). New growth has been directed to already settled areas and to the fringes of the Pinelands.

Data on the total number of development denials are not available, but it is known that the commission itself has turned down requests for waivers or exemptions on 7,000 residential units, including one for a 4,500-unit housing project in a Forest Area. Also, many applicants, apparently anticipating project denial, have withdrawn their development plans (one of these was for a retirement community of 4,400 homes in the heart of the Preservation Area). To gain approval, still other developers have redesigned their projects; this has often resulted in fewer units, relocation of construction away from wetlands, or use of alternative wastewater systems. Now that the grace period on exemptions for projects approved prior to the plan's adoption has expired, there should be no more piecemeal development in the region.

Through acquisition, more than 50,000 acres of environmentally sensitive land has been placed in public ownership, while a limited number of transactions involving PDCs and conservation easements have caused several thousand more acres to be protected in perpetuity. Numerous wetlands and habitats of endangered plants and animals have been saved, and the commission has successfully warded off several attempts to site new landfills in the Pinelands or to expand faulty existing facilities. The commission also has prodded federal installations to improve their handling of hazardous and toxic wastes and has aggressively opposed what may turn out to be the biggest threat yet to the Pinelands—excessive exploitation of ground water supplies.

Although these actions to protect natural resources may not be completely satisfying, there is no question that the Pinelands Commission has substantially ameliorated the situation as it existed before the commission came into being. David Moore, Executive Director of the New Jersey Conservation Foundation and a spokesman for the state's environmental groups, has acknowledged that the primary Pinelands legislative goal— protection of the natural resources—is being achieved; however, he adds that environmentalists must continually press for stronger protective actions.[8] Nan Walnut, coordinator of the Pine Barrens Coalition, though a strong supporter of the commission, feels less comfortable about the intent of municipalities to truly implement the Pinelands regulations;

> Given the inherent tendency for local officials to want to take care
> of their own and for neighbors to resist restrictions that prevent a

friend from doing what he wants to do with his land, there is never going to be a point in our lifetime where we can say that we don't have to worry about the Pinelands.[9]

Weaknesses in the Resource Protection Program. A serious weakness in the resource management program is that not all of the Pinelands National Reserve is under the jurisdiction of the Pinelands Commission. In this 221,000-acre part of the reserve, the record is less than satisfactory. A high proportion of the development now being approved probably would fail to meet the standards of the Comprehensive Management Plan, a situation not anticipated by federal or state legislators (see Chapter 8). Thus far, the Pinelands Commission has not taken aggressive action to seek stronger protection in the area outside its jurisdiction, and the federal government's liaison for the Pinelands, the National Park Service, also has chosen to remain silent on the issue. Although the state legislature has shown some interest in putting all, or part, of the excluded reserve area under the commission's jurisdiction, few expect that this will be accomplished soon.

In 1984, representatives of the most active environmental organizations in the Pinelands reported sixteen other areas of concern about resource protection; in particular, they criticized the commission's relaxation of management area boundaries and performance standards as well as the weakness of its monitoring and enforcement activities.[10] This task force also suggested a number of administrative and regulatory changes that could strengthen the resource protection efforts, some of which were preliminarily approved by the commission in January 1986 as part of a package of 272 regulatory and administrative changes prompted by the first triennial review of the Comprehensive Management Plan. At the same time, however, the commission accepted recommendations for other plan revisions that the environmental groups adamantly opposed; for example, permitting the use of alternative wastewater systems in all management areas, and the reduction of the widths of buffers surrounding sand and gravel mining operations.[11]

Need for Further Research. Divergent viewpoints about the efficacy of mechanisms for protecting Pinelands resources may result from the lack of adequate scientific information about the natural dynamics of the Pine Barrens ecosystem and the relation of its resilience to various land uses. In 1982 a group of nationally known scientists convened by Dr. Ralph Good, Director of the Division of Pinelands Research at Rutgers University, called attention to the needs for further research.[12] In early 1986 a research plan developed by the commission's newly established Council on Pinelands Research and Management incorporated many of these research recommendations.[13] This plan gives top priority to the need to know more about the biogeochemical processes affecting water quality and the impact of various land uses on these processes. As many typical and rare plant and animal species of the Pinelands depend upon highly acid, low-nutrient ground and surface waters, protection of water quality is the key to resource protection in the Pinelands. Yet whether the CMP water standards (which allow considerably higher nutrient levels than are found in undisturbed Pinelands streams), the associated minimum lot sizes specified for standard or alternative septic wastewater systems, and the wetland buffer widths are adequate to protect water quality (or even excessive) cannot now be judged with certainty. In addition, although the dissecting of the Pinelands into increasingly smaller natural areas is known to have subtle, yet destructive effects, the ecologically acceptable limits of landscape fragmentation by development, mining, and other human uses have not been determined.

Unfortunately, although the Pinelands has been recognized as one of several hundred outstanding natural areas in the world through its designation as a biosphere reserve by UNESCO, public funding for the necessary research work remains scarce. The first long-term investigation of the impact of development on wetlands and water resources was initiated in 1986; it was made possible by a private foundation grant to the Rutgers Division of Pinelands Research.

Protecting Sociocultural Resources

Although the Pine Barrens is a relative wilderness in the midst of a large metropolitan area, it has been home for many people over hundreds of years. Both federal and state legislators acknowledged a need to protect the cultural, aesthetic, and scenic resources in this living landscape but gave no guidance on specific values to seek out in the planning process.

The mainstay of the Pinelands cultural resource program is protection of historic, prehistoric, and other sites of local, state, or national importance in the region. Since 1982, annual grants from the Office of New Jersey Heritage and the U.S. Department of the Interior's Historic Preservation Fund have supported one professional cultural-resource planner on the Pinelands Commission staff. With advice from a panel of technical preservation experts, representatives from various levels of governments, and members of the public, this planner completed in 1985 a management plan for more than 500 historic sites in the Pinelands.[14] The commission's development review staff and municipal planning (or preservation) boards ensure that proposed development will not alter designated historic or prehistoric sites or structures without approval.

A few Pinelands municipalities have designated historic districts, and several Pinelands sites have been nominated to the National Register of Historic Places. The commission's cultural-resource planner attempts to foster wider public interest in regional cultural values by conducting symposia and arranging lecture programs on the history and culture of the Pine Barrens. Several citizen groups have helped to restore significant landmarks in the region. One such effort, initiated by the New Jersey Conservation Foundation, involves preservation of the historic village of Whitesbog, which includes the largest cranberry farm in New Jersey, the birthplace of cultivated blueberries, and the place where mechanized harvest of cranberries was introduced. Although a plan for the restoration and management of Whitesbog has been completed, implementation of the project has not yet been fully funded.

Protection of Folklife Values.   Identifying and protecting physical remnants of the past is far simpler than protecting traditional ways of life. In 1986 Mary Hufford of the American Folklife Center pointed out: "In fact, no guidelines yet exist for evaluating living cultural resources in the context of land-use management."[15] She and other researchers from the center have documented the rich Pinelands folklife centered in the resource-based activities of hunting, trapping, fishing, clamming, crabbing, wood-cutting, and gathering, and have described the many special qualities of place that make the Pinelands a nationally significant living landscape. But like any rural culture in America, and even more so than most, the Pinelands folklife is endangered by encroaching suburbanization and competing demands for resource use. Markets for many products associated with traditional lifeways have disappeared—first iron and glass and then charcoal; today, too, boat-building is only a minor activity, and few of the young are learning the skills needed to make the distinctive cedar boats used for hunting on the marshes ("sneakboxes") or shellfishing ("garveys").

The Pinelands Commission has sought to protect such folkways as these primarily by maintaining the large natural areas in which traditional resource-related lifestyles may be continued. Several social ecologists, however, charge that the commission's concentration on the protection of natural resources and historic sites and structures has overshadowed the need to protect traditional culture.[16] These critics claim that although the commission's policies limiting the growth of Villages are supposed to help maintain the social and cultural integrity of traditional communities, the rules regarding Village size are too rigid, making some Villages too large and others too small, while the encouragement of development in growth areas on the coastal fringes of the Pinelands will erode local lifestyles there and destroy the beauty of historic Villages—Mays Landing, in particular. The commission staff responds by pointing out that the size of Village designations is worked out with local officials during the conformance process and that the designation of growth areas on the fringes accords with the legislative intent and is responsive to the pressures for development generated by the Atlantic City casino industry.

The commission also has been criticized for its bias in formulating scenic restrictions, which show a preference for natural resource features and against such local aesthetic norms as signs and junk piles.[17] Another sociocultural provision, the so-called "Piney" exemption, has been criticized for a variety of reasons (see Chapter 8). Members of the public have charged that homes authorized under the exemption provision have not always been occupied by the individuals entitled to development approval. From a resource protection standpoint, linkage of a two-generation family residence in the Pinelands to permission for building in the Preservation or other restricted areas is highly undesirable as it fosters scattered development. Though the provision is favored by officials with land acreage in the Preservation Area, other public officials find it discriminatory. The Office of Administrative Law has upheld the policy but it has yet to be tested in the higher courts.

In emphasizing the need to consider local values of residents, social ecologists Jonathan Berger and John Sinton have proposed formally "reserving places" in the Pinelands where Pineys may have freedom from the resource use restrictions imposed on others.[18] At the same time they note (without offering any resolution) the dilemma that Pineys, while wanting to retain their resource-based lifestyles, may also want the freedom to sell their land to a developer for the highest possible price. Berger and Sinton also do not deal with external considerations, which may in some instances override local interests, for example, state responsibilities to offer recreational opportunities to nearby urban residents, to save a resource legacy for future generations, and to guard the land and water resources of the entire region from the impact of local land uses. Richard Forman, Harvard Professor of Landscape Ecology, adds that the uniqueness of the Pinelands resources demand that we view the region in its national and international perspective.[19]

Recreational Opportunities.   In keeping with the greenline concept, federal and state legislators both called for enhancement of public recreational opportunities in the Pinelands National Reserve. Few signs, however, advertise to travellers that they are passing through the Pinelands National Reserve, and there is no regional visitors' center. Nevertheless, growing numbers are seeking outdoor experiences in the Pines. Residents and visitors compete for recreational opportunities, as do recreationists of varied interests—the wilderness hiker versus the motorized bikerider, for example.

As yet, there is no integrated program that defines the optimum mix and intensity of recreational opportunities that can be offered in the Pinelands without destruction of natural or cultural resources. The state legislation left authority to manage recreational use of state-owned lands in the Pinelands in the hands of the Department of Environmental Protection. In actuality, however, management responsibility is divided between two DEP agencies, each having its own objectives for land use which are not completely compatible with legislative goals (see Chapter 9). Compounding the problem has been lack of funds for staff and facility expansion and the lack of a continuing, strong gubernatorial interest in recognizing the New Jersey Pinelands as a nationally significant resource.[20] The result has been a disappointment both to the commission and its staff and sometimes to those who come to the Pinelands for recreation.

Maintaining Economic Vitality

Although subordinating development to resource protection, one of the objectives of both the federal and state legislation was to maintain the economic vitality of the Pinelands, an aim inherent in the greenline park concept. Regional growth through compatible residential and commercial development and indigenous industry is encouraged and agriculture actively promoted.

Growth Management.   From the beginning, the commission has been sensitive to its obligation to accommodate residential and commercial development compatible with resource protection. Each issue of *The Pinelander,* the commission's bimonthly newsletter, carries an update of development approvals under the Comprehensive Management Plan. In the first six years of regulation, about 17,400 new homes and more than 1,000 commercial and industrial development projects, including a $100 million shopping mall, were approved. These figures exclude the approvals of 11,500 new housing units granted between February 1979 and January 1981 (the moratorium or interim period).

Although development in the Pinelands Area obviously has not been completely stifled, there is evidence that CMP regulations have slowed the pace of residential construction, the mainstay of Pinelands development. Commission studies released in 1985 confirm that even after taking into account the high interest rates and the economic recession of 1981 and 1982, new construction declined more in the Pinelands Area than in either other parts of South Jersey or the state as a whole (see Chapter 10). Building permit analyses indicate that new housing has been diverted from the highly restricted Preservation, Forest, and Agricultural Production areas not only to Regional Growth Areas and Towns and Villages but also to locations outside the Pinelands Area. Michael Gross, counsel for developers, notes the obvious explanation: Density restrictions have decreased the attractiveness of Pinelands sites relative to land still available in other parts of the state.[21]

Growth Issues. Opinions vary about whether housing needs within the Pinelands have been accurately projected. Although Hamilton Township officials have claimed that lower-than-expected demands from Atlantic City development make CMP projections of housing needs excessive, developers and county planners worry that these projections may not be high enough. Developers also complain that restraints on the development of wetlands and requirements for housing mix may make it difficult to achieve the densities theoretically permitted under certified ordinances.

In the initial six years of plan implementation, the greatest obstacle to achieving the targeted growth was the lack of basic infrastructure in Regional Growth Areas. Although the Pinelands CMP specified how much and where future population growth was to be accommodated, it did not identify how the infrastructure (roads, water supplies, and sewer facilities) and community services (schools, hospitals, police and fire protection) to support this growth would be provided. As it turned out, many communities targeted as growth areas under the CMP had neither the infrastructure (particularly sewer facilities) in place for high-density development nor the resources to finance that infrastructure. In 1985 the state legislature acted to correct the situation by providing a low-cost mechanism for infrastructure financing. While this infrastructure fund may solve one problem, some environmentalists are concerned that it may create another by becoming an undesirable stimulant to growth in the Pinelands.[22]

Agriculture Support Programs.   Although berry, fruit, and vegetable culture in the Pinelands has not suffered the economic reverses experienced in other parts of the country, farmers here, as elsewhere in the state, are aware of the financial benefit of turning farmland into housing sites. Overall, New Jersey has lost more than half its farmland during the last three decades, partly because the farmland tax-assessment program may encourage land speculation rather than retention of land for farming.[23]

The commission included in the CMP a number of provisions to protect both farmland and farming activities in the Pinelands. The restriction of residential development in Agricultural Production Areas to housing for farm owners or their employees was intended to prevent developers from driving up land prices beyond the purchasing power of local farmers who need to expand their operations or of young farmers who wish to set up a new operation. Further, the exclusive agricultural zoning was designed to protect farmers from the vandalism and theft frequently associated with nearby development. Bowing to the strong antipathy of the farm bloc to regulatory restrictions, the Pinelands Development Credit system was heavily weighted to benefit farmers. Much to the dismay of environmentalists, but following the legislative intent, the commission also exempted agricultural activities from many development permitting requirements, including water quality standards. Despite such concessions, farmers, supported by the state Department of Agriculture, remained persistent and vocal critics of the CMP. Finally, in 1984 Governor Kean appointed an Agricultural Study Commission, chaired by Agriculture Secretary Arthur Brown, to investigate the farmers' complaints.

In its report submitted in late 1985, the Agricultural Study Commission noted that although it could not determine whether CMP regulations had caused lowered agricultural land prices, it did find that credit sources upon which most farmers depend had been disrupted by an uncertainty over the value of Pinelands farmland as collateral.[24] The report added, however, that only marginal farmers were being affected negatively by the credit restrictions. The study group also stated that the PDC program was not "functioning as well as it could" for a variety of reasons: inadequate infrastructure in growth areas, lack of a PDC bank (which the farm bloc originally had strongly opposed), failure of the Pinelands Commission to gain conformance from all municipalities, and a sluggish real estate market.

As a result of the agricultural study, the Pinelands Commission agreed to consider the feasibility of permitting nonagricultural, clustered housing in Agricultural Production Areas as an additional benefit to landowners.[25] It also agreed with the Department of Agriculture that there was a need for an educational outreach program to acquaint both farmers and developers with the mechanics and benefits of the PDC program. Because the state Pinelands Development Credit Bank was not authorized until 1985, the commission and the Department of Agriculture postponed final evaluation of the PDC program until the time when the PDC bank will have been in operation for two years. Thus, whether the total Pinelands PDC program will become more effective remains to be seen.

Whether an effective PDC operation (either as originally intended or simply as an easement purchase program) will satisfy the Pinelands farm bloc is questionable. In public hearings held by the Agricultural Study Commission, individual farmers complained that the $10,000 value of one PDC was much too low to offer just compensation for the regulatory restrictions on their land. In all fairness, the Pinelands Commission never represented nor intended that the PDC program would provide "just compensation," since the idea of compensation only raised the worrisome "taking issue." Instead, the program was described as a form of profit sharing: PDCs would allow owners of land in highly restricted areas to share in the rise of land values realized in growth areas. Interestingly, though not completely satisfactorily, the Pinelands experience with the PDC program appears promising enough to have stimulated legislators to again seek legislation for statewide authorization of transfer-of-development-rights programs.

Despite the complaints, Pinelands farming has remained strong. Indeed, in late 1985 Secretary of Agriculture Arthur R. Brown, Jr., reported that "agriculture continues to be one of the most productive aspects of the Pinelands Area."[26]

Economic Impacts of Regulation and the Equity Issue. A staff economist monitors and reports to the commission the discernible impacts of the Pinelands regulations on the regional economy. One of the more important economic indicators attempts to measure the impact on local land values of land-use restrictions in individual management areas. The latest staff analyses show that between 1981 and 1984 the sale price of land in all CMP management areas except the Preservation Area was higher than in the premoratorium years and that the increases in prices in all management areas except Agricultural Production Areas were greater than those outside the Pinelands. In the same period, however, there was a significant drop in the average sale price of vacant land in the Preservation Area—from $1,643 to $594 per acre.[27]

In expectation of this drop, many municipalities reduced assessments on vacant land in the Preservation Area and other highly restricted management areas when the Pinelands management plan became effective, thereby increasing the tax burden on developed property and causing a loss of ratable base in twenty-eight Pinelands municipalities. Although the loss amounted to 1.5 percent or less in twenty-five of these townships, in 1984 the state legislature, in response to a recommendation of the Pinelands Commission, enacted a three-year program (at an annual cost about $600,000) to reimburse municipalities for the loss of ratables. The legislature, however, has failed to act on another commission recommendation calling for a continuing in-lieu-of-tax reimbursement to Pinelands municipalities based on full tax equivalency for public land acquisitions.

Although some environmentalists oppose both types of reimbursement, arguing that they are unjustified and set bad statewide precedents, it is apparent that the commission's efforts to win legislative support for these programs, as well as its positive actions to help municipalities generate more ratables through the development of industrial parks, has gained goodwill from public officials.[28] Had such economic support programs as these been in place from the outset, the Comprehensive Management Plan and the conformance process might have been more easily accepted by municipalities.

Individuals owning land in the Preservation, Agricultural Production, and Special Agricultural Production areas are eligible for benefits under the PDC program. Assuming that one PDC is worth $10,000 (the value at which the state bank is authorized to redeem a credit), a premoratorium owner of a land parcel of 0.1 acre or more will be entitled to the minimum payment of $2,500. Above the minimum threshhold, PDCs translate into a value of $512 per acre for larger farmland tracts in the Preservation Area. Wetlands carry a lower benefit value. Even though a landowner redeems to the bank, or sells privately, the PDC credits allocable to a land parcel, residual land uses will always remain attached to the property, thereby circumventing the taking issue.

The only mechanism available to compensate individual landowners for hardships resulting from the land-use restrictions is the PDC program. Although the commission has treated the question of equity as a moral rather than a legal issue, individual commission and staff members have not been insensitive to the economic hardships suffered by some small property owners (see Chapter 8). Former Pinelands Commissioner Robert Shinn acknowledged that "some little people have been caught in the middle, particularly in the early implementation years."[29] Executive Director Terrence Moore has sometimes wished that he had "100 development approvals to give out at will."[30] Moore has suggested the desirability of having a new independent, nonregulatory state agency (a Pinelands

Conservancy) to deal with hardship cases and to perform other services for landowners and developers including PDC banking. It would be not unlike the California State Coastal Conservancy.

The problem of equity in individual cases may diminish with time. In 1986 State Senator Daniel J. Dalton, whose district includes part of the Pinelands, observed that "a lot of people have just resigned themselves to the fact that their land is not going to be developed. They're not happy, but they're learning to live with it."[31] Overall, however, the equity (or justice) issue has not been squarely faced in the Pinelands where the benefits of protection are enjoyed by many who do not as yet share the costs.

Enlisting Public Participation

Legislators mandated that the Pinelands program "provide for the maximum feasible . . . public participation in the management of the Pinelands Area" (PPA 13:18A–8h). Commission experiences, however, indicate that it is easier to incorporate public involvement in planning activities than in day-to-day decision-making.

During the formulation of the CMP, public comments resulted in significant changes in the plan. With few exceptions, though, there has been relatively little public participation in the conformance process, and environmentalists generally have found the opportunities for public involvement in development review decision-making less than satisfactory. Meetings of the Pinelands Commission and its subcommittees (which are public except when litigation, land acquisitions, or personnel evaluations are discussed) are usually attended by only a handful of people, mostly representatives of environmental organizations and occasionally of development interests. Attendance is larger only when the commission is discussing issues of unusual concern to a particular segment of the local population. For example, discussions involving siting of a landfill, pollution of water supplies by toxic wastes at federal installations, and granting of a waiver for a large development have brought out larger audiences.

Starting in late 1983 the commission made a special effort to enlist public involvement in the triennial plan review process. More than 2,400 persons were encouraged to submit comments on the need for revisions in the Comprehensive Management Plan. Copies of commission reports and staff discussion papers were sent to anyone requesting them, and public hearings and numerous meetings of the Commission's Plan Review Subcommittee were held to discuss proposed revisions to the plan.[32] Though the Pinelands Commission made it clear that it was willing to listen to anyone, public response was dominated by representatives of special-interest groups.

Spokespersons for these groups have been highly effective in articulating positions on critical issues, in gaining attention from the region's major newspapers, and ultimately in influencing the decision-makers. Throughout the planning and implementation periods they have aggressively presented to the commission the interests of environmentalists, farmers, builders and developers, sand and gravel pit operators, and municipal and county officials. Sportsmen and other recreationists, and operators of campgrounds and canoe rental services, have been represented to a lesser extent. Individual wood-cutters and utility company executives have spoken for themselves. The state Public Advocate has intervened in favor of the economically disadvantaged, pressing for enforcement of affordable housing programs.

As noted by Philip Burch, professor at the Rutgers Bureau of Government Research, in New Jersey special-interest groups represent a critical link between citizens (public opinion) and the government because the political parties are not issue oriented.[33] Burch suggests another finding borne out in the Pinelands experience—farmers in New Jersey, despite their limited numbers, have held unusual political power.

Although many residents of the Pinelands are represented by one or more special-interest groups, others are not. Pineys as a group, for example, are said to be alienated from the power structure, and claim that their voices are not heard by the commission.[34] Military personnel, senior citizens, and other newcomers who moved into the Pinelands in the 1960s and 1970s actually represent the largest segment of current population in the Pinelands but their concerns are seldom heard in commission meetings except when they happen to be represented by one of the interest groups. Mostly it is small property owners who speak up at meetings and then seek recourse from the commission. Some come to appeal for favorable action on waiver requests; others denounce the commission for particular plan restrictions such as the minimum lot sizes, the need to use waterless toilets on substandard-sized lots, or wetland buffers. One such landowner emotionally complained several times about the "loss of God-given rights" and the "violation of his constitutional rights," and accused the commission of listening too much to the environmentalists—"the free-loaders, who are getting use of the land for free"—and of "not getting input from where the damage is done."[35]

The commission recognizes the physical difficulty of gaining wider public participation: Most meetings are held in the daytime in a Pinelands township hall or at the commission office, a location that may require an hour or more drive by some residents of the Pine Barrens. For this reason, efforts have been concentrated on information outreach programs. A staff of two professionals generates frequent news reports and press releases, publishes a bimonthly newsletter, and disseminates information packets to realtors and prospective home buyers as well as guides to recreation resources. The greater part of staff time, however, is devoted to handling telephone, written, and walk-in requests for information about the Pinelands. Most inquiries concern permitted uses of private property or how to gain approval for development. As an aid to these landowners and prospective builders, simplified explanations of CMP requirements have been prepared. For the general public there is an attractive brochure containing a copy of the land-use management map and a brief description of the Pinelands resources.

Private foundations have underwritten development of an audiovisual program on the Pinelands that has been presented to many school and civic groups throughout the state. A staff educational coordinator, with help from an Educational Advisory Council, has developed elementary curriculum units on the Pinelands, and has fostered widened interest in the region through annual essay and poster contests. The National Park Service has proposed to develop (with the Department of Environmental Protection and the commission) a much-needed interpretive program for public lands. These efforts to inform and educate should create greater awareness of the value of the Pinelands resources, the issues involved in protecting them, and the need for land-use regulatory programs, and may well be the most effective way of stimulating public participation in commission activities and acceptance of the program.

Long-Term Viability of the Pinelands Program

Despite the program flaws already mentioned, mechanisms for implementing the CMP are working well. Although the authority to regulate development is lodged with local government, the traditional base of power in New Jersey, there is regional oversight. Duplicate permitting and ad-hoc decision-making have been minimized to facilitate the development review process for applicants and to help ensure more consistent outcomes. Such organizational features as the detachment of regional authority from the state bureaucracy and its Trenton headquarters, capable and generally nonconfrontational commission representation of both local and statewide interests, a well-managed and hard-working professional staff, and the conduct of planning and implementation decision-making in open sessions have helped to institutionalize the program at local levels and to defuse much of the early animosity. Given the location of the Pinelands, however, in the midst of megalopolis, with a growth-stimulating casino industry on the doorstep, will today's program work effectively in the decades to come?

Future Threats.   It is impossible to predict with any certainty all future claims that will be made on Pinelands resources and just how the protection program will hold up under competing resource demands. At least two threats of great significance appear inevitable, however; one is already present.

The Demand for Pinelands' Groundwater. Who will get to use the huge supply of water underlying the Pinelands? Although opponents of the CMP often argued that the plan was nothing more than an instrument to save this water for North Jersey, the first real threat to use it came from South Jersey. In 1985, upon request of a water purveyor, the Department of Environmental Protection started investigating whether the Cohansey aquifer could be tapped to supply the needs of metropolitan Camden, whose normal supplies drawn from the Potomac, Raritan, and Magothy aquifer were contaminated. By early 1986 it had also become apparent that Monmouth and Ocean counties and Atlantic City were facing critical water-supply problems.

The Pinelands Commission, reinforced by scientific studies of the deleterious ecological impacts of excessive groundwater pumping from the Cohansey aquifer, and with the strong support of farmers dependent on adequate local water supplies, has opposed the export of surface or ground waters from the Pinelands National Reserve except as an emergency measure or if no alternative is available. State legislation to affirm this policy has been introduced; by early 1987, however, no legislative action had been taken and the Department of Environmental Protection still remained unwilling to exclude consideration of the Cohansey as the preferred water source for a much wider area of the state.

The Pressure of Growth. In the early 1980s New Jersey's population grew almost twice as fast as it had in the 1970s, and more than one-quarter of this growth occurred in four Pinelands counties—Atlantic, Cumberland, Ocean and Cape May—generating in each strong demands for new housing.[36] In 1985 the Federal Aviation Administration announced plans for a $2.5 billion expansion of its technical center in Pomona (Atlantic County), and business leaders, public officials, and developers began to tout the advantages of South Jersey as a "high-tech" center and a desirable location for corporate campus development.

Governor Kean has fueled these growth hopes by pledging state help to expand the road system, develop a major airport, and provide a rail link between Atlantic City and New York and Philadelphia.[37] New or expanded transportation routes connecting South Jersey's coastal areas with Philadelphia, Camden, or Trenton, however, cannot be built without encroaching on the Pinelands National Reserve.

Given the present growth trends in South Jersey, it appears inevitable that at some future time, beyond the vision of current planners, the development potential built into the Pinelands Comprehensive Management Plan will be exhausted. Once Regional Growth Areas, Municipal Reserves, Towns and Villages, and then Rural Development Areas are built to capacity, will members of the Pinelands Commission continue to hold firmly to the goal of protecting the integrity of the total Pinelands ecosystem and its natural resource components? Will the limitations on growth be continued in the critical Preservation and Forest management areas? And will development uncompromisingly be diverted to areas outside the Pinelands? Answers to these questions will depend primarily on the attitudes of future governors, and on the degree of continuing public support for Pinelands protection.

Gubernatorial Attitudes.   The governor plays a powerful role in determining the success of the Pinelands program. As the state's executive, he not only sets the tone for both legislative action and interagency cooperation, but also has veto authority over actions of the Pinelands Commission and the right to appoint seven of its fifteen commissioners. Governor Brendan Byrne fought for strong legislation to protect the Pine Barrens and nursed the commission's efforts through the planning stage and the first year of plan implementation despite strong and vocal opposition from a number of quarters. Byrne's successor, Governor Thomas Kean, has not been a strong supporter of the Pinelands Commission, at least during his first six years of office. He has neither initiated legislation for the economic support programs nor encouraged increased appropriations for key staff operations. Kean's failure to give high priority to Pinelands protection efforts also is partly reflected in the negative attitudes of state agencies toward the Pinelands program.[38]

More important, however, in the long run are the imprints left by gubernatorial appointees. Pleasing developers and farmers and outraging environmentalists, Kean replaced two of the most pro-regulation members of the commission with appointees who markedly changed the strong dedication to resource protection that characterized the initial Commission.[39] One Kean appointee, a cranberry and blueberry grower, had actively opposed both the state legislation and the adoption of the Comprehensive Management Plan; since becoming a commissioner, he has aggressively supported agricultural interests and emphasized the need for farmers to be fairly compensated for the loss of alternative land uses. The voting record of the second Kean commissioner, an architect with close ties to Ocean County political circles, has favored development rather than environmental protection. A third Kean appointee (1987) was distinguished in Republican politics, but not known for conservation work.

Initially, the biases of Kean's appointees were offset by four county representatives (those from Burlington, Camden, Cumberland, and Gloucester) who usually favored protection of resources threatened by development. The commission's ideological emphasis on resource protection became less discernible when Burlington's Bob Shinn resigned in 1985 to take a seat in the state assembly. Shinn, vice-chairman of the Commission since its formation, though originally opposed to the Pinelands legislation, had turned out to be one of its most effective advocates, particularly persuasive in the areas of PDCs and farmland preservation programs. His successor has been less so.

Further erosion of the present county support for resource protection, or replacement of any of the remaining initial four gubernatorial appointees with individuals more accommodating to development, could seriously hurt the Pinelands protection efforts. Domination by local agriculture and development interests may transform the commission into a body little better than its ineffective predecessor, the Pinelands Environmental Council. As Frank Popper has observed, several other land-use reform programs have been weakened by the entrenched opposition achieving substantial representation in the implementing agency.[40]

Strength of Public Support. Since adoption of the Comprehensive Management Plan, the sources of support for the Pinelands protection effort have shifted and broadened; in part the movement has been away from environmental groups and toward developers, builders, and mining operators (the commission's clients) and municipal officials (its management partners). Statewide citizen support was reaffirmed in 1985 when voters approved by an overwhelming majority the Pinelands infrastructure bond referendum.

Given New Jersey's history of strong voter support for environmental controls, it seems reasonable to expect that protection of the Pine Barrens legacy will remain high on the public agenda. According to a recent poll, South Jersey residents worry most about manmade environmental threats, especially mishandling of toxic wastes and landfills and negative impacts

of development on the rural landscape.[41] The Pinelands program addresses both these areas, and commission actions on these and a variety
of other regional issues—illegal dumping, infrastructure needs, and water
export—have won enthusiastic support from many local officials, community groups, and individuals, many of whom were initially antagonistic to
its efforts. In a Commission meeting, one resident of Mullica Township
volunteered:

> I'm one of the little people. When the Pinelands Act was first passed
> we were uncomfortable with the state telling us what to do. But
> now with the landfill problem we have come to appreciate the Act
> and the commission actions to protect the environment which we
> feel so strong about.[42]

These remarks mirror a growing statewide recognition that 567 municipalities acting independently cannot deal with complex environmental
and social issues, such as landfill siting and hazardous-waste cleanup,
maintenance of unpolluted water supplies, and fulfillment of affordable
housing needs.[43] In 1985 the state legislature created a State Planning
Commission to "promote suitable use of land," mandating that the new
commission rely on the Pinelands Comprehensive Management Plan for
management policies in that region.[44]

Another item on the public agenda, tax reform, may also favor the
Pinelands program. As an observer of the New Jersey scene has noted:
"Effective management of land-use is not impossible without tax reform,
but it is ten times harder."[45] If property tax relief is achieved, the lust for
ratables and the fiscal stress caused by land-use restrictions should be reduced in the Pinelands.

The future effectiveness of the Pinelands protection effort also will depend greatly on strengthened support from environmental groups. The
environmental movement, usually ideologically pluralistic, showed remarkable unity through the legislative fight, but its undivided support
began to unravel before completion of the Comprehensive Management
Plan, as some groups grew increasingly strident in their criticisms of the
commission. Representatives of the West Jersey chapter of the Sierra
Club, for example, urged the Governor and the Secretary of the Interior
not to approve the plan; they thought its protection of the environment
too weak. During the first six years of plan implementation, a few members of this group continued to be highly critical of commission actions,
and in early 1986 they formed a new organization, the Pine Barrens Al-
liance, to take legal action against the commission for its certification of

Berkeley Township. The state Sierra Club officers, however, did not endorse this action.

Other state environmental groups (primarily the New Jersey Conservation Foundation, the Pine Barrens Coalition, the New Jersey Audubon Society, and the New Jersey Environmental Lobby), less militant but still resolved that the Pinelands be protected, have worked effectively to persuade the commission to take stronger preservation actions. With the exception of the Natural Resources Defense Council and the Environmental Defense Fund, national groups which joined to secure passage of the legislation are no longer actively involved.

In six years of plan implementation there has been only one full-time, professional representative of environmental interests in the Pinelands. Maintaining involvement in issue discussions at commission, staff, and legislative levels requires more than one professional. In addition, to effectively counterbalance future competing claims for land uses, environmental groups must find the financial resources to establish a more formal and extended network for monitoring activities of the commission and local implementing actions.

Conclusion

Against almost overwhelming odds, the radical land-use management program in the Pinelands has been made to work. Protection of unique resources on privately owned lands has been effectively achieved, without successful legal challenge, through the use of state and local regulatory powers. Public officials, developers, and residents have gradually come to accept the program's stringent regulations. At minimum, designation of the region as a National Reserve provided a much-needed breathing period during which critical resources threatened by development could be acquired. Institutionalizing of the plan's provisions in municipal zoning ordinances will tend to have lasting value.

Protection of New Jersey's priceless legacy, the Pine Barrens, should remain an attainable goal for many years to come. As in the past, however, success will require statewide public interest, continuing involvement and vigilance by environmental groups and, at minimum, gubernatorial neutrality.

13. Lessons of the Pinelands Experiences

Beryl Robichaud Collins

Worldwide, growing populations and their dispersals from metropolitan areas are generating conflicting demands for the use of our diminishing natural resources, in particular for undeveloped land and unpolluted water. As urbanization spreads, landscapes become fragmented, destroying cultural and community values and impoverishing natural biological diversity. Fertile farmlands are lost. In this country at least, traditional governmental structures are increasingly unable to deal with the competing interests for resource use. The results are evident everywhere—pollution or inadequacy of water supplies, mismanagement of toxic and nontoxic wastes, traffic congestion, lack of access to affordable housing and to recreation resources, destruction of terrestrial and aquatic habitats that serve as sources of food supplies, and decline of older cities.

Since the 1960s innovative programs to avoid environmental degradation through improved land-use (or growth) management have been initiated at local, regional, and state levels. Hundreds of local governments from Petaluma, California, to Ramapo, New York, to Boca Baton, Florida, have adopted measures to direct and phase future growth. In the 1960s and 1970s federal grants encouraged regional approaches to resource planning, particularly for water-basin and coastal-area management.[1] Although states have ultimate authority over local planning and zoning actions, few have assumed an activist role in land-use or growth management.[2] As exceptions, New York set up the Adirondack Park Agency, and California and Nevada, the Tahoe Regional Planning Agency. California and North Carolina established coastal planning commissions, and Florida, critical area planning units. Vermont and Colorado, and more recently New Jersey, have assigned broader planning roles for the state, but to date only Hawaii, Oregon, and Florida have legislated strong mandates for total statewide land and growth management. The successes and failures of these ventures into more-innovative land-use management are well documented.[3]

The experiences with the New Jersey Pinelands National Reserve now offer additional insights into the issues of land-use and growth management in more-settled areas of the country. The Pinelands National Reserve provides a classic illustration of the conflict in the complex interrelationships of land use and water resources (one that transcends political boundaries), the impact of so-called "buckshot" urbanization of a rural landscape, and the impracticality of attempting to protect a settled landscape solely through fee simple acquisition. Unlike New York's program for the Adirondack Park or federal efforts to achieve resource protection through the traditional National Park system, the Pinelands National Reserve program calls for an innovative federal-state-local partnership to manage the reserve's one million acres.

When Congress authorized the Pinelands National Reserve, legislators viewed the action as an experimental prototype of a greenline park which, if successful, could be applied to many other situations. The federal government asked that New Jersey use state and local regulatory and police powers to protect land and water resources to an extent previously untested. In return, it provided funding for limited land acquisition.

European countries have a heritage of "countryside," or regional landscape parks that are created on mostly privately owned lands under governmental incentive and regulatory programs. Richard Babcock and Frank Popper, in writing about the special privileges granted ownership of land by Anglo-American law, pinpoint the primary obstacle to acceptance of the greenline park concept of resource protection in United States—the pervasiveness of the idea that "owners feel that their land is theirs, to do with as they please."[4] For this reason there has been in this country a reluctance to use zoning rather than land acquisition or easement purchase as the prime method for protecting valuable resources. This reluctance has been particularly strong in New Jersey, where home rule is reinforced by a tax system dependent on property values.

That resource protection on a large scale can indeed be effectively achieved by the exercise of state and local regulatory and police powers over the use of privately owned lands is the most noteworthy lesson to be drawn from the Pinelands experience. The land-use restrictions and performance standards established in the Pinelands program are as stringent as any in the country and yet they have survived judicial scrutiny in an environment of strong home rule. Furthermore, there has been growing public acceptance of the program and its underlying concepts of land-use management. The validation of the greenline concept on a regional scale thus has broad implications for protection of critical resources and regional landscapes throughout the country.

The Pinelands program also offers a viable model for a local, state, and federal partnership to manage land and water resources. The Pinelands experience demonstrates that implementation of regional plans may be effectively delegated to traditional local jurisdictional units if regional (or state) land-use standards, policies, and regulatory mechanisms are incorporated into local master plans and ordinances by a formal certification process. Regulatory mechanisms that provide both a minimum of local ad-hoc decision-making and a continuing regional oversight of outcomes will ensure greater consistency with plan objectives. Local acceptance of a restrictive land-management program appears to depend largely upon enough flexibility in the certification process to allow local modifications to the greatest extent consistent with the program goals.

Under the Pinelands Comprehensive Management Plan, certified municipalities and counties exercise initial responsibility for development permitting within their jurisdictions, while the regional body (the Pinelands Commission) retains oversight authority for approved development. Another (and perhaps better) division of responsibility would be to delegate to municipalities initial review authority for the many projects of only local impact while retaining in the hands of a higher-level body both initial review authority for projects (usually few in number) having regional impact and oversight authority for all approved development.

The weakest link in the Pinelands intergovernmental partnership has turned out to be the state agency partners, a problem compounded by an unexpected weakening of gubernatorial support for the program. In the absence of a strong executive interest, it is apparent from the Pinelands experiences that state agencies may be less than cooperative in assuring that their implementing actions are consistent with the regional plan. Jurisdictional incompatibilities could have been mitigated had the state's enabling legislation made the borders of the state Pinelands Area completely coincident with those of the federal reserve. Changes in executive attitudes can be counterbalanced only by continuous and careful public scrutiny of decision-making.

Federal sponsorship of the national reserve, and seed money for planning and land acquisition, were essential to drive the Pinelands program, first to gain initial program acceptance and then to leverage supporting state funding. Shortly after the Pinelands program became effective, the role of the federal partner changed. Washington's interest in the innovative land-use experiment declined. Although the federal presence becomes less important as the reserve ages, the federal government has ongoing obligations to fulfill, particularly with respect to ensuring that adequate recreational facilities and programs are provided to accommodate visitors attracted to the national reserve and that the land acquisition program is completed. The reserve concept of land protection demands, too, that adequate efforts be made to protect privately owned lands from damage by visitors. Without assurance of continuing federal involvement, other states may find it less attractive to undertake a regional protection effort on the scale of the Pinelands.

As mandated by both federal and state legislation, the Pinelands program is strongly biased for resource protection, but it serves also as a growth management program channeling compatible development to appropriate locations and promoting certain resource uses without sacrificing fundamental environmental goals. The Pinelands experience confirms the growing consensus that landscape protection is a goal that must be vigorously pursued, but such protection cannot be a sole objective.[5] Protection must be rooted in a program that also considers regional growth needs and ways to mitigate the costs of protection. In fact, the success of a large-scale resource-protection program depends upon the coexistence of a workable, complementary economic program. The Pinelands experience illustrates too that the needs for capital improvements to support the planned growth potential, and the means for financing these should be clearly delineated in the planning phase. Ideally, minimum funding for the economic support programs should be authorized before the regulatory program is implemented.

Elements of the Pinelands program that have worked well may serve as models for many other situations, and program failures also provide valuable insights:

> *Assigning regional or statewide planning authority without concomitant implementation responsibility will usually fail to produce the desired results.* New Jersey learned this lesson when a predecessor of the Pinelands Commission, the Pinelands Environmental Council, failed in its attempt to protect the resources. Sensitive to this experience, the New Jersey legislature prescribed and assigned unusually strong implementation authority to the Pinelands Commission. Combining implementation and planning authority in a single agency has worked well for the Pinelands where the regional body (the commission) has been able to delegate effectively some of its implementation responsibilities while retaining oversight authority.
>
> *Regional or statewide land-use (or growth) management requires adequate state appropriations to cover planning and implementation costs.* Where resource considerations dictate that land-use restrictions are not equitably apportioned to local governing units and where tax-sharing is not feasible, additional funding may be appropriate to help offset the so-called "wipeout" costs associated with the regulatory measures. As illustrated by the Pinelands experi-

ence, a state program to reimburse municipalities that suffer disproportionate net losses in ratables because of decreases in the value of restricted vacant lands can help gain public acceptance for a regulatory program. Continuing reimbursement for the full loss of ratables acquired as public lands would win even more support.

A regional (or statewide) transfer-of-development-rights (TDR) program offers great promise as an effective means to provide landowners in highly restricted areas with opportunity to share in the rise of land values in growth areas. Experiences with the Pinelands Development Credit (PDC) program, however, emphasize the need for adequate mechanisms to ensure the marketability of allotted rights or credits. It also suggests that a TDR program alone may not be sufficient in a moral (versus legal) sense to mitigate personal losses associated with the imposition of restrictive land uses. The issue of equity, where the benefits of a broad land-use management program (particularly in an urbanized area) are enjoyed by many and the costs borne by a few, has not been fully resolved in the Pinelands.

A regional authority may represent both local and statewide interests and still be an effective planning and management body. To gain public confidence and acceptance, however, the regional agency should conduct its business openly and provide effective means for the public to receive attention. In New Jersey it also has been helpful that the professional staff of the Pinelands Commission is lean in personnel as well as administratively and physically detached from the state bureaucracy.

The Pinelands experience offers other lessons to public officials, planners, and members of land-use interest groups. Often it is suggested that successful regional planning demands ample time to gain input and win support from all affected constituencies.[6] Admittedly, the Pinelands Commission, working within the strict time constraints imposed by the legislature for the planning process, was not successful in establishing formal communication channels with municipal officials, county planners, and segments of the population not represented by special-interest groups. Given a longer time, some parts of the plan might have been better developed and greater local acceptance enlisted.

On the other hand, as John DeGrove has suggested, shorter planning periods do have benefits, one being the production of more-concise plans.[7] Clearly, in the Pinelands a stronger protection plan was favored by the shorter planning period: President Carter's Administration was able to approve the plan before leaving office and Governor Byrne to oversee its initial implementation problems. Adoption of a strong Pinelands protection program also was favored by the unusually powerful executive authority that exists in New Jersey. Had the Comprehensive Management Plan required legislative approval, it probably would have been weakened.

The mixed benefits of development moratoria during the planning phase are also illustrated by the Pinelands experience. On the one hand, interim building restrictions prevented development that would have destroyed critical resources before they could be protected and also introduced a certain reality into the planning process; on the other hand, they generated hostility and crystallized opposition before the plan was even completed. This negative effect might have been reduced by increasing the interim threshold for exemptions from the regulations.

Finally, the Pinelands experience confirms several truisms about the genesis of innovative land-use management programs:[8]

> *Regional or state land-use management programs that override traditional local authority usually come into existence only when the public perceives a threat of crisis proportions.* There must also be hard evidence that valuable resources (a water supply or an historic landscape, for example) are endangered or that extremely undesirable social effects (such as traffic congestion or no public access to coastal areas) have occurred. In the case of the Pinelands, sound scientific research also has served to satisfy judicial scrutiny of resource protection policies.
>
> *There must be strong gubernatorial support for a regional solution as well as a strong grass-roots recognition that multiple local jurisdictions cannot effectively deal with the competing demands for use of land.* In the Pinelands program, adoption also required an extraordinary effort by a well-organized environmental-interest group to combat the entrenched and well-financed representatives of development and agricultural interests.[9] Involvement of effective and interested legislative leadership was equally important.

The Pinelands Comprehensive Management Plan has been labeled an extreme expression of the greenline park concept, and indeed its stringent land-use and performance standards may not be needed or appropriate in all circumstances.[10] However, the Pinelands model still provides a prototype for a variety of situations. The National Parks and Conservation Association has identified scores of sites in the nation as possible candidates for greenline park consideration.[11] The staff of the National Conference of State Legislatures has concluded there is need for regional action to protect valuable farmlands, forest areas, aquifer recharge zones, wetlands, and floodplains.[12] Others add to this list mountain and coastal resort areas and other unusual scenic or historic sites that are suffering under local jurisdiction. The Pinelands program not only offers a model for state-wide planning in New Jersey and other states, but also suggests one way in which the nation may meet its pressing need for new and expanded national parks.

The opportunities for protection of the nation's diminishing critical resources are many. And, as the Pinelands experience is proving, although the efforts and the costs needed to ensure success are considerable, the potential rewards can be enormous.

Appendix

Table A–1. Scientific Names of Plants and Animals (Prepared by Norma F. Good)

Common Name	Scientific Name
Plants	
bracken fern	*Pteridium aquilinum* (L.) Kuhn
chain fern	*Woodwardia virginica* (L.) Sm.
curly grass fern	*Schizaea pusilla* Pursh
blackgum	*Nyssa sylvatica* Marsh.
blackjack oak	*Quercus marilandica* Muenchh.
black huckleberry	*Gaylussacia baccata* (Wang.) K. Koch
black oak	*Quercus velutina* Lam.
bog asphodel	*Narthecium americanum* Ker
broom crowberry	*Corema conradii* Torr.
broomsedge	*Andropogon virginicus* L.
bullsedge	*Carex bullata* Schkurh
chestnut oak	*Quercus prinus* L.
cowwheat	*Melampyrum lineare* Desr.
cranberry	*Vaccinium macrocarpon* Ait.
dangleberry	*Gaylussacia frondosa* (L.) T.&G.
dwarf chestnut	*Quercus prinoides* Willd.
false heather	*Hudsonia ericoides* L.
golden club	*Orontium aquaticum* L.
gray birch	*Betula populifolia* Marsh.
highbush blueberry	*Vaccinium corymbosum* L.
leatherleaf	*Chamaedaphne calyculata* (L.) Moench
lowbush blueberry	*Vaccinium vacillans* Torr.
mountain laurel	*Kalmia latifolia* L.
Pine Barrens gentian	*Gentiana autumnalis* L.
pitch pine	*Pinus rigida* Mill.
pitcher plant	*Sarracenia purpurea* L.
post oak	*Quercus stellata* Wang.
pyxie moss	*Pyxidanthera barbulata* Michx.
rose pogonia	*Pogonia ophioglossoides* (L.) Ker
sand myrtle	*Leiophyllum buxifolium* (Berg.) Ell.
sassafras	*Sassafras albidum* (Nutt.) Nees
scarlet oak	*Quercus coccinea* Muenchh.
scrub oak	*Quercus ilicifolia* Wang.
sheep laurel	*Kalmia angustifolia* L.
shortleaf pine	*Pinus echinata* Mill.
southern red oak	*Quercus falcata* Michx.
southern white cedar	*Chamaecyparis thyoides* (L.) BSP
sphagnum moss	*Sphagnum* spp.
staggerbush	*Lyonia mariana* (L.) D. Don
sundew	*Drosera* spp.
swamp azalea	*Rhododendron viscosum* (L.) Torr.
sweet fern	*Comptonia peregrina* (L.) Coult.
sweet pepperbush	*Clethra alnifolia* L.
sweetbay	*Magnolia virginiana* L.

Table A–1. *(continued)*

Common Name	Scientific Name
trident red maple	*Acer rubrum* var. *trilobum* K. Koch
turkey beard	*Xerophyllum asphodeloides* (L.) Nutt.
virginia pine	*Pinus virginiana* Mill.
white oak	*Quercus alba* L.
wintergreen	*Gaultheria procumbens* L.

Animals

Amphibians and Reptiles

carpenter frog	*Rana virgatipes*
corn snake	*Elaphe guttata guttata*
eastern king snake	*Lampropeltis getulus getulus*
eastern mud salamander	*Pseudotriton montanus montanus*
ground skink	*Scincella lateralis*
northern pine snake	*Pituophis melanoleucus melanoleucus*
northern red-bellied snake	*Storeria occipitomaculata occipitomaculata*
northern scarlet snake	*Cemophora coccinea copei*
Pine Barrens treefrog	*Hyla andersoni*
rough green snake	*Opheodrys aestivus*

Fish

alewife	*Alosa pseudoharengus*
American shad	*Alosa sapidissima*
banded killifish	*Fundulus diaphanus*
banded sunfish	*Enneacanthus obesus*
blackbanded sunfish	*Enneacanthus chaetodon*
blueback herring	*Alosa aestivalis*
eastern mudminnow	*Umbra pygmaea*
golden shiner	*Notemigonus crysoleucas*
ironcolor shiner	*Notropis chalybaeus*
mud sunfish	*Acantharchus pomotis*
mummichog	*Fundulus heteroclitus*
pickerel	*Esox niger*
pirate perch	*Aphredoderus sayanus*
pumpkinseed	*Lepomis gibbosus*
redbreast sunfish	*Lepomis auritus*
striped bass	*Morone saxatilis*
swamp darter	*Etheostoma fusiforme*
white perch	*Morone americana*
white sucker	*Catostomus commersoni*
yellow bullhead	*Ictalurus natalis*
yellow perch	*Perca flavescens*

Birds

American kestrel	*Falco sparverius*
American redstart	*Setophaga ruticilla*

Table A–1. *(continued)*

Common Name	Scientific Name
black-and-white-warbler	*Mniotilta varia*
blue jay	*Cyanocitta cristata*
northern bobwhite	*Colinus virginianus*
brown thrasher	*Toxostoma rufum*
Carolina chickadee	*Parus carolinensis*
Carolina wren	*Thryothorus ludovicianus*
gray catbird	*Dumetella carolinensis*
chipping sparrow	*Spizella passerina*
downy woodpecker	*Picoides pubescens*
eastern bluebird	*Sialia sialis*
eastern prairie chicken	*Tympanuchus cupido cupido*
eastern wood-pewee	*Contopus virens*
mourning dove	*Zenaida macroura*
common nighthawk	*Chordeiles minor*
northern mockingbird	*Mimus polyglottus*
ovenbird	*Seiurus aurocapillus*
pine warbler	*Dendroica pinus*
prairie warbler	*Dendroica discolor*
red-eyed vireo	*Vireo olivaceus*
red-winged blackbird	*Agelaius phoeniceus*
rock dove	*Columba livia*
ruffed grouse	*Bonasa umbellus*
rufous-sided towhee	*Pipilo erythrophthalmus*
screech owl	*Otus asio*
sharp-shinned hawk	*Accipiter striatus*
dark-eyed junco	*Junco hyemalis*
tufted titmouse	*Parus bicolor*
turkey vulture	*Cathartes aura*
whip-poor-will	*Caprimulgus vociferus*
wild turkey	*Meleagris gallopavo*
common yellowthroat	*Geothlypis trichas*
yellow-throated vireo	*Vireo flavifrons*

Mammals

beaver	*Castor canadensis*
big brown bat	*Eptesicus fuscus*
black bear	*Ursus americanus*
bobcat	*Lynx rufus*
eastern chipmunk	*Tamias striatus*
eastern cottontail rabbit	*Sylvilagus floridanus*
eastern mole	*Scalopus aquaticus*
eastern coyote	*Canis latrans*
eastern pipistrelle	*Pipistrellus subflavus*
gray fox	*Urocyon cinereoargenteus*
gray squirrel	*Sciurus carolinensis*
house mouse	*Mus musculus*

Table A–1. *(continued)*

Common Name	Scientific Name
least shrew	*Cryptotis parva*
little brown bat	*Myotis lucifugus*
long-tailed weasel	*Mustela frenata*
masked shrew	*Sorex cinereus*
meadow jumping mouse	*Zapus hudsonius*
meadow vole	*Microtus pennsylvanicus*
mink	*Mustela vison*
muskrat	*Ondatra zibethicus*
Norway rat	*Rattus norvegicus*
opossum	*Didelphis virginiana*
pine vole	*Pitymys pinetorum*
raccoon	*Procyon lotor*
red-backed vole	*Clethrionnomys gapperi*
red fox	*Vulpes fulva*
red squirrel	*Tamiasciurus hudsonicus*
rice rat	*Oryzomys palustris*
river otter	*Lutra canadensis*
short-tailed shrew	*Blarina brevicauda*
southern bog lemming	*Synaptomys cooperi*
southern flying squirrel	*Glaucomys volans*
star-nosed mole	*Condylura cristata*
striped skunk	*Mephitis mephitis*
white-footed mouse	*Peromyscus leucopus*
white-tailed deer	*Odocoileus virginianus*
wolf	*Canis lupus*
woodchuck	*Marmota monax*

SOURCES: Nomenclature follows: M. L. Fernald, *Gray's Manual of Botany,* 8th ed. (New York: American Book Co., 1950) (plants); R. W. Hastings, "Fish of the Pine Barrens," *in Pine Barrens: Ecosystem and Landscape,* ed. R. T. T. Forman, (New York: Academic Press, 1979) (fish); R. Conant, *A Field Guide to Reptiles and Amphibians* (Boston: Houghton Mifflin, 1958) (amphibians and reptiles); C. F. Leck, *The Status and Distribution of New Jersey's Birds*(New Brunswick, N.J.: Rutgers University Press, 1984) (birds); and W. H. Burt and R. P. Grossenheider, *A Field Guide to the Mammals* (Boston: Houghton Mifflin, 1959) (mammals).

Table A–2. Population and Land Size of Fifty-two Pinelands Municipalities

County and Municipality[a]	Date Certified[b]	1980 Population[c]	Total	Total Pinelands Area	Pinelands National Reserve Only[d]
Atlantic County					
Buena	9/85	3,642	7.40	3.54	—
Buena Vista	NC	6,959	41.83	37.66	—
Corbin City	10/82	254	8.30	0.18	8.79
Egg Harbor City	10/86	4,618	10.89	10.89	—
Egg Harbor Twnshp	NC	19,381	67.94	28.05	7.69
Estell Manor	8/83	848	53.75	35.25	18.28
Folsom	NC	1,892	8.40	8.40	—
Galloway	11/86	12,176	91.75	40.62	34.38
Hamilton	3/85	9,499	113.40	110.27	1.50
Hammonton	11/84	12,298	41.80	41.80	—
Mullica	2/84	5,243	56.50	56.50	—
Port Republic	NC	837	8.10	1.75	1.09
Weymouth	NC	1,260	12.00	10.02	—
Total		78,907	522.06	384.93	71.73
Burlington County					
Bass River	7/82	1,344	77.35	67.90	10.39
Evesham	7/83	21,508	29.65	16.43	5.78
Medford	5/83	17,622	40.29	31.27	0.16
Medford Lakes	2/83	4,958	1.25	1.25	—
New Hanover	7/81	14,258	21.85	19.36	—
North Hanover	2/82	9,050	17.30	0.73	—
Pemberton	6/83	29,720	64.67	58.95	—
Shamong	NC	4,537	46.61	46.61	—
Southampton	5/83	8,808	43.31	32.11	—
Springfield	9/81	2,691	29.34	0.73	—
Tabernacle	9/85	6,236	47.64	47.64	—
Washington	8/83	808	107.32	107.32	—
Woodland	9/83	2,285	95.38	95.38	—
Wrightstown	8/81	3,031	1.65	1.22	—
Total		126,856	623.61	526.90	16.33
Camden County					
Berlin	6/83	5,786	3.56	0.35	—
Berlin Township	6/83	5,348	3.27	0.57	—
Chesilhurst	2/83	1,590	1.72	1.72	—
Waterford	7/83	8,126	36.11	36.11	—
Winslow	4/83	20,034	57.78	46.58	—
Total		40,884	102.44	85.33	—

Cape May County					
Dennis	9/83	3,989	64.97	24.46	32.39
Upper	7/83	6,713	63.70	21.44	32.26
Woodbine	5/83	2,809	8.00	7.59	0.27
Total		13,511	136.67	53.49	64.92
Cumberland County					
Maurice River	12/82	4,577	94.70	66.31	21.68
Vineland	9/82	53,753	69.50	4.90	—
Total		58,330	164.20	71.21	21.68
Gloucester County					
Franklin	11/82	12,396	56.47	20.43	—
Monroe	9/83	21,639	46.96	31.48	—
Total		34,035	103.43	51.91	—
Ocean County					
Barnegat	4/83	8,702	34.90	24.39	13.64
Beachwood	1/83	7,687	2.80	0.68	—
Berkeley	9/85[c]	23,151	41.90	15.59	14.91
Eagleswood	4/83	1,009	16.50	3.85	12.75
Jackson	7/83	25,644	100.30	47.78	7.02
Lacey	NC	14,161	84.60	65.60	18.14
Lakehurst	2/83	2,908	0.95	0.82	0.08
Little Egg Harbor	1/83	8,483	49.50	16.30	29.84
Manchester	7/83	27.987	82.50	59.52	12.65
Ocean	1/83	3,731	20.62	11.75	8.90
Plumsted	7/83	4,674	40.70	21.24	0.63
South Toms River	NC	3,954	1.20	0.45	0.03
Stafford	10/83	10,385	47.05	18.70	26.08
Total		142,476	523.52	286.67	144.67
Total for 52 Municipalities		494,999	2,175.93	1,460.44	319.33

[a] Fifty-two municipalities with land in the Pinelands Area.

[b] Month and year of final certification; NC means not certified by September 1, 1987.

[c] Population from 1980 census figures.

[d] The following four additional townships have land only in the Pinelands National Reserve:

Atlantic County—Brigantine (4.22 sq. mi.)

Cape May County—Middle (16.47 sq. mi.)

Ocean County—Dover (1.56 sq. mi.)

Ocean County—Tuckerton (3.88 sq. mi.)

Notes

Throughout the text, the abbreviation "CMP" refers to The New Jersey Pinelands Commission, *Comprehensive Management Plan for the Pinelands National Reserve* (New Lisbon, N.J.: 1980). References to material in Part I of the CMP (which is in narrative form) show page numbers. References to material in Part II (which contains the agency regulatory provisions) show article and section numbers.

The federal Pinelands legislation is indicated by "NPR," an abbreviation for the National Parks and Recreation Act of 1978, S. 719, Sec. 502. The state Pinelands legislation is indicated by "PPA," an abbreviation for New Jersey Pinelands Protection Act of 1979 (N.J.S.A. 113:18 A–1 et seq., or sometimes P.L. 1979, Ch. 111).

Preface

1. Although through 1986 the Pinelands National Reserve was by far the largest of its kind, at the time it was established there were two other land areas in the United States classified as national reserves. Both are relatively small and of specialized designation: Ebey's Landing National Historical Reserve in the state of Washington is 8,000 acres, and the Ice Age National Scientific Reserve in Wisconsin is 32,500 acres.

Chapter 1. The Landscape of the New Jersey Pine Barrens

1. John W. Harshberger, *The Vegetation of the New Jersey Pine Barrens: An Ecological Investigation* (Philadelphia: Christopher Sower Co., 1916), p. 9.

2. The material in this section draws heavily on Beryl Robichaud, *A Conceptual Framework for Pinelands Decision-Making* (New Brunswick, N.J.: Rutgers University Center for Coastal and Environmental Studies, 1980); portions of this work were also directly incorporated into chapters 2 and 3 of the CMP. The principal sources of ecological information for this section are Richard T. T. Forman, ed., *Pine Barrens: Ecosystem and Landscape* (New York: Academic Press, 1979) and the inventories of Jack McCormick published in McCormick, *A Study of the Significance of the Pine Barrens of New Jersey* (Philadelphia: Academy of Natural Sciences of Philadelphia, 1968), which was later republished under the title *The Pine Barrens: A Preliminary Ecological Inventory* (Trenton, N.J.: New Jersey State Museum, 1970).

3. See Marco L. Markley, "Soil Series of the Pine Barrens" in Forman, p. 81.

4. Charles T. Roman and Ralph E. Good, *Wetlands of the New Jersey Pinelands: Values, Functions, Impacts and a Proposed Buffer Delineation Model* (New Brunswick, N.J.: Rutgers University Center for Coastal and Environmental Studies, 1983), p. 53.

5. At the June 17, 1986, Pinelands Field Station meeting of the Site Advisory Committee in New Lisbon, N.J., David E. Fairbrothers, botanist, said that al-

though the figure of 800 to 850 plant species has been talked about for a number of years, he believes that the number of plant species in the Pinelands is closer to 1,035 and that 18 to 20 percent of these are threatened or endangered.

6. For a summary of research evidence see Ralph E. Good, et al., "The Pine Barrens Plains" in Forman, pp. 289–291.

7. Leonard J. Wolgast, "Mammals of the New Jersey Pine Barrens" in Forman, p. 443.

8. Robert W. Hastings, "Fish of the Pine Barrens" in Forman, p. 490.

9. Roger Conant, "A Zoogeographical Review of the Amphibians and Reptiles of Southern New Jersey, with Emphasis on the Pine Barrens" in Forman, pp. 467–486.

10. Identifications of common species and their habitats are from Charles F. Leck, "Birds of the Pine Barrens" in Forman, pp. 457–466.

11. See Richard Lehne and Alan Rosenthal, editors, *Politics in New Jersey* (New Brunswick, N.J.: Rutgers University, Eagleton Institute of Politics, 1979), pp. 88–99.

12. Alan Rosenthal and Maureen Moakley, *The Political Life of the American States* (New York: Praeger Publishers, 1984), p. 223. For a description of South Jersey characteristics and geographic boundaries see Edward Reimer and Barbara Reimer Jones, "New Jersey: The South" in *The Outlook on New Jersey,* ed. Silvio Laccetti (Union City, N.J.: William H. Wise & Co., 1979), pp. 39–60.

13. "Secessionist Leader is Choice for Seat on the Pinelands Panel," *Asbury Park Press,* 22 March 1985.

14. "Secessionist Movement Isn't Dead," *Asbury Park Press,* 22 April 1984.

15. John McPhee, *The Pine Barrens* (New York: Farrar, Straus & Giroux: 1968), p. 77.

16. Henry Charlton Beck, Forgotten Towns of Southern New Jersey (New Brunswick, N.J.: Rutgers University Press, 1983), p. 20.

17. See Kenneth Buchholz and Ralph E. Good, *Compendium of Archaeological, Cultural and Historical Literature of the New Jersey Pine Barrens* (New Brunswick, N.J.: Rutgers University Center for Coastal and Environmental Studies, 1983).

18. Nora Rubinstein, *A Psycho-Social Analysis of Environmental Change in New Jersey's Pine Barrens* (Ph.D. diss., City University of New York, 1983), p. 191.

19. Jonathan Berger and John W. Sinton, *Water, Earth and Fire* (Baltimore: Johns Hopkins University Press, 1985), p. 13.

20. James E. Applegate, Silas Little, and Philip E. Marucci, "Plant and Animal Products of the Pine Barrens" in Forman, p. 29.

21. Mary-Ann Thompson, "The Landscape of Cranberry Culture" in *History, Culture and Archaeology of the Pine Barrens,* ed. John W. Sinton (Pomona, N.J.: Stockton State College, 1982), pp. 193–209.

22. James B. Durand and Bonnie Zimmer, *Pinelands Surface Water Quality* (New Brunswick, N.J.: Rutgers University Center for Coastal and Environmental Studies, 1982), pp. 25 and 119.

23. New Jersey Division of Parks and Forests, "New Jersey Pinelands" (a report prepared for the Governor's Pinelands Review Committee, Trenton, N.J., 1978), p. i.

24. Arthur Pierce, *Iron in the Pines* (New Brunswick, N.J.: Rutgers University Press, 1957), p. 5.

25. A. T. M. Lee, "A Land Development Scheme in the New Jersey Pine Area," *N.J. Agricultural Experimental Station Bull.*, No. 665 (1939), p. 13.

26. J. K. Hauck and A. T. M. Lee, "Land Subdivision in the New Jersey Pines," *N.J. Agricultural Experimental Station Bull.*, No. 701 (1942), pp. 14–16.

27. Richard T. T. Forman and R. Boerner, "Fire Frequency and the Pine Barrens of New Jersey," *Bull. of the Torrey Botanical Club* (1981) 108:34–50.

Chapter 2. The Backdrop for Pinelands Legislation

1. Actual population figures are not available for the Pinelands National Reserves or for the Pinelands Area. Figures quoted in this chapter have been extrapolated from data in the CMP, pp. 126 and 161.

2. See Jack McCormick and Richard T. T. Forman, "Introduction: Location and Boundaries of the New Jersey Pine Barrens" in *Pine Barrens Ecosystem and Landscape*, ed. Richard T. T. Forman (New York: Academic Press, 1979), pp. xxxviii–xlii.

3. Dorothy Evert, "Pine Barrens Conservationists," *The Pitch Pine*, Feb., 1968, p. 2.

4. "Burlington County Seeks Jet Airport," *New York Times*, 16 May 1967.

5. James T. Pyle, Administrator of the Civil Aeronautics Administration, letter to the Planning Director of Burlington County, 21 March 1958.

6. Cam Cavanaugh, *Saving the Great Swamp* (Frenchtown, N.J.: Columbia Publishing Company, Inc., 1978).

7. Burlington County Freeholders, Resolution No. 44, 9 February 1960.

8. Pinelands Regional Planning Board, "The New Jersey Pinelands Region: A Framework for Planning" (West Trenton, N.J., 1963), pp. 4–5.

9. Pinelands Regional Planning Board, "Future Development Plans for the Pinelands Region" (West Trenton, N.J., 1964), p. 1.

10. Albert E. Blomquist, "A Future System of Airports for New Jersey" (a report prepared for the Governor's Economic Evelution Committee for an Intercontinental Jetport for New Jersey, July 1968), pp. xviii–xix.

11. "Questionnaires for Candidates," *The Pitch Pine*, September 1969, p. 3.

12. C. Gordon Jildine (acting assistant director of the U.S. Dept. of the Interior National Park Service), in a letter to Richard Thorsell, 2 February 1965.

13. Jack McCormick, *Significance of the Pine Barrens*, p. 6.

14. *Pinelands Environmental Council: History* (Barnegat Light, N.J.: Ocean Nature & Conservation Society, September 1976).

15. News release from Burlington County Freeholder Board, 23 October 1968.

16. National Park Service, "Pine Barrens of New Jersey" (study report, Washington, D.C., n.d.), pp. 24–34.

17. A. Morton Cooper, "The President's Message," *The Pitch Pine*, December 1970.

18. N.J.S.A. 13:18–8 (January 1972).

19. David Bardin, letter to Garfield DeMarco (chairman of the Pinelands Environmental Council), 22 April 1975; Jack McCormick, letter to Floyd West (Bass River Township Committee), 24 March 1975.

20. Pinelands Environmental Council, "Plan for the Pinelands" (Browns Mills, N.J.: 1975), p. 11.

21. James B. Kennedy (Ocean County administrator), as quoted in "Retirement Villages Flourishing in Fields Where Jersey Corn Once Grew," *New York Times*, 5 March 1984.

22. Robert Glasser (Ocean County freeholder), as quoted in "Pinelands Plan Offered," *Toms River Daily Observer*, 17 June 1977.

23. Nathaniel P. Reed (U.S. Dept. of the Interior, Assistant Secretary for Fish and Wildlife and Parks), letter to the directors of the Bureau of Outdoor Recreation, the Fish and Wildlife Service, and the National Park Service, 6 October 1975.

24. "New Jersey Pine Barrens: Concepts for Preservation" (report of the U.S. Dept. of the Interior, Bureau of Outdoor Recreation, Washington, D.C., 1976), pp. 8 and 9. This is the report referred to in the text as the "BOR Report."

25. John McPhee, *The Pine Barrens* (New York: Farrar, Straus & Giroux, 1968), p. 4.

26. Donald Linkey (assistant counsel to the governor), letter to Governor Brendan T. Byrne, 18 November 1976; Alan B. Handler (special counsel to the governor), briefing memo to Governor Byrne, 14 October 1976.

27. "Pines Water Proposal Under Fire," *Atlantic City Press*, 15 February 1977.

28. "Pines Water Standards Upheld," *Ashbury Park Press*, 13 June 1979.

29. Governor's Pinelands Review Committee, "Planning and Management of the New Jersey Pinelands" (Trenton, February 1979), pp. 2–4.

30. Brendan T. Byrne quoted in "Byrne's Busy Day: Pine's Zoning, He Supports It," *Philadelphia Evening Bulletin*, 22 July 1978. See also "Byrne Report: Strict Zoning for the Pinelands," *Philadelphia Evening Bulletin*, 12 July 1978.

31. Garfield DeMarco, as quoted in "Steep Cost Likely to Preserve the Pines," *Philadelphia Evening Bulletin*, 13 July 1978.

32. A. Morton Cooper, "The President's Message," *The Pitch Pine*, March 1971.

33. A more detailed description of the various social and political forces that were involved early in the Pine Barrens land-use conflict may be found in Joan Goldstein, *Environmental Decision-Making in Rural Locales* (New York: Praeger Publishers, 1981).

34. Rosenthal and Moakley, *Political Life*, p. 222.

35. McPhee, *Pine Barrens*, p. 156.

Chapter 3. Federal and State Pinelands Legislation

1. Charles E. Little, *Green-Line Parks: An Approach to Preserving Recreational Landscapes in Urban Areas* (Washington, D.C.: Library of Congress, Congressional Research Service, Environmental Policy Division, 1975), pp. 1–2. Little hyphenated "green-line"; most users since then have used the word unhyphenated, and we shall follow this practice.

2. *Congressional Record*, Vol. 123 (4 November 1977), p. 37250.

3. Little, *Green-Line Parks*, p. 23.

4. Paul Bea, "Pinelands: Possible Senate and Department Action," memo to Daniel O'Hern (commissioner of the N.J. Dept. of Environmental Protection), et al., 13 June 1978.

5. "Andrus Vows Pines Backing," *Asbury Park Press*, 29 September 1977.

6. Elmer Rowley (chairman of the Pinelands Preservation Committee of the N.J. Audubon Society), in testimony on the Hughes/Forsythe bill (HR 9535, HR 9539) before the House Committee on Merchant Marine and Fisheries at Stockton State College, 28 October 1977.

7. Bea, memo to O'Hern.

8. "Pine Barrens Legislation Passed," *Jersey Sierran*, January–February 1977.

9. Hearing on the National Parks and Recreation Act before U.S. Senate Subcommittee on Parks and Recreation of the Committee on Energy and Natural Resources, 4 August 1978.

10. *Evening Bulletin*, 28 September 1978.

11. Edwin Forsythe and William Hughes, Letter to the Editor, *Philadelphia Evening Bulletin*, 22 September 1978.

12. Mae Barringer, Letter to the Editor, *Philadelphia Evening Bulletin*, 29 September 1978.

13. Minutes of a meeting between officials of the Dept. of Environmental Protection and the Dept. of Community Affairs, 6 November 1978.

14. "Pines Ban Endorsed by Andrus," *Asbury Park Press*, 17 March 1979.

15. Michael Catania, interview with the author, 18 June 1980.

16. "Pine Barrens Moratorium Triggers Jeers and Cheers," *Asbury Park Press*, 21 March 1979.

17. Anonymous, "Suggested Executive Strategy—Pinelands," memo, DEP files, December 1978.

18. Daniel O'Hern, memo to Governor Brendan T. Byrne, 26 October 1978.

19. "Pine Barrens Construction Ban Stirs up an Emotional Debate," *New York Times*, 25 March 1979.

20. Thomas Paparone (president of the N.J. Homebuilders Association), as quoted in *Philadelphia Evening Bulletin*, 20 May 1979.

21. Hazel Gluck, in testimony on S 3091 before the N.J. Senate Energy and Environment Committee, 22 February 1979.

22. Joseph P. Merlino, in testimony on S 3091, 22 February 1979.

23. Jim Christy (local businessman), as quoted in *Burlington County Times*, 10 March 1979.

24. David Moore, in testimony on S 3091, 22 February 1979.

25. *Burlington County Times*, 12 March 1979.

26. Catania interview.

27. James Florio, *Congressional Record*, Vol. 123 (30 April 1977), pp. 11474–11476.

Chapter 4. Pinelands Commission: Startup and Interim Development Regulation

1. B. Budd Chavooshian, interview with Emily Russell, 28 April 1980; and Richard A. Liroff and G. Gordon Davis, *Protecting Open Space* (Cambridge, Mass.: Ballinger Publishing Co., 1981), pp. 10, 14, and 16–18. Much of the information in this chapter comes from minutes of commission meetings and hearings.

2. Pinelands Commission, minutes, 23 May 1980.

3. All development review statistics used in this chapter come from an analysis of Pinelands interim applications made by Beryl Robichaud Collins with research assistance from Matthew Gordon and Kevin Kerlin.

4. Pinelands Commission, "Interim Rules and Regulations for Review and Approval of Applications for Development of Construction under the Pinelands Protection Act," adopted 27 July 1979.

5. Denial figures do not include denials on applications that had previously been denied by the Review Board.

6. For example, see "Factual and legal contentions submitted by the staff and executive director of the Pinelands Commission in the matter of the application of the Atlantic Utility Construction Company [Hanada Development Corporation]," Pinelands Application No. 79–0519 (OAL Dkt. No. EPC 0701–80), 5.

7. Orleans Builders and Developers, Inc. v. Governor Brendan T. Byrne, N.J. Super. App. Div. A–503–80T (Pinelands Application No. 79–1026).

8. "Pinelands Building Moratorium," *Central Record* (Medford, N.J.), 15 February 1979.

9. Pinelands Commission, "Economic and Fiscal Impacts of the Pinelands Comprehensive Management Plan" (New Lisbon, N.J., June 1983), pp. 37–73.

10. "Pine Barrens Construction Ban Stirs up an Emotional Debate," *New York Times*, 25 March 1979.

11. Edwin B. Forsythe, "Weekly Report," 2 July 1979.

Chapter 5. Preparation of the Comprehensive Management Plan: Issues and Procedures

1. Pinelands Commission meetings, 22 February and 2 May 1980. Much of the information in this chapter comes from the author's observations of more than thirty meetings of the Pinelands Commission, as well as many subcommittee meetings, public workshops, conferences, and hearings. Where appropriate, the specific date of a meeting at which a particular action or decision occurred will be

given in a note; textual commentary often results from integrating the material presented at several meetings.

2. Suggestions along this line were made when the DEP's critical water standards were proposed in 1977. See the comments on the proposed regulations submitted by Maurice Arnold (regional director of the Bureau of Recreation, U.S. Dept. of the Interior), 8 February 1977; The Delaware Valley Regional Planning Commission, 31 January 1977; and Fellows, Read and Weber, Inc. (consulting engineers), 14 March 1977.

3. Pinelands Commission meetings, 25 April, 13 June, and 18 August 1980.

4. Gerald E. Speitel Assoc., "Review of Water Quality Planning Aspects of the Draft Comprehensive Management Plan," in *Technical Issues*, Vol. 1 of *Report to the Pinelands Commission on the Protection Area* (Trenton: Coalition for the Sensible Preservation of the Pinelands, n.d.), p. 24.

5. Pinelands Commission meeting, 3 April 1980.

6. Ross, Hardies, O'Keefe, Babcock and Parsons (Pinelands Commission consultants), "The Taking Issue and Vested Rights" (a report to the Pinelands Commission, New Lisbon, N.J., 1980).

7. B. Budd Chavooshian, interview with the author, 28 April 1980.

8. John W. Sinton, et al., "Position Paper" (New Lisbon, N.J., Pinelands Commission files, n.d.).

9. Pinelands Commission meeting, 25 April 1980, and statements by the Coalition to Save Agriculture at a special meeting of the Pinelands Commission, 26 July 1980.

10. Pinelands Commission meeting, 25 July 1980.

11. A question on this subject was asked by Lester Germanio (commissioner from Cape May County) and answered by Deputy Attorney General Richard Hluchan at a meeting of the Pinelands Commission, 9 May 1980.

12. Pinelands Commission meetings, 28 June, 25 July, and 14 November 1980.

13. See Richard A. Liroff and G. Gordon Davis, *Protecting Open Space* (Cambridge, Mass.: Ballinger Publishing Co., 1981), *passim.*

14. Pinelands Commission meetings, 2 May and 16 May 1980.

15. Liroff and Davis, *Open Space*, p. 33.

16. Brendan T. Byrne, interview with the author, 1 July 1980.

17. Haig Kasabach (NJDEP Division of Water Resources), interview with the author, 25 March 1980.

18. Byrne interview.

19. "Pinelands Plan's in for Fight," *Philadelphia Inquirer*, 29 September 1980.

20. Senator Frank Dodd, in comments after the hearing on the Pinelands Protection Act before the N.J. Senate Energy and Environment Committee, 6 February 1980, as reported in "Pinelands Act Escapes Unscathed," *Asbury Park Press*, 7 February 1980.

21. Mae Barringer, Interview with the author, 31 March 1980.

22. Mae Barringer (chairperson of the Pine Barrens Coalition), "Position Paper," (Vincentown, N.J., 2 April 1980; document in the Pinelands Commission files, New Lisbon, N.J.), p. 3.

23. Howard Butensky, written statement presented at a hearing on the draft CMP before the Pinelands Commission, 16 July 1980.

24. Nelson Johnson, written statement presented at a meeting called by Stockton State College to review the draft CMP, Galloway Township, 16 July 1980.

25. For a fuller consideration of some local resentments, see Jonathan Berger and John W. Sinton, *Water, Earth and Fire* (Baltimore: Johns Hopkins University Press, 1985).

Chapter 6. Pinelands Comprehensive Management Plan

1. Ian McHarg, comments made in a Pinelands Commission public meeting for plan review, 3 June 1985.

2. The CMP calls for the construction of about 240,000 new housing units, divided as follows: 141,350 as base density units in Regional Growth Areas with an additional 30,000 units as PDC bonus units; 32,800 units in Forest Areas; and 10,850 units in Pinelands Towns and Villages. The remaining units are for construction in all areas under the exemption provisions.

3. Pinelands Commission, Letter of Interpretation No. 233.

4. Pinelands Commission, Letters of Interpretation Nos. 87, 117, 193, and 233.

5. In re: Certification of Master Plan and Land-Use Ordinance of the Township of Berkeley, N.J. Super. App. Div., Dkt. No. A–2082–85T7.

6. Pinelands Commission, "Comprehensive Management Plan: A Progress Report on the First Three Years of Implementation" (New Lisbon, N.J., 1983).

Chapter 7. Management of the Pinelands: An Intergovernmental Partnership

1. Terrence Moore, interview with the author, 22 September 1982.

2. Unpublished statistics developed by Susan Sullivan of the Pinelands Commission staff. The degree of development activity is based on changes in population, building permits issued, and vacant land sales.

3. League of Women Voters of New Jersey, *New Jersey: Spotlight on Government,* ed. Elizabeth Brody (New Brunswick, N.J.: Rutgers University Press, 1972), p. 167.

4. Ross, Hardies, O'Keefe, Babcock & Parsons, "Local and State Regulations of Potential Relevance" (report to the Pinelands Commission, New Lisbon, N.J., 1980), p. 44.

5. Teuvo M. Airola, "Municipal Land Use Planning Issues in the New Jersey Pine Barrens" in *Natural and Cultural Resources of the New Jersey Pine Barrens,* ed. John W. Sinton (Pomona, N.J.: Stockton State College, 1978), p. 282.

6. "Freeholders Vote to Boycott Pinelands Commission Orders," *Asbury Park Press,* 13 March 1981.

7. "Attempt Seen to Discredit Kean's Stand on Pinelands," *Footprints* (newsletter of the N.J. Conservation Foundation, Mendham, N.J.), March/April 1982.

8. Commissioner Nanzetta of Atlantic County strongly objected to the subcom-

mittee (see minutes of Pinelands Commission meeting, 1 May 1981). Conclusions about the conformance process, its operation and its impact, are drawn from observations by the author, who, over a period of five years, attended most of the commission's subcommittee meetings as well as regular monthly meetings of the Pinelands Commission and numerous public hearings.

9. John Stokes, interview with the author, 22 February 1985.

10. William Harrison, interview with the author, 7 November 1983.

11. Gary Patterson and Debbie Miller, "Pinelands Review Conformance Process," in "A Task Force Report to the Plan Review Subcommittee on the Comprehensive Management Plan" (unpublished report, New Lisbon, N.J., May 1984), p. 7. Patterson and Miller were speaking for one N.J. chapter of the Sierra Club.

12. Minutes of the Pinelands Commission meeting, 7 November 1983.

13. Remarks made by Michael Garabedian at the Pinelands Commission meeting, 1 November 1983.

14. Gary Patterson and Michael Garabedian, letter to Governor Thomas Kean, 6 November 1985; In re: Certification of Master Plan and Land-Use Ordinance of the Township of Berkeley, N.J. Super., App. Div. Dkt. No. A–2082–85T7; appellate court decision dated 22 December 1986.

15. Carlo M. Sardella, "Pinelands is Suffering Growing Pains," *New York Times*, 8 April 1984.

16. Even Congressman James Florio, a champion of strong protection for the Pinelands complained that the PDC program "has not been pushed or advocated and yet that is the heart of the fairness of the system" (as quoted in "Pinelands Regulation: 2 State Reviews Due," *New York Times*, 1 April 1984).

17. Richard Hluchan, statement to the Pinelands Commission Conformance Subcommittee, 22 February 1985.

18. Alice D'Arcy, interview with the author, 23 June 1983.

19. Bennett Barfeld, remarks to the Pinelands Commission Conformance Subcommittee, 4 December 1981.

20. "Stafford Twp. Moves to OK Pines Codes," *Asbury Park Press*, 11 August 1983.

21. Southern Burlington County NAACP v. Mount Laurel Township, 456A. 2d 390, 410 (1983).

22. D'Arcy interview.

23. Berlin Township (Camden County) was fully certified in June 1983.

24. Egg Harbor Township Planning Board v. the New Jersey Pinelands Commission, OAL Dkt. Nos. EPC 9259–82, 18717–82, 10993–82 (1982).

25. "Officials to Fight Undemocratic Pinelands Law," *Atlantic County Record*, 26 April 1984.

26. Egg Harbor Township Planning Board v. Pinelands Commission and James F. Tsafos et al., OAL Dkt. No. EPC 4703–84 (1984).

27. "Lacey Township to Comply with Pinelands Act," *Asbury Park Press*, 8 November 1985.

28. Ross, Hardies, O'Keefe, Babcock & Parsons, Introduction, Summary, and Analysis, Vol. 1 of Procedural and Substantive Land Management Techniques of

Potential Relevance for the New Jersey Pinelands (a report to the Pinelands Commission, Chicago, Ill., 1980), p. 38.

29. Patterson and Miller, *Conformance Process*, p. 8.

30. Terrence Moore, interview with the author, 22 February 1985.

31. "In Evesham the Focus is Planning," *Burlington County Times*, 17 February 1984.

32. Mayor Arthur Bird of Hamilton Township, comments made at the 26th Annual State Planning Conference, 22 March 1985.

33. Michael N. Ingram, letter to the Pinelands Commission, 1 August 1983.

34. Minutes of the Pinelands Commission, 7 July 1983.

35. "Pines Officials, Hamilton Agree on Zoning Pact," *Atlantic City Press*, 10 December 1984.

36. For example, on 3 January 1986, Ocean County Commissioner Alan Avery cast the only vote opposing adoption of a comprehensive package of policy recommendations by the Plan Review Subcommittee; the reason for his negative vote was Ocean County's objection to one provision dealing with airport expansion.

37. "Worthington's Reign Marked Era of Change," *Atlantic City Press*, 21 November 1983.

38. Beryl Robichaud, *Protecting That Portion of the Pinelands National Reserve outside the Jurisdiction of the Pinelands Commission: Is Regulation under CAFRA Adequate? Final Report* (New Brunswick, N.J.: Rutgers University Center for Coastal and Environmental Studies, 1984), p. 34.

39. Pinelands Commission meeting, 6 November 1981.

40. "Pinelands Commissioners Named," *Dimensions* (newsletter of the N.J. Builders' Association), March 1983.

41. Statement made by Garfield DeMarco in conversation with Michele Byers, 19 May 1986, and reported by Byers that day to the author.

Chapter 8. Development Regulation: Processes and Outcomes

1. The requirement for public notice was added in 1985, along with other procedural changes that provided for commission action when a request for an OAL hearing is not filed by an interested party. These changes were part of the commission's response to the appellate court decision on rights of certified municipalities, issued 9 May 1984. (See In re: John Madin, N.J. Super. App. Dkt. No. A 4343–83T6.)

2. Pinelands Commission, Letters of Interpretation Nos. 9 and 129.

3. Terrence Moore, statement made in a meeting with representatives of the Pine Barrens Coalition, 16 December 1982.

4. Pinelands Commission, Letter of Interpretation No. 319.

5. Kenneth and Debra Foster, Pinelands Application No. 81–1681.

6. Elizabeth M. Domako, Pinelands Application No. 82–10,010; and Frank and Blanche Renz, Pinelands Application No. 82–2483 (OAL Dkt. No. EPC 8057–82).

7. Pinewald Pioneer Forest Fighters, Pinelands Application No. 81–0127P.

8. State of New Jersey Dept. of Corrections, Pinelands Application No. 82–4123P.

9. Cape May County Municipal Utilities Authority, Pinelands Application No. 81–0837.

10. Statistics on waiver actions are derived from the author's analysis of waivers approved and denied during the three-year period from 14 January 1981 to 31 December 1984.

11. Oxly, Inc., OAL Dkt. No. EPC 0828–83 (Pinelands Application No. 81–1050).

12. ROC Investment Corp., OAL Dkt. No. EPC 2543–82 (Pinelands Application No. 81–1411); ROC Investment Corp v. the New Jersey Pinelands Commission, N.J. Super. App. Div. A–5558–82T2 (decided 17 May 1984).

13. Crestwood Village, Inc. (Pinelands Application No. 83–505) was withdrawn on 16 January 1984, two days after the expiration of the CMP's hardship provision under which it would have been considered.

14. Pinelands Commission, "A Progress Report on the First Three Years of Implementation" (New Lisbon, N.J.: December 1983), III:10–12.

15. Sean Reilly, as quoted in "Pinelands Preservation Development Pace and Patter," *Bus. Digest*, I:2 (November 1984), n.p.

16. Coastal Area Facility Review Act: N.J.A.C. 13:19–1 et seq.

17. Coastal Resource and Development Policies: N.J.A.C. 7:7E–1.1 et seq.

18. See Beryl Robichaud, *Protecting That Portion of the Pinelands National Reserve outside the Jurisdiction of the Pinelands Commission: Is Regulation under CAFRA Adequate? Final Report* (New Brunswick, N.J.: Rutgers University Center for Coastal and Environmental Studies, 1984).

19. "Cumulative Impacts of Unregulated Development in New Jersey's Coastal Zone (a staff issue paper, N.J. Dept. of Environmental Protection, Divison of Coastal Resources, March 1981), pp. 9–25.

20. See Beryl Robichaud, *Enforcing the Provisions of the Pinelands Comprehensive Management Plan: A Preliminary Analysis* (New Brunswick, N.J.: Rutgers University Center for Coastal and Environmental Studies, November 1984).

21. William Harrison, interview with the author, 6 September 1985.

22. Jim Jubak, "The People and the Pinelands," *National Parks Magazine*, September/October 1984.

23. See recommendation 168 of Pinelands Commission, in "Reviewing the Comprehensive Management Plan" (New Lisbon, N.J., October 1985).

24. Daniel H. Pincus, "President's Comments," *Dimensions* (newsletter of the N.J. Builder's Association), September 1985.

25. Thomas Norman, conversation with the author, 9 August 1985; and Michael Gross, conversation with the author, 4 April 1986.

26. See the comments of Michele Byers, speaking for the N.J. Conservation Foundation, in "A Task force report to the Pinelands Plan Review Subcommittee on the Comprehensive Management Plan" (New Lisbon, N.J., May 1984), p. 16. Also see the comments of David W. Hoskins and James T. Tripp, speaking for the Environmental Defense Fund, *Ibid.*, pp. 65–66.

27. Until late 1986 the listing was sometimes delayed, and it did not consistently contain an adequate project description or an identification of the management area in question. A computerized system for preparation of the list was put into effect in September 1986 and appears to have corrected these problems.

28. Margaret and Edward Kelley, Pinelands Application No. 84–0145C.

29. Frank and Blanche Renz, Pinelands Applications No. 82–2483.

30. Roland and Johanna Levrault, Pinelands Application No. 81–1897.

31. Frank and Camile Babusik, Pinelands Application No. 81–0106P.

32. Anton C. Barthel, Pinelands Application No. 81–1373.

33. Connolly and Esposito, Pinelands Application No. 83–5733.

34. Country Village Homes, Pinelands Application No. 83–10,666.

35. "Environmental Roadblocks Turn Dream into a Nightmare," *Asbury Park Press*, 13 December 1983.

Chapter 9. Acquisition, Management, and Use of Public Lands

1. New Jersey Forest Park Reservation Commission, *First Annual Report of the Forest Park Reservation Commission of New Jersey for the Year Ending October 31st, 1905* (Trenton: 1906), pp. 9–10.

2. J. Gifford, *A Preliminary Report on the Forest Conditions of South Jersey, Annual Report of the State Geologist, 1894* (Trenton: N.J. Geological Survey, 1895), pp. 245–286.

3. New Jersey Board of Conservation and Development, "Program for State Ownership of Park and Forest Land in New Jersey" (Trenton, 1931), pp. 3, 4, 23, and 26.

4. New Jersey Forest Park Reservation Commission, *Eighth Annual Report of the Forest Park Reservation Commission of New Jersey for the Year Ending October 31, 1912* (Trenton: 1913), p. 10; and Board of Conservation, "State Ownership," p. 21.

5. A. D. Pierce, *Iron in the Pines* (New Brunswick, N.J.: Rutgers University Press, 1957), pp. 3–6.

6. *Ibid.*, pp. 6–7.

7. Ronald A. Foresta, *Open Space Policy: New Jersey's Green Acres Program* (New Brunswick, N.J.: Rutgers University Press, 1981), pp. 66–67.

8. Beryl Robichaud, *Goals and Actions for the Pinelands Preservation and Land Acquisition Program* (New Brunswick, N.J.: Rutgers University Center for Coastal and Environmental Studies, n.d.), pp. 6–26; P. G. Rissler, moderator. "Ecosystem Fragmentation in the Pinelands of New Jersey" in *Ecological Solutions to Environmental Management Concerns in the Pinelands National Reserve*, ed. Ralph E. Good (proceedings of a conference held by Rutgers University Center for Coastal and Environmental Studies, New Brunswick, N.J., 1982), pp. 5–10.

9. J. F. Hauck and A. J. M. Lee, "Land Subdivision in the New Jersey Pines," *Bull. of the N.J. Agricultural Experiment Station*, No. 701 (1942), pp. 31–32; C. B. Cranmer, "Future of the Pine Barrens," *Bartonia*, No. 56 (1952), pp. 53–60.

10. The following summary of the recreational uses of state lands and the management practices employed on these lands is based primarily on information presented in unpublished draft management plans prepared by the N.J. Division of Parks and Forestry and the Division of Fish, Game, and Wildlife.

Chapter 10. Economic and Fiscal Support Programs

1. "Byrne Signs Pinelands Control Bill in Emotional Trenton Ceremony," *Newark Star-Ledger*, 29 June 1979. During the 1979 signing of the Pinelands Protection Act, Governor Byrne told reporters that the only legislative struggle that matched the Pinelands conflict in bitterness and intensity was the battle over the state income tax. Furthermore, the governor's feelings about the Pinelands struggle changed little over the years. During a February 1986 conversation with Dr. Conant, the former governor said that he had "lots of scars" from the Pinelands struggle.

2. Group support for the Pinelands Protection Act and the CMP came from about fifty different entities, which united under an umbrella organization called the Pine Barrens Coalition. The opposition groups included the South Jersey Chamber of Commerce, the Homebuilders' League of South Jersey, the Coalition for the Sensible Preservation of the Pinelands, and the Pinelands Municipal Council.

3. In addition to the economic and fiscal support programs, one other concession was particularly important: a one-year grandfather clause that allowed anyone who had received a municipal construction permit prior to the protection plan to build, even if this construction violated the plan's minimum lot sizes.

4. Because there are no unincorporated areas in New Jersey, all land is included within the boundaries of a municipality; consequently, our use of the term "municipality" refers to all of the land areas in the referenced area and should not be interpreted as a reference only to villages or built-up urban areas.

5. "Viewpoint: Pinelands Progress," *Newark Star-Ledger*, 8 October 1979.

6. *Idem.*

7. Paid advertisement, *Burlington County Times*, 6 August 1980, p. 36.

8. "Byrne Signs," *Star-Ledger.*

9. "Pinelands Plan Will Kill Economy, Builders Predict," *Burlington County Times*, 23 May 1980.

10. "Byrne Hears All Sides on Pinelands Control," *Newark Star-Ledger*, 17 September 1980.

11. "South Jersey Chamber Opposes Pines Plan," *Burlington County Times*, 2 October 1980.

12. "Byrne Hears," *Star-Ledger.*

13. Gloria Christian, James C. Nicholas, and Joan E. Towles, "Economic Analysis of the Comprehensive Management Plan" (a report for the Pinelands Commission, 20 November 1980), pp. 8–11.

14. *Ibid.*, p. 12.

15. *Ibid.*, p. 80.

16. *Ibid.*, p. 79.
17. *Ibid.*, p. 102.
18. *Ibid.*, p. 99.
19. *Ibid.*, p. 109.
20. "Probe Takes Aim at 'Plot' by Tax Boards to Scuttle Pines Plan," *Newark Star-Ledger*, 19 February 1981.
21. "Pinelands Plan Stirs Medford Tax Appeals," *Burlington County Times*, 4 September 1980. The total dollar amount of appeals granted, however, was approximately $2 million.
22. New Jersey Pinelands Commission, "Economic and Fiscal Impacts of the Pinelands Comprehensive Management Plan" (New Lisbon, N.J., July 1983), p. vii.
23. *Ibid.*, p. 7.
24. *Ibid.*, pp. ix–x.
25. *Ibid.*, p. ix.
26. *Ibid.*, p. xi.
27. New Jersey Pinelands Commission, "Economic and Fiscal Impacts of the Pinelands Comprehensive Management Plan" (New Lisbon, N.J., November 1985), p. 77.
28. *Ibid.*, p. 78.
29. This argument, that the Pinelands land-use regulations reinforced rather than altered existing development patterns, seems to be the foundation on which the predictions of minimum adverse effects are built. See for example, Pinelands Commission, "Fiscal Impacts," p. 8.
30. John Stokes (assistant director of the Pinelands Commission), memo to Pinelands Commission Conformance Subcommittee, 18 October 1984.
31. Matlack v. the Board of Chosen Freeholders of the County of Burlington, 191 N.J. Super. 236 (1983).

Chapter 11. Legal and Legislative Challenges

1. See, for example, Agins v. City of Tiburon, 447 U.S. 255 (1980). "The application of a general zoning law . . . effects a taking if the ordinance . . . denies an owner [all] economically viable use of his land."
2. CMP, 4–505: "An application for a waiver shall be approved only if the Executive Director finds an extraordinary hardship or compelling public need under the following standards:

A. The particular physical surroundings, shape or topographical conditions of the specific property involved would result in an extraordinary hardship, as distinguished from a mere inconvenience, if the provisions of the Plan are literally enforced. The necessity of acquiring additional land to meet the minimum lot size requirements of this Plan shall not be considered an extraordinary hardship, unless the applicant can demonstrate that there is no adjacent land which is reasonably available. An applicant shall be deemed to have established the existence of extraordinary hardship only if he demonstrates, based on specific facts, one of the following:

1. The subject property is not capable of yielding a reasonable return if used for its present use or developed as authorized by the provisions of this Plan, and that this inability to yield a reasonable return results from unique circumstances peculiar to the subject property which (a) do not apply to or affect other property in the immediate vicinity; (b) relate to or arise out of the characteristics of the subject property rather than the personal situation of the applicant; and (c) are not the result of any action or inaction by the applicant or the owner of his predecessors in title; or

2. The applicant can demonstrate that in good faith reliance on a valid municipal development approval, he has made expenditures of such a nature and amount that he is unable to secure a minimum reasonable rate of return on those expenditures under a strict application of the minimum standards of this Plan. In determining whether an applicant can secure a minimum reasonable rate of return, the Commission shall employ the following criteria:

    (a) the rate of return shall be related to the applicant's debt to equity ratio in the project;

    (b) expenditure for legal or other professional services that are unrelated to the design or construction of improvements shall not be considered as development expenditures;

    (c) taxes paid shall be considered as development expenditures except for any increase in taxes which result from the governmental approval or improvements actually constructed on the property.

3. For applications filed within two years of the effective date of this Plan, a valid final subdivision approval under the Municipal Land Use Law for the property proposed for development in the Protection Area was in effect on February 7, 1979, provided that all lots proposed for development have an area of at least one acre, unless sewer is available, and the proposed development is in conformance with the minimum standards and guidelines of Article 6 [Management Programs and Minimum Standards] of this Plan.

B. An applicant shall be deemed to have established compelling public need if he demonstrates, based on specific facts, that the proposed development will serve an essential health or safety need of the municipality in which the proposed development is located, that the public health and safety require the requested waiver, that the public benefits from the proposed use are of a character that overrides the importance of the protection of the Pinelands as established in the Protection Act of the Federal Act, that the proposed use is required to serve existing needs of the residents of the Pinelands, and that there is no alternative available to meet the established public need; and

C. The granting of the waiver will not be materially detrimental or injurious to other property or improvements in the area in which the subject property is located, increase the danger of fire, endanger public safety or result in substantial impairment of the resources of the Pinelands Area; and

D. The waiver will not be inconsistent with the purposes, objectives or the general spirit and intent of the Pinelands Protection Act, the Federal Act or this Plan; and

E. The waiver granted is the minimum relief necessary to relieve the extraordinary hardship, including the granting of a residential development right to lands in Forest Areas and Rural Development Areas that may be transferred or clustered to land which is suitable for clustering under the provisions of Section 5–310 of Article 5 [Minimum Standards for Clustering Residential Rights] or other developable land in the Rural Development Area, or to satisfy the compelling public need; and

F. Any waiver approved under the final subdivision standard of Subsection A(3) of this Section shall be subject to the condition that the waiver shall expire after two years if substantial construction of improvements is not commenced, or if fewer than 10% of the total number of lots in the subdivision are sold or built upon within any succeeding twelve-month period.

3. Township of Folsom et al. v. State of New Jersey, N.J. Super. App. Dkt. No. A–1675–80 (decided 12 January 1981).

4. *Ibid.*

5. The scheduling of the Secretary of the Interior's approval was considered critical in many quarters because Ronald Reagan had been elected President of the United States just prior to the adoption of the CMP, and there was concern that the new Reagan Administration might not be as sympathetic as the Carter Administration to the plan's strict regulations.

6. Orleans Builders & Developers v. Byrne, 186 N.J. Super. 432 (App. Div. 1982).

7. Matlack v. Board of Chosen Freeholders of the County of Burlington, 191 N.J. Super. 236.

8. Fine v. Galloway Township, 190 N.J. Super. 432.

9. Matter of Egg Harbor Assoc. (Bayshore Centre), 464 A.2d 1115 at 1121.

10. Centennial Pines Club v. Pinelands Commission, N.J. Super. App. Dkt. No. A–5032–82T–6 (decided 17 April 1985).

11. The Ackerman Organization v. State of New Jersey Pinelands Commission, OAL Dkt. No. EPC 0765–82 (10 December 1982).

12. Brighton Industries, Ltd., Mobile Home Park v. The New Jersey Pinelands Commission, OAL Dkt. No. EPC 4768–82 (1 July 1983).

13. Joseph and Patricia Tordella v. The State of New Jersey Pinelands Commission, OAL Dkt. No. EPC 6085–82 (2 July 1984).

14. In re: John Madin, N.J. Super. App. Dkt. No. A 4343–83T6 (decided 9 May 1985).

15. *Ibid.*

16. Sierra Club v. Pinelands Commission and Hovsons, Inc., OAL Dkt. No. EPC 3908–83 (25 April 1984).

17. Orleans Builders, *op. cit.*

18. Rober A. Greenbaum, "New Jersey Pinelands and the 'Taking' Question," *Columbia J. Env. Law*, 7 (1982), p. 230.

Chapter 12. How Is the Pinelands Program Working?

1. "Pinelands Learns to Live with a Plan," *Philadelphia Inquirer*, 16 December 1984; "Pinelands Plan, Rules Settling In," *Burlington County Times*, 26 February 1984; "Saving the Pinelands: It's a Difficult Process, but It's Working" (editorial), *Asbury Park Press*, 25 November 1985; "Fire over Pinelands Has Raged Too Long," *Newark Star-Ledger*, 19 August 1984; and "New Jersey Is Winning Its Battle in the Pinelands," *New York Times*, 10 August 1986; "The War Is Over" (editorial), *Atlantic City Press*, 17 November 1986.

2. John Heinz (former mayor of Egg Harbor Township), in a personal conversation with the author on 28 February 1986 in Princeton, N.J., volunteered that the commission and its plan were here to stay. While serving as mayor, Heinz, a vocal critic of the CMP and of the commission, had refused to seek certification of the township's master plan and ordinances. David Fisher of the New Jersey Homebuilders' Association in a personal conversation with the author on 10 March 1986 expressed the opinion (which was repeated on 4 April 1986 by Michael Gross, a prominent lawyer for real estate interests) that developers and the building industry have accepted the permanence of the Pinelands Commission and its plan, although they believe that some provisions are too restrictive—water quality, for example. Stephen Lee, III (farmer and active member of the farm group that opposed passage of the PPA and the adoption of the CMP), in a personal conversation with the author on 18 April 1986, also expressed the belief that the commission was a permanent agency and that the regional planning approach can work if more attention is given to restoring equity to landowners. Finally, Garfield De Marco, one of the most formidable critics of the Pinelands legislation and the CMP, acknowledged to Michele Byers on 19 May 1986 that "the program is working fairly well."

3. William E. Odum, "Environmental Degradation and the Tyranny of Small Decisions," *Bioscience*, 32:9 (1982), p. 729.

4. Franklin Parker (chairman of the Pinelands Commission), "Is Pinelands Plan a Success? Even Disinterested Say It Is," *New York Times*, 8 July 1984.

5. Patterson's comment was made in a meeting of the Pinelands Commission on 8 July 1985. In "Tax Lawyer Mary-Ann Thompson Has Found Peace in the Pines—and a Passion for Saving Its Buildings," *Trenton Sunday Times*, 11 November 1984, Attorney Thompson, who played an active role in securing passage of the federal and state legislation, is quoted as saying that "the commission is giving the Pine Barrens away, piece by piece, allowing too many variances for development in sensitive areas."

6. Michele Byers, personal conversation with Floyd West, 4 April 1986. See also, "Pinelands," *Asbury Park Press*, 10 November 1985.

7. Fisher and Gross, conversations with the author (see Note 2).

8. David Moore, conversation with the author, 2 April 1986.

9. Nan Walnut, conversation with the author, 26 October 1985.

10. "A Task Force Report to the Pinelands Plan Review Subcommittee on the Comprehensive Management Plan," (New Lisbon, N.J., May 1984). Participants in the Task Force included representatives of the Environmental Defense Fund, Friends of the Pine Barrens, Friends of Warren Grove, Natural Resources Defense Council, New Jersey Audubon Society, New Jersey Conservation Foundation, and the Sierra Club—West Jersey Group.

11. Most of the remaining changes approved by the commission were technical refinements that provoked little public debate. Fourteen highly debatable topics were scheduled for priority study, including an evaluation of the overall ecological implications of the CMP, the permitting of nonagricultural housing in Agriculture Production Areas, and the cumulative environmental impacts of mining in the Pinelands. As of mid-1987, the first triennial review was still far from complete; although the commission had approved 272 recommendations for revisions on 3 January 1986, many of the specific regulations to implement these recommendations remained unwritten. Moreover, once written, the revisions would have to be presented at a public hearing and approved by the governor of New Jersey and the United States secretary of the interior.

12. Ralph E. Good, ed., *Ecological Solutions to Environmental Management Concerns in the Pinelands National Reserve* (New Brunswick, N.J.: Rutgers University Center for Coastal and Environmental Studies, 1982).

13. Pinelands Commission Council on Pinelands Research, "A Long-Term Research and Management Plan for the New Jersey Pinelands" (New Lisbon, N.J., March 1986).

14. Pinelands Commission, "Pinelands Cultural Resource Management Plan for Historic Period Sites" (draft report, New Lisbon, N.J., November 1985). The Pineland study units include the following as examples of historic sites: agriculture sites, grist mills, iron forges and furnaces, sawmills, and vernacular architecture.

15. Mary Hufford, *The Pinelands Folklife Project* (Washington, D.C.: Library of Congress American Folklife Center, 20 February 1986), pp. 4–5. For discussion of folklife also see Rita Zorn Moonsammy, David Steven Cohen, and Lorraine E. Williams, eds., *Pinelands Folklife* (New Brunswick, N.J.: Rutgers University Press, 1987).

16. Jonathan Berger and John W. Sinton, *Water, Earth, and Fire* (Baltimore: Johns Hopkins University Press, 1985), pp. 147–175.

17. *Ibid.*, pp. 196–197.

18. *Ibid.*, p. 175.

19. Richard T. T. Forman, letter to the book review editor, *American Studies*, 18 November 1985.

20. In 1986, New Jersey's Division of Travel and Tourism still failed to identify the Pinelands as one of the state's distinctive regions of interest to tourists from either within or outside of the state. (Six regions are so identified, one being Atlantic City; the Pinelands is classified only as part of the Delaware River region.) An official of the Department of Environmental Protection has acknowledged off the record that "Governor Kean's office wants the Pinelands played down."

21. Michael Gross, interview with the author, 4 April 1986.

22. David Moore, interview with the author, 8 August 1986.

23. More than 50 percent of New Jersey's farmland is owned by nonfarmers. This may be attributed in part to the three-year rollback period for which the tax differential must be paid on farmland converted to development. See Thomas M. Seiler, "The Farmer is Being Strangled," *New York Times*, 28 July 1985; and Dan Jones, "Betting the Ranch," *New Jersey Reporter* (Feb. 1983).

24. N.J. Department of Agriculture, *Report of the Pinelands Agricultural Study Commission* (Trenton: Dept. of Agriculture, 1985). Commission studies made in 1985 show that the sale prices of agricultural land increased between 1981 and 1984 over the pre-CMP years, although this increase was not as much as the increase in land values in less restricted management areas. There has been no evidence that credit institutions make loans based on the value of potential development of farmland.

25. In August 1987, the Plan Review Subcommittee recommended a change in the CMP to permit nonagricultural housing in Agricultural Production Areas at a density of one unit per forty acres.

26. Arthur R. Brown, Jr., *New Jersey Report of Agriculture News*, 25 November 1985, p. 2.

27. See Chapter 10 for commission analyses. In a conversation with the author on 8 August 1986, David Moore questioned the commission's judgment of land values in the Preservation Area. Using as a guide the experience of the N.J. Conservation Foundation with land acquisition in the Pinelands during the premoratorium period, Moore said he thought that the price of typical land in the Preservation Area should not exceed $600 per acre.

28. In the same conversation on 8 August 1986, Moore also expressed the opinion that Pinelands municipalities created their own ratable problems by assessing currently vacant land at future development values. He claimed that economic support programs are not justified, first, because the programs make no provision to capture windfall profits resulting from increases in land values and, second, because municipalities have no unreimbursed service costs for public lands.

29. Robert Shinn (former Pinelands Commissioner), conversation with the author, 28 February 1986.

30. Terrence Moore, conversation with the author, 11 March 1986. For a discussion of this issue see Frank Popper, *Politics of Land Use Reform* (Madison: University of Wisconsin Press, 1981), pp. 230–232.

31. "New Jersey Is Winning the Battle in the Pinelands," *New York Times*, 10 August 1986.

32. Pinelands Commission, "Reviewing the Comprehensive Management Plan" (Draft report of the Plan Review Subcommittee, New Lisbon, N.J., April 1985), pp. 1–5.

33. Philip H. Burch, Jr., "Interest Groups in Politics" in *Politics in New Jersey*, ed. Richard Lehne and Alan Rosenthal (New Brunswick, N.J.: Rutgers University Eagleton Institute of Politics, 1979), pp. 109–122.

34. Berger and Sinton, *Water, Earth, and Fire*, p. 175.

35. Phil Swastick (Shamong Township), comments at Pinelands Commission hearings on the plan review, 3 June 1985 and 12 July 1985.

36. "South Jersey Leads State in Growth," *Atlantic City Press,* 17 October 1985. Cape May and Ocean counties were the state's fastest growing counties between 1980 and 1984.

37. Comments made at the Southern Council's awards dinner at the Atlantic Casino Hotel, 22 May 1985.

38. At least one top administrator in DEP advised his employees "not to go over the line in working with [commission staff]," while a staff member concerned with state tourism admitted, "We can't promote the Pines, [it's] too controversial." (Sources unidentified, by request of the speakers.)

39. A member of the governor's staff, off the record, suggested that the governor intended to "buy off" opposition to the protection effort through these appointments.

40. Popper, *Politics of Land Use,* p. 216.

41. Poll conducted by the Rutgers University Eagleton Institute of Politics. For a summary of poll results, see "Environmental Threats Chief Concern in S.J., Poll Finds," *Atlantic City Press,* 8 May 1986.

42. Comments made at a Pinelands Commission Plan Review Subcommittee meeting held in Atlantic County, 21 May 1984.

43. Alan J. Karcher (speaker of the N.J. Assembly), comments made during a panel discussion, "Grappling with Growth," Princeton University Institute for Advanced Study, 24 November 1985. Karcher decried New Jersey's ingrained commitment to the home-rule concept. Jon Kimmel, Thomas O'Neill, and others in the September 1984 issue of *The New Jersey Reporter,* point out the failures of home rule and the need for regional planning. Home rule also took a beating in the New Jersey Growth Management Conference held 28 February 1986 at the Woodrow Wilson School of Princeton University, where state senator Gerald Stockman and many other participants spoke of the need for regional planning and land-use management to cope with current, complex land management problems in New Jersey.

44. New Jersey State Planning Act, P.L. 1985, Ch. 398. The appointment of Candace Ashmun to the state planning commission should reinforce efforts to protect the Pinelands, since she has been a Pinelands Commissioner from the outset and was a strong force in molding the Pinelands land-use management strategy.

45. Thomas O'Neill, comments at the Growth Management Conference, 28 February 1986. In 1986 property taxes in New Jersey generated more than 46 percent of combined state and local revenues.

Chapter 13. Lessons of the Pinelands Experiences

1. For a description of New Jersey's coastal management program see chapter VI of Daniel J. Van Abs, "Regional Environmental Management in the Pinelands National Reserve" (Ph.D. diss., State University of New York, College of Environmental Science and Forestry, Syracuse, 1985).

2. John M. DeGrove, *Land Growth & Politics* (Chicago: American Planning Association, 1984), p. 2.

3. For Adirondack Park experiences, see Richard A. Liroff and G. Gordon Davis, *Protecting Open Space* (Cambridge, Mass.: Ballinger Publishing Co., 1981). For a description of the Hawaiian experiences, see David L. Callies, *Regulating Paradise: Land Use Controls in Hawaii* (Honolulu: University of Hawaii Press, 1984). For descriptions of state land-use experiences in California, North Carolina, Florida, Vermont, Colorado, Hawaii, and Oregon, see DeGrove, *Land Growth;* Council of State Governments, "Land Use Policy and Program Analysis," No. 1 (Lexington, Ky., September 1974); H. Charles Foster, *Experiments in Bioregionalism: The New England River Basins Study* (Hanover, N.H.: University Press of New England, 1984); F. R. Steiner and H. N. Van Lier, eds., *Land Conservation and Development: Examples of Land-Use Planning Projects and Programs* (New York: Elsevier, 1984); and Robert G. Healy, *Land Use and the States* (Washington, D.C.: Resources for the Future, Inc., 1979).

4. Frank Popper, *The Politics of Land-Use Reform* (Madison: University of Wisconsin Press, 1981), p. 212. See also Richard Babcock, "Regulating Land Development: Some Thoughts on the Role of Government" in *Land-Use: Tough Choices in Today's World.* Proceedings of a national symposium, Omaha, Neb., 21–24 March 1977 (Ankeny, Iowa: Soil Conservation Society of America, 1977), pp. 37–39.

5. Popper, *Politics of Land-Use,* pp. 208, 223–224; and Cecily Kihn, "The Greenline Concept," a background paper written for a policy forum on "The Future of the Greenline Concept," *American Land Forum,* Winter 1982, p. 24.

6. Jonathan Berger and John W. Sinton argue in *Water, Earth, and Fire* (Baltimore: Johns Hopkins University Press, 1985, pp. 147, 156–60) that the Pinelands planning time was much too short and also that the process should have extended into subregional planning activities.

7. John Degrove, remarks made during a panel discussion at the New Jersey Growth Management Conference, Woodrow Wilson School, Princeton University, 28 February 1986.

8. DeGrove, *Land Growth,* pp. 371–396.

9. In his study of seven systems of state land and growth management, DeGrove found that environmental support was generally, but not always, necessary for program adoption (*Land Growth,* pp. 377–379).

10. Van Abs, "Regional Environmental Management," Ch. VII, p. 1.

11. *Greenline Parks* (Washington, D.C.: National Parks and Conservation Association, 1983), pp. 17–45.

12. Larry Morandi, Gordon Meeks, Jr., and Douglas M. Scarto, *Land Management: Sustaining Resource Values* (Denver: National Conference of State Legislatures, Oct. 1983), pp. 147–223.

Index